Robert J. Priest Editor

EFFECTIVE ENGAGEMENT
IN SHORT-TERM MISSIONS:
DOING IT RIGHT!

OTHER TITLES IN THE EMS SERIES

Robert J. Priest Editor

EVANGELICAL
MISSIOLOGICAL
SOCIETY SERIES

No. 16

EFFECTIVE ENGAGEMENT
IN SHORT-TERM MISSIONS:
DOING IT RIGHT!

WILLIAM CAREY
LIBRARY

Effective Engagement in Short-term Missions: Doing it Right!
Copyright © 2008 by Evangelical Missiological Society

Published by
William Carey Library
1605 E. Elizabeth Street
Pasadena, CA 91104
www.missionbooks.org

Naomi Bradley, editorial manager
Johanna Deming, assistant editor
Hugh Pindur, graphic designer

William Carey Library is a ministry of the
U.S. Center for World Mission
Pasadena, CA USA
www.uscwm.org

First edition published in 2008.
Second printing 2010.
Printed in the United States of America
14 13 12 11 10   6 5 4 3 2 CH

Library of Congress Cataloging-in-Publication Data
Effective engagement in short-term missions : doing it right / [edited by] Robert J. Priest.
  p. cm. -- (Evangelical Missiological Society series ; no. 16)
  Includes bibliographical references.
  ISBN 978-0-87808-005-2
  1. Short-term missions. I. Priest, Robert J.
  BV2061.3.E34 2008
  266'.02--dc22
          2008035497

About EMS

www.emsweb.org

The Evangelical Missiological Society is a professional organization with more than 350 members comprised of missiologists, mission administrators, teachers, pastors with strategic missiological interests, and students of missiology. EMS exists to advance the cause of world evangelization. We do this through study and evaluation of mission concepts and strategies from a biblical perspective with a view to commending sound mission theory and practice to churches, mission agencies, and schools of missionary training around the world. We hold an annual national conference and eight regional meetings held throughout the USA and Canada.

CONTENTS

PART III   FORGING GLOBAL PARTNERSHIPS

PART IV   CARRYING OUT SPECIALIZED MINISTRIES

INTRODUCTION

ROBERT J. PRIEST

Historically missionaries were expected to serve for life. But in 1949 the Methodist Board of Missions approved a revolutionary new program (McPhee 2005, 194ff) where recent college graduates, traveling in groups of fifty, were appointed for three-year terms of service in specific countries such as Japan or India. After six-weeks of training, these "forty-five-day wonders" (as veteran missionaries sometimes called them) served as rural development workers, mission secretaries and office staff, teachers at MK boarding schools, staff at medical hospitals, and so on.

In early years, "short-term missionaries" were those who served two or three years. But in the late 1950s and early 1960s new agencies appeared on the scene—Operation Mobilization (OM) and Youth With a Mission (YWAM)—agencies organized entirely around new paradigms of short-term service of a few months to two or three years. In 1963 Greater Europe Mission (GEM), a traditional career missionary agency, began a program of summer mission service (of eight to ten weeks) for college students (Peterson, Aeschliman, and Sneed 2003, 246). Christian colleges began to organize their own summer mission trips abroad, with Wheaton College's first mission team organized in 1958, Nazarene University's in 1966, Cedarville University's in 1971, Taylor University's in 1972, and so on. Campus ministries at secular universities also began to organize summer mission trips, with Intervarsity organizing its first summer mission trip to Costa Rica the summer of 1970 (Peterson et al., 2003, 244-246).

But gradually even shorter terms of service became normal. In 1967 Wycliffe Associates began sending construction teams to various fields (Peterson et al., 2003, 242), teams serving two weeks or less. By the 1980s and 1990s whole new organizations developed (such as Adventures in Missions or Teen Mania) specializing in short-term mission trips lasting as little as seven to fourteen days. Local church youth pastors increasingly made an annual mission trip core to their youth ministry, with destinations either domestic or abroad. Larger congregations increasingly included on their staff a designated "mission pastor" who would help lead their own mission projects, projects often organized in partnership with sister-congregations abroad and sustained through regular groups of traveling short-term missionaries.

By 2005 approximately 1.6 million adult US church members were traveling abroad every year on short-term mission trips with the average (median) amount of time spent in service abroad per trip (not counting travel time) now being eight days (Wuthnow and Offutt 2008, 218). Less than a third of short-term mission trips for young people are currently longer than fourteen days (Priest and Priest 2008). One indication of the increase in the numbers of short-term mission participants comes from Wuthnow's national random survey data where he reports:

that only two percent of those who had been
teenagers during the 1950s, 1960s and 1970s said
they had gone to another country on a short-
term mission trip while in high school, whereas
the proportion increased to five percent among
those who had been teenagers in the 1990s and
12 percent among those who had been teenagers
since the 1990s (Wuthnow and Offutt 2008, 218).

In a 2002 national random survey (N=3370) of thirteen to
seventeen year olds in the United States, it was discovered that 29%
indicate they had traveled at least once on a mission or religious
service project (either domestically or abroad), with a follow-up
survey in 2005 (n=2604) of the same population—now fifteen to
twenty years old—which found that 41% reported having gone
on such mission trips or religious service projects (Trinitapoli and
Vaisey 2008). This survey did not ask about trips abroad, and thus
this data includes domestic service projects.

If we focus only on short-term mission trips abroad, my own
survey of seminary students (n=2208) in required MDiv courses in
sixty U.S. seminaries (across denominations and including Roman
Catholic seminaries) discovered that 48% had traveled abroad on
one or more short-term mission trips. Among students in required
courses at ten Bible Colleges (n=562) it was found that 62% had done
at least one short-term mission trip abroad. In core general education
courses at thirty-one Christian liberal arts colleges (CCCU schools)
it was found that 47% of students (n=2790) reported having traveled
on short-term mission trips abroad. This contrasts with only 7% of
students (n=246) taking general education courses at five Roman
Catholic colleges (NCCAA) who had taken mission trips abroad.
Again, in my survey (n=591) of adult Sunday School classes or Bible
Studies at ten megachurches, 32% of respondents indicated that they
had traveled abroad on a short-term mission trip at least once. In

short, STM is today an enormous phenomenon, central to the ministry practices of a high proportion of American Christians.

While it is often claimed that STM is primarily practiced by Christians in the United States, in fact STM is increasingly practiced by Christians around the world. For example, in my survey of 672 Protestant pastors in Thailand, 55% reported that their current congregation has hosted a visiting group of short-term missionaries from the USA. But almost the same percent (51%) report that their congregation has hosted a visiting group of short-term missionaries from Korea. Furthermore they report that they themselves and some of their congregants have also traveled on short-term mission trips. From Peru to El Salvador, Paraguay, Singapore, Thailand, Korea or Kenya, one finds Christians not only partnering with visiting short-term missionaries, but also sending out short-term mission teams themselves, either to destinations within their own country or abroad.

From the very beginning, there have been those who were highly critical of short-term missions. For example, in 1949, an old India missionary wrote a letter to the Methodist Mission Board, complaining about the two groups of fifty recent college grads that were soon to arrive in India for three-year terms. She described a gathering of veteran missionaries in which:

> *Not one of us* could think how we could put them to work at all! . . . They will not have the language and will not be trying to get it. Neither will they have any proper preparation for any particular type of work which they could do without the language. WHAT CAN they do? We don't know! On the other hand, it's no wonder they "take it into their hands and ask to be sent out" in this way! It's a wonderful trip for them, why wouldn't they want to come out? (cited in McPhee 2005, 342).

But while it has never been difficult to find critics of short-term missions, or strong advocates, and while there is a burgeoning new body of books advocating and instructing on short-term missions, prior to 2003 very little actual research had been done on short-term missions and its role in the contemporary global mission scene. That is, there was a marked divide between the world of missiological scholarship and the practice of STM, between missiological writings and populist advocacy writings on STM. Missiological writings, historically, have rather consistently had career missions in view, not STM. The STM movement, by contrast, has been a populist movement with minimal connection either to missiology or to seminary education. Key leaders in the STM movement have sometimes exemplified strong anti-intellectual strains, while missiologists have often been dismissive of, and even hostile to, STM.

Those seminarians preparing for youth ministry will someday be expected to plan, organize and lead STM trips for their youth. But nothing in their seminary education (in most seminaries until now) will provide preparation for this part of their future job description. Across America there are today thousands of mission pastors in local congregations. They will be expected to plan, lead, and coordinate STM trips, to set-up congregational partnerships, to choose, screen and train STM team leaders, but while their seminary education may well have included missiology courses, it is unlikely that such courses taught them about best practices in STM. That is, the divide between grassroots ministry practices of local churches and what is happening in the academy has perhaps been nowhere greater than in the area of STM.

But this divide is starting to be overcome as missiological scholars increasingly recognize that new patterns of short-term mission are central to ministry today, and as such scholars attempt to develop research-based understandings to correct, strengthen and refine the new patterns of ministry associated with STM (see especially the edited collections: Priest 2006, and Priest and Paredes 2007).

This book represents the single most ambitious effort to date to understand and improve upon patterns of ministry in short-term missions. Contributors to this book have, in many cases, been interacting with each other about the subject of STM for several years. Some have been at the forefront of STM practice (e.g. Cook, Gascho), and most have at least some experience participating in, or leading, STM ministries. Some are senior scholars with a long-term interest in this topic (Adeney, Cook, Moreau, R. Priest, Slimbach, Ybarrola, Ver Beek, Zehner), and others write out of their own cutting edge Ph.D. research on STM (C. M. Brown, Park, K. Priest, Richardson, Wang). Among the authors are anthropologists (Adeney, R. Priest, Wan, Ybarrola, Zehner), sociologists (K. Priest, Slimbach, Ver Beek), missiologists (Brown, Cook, Cuellar, Park, Smith), and representatives of various other fields, such as education, law, business, and medicine. Six authors are women. Two are Chinese, one Korean, and one Peruvian.

Many Christian colleges, and most seminaries, require at least one course in missions for their students. And yet most such courses do little to link missiology with the actual experience of students. One of the best ways for college and seminary professors to introduce their students to the field of missiology, would be to include this book in the assigned readings. Why? Because this book, better than any other book currently available, builds a bridge between the world of (missiological) knowledge and the world of student experience.

The book begins by exploring contemporary links between STM and older patterns of long-term missions. Scott Moreau reviews the latest data on Protestant mission agencies, exploring trends related to STM and long-term missions. Alex Smith, himself an early practitioner of STM, but also a career missionary, explores issues that STM raises from the perspective of long-term missions. Wan and Hartt review their research on ways in which STM and long-term mission can be complementary, rather than competitive.

The second section of the book puts the focus on STM engagement with people who are socially and culturally "other." The authors discuss the sorts of knowledge that STMers must foster—with particular focus on cultural understandings.

The third section of the book focuses on the theme of partnership. Zehner explores both in the New Testament and in Thailand what healthy relations between representatives of older and younger churches ought to look like. Brown reports on his research on three congregation-to-congregation partnerships—and what can be learned from these cases. Wang provides a detailed report and analysis of the ways in which an interethnic church in New York City organized an interethnic STM team to go to Ecuador. K. Priest explores the ways in which women use STM to activate their social networks to mobilize resources for South African AIDS patients and others. Cuellar explores Latin American perspectives on what partnership in glocal church ministry should look like.

In the fourth section are chapters on various specialized ministries. O'Neill looks at medical short-term missions. Burch outlines ways in which ministries to children at risk can use STM in the very process of discipling these children. And Russell reports on his research related to business professionals exercising their gifts and training in STM.

The fifth section of the book alone is worth the price of the book. Charles Cook explores legal issues in mission, particularly in relation to tax-exempt funds and how they are treated. Walker-Adams and Ross review case law and the ways in which churches should take precautions in STM to protect themselves from legal liability.

Finally, the last section focuses on the impact of STM on participants. Ver Beek reviews the scholarly literature on this, indicating what the state of the field currently is. Kyeong-Sook Park reports on her dissertation research on Bible College students, demonstrating that STM experience alone, or intercultural education alone, do not have nearly as strong a positive impact on participants as when the two of them (STM experience and intercultural education) are combined. She calls for better patterns of bringing teaching and learning into connection with STM service and experience. Rick Richardson reports on his dissertation research with Northwestern University students in Intervarsity's summer urban immersion programs, and highlights the importance of appropriate follow-through structures if participants are to sustain the behavioral change called for by the STM experience. Murray Decker explores the culture shock and disequilibrium felt by STM participants—especially by those who participate for several months (rather than several days)—and explores the parallels and potential synergy between cross-cultural adjustment and spiritual formation. Fran Blomberg also suggests ways in which STM creates optimum opportunities for faith formation on the part of young adults, if handled rightly. And Vicki Gascho explores the importance of STM supervisors for optimum impact on STM participants.

The authors in this book consistently adopt an approach which is positive and constructive. While there are criticisms in the book, these criticisms are not directed against STM per se, but against particular ways of doing STM. That is, the goal of this book is to improve the ways in which STM is carried out and to improve the understandings needed on the part of all who are involved in short-term missions. In short, this book attempts to provide a knowledge base for those who provide leadership within the short-term missions movement. Youth pastors, mission pastors, lay leaders of STM, college and seminary students, and missiologists will all find the chapters in this book informative and relevant to their concerns.

I wish to express deep appreciation to Rochelle Cathcart and Andrew Pflederer, as well as to Naomi Bradley and her editorial team at William Carey Library, for their valuable help in preparing this book manuscript for publication.

References Cited

McPhee, Arthur G. 2005. *The road to Delhi: J. Waskom Pickett remembered.* Bangalore, India: SAIACS Press.

Peterson, Robert, Gordon Aeschliman, R. Wayne Snell. 2003. *Maximum impact short-term mission.* Minneapolis, MN: STEMPress.

Priest, Robert, guest editor. 2006. *Theme Issue on Short-Term Missions. Missiology: An International Review* 34 (4).

Priest, Robert and Tito Paredes, Guest Editors. 2007. *Special Issue on Short-Term Missions in Latin America, Journal of Latin American Theology: Christian Reflections from the Global South, Volume* 2.

Priest, Robert J. and Joseph Paul Priest. 2008. "They see everything, and understand nothing: Short-term mission and service learning." *Missiology: An International Review* 36: 53-73.

Trinitapoli, Jenny and Stephen Vaisey. 2008 unpublished paper. The transformative role of religious experience: The case of short-term missions. [Under review, *Social Forces*]

Wuthnow, Robert and Stephen Offutt. 2008. Transnational religious connections. *Sociology of Religion* 69: 209-232.

CONTRIBUTORS

Miriam Adeney is an anthropologist, Pacific Northwesterner, mother, and follower of Jesus. Among her books are *God's Foreign Policy: Practical Ways to Help the World's* Poor and *Daughters of Islam: Building Bridges With Muslim Women.* Her research interests include Southeast Asia, Latin America, indigenous oral art genres, ethnicity, gender, and religions. She is a professor at Seattle Pacific University, and currently serves as President of the American Society of Missiology.

Fran Blomberg is an adjunct faculty member in intercultural ministries at Denver Seminary, as well as being involved in training and mentoring there. She is pursuing a PhD in contextualized missiology at the International Baptist Theological Seminary in Prague, studying how to build and sustain Christian community in post-modern congregations. She and her husband Craig are currently involved at "Scum of the Earth Church" in Denver, working with youth subcultures.

C. M. Brown has spent over eleven years living in Eastern European and post-Soviet nations. He is proficient in Russian and has served in various ministry and leadership development capacities. First graduating with high scholastic honors in Geological Engineering from Colorado School of Mines, Brown later earned an MA in Religion and a PhD in Intercultural Studies from Trinity International University.

Greg W. Burch is currently a candidate for the PhD from the School of Intercultural Studies at Fuller Seminary and a professor at ESEPA Seminary in San José, Costa Rica where he teaches in cross-cultural studies and children at risk issues. After six years of ministry in Caracas, Venezuela among street-living and working children Greg is now dedicating his time to research and advocacy on behalf of children at risk in Latin America. He is a member of the Latin America Mission.

Charles A. Cook is professor of global studies and mission at Ambrose University College and Seminary. Dr. Cook holds a Doctor of Philosophy degree in intercultural studies from Trinity International University. Dr. Cook served with the Christian and Missionary Alliance (C&MA) in Bolivia, Mexico and Argentina. Born to Canadian C&MA missionaries he was raised in Colombia, Ecuador and Peru. He is founder of two STM organization; Church Partnership Evangelism and the onSite study abroad program.

Rolando Cuellar (Ph.D. Trinity Evangelical Divinity School) is from Peru. He serves as assistant professor of intercultural studies at Lee University (2003). An ordained minister of the Presbyterian Church (USA), he served as pastor of Emmanuel Presbyterian Church, Chicago, 1983 to 2003. While at Lee, he has been heavily involved in short-term missions with his students around the world. His most recent journeys have been to India, Zambia, Panama, and Cambodia.

Murray Decker serves as associate professor of intercultural studies within the School of Intercultural Studies, Biola University. Dr. Decker's interest in the intersection of soul care and cross-cultural missions has opened doors for him to publish and teach on this subject, as well as speak on this topic in a wide range of contexts, both at home in the United States, and increasingly with front-line missionaries overseas.

Vicki Gascho and her husband ministered with Greater Europe Mission (GEM) in Europe from 1984-98, prior to moving to GEM headquarters, where she now serves as International Director of Preparation and Training. For several years Vicki served as Program Director of GEM's summer ministries program, EuroCorps. She received her PhD in Educational Studies at Trinity Evangelical Divinity School, with a focus on young adult development.

Geoff Hartt is a missions pastor in Portland Oregon. He has taught pastors and planted churches in Mexico and Liberia, West Africa. He is married with two daughters. He earned his M.Div. at Western Seminary in Oregon and is currently completing his D. Miss.

Scott Moreau, after 10 years of teaching in Africa, has taught since 1991 in the Intercultural Studies Department at Wheaton College, where he is as Professor of Intercultural Studies. He has been Managing Editor of the Network for Strategic Missions Knowledge Base (over 17,000 articles on missions; www.strategicmissions.org) since 2000, Editor of *Evangelical Missions Quarterly* since 2001, and co-developer of MisLinks.org, a missions topical directory.

Daniel O'Neill is a medical doctor and an assistant clinical professor of Family Medicine at University of Connecticut School of Medicine. He has participated in or led short-term medical missions since 1992 in various locations and organizations with a broad range of approaches. He is also a graduate student in theological studies at Bethel Seminary of the East.

Kyeong-Sook Park, a native South Korean, served in Sudan. She also taught for a number of years in the Evangelical Theological Seminary of Indonesia where she helped launch its Doctor of Ministry program. She holds a Doctor of Missiology from Biola University and a Ph.D. in intercultural studies from Trinity Evangelical Divinity School. She has been teaching at Moody Bible Institute since 1997.

Kersten Bayt Priest is assistant professor of sociology at Wheaton College. She holds an M.A. in anthropology and is a Ph.D. candidate in sociology (Loyola University). Her research has focused on globalization, women, religion, congregational studies and short-term missions. She does collaborative research with Robert Priest and appreciates the research assistance and patience of her three sons, lovely daughter and wonderful students.

Robert J. Priest is professor of mission and intercultural studies and director of the Ph.D. program in intercultural studies at Trinity Evangelical Divinity School. He holds the Ph.D. in anthropology from the University of California, Berkeley. Among his more recent publications is the 2007 book, *This Side of Heaven: Race, Ethnicity, and Christian Faith* (Oxford), co-edited with Alvaro Nieves.

Rick Richardson is associate professor and director of the Masters in Evangelism and Leadership at Wheaton College. Rick is also an associate evangelist and former national coordinator for evangelism with InterVarsity Christian Fellowship. He consults widely with churches on evangelism and healing and racial reconciliation. Rick earned his M.Div. from Northern Baptist Seminary and his Ph.D. in Intercultural Studies from Trinity Evangelical Divinity School. Rick has written four books, including *Evangelism Outside the Box* and *Reimagining Evangelism.*

Scott Ross is General Counsel with New Tribes Mission, with which he has served for twenty-two years. A graduate of Gonzaga University Law School, he is licensed to practice law in the states of Idaho, Florida and Washington-and has been a licensed attorney for thirty-three years. At New Tribes he has focused on responding to missionary kidnappings, and has served as lead investigator in over 120 mission child-abuse investigations. Scott's five part video series on child abuse is used by various mission agencies in their child safety programs, and he regularly consults with other missions on related matters.

Mark Russell is Director of Spiritual Integration at HOPE International. He has a Ph.D. in Intercultural Studies from Asbury Theological Seminary, a Masters of Divinity from Trinity Evangelical Divinity School, and a Bachelors of Science in International Business from Auburn University. He has lived and worked at the intersection of business and missions in several countries. He lives in Boise, Idaho with his wife, Laurie, and their children, Noah and Anastasia.

Richard Slimbach is professor of global studies and coordinator of the global studies program at Azusa Pacific University. He founded Azusa's Los Angeles Term and Global Learning Term programs, and has extensive experience living and working abroad. He has a Ph.D. in Comparative and International Education from UCLA and continues to design cross-cultural learning programs that help students to "cherish the life of the world."

Alexander G Smith is minister-at-large for OMF International in the Buddhist World. After serving in Thailand for twenty years in pioneer church multiplication, he was OMF's Northwest Director, USA. He earned his Doctorate in Missiology at Fuller, was adjunct faculty at Multnomah Bible College and Professor for the Institute of Buddhist Studies. He helped initiate and chairs SEANET (South, East, Southeast and North Asia Network) for the 1.5 billion Buddhist influenced peoples.

Kurt Ver Beek is a professor of sociology for Calvin College. He lives with his family in Tegucigalpa, Honduras, and directs a Calvin off-campus semester there. Ver Beek has a Ph.D. in Development Sociology from Cornell University, and did his dissertation fieldwork among Honduras' Lenca Indians. Ver Beek has published a number of articles and contributed book chapters on service learning, short-term missions, Honduras' "*maquila* industry," and Christians and justice. He and his wife, Jo Ann Van Engen, are founding members of the Honduran, Christian, justice and human rights organization "la Asociacion para una Sociedad mas Justa (ASJ)."

Michelle A. Walker-Adams is an attorney in Augusta, Georgia. After earning a Bachelor of Arts in Global Economics and International Business at Cedarville University, Michelle managed economic development activities of the Chamber of Commerce in Springfield, Ohio. While obtaining a Juris Doctorate degree at Regent University School of Law, Michelle gained legal experience with global missionary organizations and hopes for a long career pursuing the same.

Enoch Wan serves as research professor of anthropology and as the director of the Doctor of Missiology Program at Western Seminary, Portland, Oregon, USA. He is the founder and editor of the multilingual online journal *www.GlobalMissiology.org*, the Executive VP of the Evangelical Missiological Society, the Vice President of Great Commission Center International and a member of LCWE-Diasporas Leadership Team and International Advisory Board of FIN (Filipino International Network).

Chin T. Wang (**John**) lived in Taiwan and Argentina before coming to the United States. He serves as a pastor of First Baptist Church of Flushing, a multiethnic and multicongregational church in New York City. He is currently a Ph.D. student at Trinity Evangelical Divinity School.

Steven J. Ybarrola is professor of cultural anthropology in the E. Stanley Jones School of World Mission and Evangelism at Asbury Theological Seminary. Dr. Ybarrola has served as a missionary with Operation Mobilization and has ongoing research in the peninsular Basque country. His recent writings include "Identity Matters: Christianity and Ethnic Identity in the Peninsular Basque Country" in *Power and Identity in the Global Church* (William Carey Library,

Fall 2008), and *Enemies & Allies, Strangers & Friends: Identity and Ideology in the Peninsular Basque Country* to be published by the University of Nevada Press.

Edwin Zehner obtained his Ph.D. in anthropology from Cornell University. His dissertation focused on Protestant Christians and religious conversions in Thailand. He has taught in Christian and secular settings and most recently has been writing on short-term missions and their implications for inter-church relations across national boundaries. Recently he spent four months in beginning Arabic studies in Yemen, and in the spring of 2008 he was a visiting scholar at Cornell University's Southeast Asia Program.

CHAPTER 1

SHORT-TERM MISSIONS IN THE

CONTEXT OF MISSIONS, INC.

A. SCOTT MOREAU

Introduction

What does short-term missions look like among the agencies found in North America? We hope to provide a partial answer to that question in this chapter. To set the stage for the chapter, several introductory comments and explanations are in order.

First, the information provided in this chapter comes from data collected through several surveys taken at roughly three year intervals from 1992 to 2005 of approximately 700 U.S. and 120 Canadian Protestant mission agencies. The surveys were conducted in preparation for the ongoing editions of the *Mission Handbook*, now in its 20th edition. While the *Handbook* (under various names) started in 1953, standardization of questions currently used was initiated in 1992, and (for STM) finalized in 1996. Thus, I limit this discussion to the five surveys conducted between 1992 and 2005

(1992, 1996, 1998, 2001, and 2005). It should be noted that most of the data presented in this chapter is found in the 2007 to 2009 edition of the *Mission Handbook* (Moreau 2007, 11-75).

Second, it must be noted that while the list of agencies surveyed was as exhaustive as possible, it did not include every known agency. For example, some did not submit a completed questionnaire; others were so new that we were not aware of them yet when the survey was sent out; still others were not formal agencies but more informal sending bodies situated in the context of local churches. Additionally, for each of the surveys sent over the years, some agencies were dropped from the list because they were disbanded, merged into another agency, or did not return a survey while others were added.

Third, the short-term focus of North American Protestant agencies takes place in the larger context of the whole of their work. While several agencies focus exclusively on STM, the vast majority do not give this component of contemporary missions their sole focus. To better understand what is happening in Protestant agency sponsored STM, it will be necessary to see what has happened over the time frame of available information in the larger picture of the agencies.

Fourth, I divide the chapter into two major sections. The first section examines the U.S. scene, and the second focuses on Canada. Within each of these sections, I will start with the broader picture and then narrow the focus down to STM. To further nuance the discussion in each section, I will distinguish two terms in the discussion of the changes seen, namely *trend* and *shift*. By *trend* I refer to a change that has been consistent over ten years or more. By *shift* I refer to a change that is seen in the 2005 survey but that was not consistent over the previous ten-year period. While somewhat arbitrary, this distinction makes it easier to distinguish changes that are long-term from those that are relatively new.

Finally, one caveat is in order. It must be noted that the tables and charts that follow have a necessary softness as a result of three factors. First, the actual numbers requested in the survey, such as the number of long-term missionaries serving in a particular country, are not steady through the year. Second, agencies use different methods for reporting their information in the survey. Some are extremely careful to report exact numbers for the time in which the survey is filled out, while others give highs (or lows) or perhaps even estimates over the year. We followed up with agencies whenever numbers appeared to be soft, but the data reported here was the best that could be obtained. This is especially true for certain categories, such as volunteers, part-time staff, and associates. Third, not all agencies interpret the survey questions in the same way. Indeed, responses vary even within the same agency from survey to survey. This will be seen, for example, in tables that are labeled as "adjusted" numbers. In most cases, the adjustment was made because there was such a large discrepancy between the 2001 and 2005 surveys that both sets of numbers had to be discarded.

U.S. Protestant Mission Agencies

U.S. Missions, Inc. Changes

The first trend seen was an increase in the reported number of U.S. citizens working for U.S. agencies (see Figure 1). Altogether, when we add the number of full-time U.S. citizens serving as residential missionaries, non-residential missionaries, tentmakers, and administrative or home-based staff, 86,461 U.S. citizens were reported to be fully engaged in the missionary task through U.S. agencies, a 20% increase over the number reported for these categories in the 2001 survey. While career and middle-term missionary numbers were down, the number of U.S. citizens working as tentmakers or non-residential missionaries, and the number of those working in the United States (whether as administrative staff or on home assignments), had risen enough to result in a net increase.

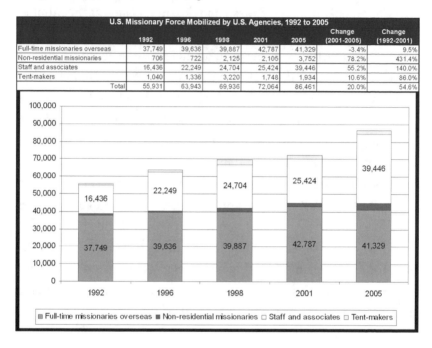

U.S. Missionary Force Mobilized by U.S. Agencies, 1992 to 2005						Change (2001-2005)	Change (1992-2001)
	1992	1996	1998	2001	2005		
Full-time missionaries overseas	37,749	39,636	39,887	42,787	41,329	-3.4%	9.5%
Non-residential missionaries	706	722	2,125	2,105	3,752	78.2%	431.4%
Staff and associates	16,436	22,249	24,704	25,424	39,446	55.2%	140.0%
Tent-makers	1,040	1,336	3,220	1,748	1,934	10.6%	86.0%
Total	55,931	63,943	69,936	72,064	86,461	20.0%	54.6%

Figure 1: U.S. Missionary Force Mobilized by U.S. Protestant Agencies

The second trend discovered was an increase in the reported number of non-U.S. citizens working for U.S. agencies (see Figure 2). The total number of non-U.S. citizens directly supported by U.S. agencies rose from 1,898 in 1992 to 86,262 in 2005, an increase of 4445%. It is important to point out that there was significant volatility in the numbers reported from 2001 to 2005. For example, eight of the organizations in the top twenty for 2005 reported zero non-U.S. citizens in 2001.

Just over 93% of the non-U.S. citizens reported in 2005 are working in their home countries. The total number of non-U.S. citizens serving U.S. agencies in their home countries has grown by more than 183% since 1996 (when this question was first asked). The gains seen between 2001 and 2005 were broadly-based; 26 agencies reported 500 or more non-U.S. citizens in 2005, up from 18 in the 2001 survey. At the same time, non-U.S. citizens serving under U.S. agencies in a country other than their own increased by 203% since 1992. The latter number is perhaps more significant, since it is more likely that those serving outside of their home country are serving cross-culturally. However, since the survey does not distinguish non-U.S. citizens serving same-culture pockets in different countries (e.g., Korean citizens under U.S. agencies working among Koreans in Japan), we do not know with certainty how many of the 5,428 people reported in this category have crossed cultural boundaries in their ministry work.

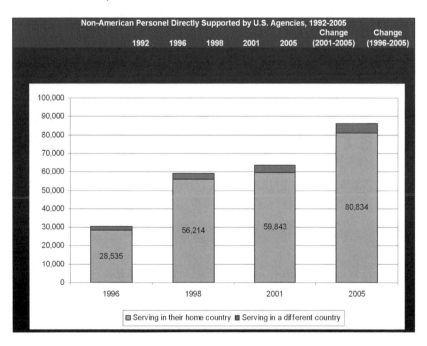

Figure 2: Non-U.S. Citizens Directly Supported by U.S. Agencies

There are at least two issues that may be raised concerning the ultimate impact of the significant increase in non-U.S. citizens working for U.S. agencies. First, it is an indication of a more globalized approach to missions. Hopefully this would include an increasingly internationalized upper leadership structure among the agencies that have employed more non-U.S. citizens, but the survey data does not include leadership composition and anecdotal evidence is spotty at best.

Second, it is likely that the longer-term stability, as well as the access to funding that U.S. agencies offer, makes working for them more attractive than for local agencies. One concern with this would be the possible extent to which U.S. agencies hiring non-U.S. citizens could potentially stifle the development of indigenous agencies as well as the creativity necessary to develop new funding models for economies that do not have as much discretionary income as in the U.S.

A third trend was the ongoing increase in the proportion of non-U.S. versus U.S. citizens working for U.S. agencies as residential workers (Figure 3). Not only did the number of non-U.S. citizens working for U.S. agencies increase, so did the ratio of non-U.S. citizens to U.S. citizens. In 1996, the first survey for which full data is available, the ratio was 0.76 to 1. As indicated in Figure 3, that ratio consistently grew until 2005, when it had reached almost 2.1 to 1.

Shares of U.S. FT Residential and Non-U.S. Citizens Working for U.S. Agencies, 1996 to 2005							
	1996		1998		2001		2005	
U.S. Citizens	39,636	56.7%	39,887	40.2%	42,787	39.7%	41,329	32.4%
Non-U.S. Citizens	30,326	43.3%	59,393	59.8%	64,872	60.3%	86,262	67.6%

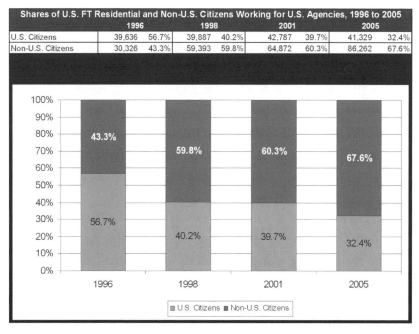

Figure 3: Shares of U.S. Full-Time and Non-U.S. Citizens Supported by U.S. Agencies

The portion of this chart representing U.S. citizens includes all full-time residential missionaries but not non-residential missionaries, tentmakers, or short-term missionaries. Eleven organizations reported 1,000 or more non-U.S. citizens (e.g., Gospel for Asia, Campus Crusade for Christ, AMG International, Partners International, Christian Aid Mission, etc.), which accounts for 60.7% of the total. This data must be seen as more soft, as several agencies reported dramatic changes from 2001 to 2005 (e.g., one organization went from 322 to 8,284; three others went from 0 to over 1,000).

A fourth trend revealed was the ongoing inflation-adjusted increase in the income reported for overseas ministries (Figure 4). The total reported income for overseas missions for the U.S. Protestant agencies in 2005 was $5,241,632,384.39. This is not the sum of the agencies total budgets; it is only what they reported as income being spent overseas. The total reported in 2005 was up 26.7% from

2001 after adjusting for inflation. The 6.7% annual growth rate is the largest seen between surveys since 1992. Altogether, since 1992, the total income for overseas ministries of U.S. Protestant agencies increased by a healthy inflation-adjusted 84.6%.

Further analysis (see Moreau 2007, 21-22), however, reveals the growth between 2001 and 2005, while large, was confined to the agencies with the largest incomes whose primary activities were related to relief and development. This make sense in light of 1) the mega-relief situations of the world context during those years (e.g., the U.S. invasions of Afghanistan and Iraq, the Indian Ocean tsunami, the earthquake in Pakistan, and so on), and 2) the change in U.S. policy to allow government funding for faith-based organizations engaged in relief and development work.

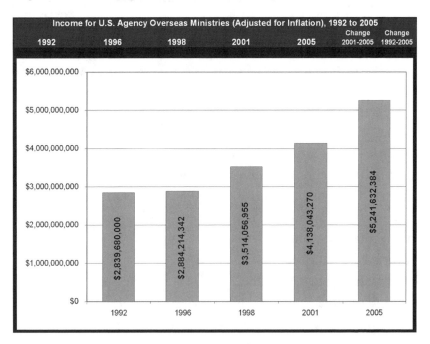

Figure 4: Income for U.S. Agency Overseas Ministries

In addition to these trends, there were two shifts that also took place among U.S. Protestant mission agencies that are important to note in setting the stage for the changes in STM.

The first shift was that from 2001 to 2005 the number of U.S. long-term missionaries decreased (Figure 5). While there was a 5.5% increase in long-term missionaries (four years or more) in the *three*-year span from 1998 to 2001, from 2001 to 2005 (a *four*-year span) there was a 3.0% decrease. This parallels the 3.4% drop in the reported number of U.S. citizens deployed full-time in overseas service for one year or longer by U.S. agencies, which was the biggest decline seen since 1992.

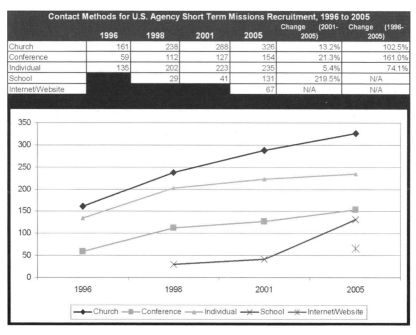

Contact Methods for U.S. Agency Short Term Missions Recruitment, 1996 to 2005						
	1996	1998	2001	2005	Change (2001-2005)	Change (1996-2005)
Church	161	238	288	326	13.2%	102.5%
Conference	59	112	127	154	21.3%	161.0%
Individual	135	202	223	235	5.4%	74.1%
School		29	41	131	219.5%	N/A
Internet/Website				67	N/A	N/A

Figure 5: Long-Term U.S. Missionaries

While the reported numbers require us to note this decline, we should point out that it might not be as severe as the reporting appears to indicate. There were 69 agencies that are newly listed in the 2005 survey, and the inclusion of those agencies to replace agencies that were previously listed but did not fill out the survey accounts for 92.5% of the decline. The agencies that did not respond to the 2005 survey, and were thus dropped, are still active and sending long-term missionaries. The fact that they were dropped makes this shift look worse than it is. In fact, if their 2001 numbers are added into the totals, there is actually a small increase in the number of long-term missionaries sent. Further, but less significant, is the fact that 353 agencies (50.4% of the total U.S. agencies) reported at least one long-term worker in 2005, while 316 agencies (45.6%) did so in the 2001 survey. This increase, however, was still not enough to offset the losses from the agencies that did not respond to the survey in 2005.

The second shift reported by U.S. Protestant mission agencies from 2001 to 2005 was a decrease in the reported number of middle-term U.S. missionaries (1 to 4 years; Figure 6). The decline was 5.2% and was the first decrease in this category since 1992. Unlike the long-term decrease, this decrease is actually more severe than indicated, as the agencies that are newly listed in 2005 accounted for 158 *more* of these middle-term mission workers than the agencies that were dropped in 2005; without the newly listed agencies the drop would be even greater. In addition, 199 agencies (28.4%) reported at least one middle-term missionary in 2005, compared to 188 agencies (27.1%) in the 2001 survey. Even with eleven additional agencies reporting at least one middle-term missionary than in 2001, the total dropped.

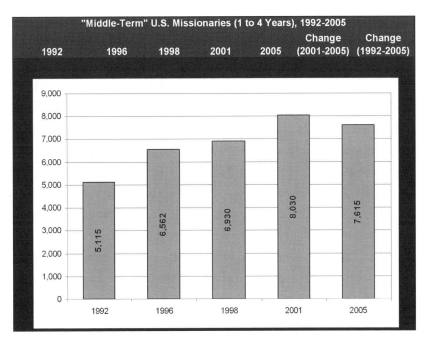

Figure 6: Middle-Term U.S. Missionaries

U.S. Missions, Inc. Short-Term Changes

The first trend in STM was an increase in the number of support staff giving time to STM for the agencies (Figure 7). Starting in 1996, agencies were asked to indicate the number of part- and full-time support personnel they dedicate to STM service. In every survey since then, there was an increase in this category from the previous survey. Three hundred sixty-three agencies (51.9% of the total) reported at least one support person (whether part- or full-time). The total number of support staff for STM has grown by almost 218% since 1996 (with full-time support staff increasing by almost 325%). Agencies are putting more and more of their resources into ensuring that STM are adequately supported. The number of regular personnel (whether in the U.S. or overseas) who had at least 10% of their time focused on STM support grew by 1,134 (60.7%)

from 2001 to 2005. Even more dramatically, those giving full-time support to STM increased by 858, a 147.4% increase.

The top five agencies (Assemblies of God World Missions; Adventures in Missions; InterVarsity Christian Fellowship/USA–Missions Department; Teen Missions International, Inc.; and Missionary Ventures International) accounted for almost three-quarters of the increase (going from a total of 46 support staff of all types in 2001, to 891 in 2005, 74.5% of the total gain).

Finally, there were 51 agencies that indicated *at least* one staff member giving part-time or greater focus on STM but with *zero* short-term missionaries sent. We assume that this is because their trips were shorter than the survey question's minimum two week time requirement, a strong indication that the number of short-term missionaries reported by the agencies is smaller than the actual number they sent.

U.S. Short Term Mission Support Personnel, 1996 to 2005						
	1996	1998	2001	2005	Change (2001-2005)	Change (1996-2005)
Part-Time (10 to 49%)	455	823	782	979	25.2%	115.2%
Part-Time (more than 50%)	150	281	503	582	15.7%	288.0%
Full-Time	339	457	582	1440	147.4%	324.8%
Totals:					60.7%	217.9%

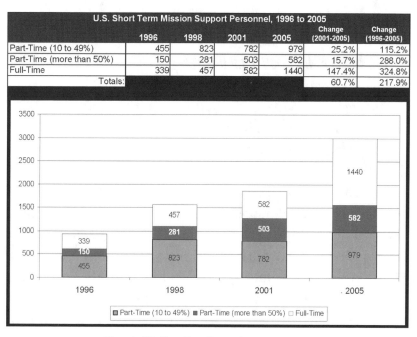

Figure 7: U.S. Short-Term Mission Support Personnel

The second trend seen was an increase of all methods used for STM recruitment (Figure 8). Nearly half (46.79%) of the U.S. Protestant agencies reported that they contact potential short-term missionaries through churches—the largest number of agencies ever. An increasing number of agencies are also using conferences to recruit for short-term trips. However, the most dramatic increase from 2001 to 2005 was in the number of agencies recruiting through schools. This number grew from 41 to 131, a gain of almost 220% (the category "school" was added in the 1999 survey, and thus no number is available for 1996). Even though it was not offered as a choice in the survey for 2005, 67 agencies indicated as a write-in that they use the Internet as a contact method. In the next survey this will be included, and that number is sure to jump significantly, as the Internet is clearly a major mobilization tool being used by agencies. In sum, it can be said with confidence that agencies are more actively recruiting for short-term trips than ever before and are using a broader variety of contact methods in their mobilization efforts.

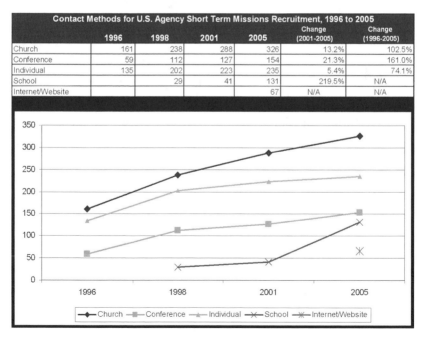

Contact Methods for U.S. Agency Short Term Missions Recruitment, 1996 to 2005					Change (2001-2005)	Change (1996-2005)
	1996	1998	2001	2005		
Church	161	238	288	326	13.2%	102.5%
Conference	59	112	127	154	21.3%	161.0%
Individual	135	202	223	235	5.4%	74.1%
School		29	41	131	219.5%	N/A
Internet/Website				67	N/A	N/A

Figure 8: Contact Methods for U.S. Agency Short-Term Recruitment

For the first time since the surveys began, there was a shift seen in the decrease in the reported number of short-term missionaries (Figure 9). In the 2001 survey, the agencies reported 346,270 short-term missionaries sent in contrast to 144,132 being reported in the 2005 survey; however, the main issue is clearly a reporting one. In this case, two agencies alone accounted for 97.5% of the total short-term losses. As a result, I adjusted the graph by dropping the 2001 and 2005 numbers of both agencies (Figure 9). Even so, there still was a loss in short-term missionaries going on two-week to one-year trips as reported by the agencies represented in this survey. Twenty agencies reported sending out 1,000 or more short-term missionaries, compared to twenty-two agencies in the previous survey. The organizations that were surveyed in 2005 for the first time accounted for 1,764 more short-term workers than those that were removed from the 2005 survey. The resulting gain was not enough to offset the overall loss, though it moderated the severity of it.

At least two possible reasons for this drop may be noted. First, as a result of the events of September 11, 2001, agencies pulled back from short-term trips to more dangerous areas and (at least in part because of ongoing conflicts in some countries) these have not yet recovered. A second possible reason is that agencies may be changing their efforts towards trips of shorter duration than the minimum two weeks required for reporting in the survey. We anticipate adding a question to the next survey that will capture the numbers of people going on shorter trips.

Because the survey asked agencies to report only those people who went on trips of at least two weeks duration, the results show only a partial proportion of those doing STM trips. Several facts support that this is only a partial picture. First, as noted above, there were fifty-one agencies which reported short-term staff support but no short-term personnel shows this is not the total number being sent by the agencies themselves. Second, a recent survey of college students, seminary students and members of adult Sunday school classes reported that more than two-thirds (67.6%) of the short-term trips they had taken were a duration of two weeks *or less* (Priest, et al. 2006, 433). Finally, the survey did not cover people sent on STM through churches or through Christian colleges (with the total number of US church members annually going on STM trips abroad estimated to be 1.6 million for 2005; Priest, et al., 432). While there is an overlap among short-terms sent by agencies, churches, and schools, each also sent out short-termers not connected to either of the other two.

When the short-term numbers are graphed together with the long-term numbers (Figure 10), there is no apparent correlation between the number of short-term people sent (showing a strong increase) and the number of middle- or long-term people sent (showing a slight increase until the 2005 survey, which showed a moderate decline). It may be mentioned that it is possible that the strong short-term increase has helped keep the decline as small as it was (contrast the U.S. number with the Canadian numbers see in Figure 21). There are several other reasons for the apparent lack of correlation.

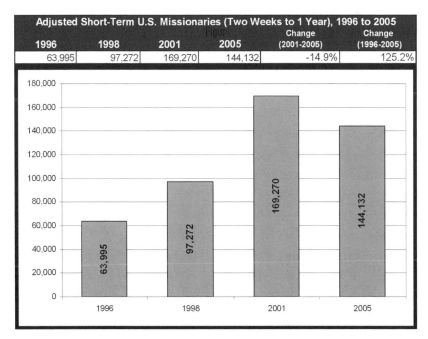

Adjusted Short-Term U.S. Missionaries (Two Weeks to 1 Year), 1996 to 2005					
1996	1998	2001	2005	Change (2001-2005)	Change (1996-2005)
63,995	97,272	169,270	144,132	-14.9%	125.2%

Figure 9: Short-Term U.S. Missionaries

First, it might be that STM experiences simply do not result in enough long-term interest for people to pursue missions as a career. Second, it could be that the shift in generations from one focused on career to one focused on shorter-term life objectives is impacting the number of career missionaries. Related to this, perhaps those taking multiple short-term trips become somehow "immune" to long-term commitment for any of a number of reasons. Finally, another possibility is that the budget of churches has shifted towards STM to such an extent that new missionaries who want to go long-term are finding it more difficult to raise and maintain their support.

	Adjusted Short-Term Workers Sent by U.S. Agency Primary Activity				
Year	Evangelism/ Discipleship	Education/ Training	Mission Agency Support	Relief and Development	Other
2001	89.3%	0.6%	5.9%	4.1%	0.1%
2005	85.3%	1.2%	5.9%	7.4%	0.2%
# Change	(28,054)	678	(1,503)	3,716	211
% Change	-22.8%	64.6%	-15.1%	53.2%	157.5%

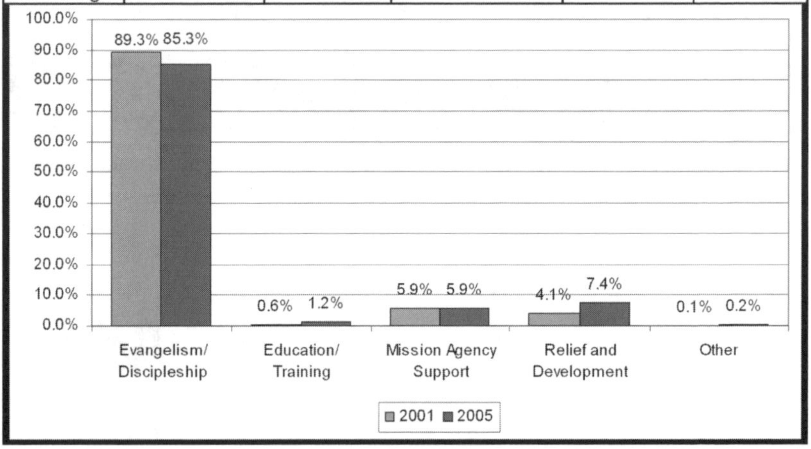

Figure 10: Short-Term and Long-Term U.S. Missionaries Compared

The final shift seen was that from 2001 to 2005 a larger percentage of all short-term workers went with agencies whose primary activities were related to relief/development and education/training and a smaller percentage went with agencies whose primary activities were focused on evangelism and discipleship. (Figure 11). In the survey, each agency was asked to choose from a list of sixty-one activities, six activities on which they focus their energy. After that, each agency was asked to indicate which of these six activities would be most commonly associated with their organization. In analyzing the survey, the activities were combined into five categories: evangelism/discipleship, education/training, mission agency support, relief and development, and other (see Table 1).

To develop Figure 11, we sorted agencies in the 2001 and 2005 surveys by the major category of their primary activity. For example, if an agency chose as its primary activity "Church establishing/planting" the number of short-term workers from that agency were counted in the "Evangelism and Discipleship" category. It must be noted that such an agency would not necessarily devote all of its activities to this category; it may also be involved in relief and development. However, for the sake of contrasting the major categories, we assumed that the primary activity of the agency was where the majority of its resources were directed.

Evangelism/Discipleship	Education/Training	Relief and Development
Apologetics	Correspondence courses	Adoption
Audio recording/dist	Education (TEE)	Agricultural programs
Bible distribution	Education, ch/schl gen Chrstn	Childcare/orphanage
Broadcasting, radio and/or TV	Education, extension (other)	Development, community
Camping programs	Education, missy (cert/deg)	Disability assistance programs
Childrens programs	Education, theological	Justice & Related
Church construction	Training, Other	Medical supplies
Church establishing/planting	**Mission Agency Support**	Medicine, incl. dental and pub health
Discipleship	Association of Missions	Relief and/or rehabilitation
Evangelism, mass	Aviation services	Supplying equipment
Evangelism, personal and small group	Furloughed missionary support	**Other**
Evangelism, student	Information services	Funds transmission
Leadership development	Management consulting/training	Other
Literacy	Member Care	Research
Literature distribution	Partnership development	TESOL
Literature production	Psychological counseling	
National church nurture/support	Purchasing services	
Support of national workers	Recruiting/Mobilizing	
Tentmaking & Related	Services for other agencies	
Translation, Bible	Short-term programs coordination	
Translation, other	Technical assistance	
Video/Film production/dist	Training/Orientation, missionary	
Youth programs		

Table 1: Activities Arranged by Category

With that methodology in mind, we saw a shift in the number of short-term workers away from agencies whose primary activity was in the evangelism and discipleship category and towards those agencies whose primary activity was in the relief and development category. This appears to parallel the shift seen in giving for overseas missions towards those agencies that focus their efforts on relief and development (Moreau 2007, 45).

Summary of U.S. Missions, Inc. and Short-Term Missions

In summary, the larger picture of U.S. Protestant agencies continues to look relatively healthy, but is not without possible warning signs. Positively, the total number of people deployed in missionary service has increased for more than a decade, as has the inflation-adjusted income for overseas ministries. While it appears that the number of long-term missionaries may have declined, and the number of middle-term missionaries has definitely declined, U.S. agencies are utilizing more non-U.S. citizens to engage the missionary task. In future surveys, it will be important to keep an eye on the number of long-term missionaries, as well as the changes of funding in the direction of the agencies with the largest budgets and those focused on relief and development.

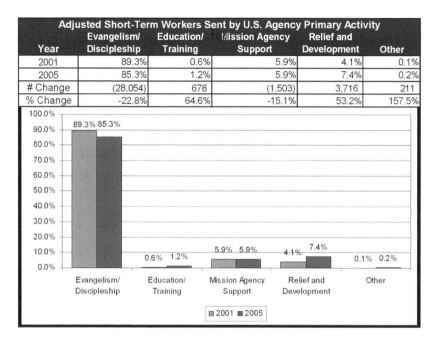

	Adjusted Short-Term Workers Sent by U.S. Agency Primary Activity				
Year	Evangelism/ Discipleship	Education/ Training	Mission Agency Support	Relief and Development	Other
2001	89.3%	0.6%	5.9%	4.1%	0.1%
2005	85.3%	1.2%	5.9%	7.4%	0.2%
# Change	(28,054)	678	(1,503)	3,716	211
% Change	-22.8%	64.6%	-15.1%	53.2%	157.5%

Figure 11: Short-Term Workers Sent by U.S. Agency Primary Activity

In this larger context, I presented two trends and two shifts in STM seen through U.S. Protestant mission agencies. The first trend was a significant increase in the number of support staff (both part-time and full-time) focused on STM recruitment. The second trend was an increase of all methods used for STM recruitment, and especially use of schools and the Internet. U.S. agencies are putting significant resources into mobilizing and administering short-term efforts, though there is no corresponding increase in long-term missionaries seen yet as a result of these efforts.

In addition to these trends, I also reported a shift seen in the decrease in the reported number of short-term (two weeks to one year) missionaries and noted possible reasons behind this reported decrease. Finally, the second shift uncovered was that a larger percentage of all short-term workers went with agencies whose primary activities were related to relief/development and education/

training and a smaller percentage went with agencies whose primary activities were focused on evangelism and discipleship. With the shift in funding changing in a parallel direction, it will be important to follow this shift in the coming years to discern whether it is a trend or an anomaly.

Canadian Protestant Mission Agencies

As with the U.S. picture, changes in the short-term focus of Canadian Protestant agencies takes place in the larger context of the whole of their work. To understand what is happening in Canadian STM, it will be necessary to see what is happening in the larger picture of the agencies. Again, as with the U.S. discussion, we split our presentation here into Canadian agency trends (10 years or more) and shifts (less than 10 years). I offer fewer conjectures on reasons behind the changes seen on the Canadian side since I am not enough aware of the shifts in Canadian society and church to offer substantive comments.

Canadian Missions, Inc. Changes

The first trend seen among Canadian Protestant missionary agencies was a decrease in the reported number of fully-supported Canadians serving overseas (this includes all full-time Canadians serving for one year or more; Figure 12).

Canadian agencies mobilized a fully-supported Canadian residential missionary force that was 9.2% smaller in 2005, than they did in 2001. This continues a trend from 1992, in which the fully-supported residential Canadian missionary force working under Canadian agencies dropped by 23.9%.

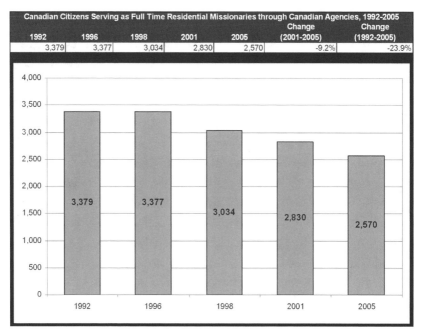

Canadian Citizens Serving as Full Time Residential Missionaries through Canadian Agencies, 1992-2005					Change (2001-2005)	Change (1992-2005)
1992	1996	1998	2001	2005		
3,379	3,377	3,034	2,830	2,570	-9.2%	-23.9%

Figure 12: Canadians Serving as Full-Time Missionaries (1 Year or More)

The second trend found was a decrease in the reported number of Canadian citizens serving as full-time, long-term missionaries (those serving 4 years or more; Figure 13). The most significant decrease for Canadian agencies has been in the number of long-term Canadian missionaries, which has dropped 33% (from 3,075 to 2,079) since 1992. The decline accelerated from 2001 to 2005, during which the long-term missionaries being reported dropped by 17.4%. The decline, and especially its acceleration from 2001 to 2005, is alarming; it is perhaps the greatest challenge facing Canadian Protestant mission agencies in the 21st century.

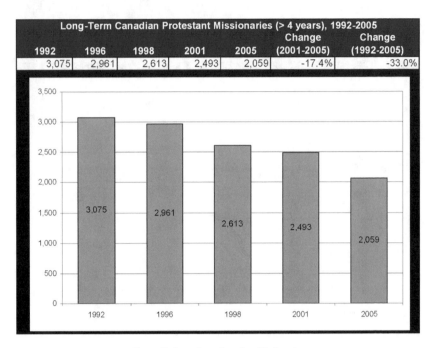

Long-Term Canadian Protestant Missionaries (> 4 years), 1992-2005						
					Change (2001-2005)	Change (1992-2005)
1992	1996	1998	2001	2005		
3,075	2,961	2,613	2,493	2,059	-17.4%	-33.0%

Figure 13: Long-Term Canadian Missionaries

The third trend seen was a modest increase in the total number of non-Canadians serving under Canadian agencies (Figure 14). Paralleling the U.S., the number of non-Canadian citizens under the support of Canadian agencies increased more than 185% since 1996. The vast majority of that increase took place during the period from 1996 to 1998 (151%). While still growing since 1998, the growth rate has significantly slowed (13.7% from 1998 to 2005). While the number of non-Canadians working in a country other than their own declined from 2001 to 2005 by 16.6%, they still increased overall from 1996 by 845%. If the current growth rates of non-Canadians working for Canadian agencies continues, we expect that Canadian agencies will have more non-Canadians than Canadians within their ranks by the time of the next survey.

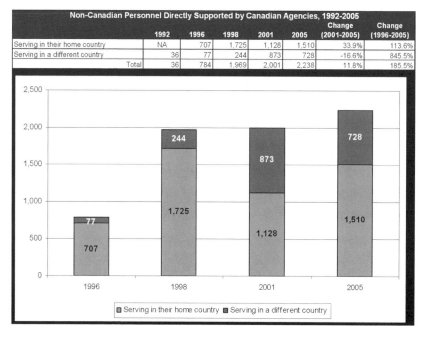

Non-Canadian Personnel Directly Supported by Canadian Agencies, 1992-2005						Change (2001-2005)	Change (1996-2005)
	1992	1996	1998	2001	2005		
Serving in their home country	NA	707	1,725	1,128	1,510	33.9%	113.6%
Serving in a different country	36	77	244	873	728	-16.6%	845.5%
Total	36	784	1,969	2,001	2,238	11.8%	185.5%

Figure 14: Non-Canadian Citizens Directly Supported by Canadian Agencies

Related to the third trend was an increase in the ratio of non-Canadian versus Canadian citizens working for Canadian agencies (Figure 15). Overall, there was growth of 44.8% in the total full-time on-location Canadian missionary force from 1992 to 2005, though the 2001 to 2005 period saw a decline of 3.9%. The overall growth is directly attributable to the number of non-Canadians working for Canadian agencies. The current ratio of non-Canadians to Canadians is .87 to 1, up from .26 to 1 in 1996.

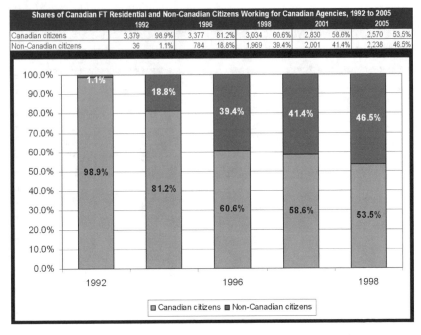

Shares of Canadian FT Residential and Non-Canadian Citizens Working for Canadian Agencies, 1992 to 2005									
	1992		1996		1998		2001		2005
Canadian citizens	3,379	98.9%	3,377	81.2%	3,034	60.6%	2,830	58.6%	2,570	53.5%
Non-Canadian citizens	36	1.1%	784	18.8%	1,969	39.4%	2,001	41.4%	2,238	46.5%

Figure 15: Shares of Canadian and Non-Canadian Citizens Supported by Canadian Agencies

The fourth and final trend seen was an increase in the reported income for overseas missions (Figure 16). Canadian agencies reported $638,142,812 in income for overseas ministries, an inflation-adjusted increase of 123.1% since 1992 (and an increase of 36.9% over the 2001 survey). In this case, the increase in income reported by the top three agencies was almost 95% of the total gain reported. Thus, the solid growth experiences in aggregate was actually confined to the top three agencies, each of which lists their primary activity as one related to relief and development.

Further, the top ten agencies received 72.6% of the total income, up from 66.7% in the 2001 survey. The top twenty agencies received 84.5% of the total income, up from 82.5%. It is clear that a larger portion of the total income for overseas work among Canadian Protestant agencies is being concentrated among fewer agencies.

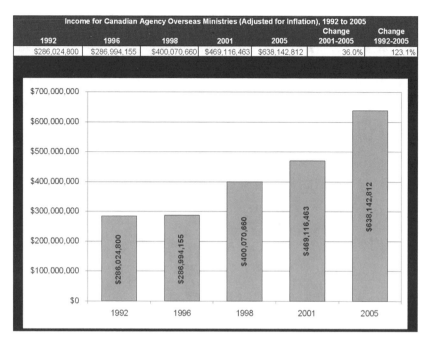

Income for Canadian Agency Overseas Ministries (Adjusted for Inflation), 1992 to 2005						
1992	1996	1998	2001	2005	Change 2001-2005	Change 1992-2005
$286,024,800	$286,994,155	$400,070,660	$469,116,463	$638,142,812	36.0%	123.1%

Figure 16: Income for Canadian Agency Overseas Ministries

Organizations which reported a primary activity focused on relief and development received 73.6% ($469,491,505) of the total income, and 93% of the inflation-adjusted gain. Thus, parallel to the U.S. Protestant agencies, the majority of the gains in income for overseas ministries among Canadian Protestant agencies was concentrated among agencies whose primary focus was relief and development activities.

In addition to these trends, one positive shift was an increase in the number of middle-term Canadian missionaries being sent by Canadian agencies (Figure 17). While the 33% decline in long-term missionaries is sobering, the fact that the number of middle-termers (serving from 1 to 4 years) rose by 68.1% between the 2001 and 2005 surveys, offers some hope for the recovery of Canadian long-term personnel.

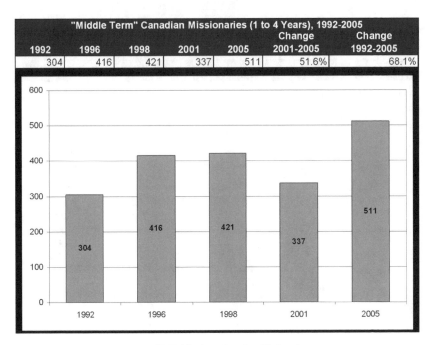

"Middle Term" Canadian Missionaries (1 to 4 Years), 1992-2005					Change 2001-2005	Change 1992-2005
1992	1996	1998	2001	2005		
304	416	421	337	511	51.6%	68.1%

Figure 17: Middle-Term Canadian Missionaries

Canadian Missions, Inc. Short-term Changes

What about short-term changes from Canadian Protestant mission agencies? *First, there was a trend seen in the continuing increase in the reported number of short-term missionaries being sent by Canadian agencies (Figure 18).*

Since 1996, the year the terminology for this question in the survey was stabilized, the number of short-term missionaries of two weeks to one year going through Canadian agencies increased by 43.1%. In the 2005 survey, seventeen agencies reported 50 or more short-term missionaries. Canadian mission agencies reported a total of 3,534 such short-term workers, a modest increase of 4.1% over the numbers reported in the 2001 survey.

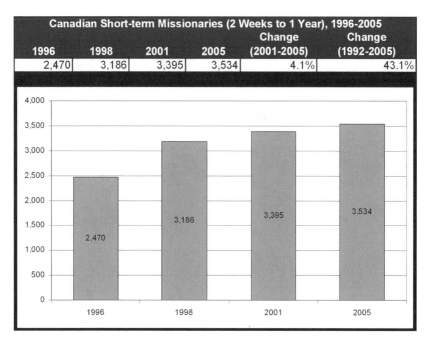

Canadian Short-term Missionaries (2 Weeks to 1 Year), 1996-2005				Change (2001-2005)	Change (1992-2005)
1996	1998	2001	2005		
2,470	3,186	3,395	3,534	4.1%	43.1%

Figure 18; Short-Term Canadian Missionaries

The second trend seen was an increase of all methods used for STM recruitment (Figure 19). How did the agencies find people for their STM projects? Figure 19 depicts the primary methods of initial contact as well as the changes from 1996 to 2005. Almost half the Canadian agencies contacted people through churches (45.9%) and more than one-third used individual contacts (38.5%). The 222.2% increase in contacts through schools reflects a surge in number of Canadian agencies (23.8% of the total) that are now using this method. Even though it was not provided as an option, seventeen Canadian agencies indicated that they used the Internet as a contact method. This will be incorporated into the next survey and we anticipate that the number indicating that they use the Internet for STM recruitment will jump dramatically.

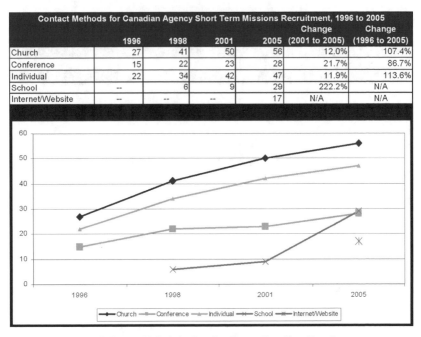

Contact Methods for Canadian Agency Short Term Missions Recruitment, 1996 to 2005					
	1996	1998	2001	2005	Change (2001 to 2005)	Change (1996 to 2005)
Church	27	41	50	56	12.0%	107.4%
Conference	15	22	23	28	21.7%	86.7%
Individual	22	34	42	47	11.9%	113.6%
School	--	6	9	29	222.2%	N/A
Internet/Website	--	--	--	17	N/A	N/A

Figure 19: Contact Methods for Canadian Agency Short-Term Recruitment

Additionally, while the aggregate number of reported short-term support personnel remained the same as in the 2001 survey (after adjusting for discrepancies) there was a shift towards more full-time staff support (Figure 20). While there was only a modest increase in the number of short-term workers, there was a 71.5% drop in the *reported* number of regular staff in Canada or overseas who have full-time responsibilities related to STM programs (from 158 to 45) and a more moderate drop in the number of part-time (10 to 49%) short-term support staff (from 130 to 86, or 33.8%) from the numbers originally reported for the 2001 survey.

However, two agencies changed reporting methods between the reports that significantly affected the results. One reported 125 full-time short-term support personnel in 2001, but 0 in 2005; another reported 30 part-time (10 to 49%) short-term support personnel in 2001 and only 4 in 2005. When the reporting of these two agencies is factored out, the resulting adjusted numbers (Figure 20) show no loss from the 2001 in the aggregate number of short-term support personnel, though we see a small shift from part-time staff (adjusted: 136 to 126) to more full-time staff (adjusted: 33 to 45).

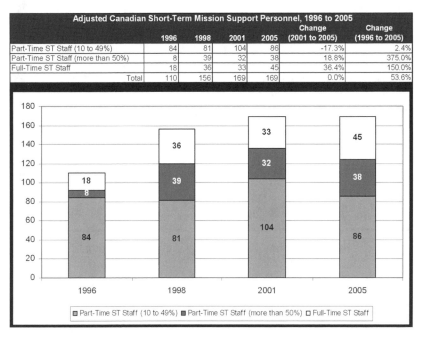

Adjusted Canadian Short-Term Mission Support Personnel, 1996 to 2005					Change (2001 to 2005)	Change (1996 to 2005)
	1996	1998	2001	2005		
Part-Time ST Staff (10 to 49%)	84	81	104	86	-17.3%	2.4%
Part-Time ST Staff (more than 50%)	8	39	32	38	18.8%	375.0%
Full-Time ST Staff	18	36	33	45	36.4%	150.0%
Total	110	156	169	169	0.0%	53.6%

Figure 20: Canadian Short-Term Mission Support Personnel

When the short-term and long-term numbers are charted, we see that there is either no correlation or perhaps a slight negative correlation between short-term and long-term Canadian missionaries (Figure 21). At best, it seems that after a decade of growth in short-term missionaries, there appears to have been no impact on long-term recruitment. It could be argued that the curve for long-term drop would be even steeper if not for short-term impact, but (as with the U.S. Protestant agencies) there is no evidence from our survey data to justify such a claim.

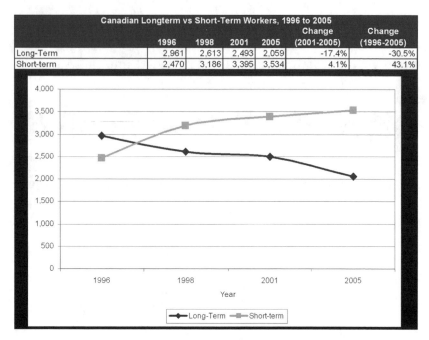

Canadian Longterm vs Short-Term Workers, 1996 to 2005					
	1996	**1998**	**2001**	**2005**	**Change (2001-2005)**	**Change (1996-2005)**
Long-Term	2,961	2,613	2,493	2,059	-17.4%	-30.5%
Short-term	2,470	3,186	3,395	3,534	4.1%	43.1%

Figure 21: Short-Term and Long-Term Canadian Missionaries Compared

The final shift seen was that from 2001 to 2005 a larger percentage of all short-term workers went with agencies whose primary activities were related to evangelism/discipleship and relief/development and a smaller percentage went with agencies whose primary activities were focused on mission agency support. (Figure 22). As noted in the U.S. section, each agency was asked to choose from a list of sixty-one activities, six activities on which they focus their energy. After that, each agency was asked to indicate which of these six activities would be most commonly associated with their organization. In analyzing the survey, the activities were combined into five categories: evangelism and discipleship, education and training, mission agency support, relief and development, and other (see Table 1 above).

To develop Figure 22, we sorted agencies in the 2001 and 2005 surveys by major category of their primary activity. For example, if an agency chose as its primary activity "Church establishing/planting" the number of short-term workers from that agency were counted in the "Evangelism and Discipleship" category. It must be noted that such an agency would not necessarily devote all of its activities in this category; it may also be involved in relief and development. However, for the sake of contrasting the major categories, we assumed that the primary activities of the agency was where the majority of its resources were directed.

With that methodology in mind, among Canadian agencies (and in contrast to U.S. agencies) we see a shift in the number of short-term workers away from agencies whose primary activity was in the mission agency support category and towards those agencies whose primary activity was in the evangelism/discipleship and relief/development categories.

Adjusted Short-Term Workers Sent by Canadian Agency Primary Activity				
Year	Evangelism/ Discipleship	Relief and Development	Mission Agency Support	Education/ Training
2001	69.7%	10.5%	18.6%	1.1%
2005	78.5%	14.3%	6.1%	1.1%
# Change	406	150	-414	1
% Change	17.2%	42.3%	-65.6%	2.6%

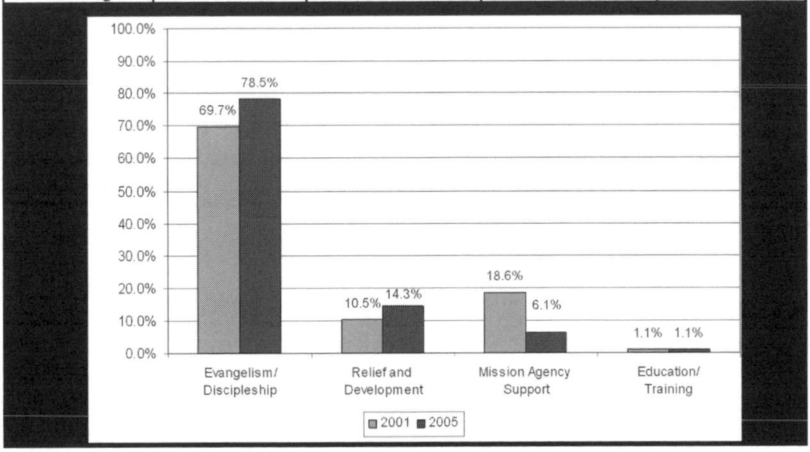

Figure 22: Short-Term Workers Sent by Canadian Agency Primary Activity

Summary of Canadian Missions, Inc. and Short-Term Missions

While Canadian mission agencies have seen some positive changes in the past several years, most notably the increase in middle-term Canadian missionaries and the increase in non-Canadians working for Canadian agencies, the overall picture is not as encouraging as one might hope. The trend of the decease in the reported number of Canadian citizens serving as full-time, long-term missionaries is especially troubling. While there is some encouragement that the trend of increasing income for overseas missions continues, the fact that the increase was concentrated among the largest agencies suggests we should exercise caution in drawing too optimistic a conclusion.

In terms of short-term work, it is encouraging that the trend of increasing numbers of short-term missionaries continues, and that the energy of Canadian agencies in recruiting and administratively supporting these efforts is also increasing. However, the fact that this does not seem to result in a higher number of long-term missionaries may be discouraging for those agencies who are hoping short-term recruitment will result in more long-term workers. In contrast to the U.S. picture, the fact that a larger percentage of all short-term workers went with agencies whose primary activities were related to relief/development and evangelism/discipleship and a smaller percentage went with agencies whose primary activities were focused on mission agency support can also be seen as a source of encouragement for Canadian agencies.

Conclusion

There can be no doubt that U.S. and Canadian Protestant mission agencies are giving increased attention to STM recruitment, support and sending. What is yet to be clearly seen is the net impact this focus has had on long-term missions. To date, no direct correlation can be drawn between the massive increase in STM and long-term sending in either country.

It is tempting to infer that without short-term missions, long-term commitments would not have held steady in the U.S. or would have dropped even more sharply in Canada, but that cannot be supported by the data collected in the survey. It is obvious that continued research into this phenomena of STM is of increasingly critical importance to the long-term health of the U.S. and Canadian Protestant agencies.

References

Moreau, A. Scott. 2007. Putting the Survey in Perspective. *Mission Handbook 2007-2009: U.S. and Canadian Protestant Ministries Overseas*, ed. Linda Weber and Dotsey J. Welliver, 11-75. Wheaton, IL: Evangelism and Missions Information Service.

Robert J. Priest, Terry Dischinger, Steve Rasmussen and C. M. Brown. 2006. Researching the Short-Term Mission Movement. *Missiology: An International Review* 34: 431-50.

CHAPTER 2

EVALUATING SHORT-TERM

MISSIONS: MISSIOLOGICAL QUESTIONS

ALEX G. SMITH

A Potent Analysis

A respected missionary practitioner and colleague recently provided increased impetus for this article when he wrote, "Short-term missions have such a profound effect on what we are doing around the world. I think it is time to make an adjustment to our course so that the whole missionary endeavor does not break up on the rocks of superficial pragmatism. They have done much to inform and involve the church in the Great Commission. I sense a lot more excitement about missions because of the sheer numbers of people who have seen first hand the needs of the field." On the other hand, a "well-thought-through strategy that helps utilize this interest to the greatest benefit of the people we are trying to reach" is often lacking. Missiologists observe "a shift in the purpose of short-term missions from reaching the lost to pleasing the goers, giving them an experience to remember" (Niphakis 2006:1).

Considerable exaggeration accompanies the claim that STM experiences are increasing the numbers of new workers that go into long-term missionary service. Some claim that "80% (of career missionaries) previously had short-term exposure" (Nicholson 2006:4). David Mays says, "Some estimate that a minimum of one million Americans go on mission trips annually at a cost of one billion dollars"(2006:312). Today some researchers say that number has doubled! But the career long-term mission force has not increased by the tens of thousands! *Mission Handbook* cites statistics of the numbers going into career missions (Welliver 2004:13). Mays reports, "The latest figures from 2001 show that the number has changed little over the last dozen years" (2006:313).

Churches have put a tremendous investment of time, money and energy into STM. Rick Warren's PEACE plan is almost exclusively based on STM. If successful, this could perpetuate the short-term missionary model. Is it not time for churches and mission agencies to look carefully at this trend and analyze the pros and cons, "before drowning the world with American enthusiasm for touchy, feely experiences?" (Niphakis 2006:1).

Several missiological issues arise. Can STM become more effective through curtailing the volume of participants and increasing the quality? Does this warrant a more careful screening of STM volunteers? How can a closer working together of agencies, churches and STM applicants foster interest in a more developmental approach? In what ways can this be focused on short-term participants so as to enhance their spiritual growth and still provide effective approaches to the peoples whom they hope to reach? What is the best use of STM workers in helping the establishment of indigenous churches, serving the long-term missionary, and maturing the volunteers themselves? What upgrades in STM training could enhance effectiveness? Is there a danger of making long-term missionaries ineffective by using them to manage large numbers of short-termers?

Another concern relates to decision making. Many short-term candidates have already been on multiple mission trips, but still say they are looking for the right sphere of ministry. Could churches and mission agencies work more with them beforehand to help them identify the most suitable opportunities? Why are all the decisions left up to the short-term volunteers as if they were customers? Why ask short-term volunteers what they want to do and then create ministries for them to fulfill their needs? "Should not the short-term model be a mirror of the long-term process where the agency (or church) decides what is needed and then recruits suitable candidates for that task? (Niphakis 2006:1). The large University Presbyterian Church in Seattle has run an effective short-term program for many years, where the church recruits, screens and selects university students, trains them, decides where they are to go, what team they are to serve on, and what their responsibilities will be. The short-term participants simply comply. The choice is not theirs to make in that church's program.

Niphakis notes that "Churches need to look at short-term service as a microcosm of long-term missions" (2006:1). Churches and agencies should invest time and energy helping volunteers think through their suitability, best placement, contribution to ministry and valid reasons for going. STM participants should go primarily as learners rather than as ministers, servers rather than as receivers. Short-term programs become apprenticeships rather than field trips, training opportunities more than holiday outlets.

Patterns from History

Biblical Examples

STM is as old as the early Church, and even predates it. God often sent Old Testament prophets for brief periods to declare His word to the nations, like Jonah to Nineveh. Other Israelite captives witnessed in foreign lands such as Daniel to Babylon, and the Jewish slave girl at Naaman's house in Syria. Even Jesus' ministry on earth was only three years! The persecution following the stoning of Stephen dispersed believers into mission opportunities throughout the regions of Judea and Samaria, followed by efforts in Phoenicia, Cyprus, Antioch and elsewhere throughout the Roman Empire (Acts 8:1, 9:31,11:19). Admittedly many of these ventures were outcomes from involuntary scattering for the disciples' preservation. But evangelism and mission were normal full-time expressions of believers. Priscilla and Aquila and others shared the faith as they traveled on business.

Surprisingly the great missionary church of Acts 13 that sent out Paul and Barnabas on their first and subsequent missions to the Gentiles was not planted by the Apostles. This church arose out of the efforts of short-term volunteer outreaches from Phoenicia, Cyprus and Cyrene in Libya (Acts 11:19-20). At first these efforts were narrow home missions to the Jews only. However, at Antioch some of these likely entrepreneurs, from Cyrene and Cyprus started mission outreach to the Greeks. These Gentiles were quite receptive, and a large number of Greeks believed and turned to the Lord (Acts 11:21).

Mission Illustrations

Andy Smith illustrates short-term mission exposures from the time of Hudson Taylor in the 1800s. Englishman Robert Landale had completed his MA at Oxford but sensed a call to China. In 1876 his barrister (lawyer) father encouraged him to go first as a traveler to

China so he could learn on site what the life of a missionary entailed, before committing to career service.

American William Borden of the celebrated wealthy dairy family had just completed high school. On a trip around the world in the early 1900s, he saw people across Asia bound in idolatry. This experience deeply burdened him and led eventually to his joining the China Inland Mission (2000:150-151).

Personal Experiences

In 1958 at age 21 I left Australia on a freighter, the SS Lakemba, for missionary training in Canada. I had never heard of STM. When we landed in Fiji, I had time on my hands. The ship was to load raw sugar over the next three weeks. I found an Australian missionary working nearby. He encouraged me to do mission among the local Tamil Indians. So I began to work in youth camps, visit in Indian homes and in the Christian hospital, play my trumpet, sing solos, pray, give testimonies and preach the Gospel. I befriended a young Tamil believer. We bonded and he later followed me to do theological education. He became a career missionary and is still serving the Lord today.

During the summer breaks at college I went on STM twice. First in 1959 I teamed up with a Scottish fellow-student. After working at a sawmill for a couple of months we took time off to sail to Britain, where we did a six-week evangelistic preaching tour of Scotland, England and Wales, which my friend's pastor had arranged. Our E-1 evangelism resulted in several being converted or revived, including some passengers from the ships on which we sailed.

The next summer of 1960 I teamed up with a South African student and the college's English mission professor for a six-week short mission in Mexico and Guatemala. We went under Harvesters International. They had an orientation and training course near the eastern border with Mexico and directed the programs of several STM teams. Our group was the only one to go into Guatemala where, with inadequate, poor Spanish we sang and played trumpet over radio broadcasts, preached and evangelized using English with interpreters, an E-2 experience. At the end of that time a communist coupe took place, which made things a bit exciting for our exit and return to Canada. Only God knows what lasting fruit came of these efforts. But those experiences are still vivid memories today.

Practical Encouragement

Four years later my wife and I, with our two infant children, were in Asia on long-term mission with OMF. During that era new missionaries first committed their lives to mission and sailed to Asia, where OMF directors then designated them to a field of service! Assigned to Buddhist Thailand with its beautiful people, difficult language, complicated culture, and intricate Folk Buddhist worldview, we realized our inadequacy to proclaim Christ effectively without divine help in that E-3 context, in spite of our previous STM experiences.

Multiplying Effort by STM

By the beginning of our second term in 1970, we had better cultural understanding and linguistic facility. Mission and evangelism were high priorities across those hot plains of central Thailand. God was doing some new things in that pioneer situation. Our resources and manpower were stretched. But I saw the strategic use of an indigenous model that battery and medicine sellers used to advantage. Day by day they drove their film vans from village to village selling their wares and showing films. Thousands came out to watch them through the night. It was a dynamic, entertaining and festive atmosphere. Our application of their model used Land Rovers to drive circuits of villages and towns to show Gospel films with Thai sound tracks, to sell Bible portions cheaply, and to proclaim Christ to the masses, particularly during the hot dry season when everyone was free after harvesting (Smith 1976: 167-169).

In order to increase the coverage for outreach in 1970, I invited a New Zealand film evangelist, who worked briefly in India, to come for several months to manage a second Land Rover film team. Usually several national believers helped on each team. Primarily the STM worker ran the technical side, maintained the equipment, drove from place to place, prayed and encouraged the indigenous Christians to evangelize. For the next few years we increased these helping hands until we had three evangelistic film teams operating simultaneously along with two larger Thai Bible College teams. Through these combined efforts the beginnings of a score of pioneer churches arose.

Investment in STM

In 1984 when I was assigned back to USA for mobilization as Northwest Director, the concept of STM was just beginning to become a mode of operation among many American mission agencies. Over the next two decades I recruited, prepared, led and debriefed many teams for STM in Asia. Usually they went for four to eight weeks. Some were teams comprised of Bible College students. Others were gathered from area churches, while a few were teams from a single church. In some cases the churches kept running their own mission teams year after year, using former experienced STM members to lead them. During these years, OMF developed several levels of short-term service: 1) Serve Asia Program for times less than a year, 2) Apprenticeship Program for two years on the Field and 3) Short-Term Associates Program for working in professional service overseas from one to three years.

From personal experience with STM programs for many years, this writer learned some key lessons. Furthermore, to get a wider view for this paper he sent a questionnaire to the main organizers and operators of STM in OMF, which works in a score of countries of Asia, where the Church is a small minority among largely folk Buddhist peoples. From that perspective, the following suggestions and evaluations may seem narrow, but the replies and responses from mission leaders and STM coordinators have shown surprising consistency. Many of those responses from thirteen home-side and field perspectives were selected for reflection below.

Pragmatic Evaluation

Value and Strengths

Over the past decade many agencies have multiplied STM programs while the number of churches involved in STM has grown considerably. This combination gives church members and young people a multitude of choices today. A variegated smorgasbord of opportunities provides an attractive market for youth, who look for exciting offerings that give instant involvement in today's intercultural global village. This volatile climate challenges mission agencies with questions like: Can they be trusted with the churches' young people? Do they have a history of experience in this STM world? Can they provide adequate care for youth? How do they provide a favorable stimulus for the appetites of the current generation's youth culture? In what ways do they use STM as an efficient part of evangelization? (Payne 2006:2).

STM volunteers can provide "worthwhile contributions to evangelization where they are integrated into a program of evangelism, follow-up and discipleship" (Eastwood 2006:1).

They usually exhibit the energy of youth, a willingness to try anything, and an ability to identify with Asian teenage groups, who reflect the current "world youth culture" (Lum 2007:2). MTV, Pop culture, immediate communications and instant gratification are some of those unifying traits, all of which carry certain dangers. Much missionary time and energy is consumed in preparing for STM and providing logistics—transportation, housing, and resources. However, from observing their youthful enthusiasm for mission, their vibrancy of faith, and their experiencing new cultures and societies, the attitudes of many field missionaries has changed towards STM (Leighton 2006:1, Thompson 2006:2). This interaction often provides them with insights into the home cultures and helps missionaries understand the current thinking of youth in their native lands (Eastwood 2006:1).

Since the enemy of the best is not the worst, but "the next to the best," missiologists must wrestle with the challenge that STM poses for long-term mission. Should agencies become more market oriented and offer more palatable services to gain more of the STM market share? Or do they rigidly maintain their distinctive goal of evangelization and primary biblical purpose of church multiplication among all unreached people groups? How do agencies measure and evaluate that they are reaching those goals? How does STM specifically contribute to that end? Are mission vision statements so broad that they do not clearly set the direction for effective evaluation? How can mission strategists hone a good thing like STM to make it more productive, and the Movement more efficient? How much do the current pluralistic cultural climate, popular universalism and consequent weakening of theology affect STM operations on the fields? What real effect does STM have on long-term recruiting? Do agencies see STM as a vital, valuable investment? How is "long term" defined? What crucial factors make STM valuable for the urgent completion of Christ's mission?

Obstacles and Weaknesses

One of six concerns noted in Phil Nicholson's unpublished article "The Dangers of Short-Term Mission" is "cultural imperialism" (p.3). Some STM participants think they are "experts" after a short time in the field and judge career missionaries for not seeing more results (Leighton 2006:1). Eastwood points out that STM can "perpetuate the idea of the foreign expert, that somehow believers from Christian countries are better," especially those from the West, Korea, and Singapore (2006:1). This ethnocentric attitude counters perceptions that mission wants to foster. Many short-term programs are run in English, usually with its accompanying western cultural connotations. This unfortunately helps reinforce the view of the Christian faith as a "foreign religion." This "is still true even when the majority of the team members have been overseas Chinese" (Eastwood 2006:1).

Naturally, many STM ministries are done in English, often to good effect, especially where they are offering a product that meets a valuable need. One STM ministry in Thailand uses qualified volunteers "to teach English to Thai High School English teachers." This uses key skills, helps local teachers, builds relationships, opens contact for the local missionaries and provides measurable satisfaction to both local teachers and those from abroad (Leighton 2006:1). Nevertheless subtle cultural imperialism can exist.

Some missionaries from the two-thirds world, for whom English is a second or third language, follow the pattern of using English classes in the community as a primary tool for evangelism. While a demand for English in many overseas lands exists, mostly for business and economic advantages, meeting that need for this smaller segment of the population falls short of evangelizing the whole nation. Even indigenous pastors holding English classes in local churches to attract people outside of the church community is common practice. National leaders use it, even when expatriate missionaries are not present, reinforcing forms of cultural and linguistic imperialism. This approach raises a problem regarding "outreach to the majority working class and lower echelons of society, for whom education was mostly a negative and degrading experience," particularly in countries like Taiwan (Eastwood 2006:1).

These cultural problems often relate to contextualization. What are better ways to multiply indigenous churches? How can STM approaches overcome contextual issues? What kinds of training are needed to preclude ethnocentric attitudes and pride? It is crucial to portray humbly that all people have equal dignity, for all are made in the image of God. Paternalistic or imperialistic attitudes are to be avoided.

The lack of the local language, church ministry experience and cultural understanding are major weaknesses of STM (Thompson 2006:2). How then can career workers expect fruitfulness in depth from STM programs in fields where language is so vital for communication? What about STM participants having too high expectations of evangelistic fruit and other successful outcomes from their brief experience?

As a consequence of these difficulties over a number of years, OMF field leaders in Taiwan restructured their STM program as follows:

First, the field determined whom to accept, decided what they would do, and assigned where they would go.

Second, they decided to accept only Chinese speakers or those who had prior relationships with their existing field missionaries.

Third, they integrated the STM program into their wider field strategy (not vice versa).

Fourth, they made the main purpose of STM to mobilize for long-term service.

Fifth, they kept expectations of STM ministry low and focused on sharing the field's vision for prayer and future workers with the participants (Nicholson 2006:1).

Effectiveness and Impact

It is important to keep the big picture in mind. Where host or home churches fail to do this, they may not feel their investment was worth the results of STM. Impact is not the only factor for measuring STM. The growth of the participants themselves, their influence on other church members, their involvement in mission programs of their home churches are also vital outcomes. A careful focus on using STM outreach through strategies integrated into church-mission programs has mostly accomplished a positive impact on the overall ministry of the churches (Thompson 2006:2).

Though effort and results are not always equal, STM provides an investment in young peoples' lives through which God uses exposure, discipleship and teaching for His higher purposes. English teaching with personal testimony have brought an international flair and flavor in lifestyles and culture. "STM is a ministry within a ministry" (Zindel 2006:3).

Teams that go each year to the same field and/or the same church situation are more effective. This allows continuity of contact and better building of relationships, which are keys to effectiveness (Payne 2006:2). STM teams "reflected Christ to the churches, especially through true servanthood. This encouraged and inspired the members, but it was difficult to transfer outside friendships made, to the local believers for follow up" after the STM classes ended (Tibbetts 2006:3).

Most impact relies on long-term relationships. The main value is adding contacts from outreach in English, which, though limited, is better among the educated classes. "The contribution of STM to evangelization is small." Similar to conditions in much of Asia, "most fruitful ministry in Taiwan depends on Chinese language and long-term relationships, especially among the majority laboring and working peoples. As to the worth of STM, the jury is still out. Some of them become prayer supporters. So far in the last ten years, out of a few hundred who joined STM in Taiwan, only one couple returned for long-term service" (Nicholson 2006:1-2). Will more time see others?

Field Leaders' Responses

The growth of interest in STM and their increased volume necessitated some fields setting aside personnel to be STM Coordinators. Their role is to help organize effective programs on the fields, to be responsible for the logistics and placements, and to monitor the recruiting and quality of participants (Thompson 2006:4, Eastwood 2006:1). One problem is that some field leaders only get involved when crises or problems arise, which seems to be rare. Often there is not adequate time for feedback between the field and home side and vice versa (Zindel 2006:3). When churches and agencies send the type of teams that the field leaders request, the key to success is the training given before departure to the field (Payne 2006:2).

Most feedback on STM teams is positive, but some individual members cause disappointment. A lot depends on the team leaders and whether they are able to provide pastoral care and bring out the best in the team. Most difficulties seem to arise from participants who are under 21. College graduates and those close to finishing, who have some work experience already, seem more mature and have more abilities to offer (Nicholson 2006:2). Most STM participants felt their exposure was beneficial and rewarding, especially in understanding the realities of what missionaries' living was like and what their agencies' ministry entailed. Most have encouraged and contributed to the blessing of the members on the field (Lum 2007:2).

The longer STM can see missions up close, the better. They then can obtain a more real view of the difficulties, and build more significant relationships. Two workers who came out for a two-year STM in central Thailand are both full-time members now (Tibbetts 2006:3).

Effect on National Believers

STM teams do challenge local Christians to do evangelism. They see the sacrifice of "young people who are not full-time workers, being willing to give up their holiday time and fly overseas, often at their own expense, to take part in mission. This causes the local believers to question how seriously they themselves are involved in mission and evangelism." Sadly, seldom are there local mission structures and opportunities to which nationals can respond (Eastwood 2006:1). How can national churches develop dynamic teams for local evangelism and mission? Some third-world churches are sending STM teams cross-culturally. In what ways can STM be used to further motivate and train their members in outreach locally and globally?

Local Christians enjoy STM volunteers. Churches often request teams to return. The best responses come from student groups around their same ages. Unfortunately, most relationships are not maintained when the teams leave. There are exceptions (Nicholson 2006:2). STM youthful presence was helpful for evangelistic camps where they invited students from colleges. Simply being there to provide a festive atmosphere even without the language was worthwhile (Tibbetts 2006:3). A strategic need is the consistent maintenance of personal relationships made from STM visits. Today's cyber-space age, electronic media, and phone technology are versatile and easy to use, but require much commitment and consistency, unfortunately not high characteristics of this active, instant generation.

Sensitivity and Fitting In

As to adaptability, STM volunteers "easily integrate into local church life on the field, and interact with members readily. Most young adults comfortably relate to unchurched students and youth. Some maintain longer-term contacts with them" (Lum 2007:2). Generally the host churches accept STM participants wholeheartedly and usually have good experiences (Thompson 2006:2).

Cultural sensitivity and acceptability are important. Nationals are often graciously quite flexible about accepting STM worker's lack of understanding of their culture. Few cultural disasters occur, but potential difficulties can arise, especially where teams are under the control of national workers, who do not always appreciate the overseas team's need of time to prepare and to get adequate rest.

Sometimes workers' immaturity and lack of sensitivity embarrasses the local church and the missionaries, particularly by the way some dress, behave inappropriately, or foster romantic infatuations (Eastwood 2006:1). Enthusiasm is commendable, but volunteers have lots to learn, and need significant mentoring. How can agencies and field missionaries foster better mentoring on the fields?

Often STM teams run "event-performance-focused" programs where people are expected to come in to them, rather than "personal friendship-relationship focused" ones whereby they go out to where the people are. Too often they also expect the local believers to do the follow up after their dramatic events (Eastwood 2006:1).

Expectations and Language Frustrations

Having realistic expectations before going out is vital (Payne 2006:3). With some significant hindrances to communication, the value of longer exposures of one to three years for STM is obvious. Language facility can be acquired with effort over time.

Previously Taiwan, like other Asian nations, "accepted individuals on STM who were frequently frustrated because of lack of language and consequently lack of fruit and fulfillment. The gap between expectations and realities disillusioned and disappointed the missionaries too. In internships of two years, non-Chinese speakers spend the first six months in language learning, are treated as full members, and given a wide range of ministry responsibilities. They can contribute input to field strategies" (Nicholson 2006:2). In Thailand apprentices usually do the full orientation and language program along with long-term career folk (Tibbetts 2006:3).

Cambodia expects even STM workers to study language at least two hours a week during their brief stays. Where local folk observe the STMers trying to learn and use their language, this produces mutual respect and opens opportunities. Missionaries who are available to mentor STM volunteers give valuable help in the early years. Taking an active role advances communication and effectiveness (Lum 2007:3).

Priority of Relationships

Bridge building and developing relationships are paramount. "Normally it takes not two years, but 8-10 years to build effective relationships" in Asia. Age is also a factor. The older and more mature one is the more one is respected. Many volunteers have not yet aged enough to gain that level of credibility. They are not known nor trusted fully (Nicholson 2006:2-3). Teams moving from place to place are not conducive to making even short-term relationships. Programs that keep the team in one location and spend more time with locals do better, despite linguistic barriers (Eastwood 2006:1). Repeat teams to the same churches or areas are often more effective.

Several members from the overseas churches served by STM have visited New Zealand through these friendships. During their exchange they received deeper discipling in the churches there and were able to go back to strengthen and encourage their local congregations better (Payne 2006:3). One former STM, who went to teach in Asia, continued nurturing his students after returning to USA. Eventually, he married one of them and that couple has served long term overseas for over fifteen years.

As observers in Japan suggest, the longer volunteers stay, the better. Effectiveness is based on relationships. Many home-sides do not encourage associate workers to go for one to three years until they have first tried STM (Thompson 2006:2). Is STM becoming a required rite of passage to longer service? Historical missiology might question that need. Has mission moved away from the primary calling of God and total dependence on Him to a human-oriented, existential, pragmatic process where faith has little place? How can the STM process be realigned with God's will? The claim that STM has become the door for long term needs careful research. How can the data and statistics be more meticulously qualified, defined and evaluated? What percentage of those joining STM, actually return long term later? How long does it take? How many new career workers were committed to long term before STM? How many after STM? Has STM become a requirement of the agencies' process and how has that affected statistical data?

Mobilization for STM

The demand to host STM workers in Japan has greatly increased in recent years. There is no problem in getting people to do STM. The money is there too (Thompson 2006:3). A Taiwan field leader noted, "More want to come on STM than we can accept, so there's no need to recruit. By contrast this field has added only one long-term worker in the last six years. In some circles STM has become a substitute for long-term commitment, an excuse not to consider long term. This is particularly true of overseas Chinese churches. Youthful Chinese frequently say they cannot go on long-term mission because their parents would never allow it! The investment of many agencies in these ethnic churches in the West may produce little fruit in long-term mission workers" (Nicholson 2006:3).

STM teams affect their sending constituencies. They bring home lots of field feedback for multiplication as well as high motivation as the STM returnees become advocates, essential to maintain and stimulate new prayer and recruiting. Relationships and connections are kept fresh. Home leaders who contact former STM volunteers can get them involved. The younger generation's culture helps break the ice in introducing mission agencies to new churches, along with their creativity for starting new church models. Agencies that make the effort to support these newer church structures in mission efforts are generally welcomed (Zindel 2006:3).

A current trend is receiving STM from many parts of the world. "Some go back to initiate a more involved and more integrated mission approach in their home churches because their STM time had impacted them to think globally" (Lum 2007:3).

Using Funds Wisely

Another pressure is the penchant of some for advocating that Western churches support national workers only, instead of their seasoned career missionaries. Churches in the West want more involvement of the laity in missions so they encourage STM trips, especially to places where they may be supporting a national worker. The trend is to have STM teams "partnering" with a national church or worker. Long-term missionaries are viewed as "expensive" (Tibbetts 2006:4).

Missiologists need to research definitively and evaluate deeply the effects of funding of national workers. How does money affect the worker, the attitude of fellow believers, the local church and potential dependency problems? What is the effect on evangelists to unreached peoples, particularly where the primary support is used for serving primarily among their own people group?

Some churches bring national workers back to America to train them in the USA, exposing them to potential cultural, linguistic, financial and theological imperialism. Recently a missionary I know brought one of the first believers of their overseas' outreach back, to baptize them at the home church so that the Australian congregation could see the fruit of their mission efforts! What effect does that have on the indigenous church and on the identity of the new believers?

Screening

More thorough screening helps STM, especially in areas of relationships, family issues, health matters, and money related problems. Are participants seriously considering mission or just riding on the wave for a free holiday? (Lum 2007:3). While many are wanting to do STM, the agencies and churches must be selective of those getting the most impact, those already in ministry, or those interested in cross-cultural outreach (Thompson 2006:4). Clear communication concerning expectations is necessary, both from the home-side and on the field. Often teams arrive with higher than realistic expectations of what they can do or accomplish on STM (Eastwood 2006:2).

A European home-side pointed out difficulties often occasioned by a short application process because of late registrations, rare references, and inadequate church experience in working with youth, music or evangelism. Training in the home churches on the call of God, the cost and risks entailed in following God, and how to do effective evangelism are frequently lacking. Many volunteers want to go to fill in the gap between the end of school and their continuing studies (Zindel 2006:1). Often they come to the fields at Christmastime or periods favored for missionary vacations (Eastman 2006:1).

Training and Debriefing

STM participants must come with a view to serve, and have attitudes of flexibility on the field. When STM volunteers came with their own agenda, want to have their own hands-on experience, to do their own pattern of evangelism, or to sightsee, they put stress on the churches and missionaries. The best teams trained together before they came, and had prepared skits, music, testimonies and stories. Coming to serve, they were ready to do anything the churches and missionaries asked. They were readily available. They also desired to build long-term relationships and returned annually with teams to the same locations to foster those links (Tibbetts 2006:2-3). Training in STM can be fruitful investment in the future for mission.

Some leaders debrief participants on the field as a group, others individually; some do both. They help them about next steps, follow-up newsletters and personal contacts, continuing to nurture and invest in them for long-term service. The home-sides also debrief participants on their return. There is no one best way for debriefing. Often this is difficult to do soon after they return home. Regular follow-up and continuing contact are essential. Many youth see STM as just one more experience in life to be crossed off their agenda. How many seriously pray about future mission commitment is difficult to determine (Payne 2006:3). A key strategy is to have field missionaries maintain contact with past STM participants for several years (Nicholson 2006:3).

STM Costs and Funding

Many STM participants earn their own money to pay for their stay in Asia. Relatives and friends also help. Participants discuss this matter with church leaders and the mission team too (Zindel 2006:4). Often churches and individuals respond to the need of the moment rather than from a thought-out strategy for missions (Payne 2006:3).

STM does detract from funding for long-term workers. Some career missionaries have personally experienced considerable loss of support because more funding is being channeled into STM programs of the local church (Tibbetts 2006:4). One missionary laments, "In my two home churches the number of supported full time cross-cultural workers dropped significantly over the last ten years. However, these churches perceive that they are more involved in missions than ever before, due to the large number of young people going out in the summer" (Eastwood 2006:2). It is "easier to raise funds for STM than to commit funds to support long-term workers" (Lum 2007:3). "STM eats much missionary budget. On the other hand, many STM volunteers often have weak links with local churches in their homelands" (Eastwood 2006:2). A serious analytical study is urgently needed on STM costs and funding to determine real criteria for evaluating their actual contribution to evangelization. How does this compare with long-termers?

"Some people see STM as a sort of pilgrimage to make each year without ever crossing over to long-term career. Young people want experiences first before exercising faith," which determines their "stickability" (Lum 2007:3). The purposes of "many STM programs are to serve the congregation, not the field ministries. Churches are tempted to think that they get more "bang for the buck" through STM, catering to the immediate gratification syndrome" (Thompson 2006:3). Exciting or sensational reports from STM stir church members. "North Americans want hands-on opportunities fitting their own thinking. They seldom understand what it takes to disciple a new believer in a foreign culture. Usually it takes at least nine months on the field before getting an inkling of appreciation about the prayer and energy it requires to see lasting fruit" (Tibbetts 2006:4).

Conclusion

STM is like people standing in the shallow waters watching the rolling ocean. They see the boisterous waves. They observe the frothy foam. But they cannot experience the deep currents underneath, or the life that crawls on the sandy bottom of the ocean depths. That can only be known, like long-term mission, through full immersion and time.

The value of STM is considerable. They have stimulated Christians to get involved in mission. The weaknesses of them relate to strategic and missiological issues of the long-range picture. Changes in the design of STM programs and better training before leaving for overseas can overcome some of these. Pastors, mission committees and missiologists must carefully evaluate STM in the light of the ultimate "kingdom" purpose of Christ's Great Commission, particularly in this age when instant and often superficial results are commonly promoted in Western culture, whether in business (corruption), entertainment (extreme fantasy), or the arts (flamboyance). In fulfilling God's mission, STM requires careful honing to guard against degenerating into self-centered satisfaction, popularity-driven programs, and exaggerated outcomes. Can current patterns of STM actually inoculate participants and churches against traditional long-term mission? Establishing clear definitions of mission and evangelization, and setting precise goals and biblical objectives will bring balance and guidance to the great STM movement of the future.

A summary of broad observations in evaluating STM attitudes for Generation X/Y raises some concerns, dangers, and warnings for the future. These include:

1. Short-sighted convenience without long-term commitment - inadequate personal vision.

2. Self-centered individualism without deep altruistic concern for others - false focus; What can I get out of this?

3. Instant gratification without distant responsibility - questionable motivation; just experience the here and now; get the biggest bang for the buck.

4. Intense activity without deliberate purpose - lacking significant eternal goals.

5. Social service participation without evangelistic proclamation - short circuited outcomes in spiritual duty.

6. Immediate satisfaction without eternal consequences—fuzzy ultimate expectations.

7. Humanistic self sufficiency without theological reflection and analysis—unevaluated self dependency.

STM investment emphasizes the person and the process of life's pilgrimage. Two closing illustrations show the importance of agencies' investing in STM. The first changed the direction of a participant, but leaves her short of total commitment to the ultimate task. The second shows the powerful impact of a well planned STM program that propelled a young man into career missions and continues to affect him decades later.

James Dougherty, a STM coordinator now serving in career mission, reported the following story:

In 2002 Stacey was a Junior studying art at a notable Christian College. She planned that, after she graduated, she would get a good art-drawing job. That summer, she served on an STM team in Taiwan, primarily doing children's ministry with a church in the southern region. She was one of the "younger" members of the team, who didn't seem to engage seriously with the work or the people there. Even though she was Chinese-American, she really struggled with Taiwanese culture and language.

Coming back from STM, she took to heart the lessons learned from that summer. A few weeks after debriefing, she wrote to the sending agency, "Thanks to OMF, now I don't know what I want to do after I graduate." She was (and still is) far from committing her life as a full-time mission worker, but her brief experience in Asia really changed her priorities and a sense of what was important in how she spent her life.

After Stacey graduated in 2003, she moved home and began studying Chinese. She went with her church on another overseas trip to China. Then, in the summer of 2004, she led a STM team of sixteen back to China to do language study and to build relationships. She was one of the better leaders. She really had a heart focused on serving her team members and helping them go through the challenges of life and ministry that she had experienced the previous two summers (N. Thompson 2006:2).

Second, Neel Roberts, a twenty-year veteran missionary, shares this personal story of his summer mission experience a quarter of a century ago.

> I learned most everything I needed to learn about STM when I was 20 years old and spent a summer with North American Indian Mission. I am grateful for that summer. I continue to apply the lessons I learned to my work in Southeast Asia even to this day. Listed below are the key elements of that effective STM program:
>
> 1. A good screening process meant that all participants were committed to serving God.
>
> 2. Senior missionaries spent considerable time with all the short-termers. They took part in our week of orientation. Then during six weeks in various Indian villages a senior missionary couple visited us regularly. We learned lessons about what others had done that worked or failed in the past.
>
> 3. We were expected to develop personal Bible study skills and were asked to share what lessons we learned from the Bible.
>
> 4. Training and debriefing times were well organized. I still remember some of the presentations I heard at that time.

5. Assignments were challenging but realistic. My co-worker and I were sent to a village with only one Christian family. Our job was to encourage them in their faith and organize some children's ministry. It was hard but do-able.

6. We were encouraged to consider long-term ministry with NAIM, but were in no way pressured to do so.

7. We were clearly told that we were only one link in the chain. Others had gone before us and, in the years to come, others would go to the villages where we were staying. Thus we were taught that the testimony of our lives was more important than individual evangelistic activities in which we might engage. We learned that one Christian does not make one convert, but it is as Christians work together over a period of time that the truth breaks into hearts and churches emerge.

8. We learned about spiritual warfare from missionaries and native Indians who had fought spiritual battles.

9. We saw that short-term work was a vital part of long-term ministry and not a substitute for it.

Roberts concludes, "I share this experience of mine because it is etched on my heart and memory. I learned and retained more from that STM experience than from many college or seminary courses that I sat through (which certainly cost more money)! To the degree that we try to reproduce these elements in short-term programs, I believe we will see positive long-term results in a) The fields of ministry, b) The efforts in recruitment, and c) The loyalty of supporters who have passed through past STM programs" (2007:1).

When mission and church leaders honestly evaluate STM from a deeper perspective of missiology, significant issues arise, demanding attention and requiring answers. Hopefully their responses to those challenges will sharpen better STM programs, mobilize more efficient participants, and produce long-lasting effects in the future for the kingdom of Christ.

References Cited

Eastwood, David. 2006. "Short-term teams." E-mail and attachment 12/18/06, Taiwan, Pp 1-3.

Leighton, Mark W. 2006. Personal E-mail 12/26/06, Thailand, Pp 1-5.

Lum, Serene. 2007. "Short-term movement – Missiological effectiveness and implications: A field side (Cambodia) perspective." Email and attachment 1/2/07, Cambodia, Pp 1-5.

Mays, David. 2006. Six challenges for the church in missions. *Evangelical Missions Quarterly* 42: 304-315.

Nicholson, Philip. 2006. E-mail and attachments 12/18/06, Taiwan, Pp 1-5.

Nicholson, Phillip. n.d. "The dangers of short-term mission," an unpublished article, Pp 1-4.

Niphakis, Steve. 2006. Personal E-mail 12/18/06, USA, Pp 1-4.

Payne, Warren. 2006. Personal E-mail 12/17/06, Pp 1-4.

Roberts, Neel. 2007. Personal E-mail 1/2/07, forwarded 1/9/07, Pp 1-4.

Smith, Alex G. 1976. How to multiply churches by film evangelism. *Evangelical Missions Quarterly* 167-172.

Smith, Andy. 2000. Faith in missions. *Evangelical Missions Quarterly* 36: 150-151.

Tibbetts, Scott. 2006. Personal E-mail 12/22/06. USA, Pp 1-5.

Thompson, Bryan. 2006. Personal E-mail with attachments 12/27/06, Japan, Pp 1-15.

Thompson, Neil. 2006. Personal Email with notes of "Rosie the riveter: Mobilization trends for the 21st century." Mission Leadership Network, Wheaton Il. 12/22/06, USA, Pp 1-6.

Welliver, Dotsey and Minnette Northcutt, eds. 2004. *Mission handbook 2004-2006: U.S. and Canadian Protestant ministries overseas.* Wheaton IL. EMIS.

Zindel, Andreas. 2006. Personal E-mail with attachments. 12/20/06, Switzerland, Pp 1-5.

CHAPTER 3

COMPLEMENTARY ASPECTS OF SHORT-TERM MISSIONS AND LONG-TERM MISSIONS:

CASE STUDIES FOR A WIN-WIN SITUATION

ENOCH WAN AND GEOFFREY HARTT

Introduction

In his recently published dissertation, George Robinson (2007) opens by summarizing the current status of short-term missions (STM) and asking a key question:

> Much harsh criticism has been dealt towards STM recently, some justified and some not. Missiologists and long-term missionaries have struggled with this paradigm shift. It seems the move to incorporate STM into mission strategy has not been taken seriously. Can anything be learned from the army of amateurs that are now dispersing annually around the world?

Ralph Winter, in an editorial for the January 2000 issue of *Mission Frontiers*, suggested:

> The burgeoning short-term phenomenon
> highlighted in this issue is a blessed, booming
> reality, but it does little more than educate the
> sending churches about churches overseas. It does
> little to expose the need of precisely the unreached
> peoples where there are no believers or churches
> to visit.

Winter was absolutely correct about short-term missions (STM) being a "booming reality" (for statistics, see Moreau and Priest in this volume). But he sees limited value in them. Is this the case? Is it possible that short-term missions can actually complement the work of long-term missions in reaching the unreached and planting new churches in new fields? Can we learn anything from this "army of amateurs" that has become a major force in missions today? We believe it is possible for short-term missions (STM) to benefit long-term missions (LTM) and that the two models can exist in harmony rather than tension.

Purpose of the Paper

If STM and LTM are to co-exist and support each other, then we need to focus on aspects of their ministry that complement their particular purposes. Rather than view STM and LTM as irreconcilable and antagonistic approaches to mission, our research intentionally focuses on potentially complementary features of STM and LTM— ways in which each can serve the other. We gathered information from people representing both STM and LTM practitioners in sending, going, and receiving contexts. While we acknowledge that there are sometimes negative elements in STM and LTM relationships, we have chosen to limit this study to the positive side only. It is hoped that by identifying potentially complementary relationships between the two, the positive can be strengthened.

Definition of Key Terms

The definition of "short-term missionary" has changed over time, with older paradigms defining short-term missions (STM) in terms of years. For example, when Hale (2003) defines short-term missionaries as those who serve between three months and five years, this reflects a rather dated paradigm. The Protestant Mission Handbook (Weber and Welliver 2007) has continued to collect data on short-term missions defined as between two weeks and one year. But even this is a dated and misleading definition, since extensive data collected by Priest and Priest (2008, 56-57) demonstrate that fully two thirds of current short-term missionaries serve for periods of two weeks or less.

In this paper, then, "short-term missions" (STM) are defined as intentionally limited, organized, cross-cultural mission efforts for a pre-determined length of time without participants making a residency-based commitment of more than two years. That is, STM field presence ranges from a few days to a maximum of two years.

"Long-term missions" are defined here as any cross-cultural mission work that is residency-based, involving a minimum of a two-year term or more, and typically involving elements of language acquisition and cultural immersion and adjustment.

Methodology

Both of us are STM practitioners, theological educators and missiologists who have an interest in both research and in the application of research findings. In this project we carried out qualitative research, being careful to contact a wide variety of people in the missions community, and interviewing them in person or by telephone or email. We focused our interviews of mission participants and leaders narrowly on the question of whether, and in what ways, STM and LTM were potentially complementary. Our understanding of the flow of missions is presented below.

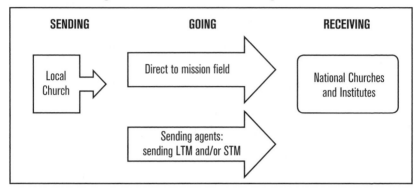

We understand that the Church is ultimately the only sending entity as it is Christ's representative in this world to pursue the *missio Dei*. Congregations (local churches) and mission organizations are intermediary agents in the big picture of "the Great Commission." Both LTM and STM are part and parcel of this global Kingdom effort. STM agencies and participants of STM are to assist the local church in carrying out its mission.

We have tried to identify and interview STM/LTM practitioners from each major continent and as many different countries as possible. Our intent was to gather data from a variety of perspectives; rather than just that of North Americans. STM teams are not only going to a variety of countries outside the U.S. today, but they are originating from many of these other countries as well.

Sending Entity

North America

In an editorial written for *Christianity Today*, Miriam Adeney (1996), missions professor at Regents College and Seattle Pacific University, identified several ways STM complement LTM through her experiences at her own church, University Presbyterian in Seattle. She stated:

> STM members can bring Christ to "restricted access" regions where missionaries are not allowed to settle. They can provide a vast pool of resources for huge events, like evangelism at the Olympics. STM members may encourage nationals in their own witness.

She identified many problem areas for STM in her article along with some areas STM can complement LTM, e.g. extending an LTM's ministry, providing a resource pool for large events, and for encouragement.

Jacksonville Chapel in Lincoln Park, New Jersey, has a large mission program. They support 35 long-term missionaries in 15 countries and also send numerous short-term teams out every year. The church contributes 18% of its budget to missions which amounts to over $5 million annually. They have leaders assigned to both long-term and short-term aspects of mission.

Walt Windish is the chairman of their missions committee. He has personally participated in STM as well as overseen the long-term commitments at Jacksonville Chapel. He identified the following as specific ways he has observed STM complementing the work of the LTM efforts.

- STM has been a source of long-term missionaries for Jacksonville Chapel. Their missions policy gives priority to LTM missionaries that go out from the body.
- STM has been a source of support to LTM. STM has provided evangelistic support and medical care as well as delivering resources to LTM.

- STM has provided training to national pastors in the field who have minimal preparation for ministry.

- STM has led to identifying national pastors to support.

Another church with a large missions program involving both STM and LTM is Village Baptist in Beaverton, Oregon. They have fifty years experience in missions work and currently support forty-seven LTM families from Village living abroad. John Jordan, their missions pastor, explained how they have restructured their program over the last decade to take advantage of the benefits STM brings to LTM work.

They report that many of their STM participants go on to LTM work. Jordan said, "16% of the people who go on a short-term trip from Village will go on to a long-term position." For Village this translates into about four families being sent out each year in partnership with LTM agencies, with as many as twenty constantly in preparation for sending.

Their philosophy is to identify gateway countries (such as Lebanon and India), assess the local churches' or LTM's needs and try to match that up with the skills available in Village's members. This results in three to four teams going out annually to conduct theological, medical or practical training.

Jordan shared a few examples of how STM has directly benefited the work of LTM. In India, a series of pastors' conferences conducted by an STM team led to greatly improved inter-denominational unity in the state where they were working. They also extended the reach of the community health training being conducted by Operation Mobilization among the Dalits. These STM teams have directly led to five families from Village now working for OM in India. One church member who traveled to India three times on STM teams from Village eventually left her marketing career in the U.S. to take an LTM position as assistant to the National Director of O.M. in India.

Another way in which STM has benefited LTM work has been through education. Training conducted by STM teams from Village in the Philippines and Lebanon has increased the theological competency of local pastors. In one case, a Korean couple from Village who participated in an STM trip to Lebanon is now in the process of moving permanently to teach at a seminary there. For Village Baptist, STM is not only a benefit to, but an integral part of, their LTM program.

First Filipino Alliance Church of Edmonton, Canada has a short history of about twenty five years. The founding pastor, Rev. Joy Tira, has motivated church members and mobilized the entire congregation for church planting within Canada and for both STM and LTM (Tira 2002). FFAC has been instrumental in the founding of the fraternal association (CFAM) of Filipino Alliance Churches in Canada and through partnership with several entities, in the forming of the Filipino International Network (FIN). He described their experience this way:

> For two decades, FFAC has sent short-term workers in collaborations with Christian organizations like Operation Mobilization, Campus Crusade for Christ, Youth With A Mission, and Samaritan Purse. In recent years we sent members of our congregation to conduct evangelism and discipleship training with the Filipino International Network in places like Japan, Singapore, Taiwan, Hong Kong, Jordan, Israel, Cyprus, United Arab Emirates, Qatar, Kuwait, Oman, and the homeland—the Philippines. All these "short-term workers" are now engaged in missions serving as lay leaders of

FFAC, pastors of C&MA congregations in Canada, and serving as C&MA missionaries in North Africa, Arabian Gulf, and South Asia (Tira 2004). FFAC also has sent out medical and dental teams to the Philippines in the past six years. Our holistic ministries in the homeland have encouraged more workers to engage in compassionate and justice ministries right here in the inner city of Edmonton.

Short-term missions, therefore, have impacted the long-term missions involvement of FFAC in very positive ways.

Below are observations by Joy Tira regarding the complementary features of STM and LTM:

- STM benefited the congregation of FFAC in several ways. The positive results and encouraging reports of participants of STM created a sense of excitement for missions, an adventure spirit to travel abroad for the Gospel and a passion for the lost.
- We plan our STM well in advance and in line with ministry goals of LTM on the field in terms of location and formation of team focus (e.g. medical team, charity mission, community development, etc.).
- Our STM seeks to partner with other parachurch organizations (e.g. Campus Crusade), and local missions (e.g. OMF) to provide strategic assistance to LTM.
- Many of our STM participants are now serving in LTM in the Middle East, Asia and Europe.
- Thus STM is a way of recruiting and training of personnel for LTM.

- Those who came out of our church serving in LTM are most helpful in planning for STM, advising and coordinating STM activities that complement LTM goals.

Going Entity

Asia

Edmond Mok is a Bible translator working in Hong Kong with Wycliffe. He described their involvement with STM:

> In our organization, STM usually means a 1-2 year commitment which they can use their expertise to serve as assistants in different allocations. As far as I know, in the past we had STM sent out from HK serving in both Asia and Africa as librarian, secretary, accountant, personnel officer, bilingual education assistant, home school teacher, etc. A couple of them have stayed in the organization for a longer term.
>
> We also have many shorter eye-opening programs of various lengths, from a week to 2 months, but not many such programs are designed for ministry purposes. We do have some going for a particular ministry depending on the needs in the field. Recently a team of four went to the Philippines to visit a Hong Kong family and helped sell the translated scripture portions in the market, set up a booth, and ran some games in a local fun fair to help promote the scriptures. Yet in most cases, people go to see what translation is all about and have a taste of living in another cultural.

Asia Vision: Short-Term Missions Project (AVSTM) began as a ministry preparing and sending missionaries to South Asia, especially from the Philippines. They have expanded to Central Asia, serving in Kyrgyzstan and Tajikistan. Geri Abordo-Ramos was the former Chairperson of the Central Committee of AVSTM. He shared

> We provide pre-field training for all STM and sufficient information for their field assignment. The training they receive builds them up to become future leaders of their churches/ denominations in mobilization for missions.

> All short-term missionaries that have gone out under AVSTM have gone back to their churches and denominations carrying with them the experiences they were allowed. Some of them have in fact started their own mobilization by forming groups and forming networks in the field so they can also send from their own churches/denominations. This has been one of the thrusts of AVSTM, so that the task of missions mobilization does not remain a monopoly of just one organization, but one that is shared by all believers, as it should be.

> David Tan is the Director of recruiting and training for OC International in Singapore. He described his role in the STM process:

> We work in creative Access Countries of East Asia, providing long-term support to our long-term workers on the field. They design the types of short-term teams they need on the field, I "match

make" and "head hunt" to recruit teams for these needs. We have returned to the same location for the past four to five years with: ESL, Basketball and Volleyball clinics. Further requests are for a radiographer to train doctors in a major regional hospital at the prefecture capital, an ESL teacher for a university, and ESL teachers and a coach for a high school.

David explained how STM contribute to his ministry's goals:

Part of long-term recruitment is meaningful exposure to reality on the field. People and churches are changed by their participation on short-term teams. Each year, we have seen one or two persons on short-term teams deciding or moving into preparation mode for long-term service on the field. Some of these people have ended up as workers with the organization. Others have joined agencies which fit them better. This helps the organization accomplish the goal of placing new workers in unreached people groups.

One key issue is visas for long-term ministry. Our short-term teams have also helped generate these visas as local governments invite new workers to help meet their needs. Long-term workers gain credibility as they help in creative-access countries with real needs.

Many helpful relationships are built with long-term workers, my family, and myself as we lead teams. Participants experience the challenges of working cross-culturally. They get to see how we live out our faith on the field. Interactions with our children allow them to value and invest in long-term relationships with them. The benefits are mutual. Children on the field make new life-long friends while team participants enjoy a cross cultural perspective to living.

Field workers are always considered an extension of church ministry. Short-term teams provide a visible expression of this concept.

David recognized many ways STM experience benefited the participants as well as the LTM:

I have worked with churches that are actively mobilizing and raising the next generation of workers. Short-term trips have helped the churches pick out those with the calling. After the trips, many will join a regular group to process and grow this calling. It becomes a visible means of assessing and evaluating those called for long-term cross cultural ministry.

Teams and leadership development: Pre-trip preparation and post-trip debriefing. We demand a 10-week preparation time before teams arrive on the field. The preparation includes daily devotions for 4 weeks before and 2 weeks after trips, team meetings, team training, team prayer time and other necessary preparation like basket, volleyball practices and ESL team meetings. All these require a good amount of leaders. Trip leaders, sub-group leaders in finance and logistical support provide good training ground for leadership. One leader was found to be suitable for eldership in the church and was elected the following year.

During the trip: There are daily devotions, prayer and worship times with field workers and leaders. There is a great amount of spiritual growth during a 2 week trip.

The focus of the trip is spiritual growth and development of participants. Helping long-term workers and participants find their calling in life is a side benefit.

Central and South America

There are a handful of Chinese churches in Panama City. A key person in Christian missions in Panama is Rev. Philip Ngo, a Filipino Chinese sent by the Hong Kong C&MA missions association. He has planted several churches and currently serves as the senior pastor of a significant Protestant congregation in the country giving birth to daughter churches in various places. He is the academic dean of the Alliance Bible School of Central and South America and the key coordinator in the training, mobilizing and sending out of a dozen or more Christians annually to do STM throughout Central and South America.

He fondly recalled his years of administrative service in the mission association in Hong Kong where he mobilized and trained many to participate in STM throughout Asia. He transferred and improved the experience and expertise from Hong Kong to become even more productive in STM ministries throughout Central and South Americas. The following is the summary of his comments on how STM and LTM can be complementary in the Great Commission.

- STM participants should receive orientation and coaching from long term missionaries with extensive knowledge of the culture, people and the country.
- The work and activities of STM team should be carefully planned ahead to line up with LTM ministry goals.
- The selection of members of STM teams is to be done carefully and methodically to match the needs and expectation of nationals; but the process can be aided by LTM participants.
- STM people are to enter into partnership with nationals and are not to be domineering; even though many STM people come with money, influence and ethnocentric pride.
- If there is any tension or conflict between personnel of LTM and nationals, STM participants are usually caught in the middle of the cross-fire and their experience will be negative. STM people should avoid entering into a situation in which they might become a liability and victim of circumstances.
- If STM trips are well planned and coordinated by leaders of LTM and national churches, their ministry will be fruitful and productive for the LTM field and the network of national churches. As a result, the complementary nature of STM and LTM will be clearly demonstrated. Those who join in STM will have a positive experience which will lead them towards the path of LTM commitment and eventual life-time involvement.
- Gratified STM participants will become good promoters for LTM and the causes of national churches. Members of STM will become financial contributors, future STM leaders and recruiters for LTM.

North America

Rick Calenberg is regional director for SIM (Serving in Mission). He has served as an LTM missionary in Nigeria but currently serves SIM with recruitment, church mobilization and retiree oversight in the Northwest region of the United States. He has led STM teams for over twenty-five years to various countries. His insights are unique in that he has experienced both aspects of missions – LTM and STM. One story from an STM experience illustrates this complementary aspect of STM to LTM.

In 2004 my wife and I led a team to do ESL in China. On that team was a wife and mother whose husband had received a strong call to serve in China; but the wife was a bit apprehensive and uncertain. This STM trip gave her an opportunity to experience the culture and minister in the context. She adjusted well and was effective in making relationships and ministry. As a result she became convinced of the fact that LTM in this country was really her calling as well. They proceeded through the application process and have recently arrived in Asia and will be moving to the very city where the STM ministry was located!

Her experience allowed her to not only prepare herself but also to prepare her two teenage daughters. Her enthusiasm helped them gain confidence and overcome some of their apprehension of leaving friends and the culture they knew. She was also miles ahead in preparing for life on the field.

In this story we can see the value in STM of serving as a conduit for LTM recruiting. The STM practitioner was able to 'test the waters' of her future mission field, affirm her calling and prepare the entire family adequately for a major transition. Rick shared another story that further illustrates this complementary aspect of STM to LTM.

> Another benefit to LTM is the change in worldview that results from those who experience an STM. A pastor and wife, with no cross-cultural experience, went with a team to Nigeria and had a very rich experience ministering through teaching. They were embraced by the SIM team there which aided their adjustment. The wife's teaching gifts and ministry were rekindled and the pastor discovered how effective he could be in a cross-cultural setting. Since their return they seriously have considered career service and are planning to return when the wife retires from her current employment. Also the impact on their church has been dramatic. Though a little church, they have caught a vision for this country and for the ministry where their pastor and wife served. This has motivated them to get involved and sizeable gifts have been given to SIM-approved projects at the school and ministry site where the pastor and his wife taught. Opportunity for recruitment and ongoing education of the congregation has ensued.

There are many complementary points in this story. One is the possibility for STM participants to change their attitude toward missions. An interesting and all-too-common reality is that a local church's pastor may have very little or no exposure to global missions.

This near-sightedness has an effect on their church's involvement in global missions. In this case, the pastor's cross-cultural experience has affected the entire church and drawn it into LTM commitments.

Mike Jorgensen is a vice president with e3 Partners Ministry, an STM organization focused on mobilizing teams from the U.S.A. into partnerships with churches in Asia, Africa and Latin America. When asked how his organization relates to the LTM entity he responded with the following:

> We serve the nationals. The Body of Christ in a country is the primary tool God is going to use to take that country for Christ. So we must serve them in their vision and strategy to reach their country. Having said that, we also realize that at times no one in a country has a vision or strategy for reaching the entire country. So sometimes we "carry the vision virus" with us when we arrive. But that vision must become theirs.

When asked about how his organization specifically supports the mission of the local church, Mike answered:

> by equipping their people to do the work of ministry. Our campaigns are designed to be on-the-job training in evangelism, discipleship and church planting. The focus of our teams is not to do the work of ministry so the North Americans have a great experience, but to have the North Americans model a simple, biblical, transferable method of multiplying churches using laymen. We also provide simple, biblical, transferable tools to do this ministry: EvangeCubes, First Steps training manuals, discipleship materials, etc.

As an example of their efforts he offered this example.

> We have been working in Bolivia for five years. Up to this year, we have not found any church, denomination, ministry or individual that had a vision or plan for saturating the country with new churches. So we did First Steps leadership conferences and brought teams of North Americans. We constantly cast vision for church planting and modeled a simple church planting process and equipped local believers to use simple tools.
>
> Recently, the national director of Campus Crusade invited us to partner with them in planting 1600 new churches over the next five years. When we asked what their plan was, we were delighted to hear that it essentially was the church planting process we have modeled there, with the added components of Jesus Film mass evangelism, ongoing leadership development, and discipleship through audio New Testament listening groups.

After serving with Wycliffe in Africa as a practitioner of LTM for fourteen years, Richard Gardner now is based in the US Northwest and makes a half-dozen trips to Nigeria annually. Having done both STM and LTM in Africa, he comes with a wealth of on-field experience as a traditional long term missionary. In the last two years he has been successfully mobilizing American churches and organizing/coordinating STM teams to West Africa. He described the complementary relationship between STM and LTM as follows:

- Both STM and LTM participants are to see the big picture and work towards the shared goals if they are to be complementary.
- STM visits can bring in resources (personnel, finances, expertise, etc.) to aid the national and LTMers by regular and repeated visits to the same place working with the same national entity.
- There are many types of ministry that STM people can help, e.g. showing the Jesus film, doing medical outreach, conducting children's ministries, etc.
- I usually provide country-specific orientation to members of STM six to eight weeks prior to their departure. I coordinate and match the needs of the national with the expertise of STM group members. I serve as their team leaders, translate for them, supervise them and am a liaison with the national Christians and churches. Effective outcomes and satisfactory STM can be accomplished when there is a good fit of LTM goals and STM participants' expertise and expectation. As the coordinator, I always follow the goals and objectives of LTM planning and then form STM teams and recruit members accordingly.
- There are more and more local congregations catching the vision for missions and taking action to participate in STM in the Pacific Northwest. Therefore, though I am now stationed in Portland, I can continue my ministries in Africa through the STM format. I utilize my expertise and African network to plan and coordinate STM teams effectively by coinciding with the broader goals of LTM for the particular field.

To illustrate this point, Richard explained how during his recent STM trips of two weeks to Nigeria, he was able to bring along key individuals with him to assist with the initial planning with the Luis Palau Association for a major event - training 15,000 evangelists in

Nigeria from Sept. 10–14th and then a public rally Sept. 15–16th . He knows the country and the people. He has an extensive network developed throughout a long period of time of LTM service and thus can get a substantial amount of preparatory work done even going now as a practitioner of STM. Richard summed his statements up with, "STM can be an effective way to complement LTM."

Paul Lee works with Partners International sending U.S. based teams to East Asia. He described their role as a sending agency.

> As an STM practitioner, I think one of our most important roles in relation to the LTM/receiving entity is to build and maintain a close and healthy relationship. In some STM trips I have played another role, which is the coordinator. This is a mediator between the two parties— STM teams and the LTM/receiving side. The coordinator is very important to the relationship of the two.

He listed the following as specific ways they support the LTM.

- Supplying/bringing the necessary materials they need for their ministry such as food, teaching materials, transportation, and medicines to them
- Providing additional biblical/theological/practical trainings for them
- Prayers

Aaron Palmatier is the Director of Third World Economic Development and Ministry Director of Asia and Native Americans for Missions Door. He has worked with STM teams in Mexico and Cambodia. He identified three ways that STM has helped their organization achieve its goals. STM has:

- attracted new people to the church
- advanced construction projects, and
- encouraged the local church

He identified a key ingredient for success, "STM works well in our organization because we insist that the receiving national church association set the agenda 100% and control how the money is spent."

Receiving Entity

Asia

James Lai is the director/CEO of the South East Asia Christian Nationals' Evangelism Commission. He comments:

> In this year we received 20–30 STM teams in Myanmar, Thailand, Kalimantan, Malaysia, Cambodia, Laos and China. Members from STM teams came to help in the areas of teaching English, technical support, micro-enterprise projects, Bible teaching, children's ministry and youth camps. They became an encouragement to the national churches and leaders and later provided funding for various local ministries after their STM trips.
>
> Members of LTM and mission executives also contributed to the STM participant's development by providing opportunity for professionals to use their expertise to contribute to the mission field. We educate the STM teams to know more about missions prior to their departure. We even

conduct classes for the teams on missions while they are in the field. We bring vision, challenges and opportunity to STM members to help them understand God's calling for their lives for the particular countries where they contemplate going.

James Lai also described the positive working relationship between STM and LTM in the points listed below:

- The best way to educate the church members in missions is to send them to the mission field.
- The best way meaningfully to raise funds is to bring the sponsors into the field to see for themselves.
- The best way to involve professionals in missions is to give them opportunity to use their expertise in the mission field.
- STM participants will contribute in funds and human resources if the missions organization would be willing to take them to the field, educate them, and give them opportunity to contribute to the field.
- STM is a resource itself both to the mission organizations and the mission fields.

James added one final point in relation to the benefits of STM:

Concerning the STM, it is a way in which the church can satisfy and mobilize the postmodernists. The postmodernist congregation does not like just to be told about missions but to be hands on themselves. They always crave experiences and thus STM is a way which appeals to and can help the postmodernists know missions through their own experiences.

Paul and Diana Mayhugh are a seasoned missionary couple from the U.S. serving as the field chairman of WorldVenture in Hong Kong. They have mastered the language and earned the respect of the nationals. Paul is pursuing a Ph.D. at the China Graduate School of Theology in Hong Kong though he is stationed in Macau. Paul and Diana receive STM members annually and have a positive perspective on STM. Paul recognized that STM teams have contributed to the goals of LTM. In his own word:

> STM is primarily about experiencing missions first hand. Generally speaking, any person that is able to leave their home church and culture to experience life and ministry in a dissimilar culture will benefit. WorldVenture Macau is generally about building God's Kingdom and particularly about helping build the church in the Chinese world. Every believer (no matter what country) that comes to Macau for an STM trip is being enriched in Christ and helping to either build the Chinese church or become a more impassioned and knowledgeable advocate for the Chinese church.

Paul also noted that as a career missionary, his LTM ministry contributed to the STM participant's development in the following way:

> From my twenty-one years of experience, receiving 100–200 STMers a year here, STM are largely 80% what they receive from the

experience and about 20% of what the hosting ministry receives. Most of the participants' lives are eternally changed because of their coming to Macau. Macau ministries are not necessarily extra-normal but God seems to use this small place in a big way in many people's lives. One Taiwanese church sends two STM teams a year to work with us. It is their strategy that by doing this regularly, the majority of their church members will have gone on a mission trip. In addition their church has had over fifteen young people make the decision to go into "full time" ministry because of their Macau STM experience. Many church pastors comment that their church members come back from Macau changed. They are more aggressive in evangelism. They are more hungry in Bible study and more eager to go on mission trips or support missions in their local church.

In conclusion, Paul made a simple and strong statement: "STM are a win-win ministry experience from our perspective."

Another American missionary serving in Kazakhstan, who preferred to remain anonymous said that STM teams had contributed to his ministry as a career missionary. He said,

They did evangelism among college students through providing conversational English practice. Advantage: valuable, direct ministry takes place without dependence on translators. Many Kazakh students have come to Christ through short-term teams in this way. In the 90's my team also received medical STM (very helpful when well organized), prayer teams (good if they are well-led by seasoned prayer ministry workers), teams that did VBS for MK's (good results) and teams that came to do street evangelism (not good, because every pair of foreigners needed a local guide/ translator).

He commented that his ministry had also contributed to the STM participants' development in the following way:

They learn cross-cultural adaptation, and are able to assess their own suitability for long-term service in Kazakhstan, Central Asia or elsewhere. Many have returned on additional short-term teams, and five participants have returned to Central Asia for longer term service.

He concluded by commenting on the positive working relationship between STM teams and his mission:

Most of our STMers have been recruited by our mission organization. In the past I have received short-term missionaries from other organizations. This sometimes results in clashes of expectations and goals, so there must be clear communication about these things beforehand. This is sometimes difficult by email, and things work better if there is a face-to-face meeting.

Jim Latzko is a missionary with the Association of Baptists for World Evangelism in the Philippines. He shared that STM teams have been a positive experience for them. Musical teams have joined them to assist with public outreaches and several pastoral teams have conducted seminars and brought encouragement and training to local pastors. Speaking of the STM participant's experience Latzko stated:

> We provide both pre-field briefings and debriefings. We try to provide a mix of ministry, personal enrichment, cultural training, and relaxation. Many participants were greatly encouraged to see the growth of the Body of Christ in the world. One of our STM participants is now in full-time missionary ministry, while another is in preparation for full-time missionary ministry.

Rev. Jorge de Ramos is a Missions Mobilizer for the Conservative Baptist Association of the Philippines. He works with STM teams deployed to China, Pakistan, Cambodia, Hong Kong and the Philippines. Asked how STM teams have contributed to his ministry he replied:

> They were able to accomplish certain objectives related to raising awareness of the field, discovering God's calling for cross-cultural missions, being able to explore new platforms for presence in the host countries. In the long run these accomplishments through the short-term teams will contribute to the purposes and aims of our organization.
>
> STM, especially when they have had positive experiences in the field, will prove to be an effective "mouthpiece" for your organization and what it represents. They draw more involvement and resources to the task.

He also identified some benefits that assist with the development of the STM participants:

> General orientation to cross-cultural missions, vocational counseling - the participants generally begin to have a broader perspective for their personal ministry and calling. The experience of having contributed to the needs of the field gives them a deeper sense of fulfillment. STM also gives them a deeper understanding of the missionary life.

Christ Community Alliance Church in southwest China has received 3 teams over the last several years. Rev. Alfred Tai shared that they have assisted with teaching English at the primary/high school level and bringing medical services. He said:

> STM bring a sense of real participation to missions, rather than just giving money (not that offering to the missions fund is not important.) STM have changed the lives of everyone who has been on the field positively to be a little more of a mature Christian.

Africa

Rev. Hilary Gbotoe, Jr. is the Bishop of Kingdom Harvest Ministries in Monrovia, Liberia, West Africa. This network of churches and ministries throughout the capital area has received many STM teams in the past. He is responsible for leadership development, project planning and implementation of their strategy to plant churches in the country. The following were some of his observations about STM:

> My observation is that short-term missions always bring focus to the long-term mission of the work. It is often easy to lose track of the long-term mission and get distracted. Here is an example of how short-term missions complement long-term missions by bringing focus to the group.

> The Kingdom Harvest Ministries was primarily established to plant churches throughout Liberia. About two years ago, the leadership in Liberia got distracted over the allocation of resources to the already established churches instead of using the resources to plant more churches. When I took a short-term missions team to Liberia, the team had a series of outreaches to win more people to the Lord. The meetings were so fruitful that the leadership in Liberia repented and decided to keep using every resource provided to plant churches instead of trying to build huge buildings (although there is nothing wrong with building decent buildings for worship).

As we can see here, the STM team was able to re-energize the national church-planting ministry and to refocus them on their own stated goal. It is important to note that the STM team was led by a national and was in harmony with the aspiration and agenda of local churches.

Mark Dunker, the BA Program Director at International Christian Ministries (ICM) in Dar es Salaam, Tanzania serves as an LTM educator. He administrates the BA program at the Bible

College and coordinates STM teams sent from the United States to assist them. They regularly host visiting teachers and work teams at the school. Mark commented, "Teaching at the seminary and doing building projects have been clear fits. As an educational mission, we have practitioners and teachers who bring their years of experience. This very positively impacts our ability to train our pastors."

Another area that STM have complemented is the financial aspect. Mark recognized, "Having teams come minister along side us has been beneficial financially. We've been able to do some ministry that otherwise wouldn't have happened." He also observed that one STM teacher to the school had become a donor to the ministry through their teaching experience. Mark also saw the importance of building donor relations. Both the LTM practitioners in the field and the national staff members, benefit from the connection that can happen when STM teams come to encourage LTM staff.

Amos Magezi is the Director of the Uganda Bible Institute in Uganda. He described his STM experience.

> We have been receiving short-term teams in Uganda from USA, Canada, New Zealand, and UK. Some of these help us doing Bible studies, construction, youth evangelism, sports ministry, VBS and teaching some classes at UBI. The short-term teams are very effective if the schedule is drawn very well. It also works well if the relevant people with relevant skills come for specific ministries. Or else the time is wasted.

In Ethiopia, Ayasu Malfamo is the country coordinator for Bible Training Centre for Pastors (BTCP). He has worked with numerous STM teams serving local denominations and Ethiopian churches. These teams have conducted evangelistic outreaches and supplied teachers to assist with the training BTCP conducts. Malfamo noted the STM participants often return encouraged by both the success of evangelistic outreaches and the level of participation by the national believers.

Sammy and Winny Ndumu serve with AIC Kisima Ministry Fellowship in Kenya. They described their relationship with the STM teams that have visited them and projected some of the ways STM could help their ministry:

> We make the plans for STM teams to visit us. We have health services to HIV/AIDS victims where nurses and doctors can visit and minister with us. We have teaching opportunities in which teachers can come for short-term teaching engagements. We have HIV/AIDS orphans and widow/widowers who need emotional support, counseling and financial support. We have Sunday school kids who need teaching materials and equipment for teaching them.

The Ndumu's final comment on STM was "There is so much you can partner with us!"

Seth Anyomi with African Christian Mission shared they had hosted STM for over twenty years supporting their ministry in Ghana. He noted the teams had, "Given time, skills and money to areas of ministry where they served." He stated they arranged lodging and created the setting for their ministry involvement. "Such partnerships have been cordial and some of the teams have repeated their visits many times following."

Fullstature Missions International of Nigeria both trains and sends out long-term missionaries to Ghana, Guinea Bissau, Togo and Nigeria, and also receives STM teams to work with these LTM. Isaiah Lawon is their International Director. He described the role the STM teams play in helping them reach un-reached people groups:

> The STM serve in several capacities: in medical mission, in teaching and equipping, in assistance to farmers with input, in evangelism, building and missions awareness, Bible distribution and material and financial supply.

He added:

> The working relationship between STM team and our organization have produced profound changes reinforcing the desire to see the ends of the world evangelized. This has brought the team to see the situation differently and then become challenged to do more for the fields. Some of these have become missionaries because of the trips.

Central and South America

American missionary Marcos Vance is the field missionary area coordinator with CrossWorld in northern Brazil. He recognized that STM teams contributed to the goal of his career ministry through the following:

- Increasing involvement with our home churches;
- Providing opportunities to connect with our other ministries here in Brazil;
- Meeting of physical needs in the ministries;
- Through translation, helping with proclamation and testimony.

When asked how the experience contributes to the STM participant Marcos stated, "We see it as an opportunity to disciple participants and move them ahead a few steps in their walk with the

Lord and especially in their mission's involvement." He commented additionally on the positive working relationship between STM team and his missions: "Some good long-term intercultural relationships develop this way."

Don and Zoe Peffer serve with CrossWorld in Cuiaba, Brazil. They responded to our research on STM with the following:

> They have encouraged supporting churches to be actively involved in our ministries and they have encourage the national brethren with their presence and willingness to serve the Lord. They have helped physically with the building of cabins for our camp, buildings and repairs for churches in town, and even some missionary home improvements. Teams have also been a great blessing to our family.

North America

Working among Native Americans in Oregon and Washington with Christian Hope Indian Eskimo Fellowship, David Hopkins has worked with STM teams on several reservations. They conducted building projects in the morning and then visited people in the afternoons in their homes. David indicated that, "The summer projects on the Warmsprings Reservation helped to open the doors for our teaching ministry with CHIEF called 'The School Without Walls.'"

Middle East

An unnamed field director for a missions agency in the Middle East told us that they easily blend STM teams into their LTM work as many of the LTM personnel are in tent-making jobs. Some of the activities the STM have been involved with were:

- prayer walking
- friendship evangelism
- teaching English at the language institute
- administrative support
- hospitality
- conference support
- evangelism at public events that the LTM's weren't able to do

Conclusion

In this paper we have interviewed numerous STM/LTM practitioners regarding the complementary aspect of STM/LTM. We have relied on our personal contacts among the missions community, interviewing them by telephone or e-mail. The data we have collected represents both emic and etic perspectives from a global perspective. These case studies have demonstrated to us that STM and LTM can be a win-win situation, complementing each other and bringing benefits to both elements of missions work.

Listed below are the un-duplicated benefits identified by the interviewees. Our desire is that those who have had a low opinion of STM will begin to see its value to LTM, and that more research might be done on the STM phenomena.

Complementary aspects of STM to LTM

They become a…
- source for recruiting and training LT missionaries
- source of financial support for LTM
- resource pool for large-scale events
- means of congregational education

They…

- create the ability to deliver resources to the field
- provide training to national pastors
- identify national pastors to support
- extend an LTM's reach
- provide access to areas restricted to missionaries
- encourage national believers
- educate sending churches about overseas churches
- conduct pastor's conferences
- provide pastoral training
- improve inter-denominational unity
- create excitement for missions in the home church
- provide strategic assistance
- increase involvement with missions
- cast vision for church planting
- re-energize the national church-planting ministry
- provide encouragement to LTM staff
- create opportunity for professionals to use their expertise in the mission field (medical, dental, agriculture, etc.)
- promote LTM at home
- provide support for MK's
- meet physical needs
- provide musical help with public outreaches
- provide teachers
- create interest in educational programs
- prayer walk
- provide administrative support
- provide hospitality
- enable evangelism at public events closed to missionaries
- contribute to the formation of new groups and sending networks

Complementary aspects of LTM to STM:

They…
- change worldviews through experience
- change attitudes toward missions
- help people catch the vision for church planting
- develop relationship with short-term missionaries
- help give a positive experience moving STMers toward LTM commitment
- foster increased involvement in evangelism
- encourage increased interest in Bible study
- give assessment of suitability for LTM
- encourage
- encourage engagement in compassion and justice ministries at home
- increase understanding of God's calling in their lives
- increase understanding of the LTM's life and challenges
- strengthen desire to see the ends of the world reached

References

Adeney, Miriam. 1996. McMissions: Short-Termers have their place, but not at the expense of career missionaries. *Christianity Today*, Nov. 11, p. 15.

Bromley, D. B. 1990. Academic contributions to psychological counseling: A philosophy of science for the study of individual cases. *Counseling Psychology Quarterly 3*(3): 299-307.

Hale, Thomas. 2003. *On Being a Missionary*. Pasadena, CA: William Carey Library.

Priest, Robert J. and Joseph Paul Priest. 2008. "They see everything, and understand nothing!": Short-term mission and service learning. *Missiology* 36: 53-73.

Robinson IV, George G. 2007. "The Ministry of e3 Partners As a Case Study of Strategic Cross-Cultural Short Term Missions". D. Miss. dissertation, Portland, OR, Western Seminary, April 2007. Forthcoming book *Striking the Match: Strategic Short-term Missions in the Age of Church Planting Movements.* E3 Resources.

Tira, Sadiri Emmanuel. 2002. *Global missions and local congregation: A case study of the First Filipino Alliance Church in Edmonton, Alberta, Canada.* D. Min. dissertation. Jackson, Mississippi: Reformed Theological Seminary.

Tira, Sadiri Emmanuel. 2004. Filipino International Network: A strategic model for Filipino Diaspora glocal missions. *Global Missiology, www.globalmissiology.net.* Oct.

Weber, Linda and Dotsey Welliver, eds. 2007. *Mission handbook: U.S. and Canadian protestant ministries overseas 2007-2009.* Wheaton, IL: EMIS.

Welliver, Dotsey and Miente Northcutt. 2004. *Mission handbook: U.S. and Canadian protestant ministries overseas 2004-2006.* Wheaton, IL: EMIS.

CHAPTER 4

AVOIDING THE UGLY MISSIONARY:

ANTHROPOLOGY AND SHORT-TERM MISSIONS

DR. STEVEN J. YBARROLA

On New Years Eve, 1974, a man named Jonathan McCrostie attended a Bible study we were having at our small house church in Stockton, California. We were a ragtag bunch of ex-hippies, ex-druggies, bikers, and young people who did not feel comfortable in the institutional American church and were trying to live by the precepts, as we understood them, of the New Testament. Jonathan was visiting his parents who lived in Stockton, somehow heard of our Bible study, and decided to ring in the New Year with us. None of us knew Jonathan, but he brought a message to us that would change the trajectory of many of our lives. Jonathan was one of the leaders of a short-term mission organization called Operation Mobilization, or OM. On this night he shared with us the missionary task and challenged us to consider participating in OM. The following summer five of us from the house church went with this organization, working on a campaign they were carrying out in France. I spent a month in

Brest and a month in Nancy, and came back changed forever. The following year I rejoined OM. I ended up spending two more years working in Austria, where we took Bibles and Christian literature to believers living behind the Iron Curtain, and one year on the ship Doulos visiting ports along the east coast of South America. I am an anthropologist today largely as a result of the experiences I had while with OM.

Since my time with OM, the increase in STM has skyrocketed. An article in *Christianity Today* a few years ago (October 2003:30) stated that in 1979, my last year with OM, approximately 22,000 lay people from the United States were involved in short-term missions programs ranging in length from a few days to four years. Current estimates, based on national survey data, are that 1.6 million US church members annually travel abroad on short-term mission trips (Wuthnow and Offutt 2008, 218). In the 1970s organizations like OM were viewed fairly negatively by traditional mission organizations, whereas today there is much greater acceptance of the role short-term missions can play in the overall missionary task. Indeed, many traditional mission organizations now have their own short-term programs that they use to expose people to the need and work of missionaries, and as a means of recruiting long-termers.

Still, short-term missions come under heavy criticism for their alleged "superficiality, cross-cultural ignorance, and poor stewardship of resources" (*Christianity Today*, October 2003:30). These criticisms led a coalition of organizations that sponsor short-term work, such as Campus Crusade for Christ, YWAM, InterVarsity, and the Southern Baptist Convention, to develop a set of "Standards of Excellence in Short-Term Mission." Included in these Standards are the need for "appropriate training" and "thorough follow-up." It is these two areas I wish to focus on in this paper—preparing people to participate on short-term projects and helping them with their re-entry when they return. Specifically, I will explore how the "tools" of cultural anthropology can be used to help students better understand the cultures of the people to whom they are going to, in turn, better understand their own.

Personal Background

To begin, let me address how my interests developed in this area. As I previously indicated, I came to anthropology through missions. My OM experience gave me a lot of "data" to work with, but it was while attending classes at the U.S Center for World Mission in Pasadena, California that I was first exposed to the anthropological concepts that provided the analytical framework to interpret my mission experiences. Many of the guest lecturers, including Don Richardson, James Buswell, Robertson McQuilkin, and David Hesselgrave, applied anthropological methods and concepts to the study of contemporary missions. The interplay between anthropology and missions caught my interest, and I knew at that time that I wanted to go on in anthropology—but always with an eye on missions. In my current position as professor of cultural anthropology at Asbury Theological Seminary, I am able to focus more explicitly on the interplay between anthropology and missions, examining how the former can be applied to assist the latter.

During my fifteen years of teaching anthropology at a liberal arts college, I was involved at various levels with students participating in STM projects. It is through working with these students, as well as reflecting on my own experience with STM, that I have come to appreciate the role cultural anthropology can play in helping people get the most out of their missions experience.

Two Related Problems

As I have worked with students preparing for STM projects, I have detected two related problems that hinder their pre-departure preparation and on-field effectiveness. The first has to do with the inherent tension between the universal and particular nature of the Gospel, and the second is an emphasis on "doing" rather than "learning." I find that students interested in missions often focus on the universal nature of the Gospel—i.e., there is neither Jew nor Greek, male nor female, slave nor free--and either downplay or totally ignore the particular cultural and social context in which the people they hope to reach actually live. This is particularly true for the type of student I typically dealt with—white, middle-class, and from smaller towns in the Midwest. Take the issue of ethnic identity, my area of expertise in anthropology and one in which I offer several courses. For most of my students their ethnic ancestry plays no role in their day-to-day lives—indeed, it plays virtually no part in their self-identity whatsoever. As a result, it is difficult to get students to appreciate the foundational role such identities often play in the lives of people in much of the rest of the world, and how these identities can affect almost every sphere of their lives—social, cultural, political, and economic. The assumption seems to be that since ethnicity is meaningless to the students, it is therefore meaningless for others as well. If more of my students came from minority populations in the United States, they would probably have a very different understanding of, and appreciation for, the role of ethnicity and race in daily life. By being ignorant of, or ignoring, the importance of ethnic identity in the lives of the people students are going to "reach" with the Gospel, they may inadvertently offend the native population, resulting in a rather "cold" reception at best. I will return to this point in a moment.

By focusing on doing rather than learning, students risk not understanding the local situation and therefore being less effective with what they understand to be their "task," i.e., sharing the Gospel with others. As the evangelical historian Mark Noll has noted, American evangelical Christians, reflecting their cultural context, value action over careful thought and analysis. He states that "its crusading genius, whether in religion or politics, has always tended towards an oversimplification of issues and the substitution of inspiration and zeal for critical analysis and serious reflection" (1994:12). We can certainly see this characteristic among many who participate on STM projects. Often when I hear presentations by students who have gone on such projects—over winter or spring breaks, summers—they tell of all they accomplished, and how many people were "saved" at the end of their one to four week experience. Far too seldom do I hear them speak of what they received from the local people, as if there was nothing to learn from the "natives." After all, the students were the ones with the Good News to share and the natives were in darkness. This was brought home to me a few years ago when my wife and I were helping with an evangelistic campaign being conducted by a local church in a small town in the Basque Country of Spain. A group of Campus Crusade for Christ students from the United States had come over to help with the campaign, where the church was showing the *Jesus* film in the local cinema. After being there for a few days one of the female students approached my wife and I, expressing her frustration. Even though she had studied Spanish in high school and college for several years, she found that she could neither speak nor understand the language well enough to share the Gospel with the local people. She told us that since God had "called" her to work on this project, and since she could not "share" the Gospel with these people, she saw no reason why she should stay. My wife and I tried to convince her that perhaps God *had* called her to be there, but that He had something else in mind for her. Perhaps He had something for her to *learn* about herself and others. I'm not sure how well she received this, but she did end up staying for the rest of the campaign.

The danger of focusing on the universal at the expense of the particular and on "doing" rather than "learning" is that students are then uncritical and unreflective when it comes to the impact their own culture has on how they understand what the Gospel is, and how they present it to others. Ethnocentrism appears to be a universal phenomenon where the "assumed givens" of social life in a particular culture are believed to be "natural" and "good," whereas those of other cultures are viewed as "weird" and "wrong." There are enough stories about ugly Americans who travel to other cultures and expect the natives to adjust to them, to speak English, dress the same, live on the same time schedule, and eat the same foods—which, thanks to the McDonaldization of the world, gets easier every day. Unfortunately, the same is true for many Americans who go on STM projects; because they tend to be unreflective of their own culture, much of what they "give" to others is the Gospel neatly wrapped in American culture (see Loewen 1976).

Short-Term Missions and Cultural Anthropology

Having outlined two related problems associated with Americans involved in STM, I now want to examine how cultural anthropology provides the "tools" or perspective needed to help overcome these obstacles. I will look at how its holistic perspective, its emphasis on understanding the native's point of view, and its reflexive nature can provide a framework to help those going on short-term projects effectively deal with their ethnocentrism and be more effective in the missionary task.

Holism

One of the principle tenets of cultural anthropology is that different aspects of a society or culture cannot be examined in isolation. When anthropologists conduct fieldwork even though they typically have a particular question they are interested in exploring, they realize that they have to understand that question in its broader context. For example, my research question had to do with the affect the Spanish immigrants to the Basque Country were having on Basque society and culture. Were they integrating or remaining separate? To what extent were they changing the local scene? How did they view the native population? How were they viewed by natives? Were the terms "immigrant" and "native" still meaningful as social categories? In pursuing answers to these questions I needed to understand the local political situation (i.e., Basque nationalism and Spanish nationalism), the economic situation (the changes in industrial output and the affect on jobs), the housing situation (how different barrios developed and how they affected intergroup relations), the voluntary associations (who belonged to which associations, and why), the local language policies (the Basque language vs. Spanish), and the educational system (who is educated, where, and why), to name but a few. In cultural anthropology we refer to this as the holistic perspective. People do not live in worlds where these various elements are nicely segregated, and therefore, we must study how all of these parts affect the particular problem we are interested in.

When the Campus Crusade group referred to above came to the Basque town of Tolosa to help with the evangelistic campaign, one of the things they did was to share the Gospel with in a way peculiar to Campus Crusade—they used "The Four Spiritual Laws." This was an evangelistic tool developed on university campuses as a "bridge" to reach college students who are used to dealing with different laws, particularly in the natural sciences. In this context, to speak of "spiritual laws" was a connection students could make— "Just as there are natural laws, so, too, there are spiritual laws." Campus Crusade developed a tract that could be used to walk students through the "Four Laws."

However, the same context was not found in the small town of Tolosa. The Basque people suffered for nearly forty years under the oppressive laws established by the Franco regime. These laws prohibited Basques from using their own language or having any other external symbols reflecting their distinct culture and identity. This caused Basque culture to go underground, and relegated the Basque language to the home. Now, at the time of the evangelistic campaign in 1984, less than a decade after the death of Franco and the establishment of a constitutional monarchy, here were young Americans (a nationality not held in high esteem) stopping people on the street and trying to read to them from their "Four Spiritual Laws" tract. There is little doubt that when Basques heard the word "laws," it had a very different connotation to them than it did to their foreign visitors. In addition, when debriefing after a day of evangelism in Tolosa, one of the Campus Crusade students described how he had been invited by a man to go to a local pub and, after making clear to the other Campus Crusaders that he had consumed no wine with the gentleman, he reported that they had had a wonderful conversation. Still, the student stated with a sense of failure, he had not been able to share "the laws" with him yet, but hoped to meet with him again to do so. Here we have a situation where, because the students had no understanding of Basque culture or history, their efforts to communicate the universal aspect of the Gospel by means of the "Four Spiritual Laws" inadvertently communicated a very different message to their listeners than they intended. As Loewen notes, "Differing cultural backgrounds and their concomitant presuppositions will cause people to *hear* a differing content from the same message" (1979:160).

I recall walking around the streets of Buenos Aires in 1979, thinking how much it reminded me of European cities and how it was unlike other cities in Colombia and Venezuela we had visited on the Doulos. I was totally unaware of the fact that at that time people were "disappearing" from those same streets, never to be seen again. Politically, it was not that different from other corrupt and totalitarian regimes in Latin America. How can one communicate the Gospel effectively when he or she is unaware of the broader context in which people are living their lives?

The Natives' Point of View

Within anthropology it is common to speak of the "native's" perspective. This is not meant to refer to people from "primitive" or traditional settings in contrast to others, but is used simply to refer to the cultural insiders in any social community. In this "strict sense of the term" (Geertz 1983: 56), I am a "native" Californian. As the anthropologist Clifford Geertz has so poetically stated, humans are suspended in "webs of significance" they themselves have spun, and as such, the task of cultural anthropology is "an interpretive one in search of meaning" (Geertz 1973:5). In order to understand the great diversity of meaning embodied in different cultures, anthropologists attempt to get at the natives' point of view, or, as Geertz puts it, "trying to figure out what the devil [the natives] think they are up to" (1983:58). This is certainly no easy task, as any anthropologist can attest, but if it is "native" meaning we are after then we must put in the time and effort necessary to approximate this meaning.

An example from my own experience might help illustrate what can happen when we are ignorant of local meanings. In the late 1970s I took a trip to Turkey with two other Americans. We were with Operation Mobilization at the time, and had traveled through Yugoslavia and Bulgaria distributing Christian literature in a clandestine manner along the way. When we arrived in Turkey, we went to a bank to exchange money. One of my friends and I took a seat on a small couch while the other went up to the teller. In front of us was a coffee table with two chairs facing us on the other side. Shortly after we sat down, a Turkish gentleman entered the bank and took a seat across from us. As we two Americans interacted with one another my friend put his foot up on the edge of the coffee table, as many Americans do. The Turk on the other side glared at us, stood up, said something in Turkish which we did not understand, and proceeded to knock my friend's foot off of the table. We were shocked! What had just happened, and why?

The best meaning we could give at the time was that Turks must not like people putting their feet on furniture. It was not until a few days later we were told that, by showing the bottom of his shoe, my friend had greatly insulted the Turkish gentleman. In a culture that puts a high premium on honor and shame, this man evidently felt compelled to defend his honor in the face of this obvious insult. We had absolutely no frame of reference to know how insulting my friend had been, nor why the Turk acted in what we considered to be a violent and aggressive manner.

Traditionally, missionaries have outshone anthropologists when it comes to the amount of time they spend with a people. But when it comes to STM participants this is a very different story. Far too often, I'm afraid, there has not been enough effort given to prepare short-termers to understand the meanings of the local cultures they will be entering, which can lead less effectiveness, and can actually harm the missionary cause. Let me illustrate. A few years ago a group of students from the college I was teaching at went with an STM team to China. Each American lived with a Chinese student at a college catering to China's ethnic minorities. They were to live together for over a month, spending time with their roommates and trying to share the Gospel in word and deed. After being there for a couple of weeks, the American students decided they would have a foot-washing ceremony to show humility and servanthood to their Chinese counterparts. The Chinese students balked at this idea, but the Americans insisted, carrying out what was to them a very meaningful act. It was meaningful to the Chinese students as well—unfortunately in a very negative way; they interpreted the American students' actions as an indication that they thought the Chinese students were dirty and needed to bathe. Whatever rapport had developed was lost, and many of the Chinese students wanted nothing to do with their American roommates after this act.

One of the leaders of the mission trip to China wrote to me with examples of how our students had been culturally insensitive. He stated,

> The major issue is misattribution which stems from a basic failure to enter the point of view of the other culture. The ... students consistently interpreted their Chinese roommates' behavior from their U.S. point of view and thus made faulty interpretations of behavior and misattributed motives to those behaviors....We need to anticipate the places where our cultures differ and be ready to be proactive.

He asked for my help in "stressing how important it is that [the] students go as culture learners."

Of course, students can purchase books like *Do's and Taboos Around the World* (Axtell 1993) which can help them become more aware of taboo hand gestures in different cultures (anyone remember Dan Quayle giving the "O.K." sign in Latin America?), gift giving and receiving, jargon and idioms, and perhaps even what showing the bottom of your shoe means in Middle Eastern cultures. But, while these aspects of culture are not unimportant (as my Turkish experience), it is imperative that students also understand the deeper, more historical aspects of cultures as well—what has often been referred to as "worldview" in the missiological literature (see, for example, Kraft 1996:11). I have overseen several student STM projects to Mexico, usually done for a week or two during spring or winter break. One of the things I try to get my students to understand is the role that honor and shame, patron/client relations, and limited good play in the everyday lives of people in Mexico—how these create "webs of significance" that affect all of life, including how the Americans themselves will be perceived. I tell the students about the first time I became aware of the concept of limited good. A colleague (who is a Latin Americanist) and I were interviewing an immigrant from El Salvador who had settled a few years earlier with his family in a small Iowan town. When we asked him if he had many Latino friends he said "no," and went on to explain that whenever he and his family experienced difficulties, the other Latinos were happy; it was the Anglos who offered him and his family comfort and support. When I later asked my colleague about this he explained to me the idea of "limited good," a cultural construct that is below the surface in many peasant communities of Latin American—i.e., that there is a limited amount of "good" to go around, so if something bad is happening to someone else, it means that there is more good out there potentially for you. Our narrator's experience shows how this concept can affect daily interaction and the formation of friendships.

Another cultural difference with Mexico that students often noticed right away is how time is conceived—Mexicans always seem to be "late" or "wasting time." What students often fail to recognize, however, is how time in Mexico ties into broader cultural constructs such as honor and status. I have students read a chapter from Glen Dealy's book, *The Latin Americans*, entitled "Homo Políticus," in which the author goes into some detail on how Mexicans and other Latin Americans often manipulate time as a way of establishing their status and social ascendancy in relation to others. Making people wait on you is a way of exerting power over them. After a conversation with a Mexican student, in which he learned that their persistent tardiness was intentional, Dealy writes,

> This exchange marked a coming of age with regard to the Latin American way of life. Despite having previously vacationed and lived in Central and South America, only at that moment did I truly "see." As if through religious enlightenment, my

frame of reference changed; however haltingly, I began to grasp the mainsprings of that culture…. The Latin Everyman dreams not of winning impersonal deference through faceless material accumulation, as does the capitalist, but of directly earning and receiving esteem (1992:54, 55).

After reading this chapter, a student planning to go to Mexico asked the insightful and important question, "How will they view us as Americans?" He had come to realize that they, too, could be used as a way for certain people they encountered in Mexico to earn and receive esteem. Whereas the Americans would almost certainly focus on the material poverty of the people—indeed, one of their main tasks was to help with the construction of a house—many of the Mexicans, particularly those with a degree of local power, would be focusing on honor and esteem. These are two fundamentally different ways of constructing the situation that profoundly affect the meaning given to social interaction.

A word of caution is perhaps warranted here. While recognizing these deeper, "worldview" aspects of a culture, students also have to be aware of the fact that not everyone in a particular culture acts the same, thinks the same, or gives the same meanings to events around them. This should be somewhat self-evident—all a person has to do is be cognizant of the diversity found within his or her own culture—but probably needs to be made explicit. For over ten years, during summer breaks, I directed ethnographic field schools with American students in the Basque Country and Wales. The main question I had students address was how Basqueness or Welshness was defined. As students explored this issue they became aware that identity was quite complex. People defined Basqueness or Welshness in different ways, employing a variety of criteria. What the students found was that people often defined ethnic identity in a way that included themselves. For example, if they spoke Basque or Welsh, then language would often be the key defining characteristic; if they did not, then place of birth, emotional attachment to the country, political affiliation, or any combination of these would take precedence. Through this research students came to appreciate the diversity of opinion and belief found within the cultures being studied. Awareness of this diversity does not negate the deeper cultural constructs, it just mitigates the belief in a universal uniformity (see Douglass 2000 for a discussion of essentialism in anthropology).

Approximating the natives' point of view has very practical implications for missions in general, and STM in particular. Attempting to "enter into," or understand, the natives' point of view will not only make sharing the Gospel more effective as students are better able to grasp the natives' "felt needs," but it will also help them develop a truly humble attitude as they take on the role of learners.

Reflexivity

One of the metaphors for cultural anthropology is a two-edged sword—that is, studying other cultures causes one to reflect on and analyze one's own. Since much of culture is tacit, or below the surface, this reflexive aspect of anthropology is quite important in understanding our own underlying cultural assumptions. For example, one of the things students learn in going to China is the difference between egocentric and sociocentric societies. On many occasions students returning from China have commented on how, when they asked their roommates what they thought about a particular subject, the answer they received was "We Chinese think…" rather than "I think…." For many of the Americans, this was baffling. However, once they returned home they could think about how that response reflected the "communal" worldview of the Chinese in contrast with their own "individual" worldview.

Still, although being exposed to another culture may cause a person to reflect on his or her own, that reflection is not naturally critical. Ethnocentrism is often subtle and difficult to break. I find this to be true in the courses I teach, as well as with students who go on short-term mission projects. All too often, both blades of the two-edged sword are used against the culture one is in or is studying. For those immersed in another culture, this can be a manifestation of culture shock. I recall the difficulty an American roommate of mine in Austria had with the local culture. Regularly he would compare things Austrian with their American counterparts, with the former always coming up short. I did not know what to call it at the time, but I knew he was not adjusting well when he came into our room one evening ranting and raving about the "stupid" Austrian traffic lights that blinked green before turning red and showed both red and yellow prior to turning green. I have to admit that at the time I was more concerned about an exit strategy from the room than I was with the symptoms of his culture shock.

Returning to the short-termers in China, not all of them initially handled the egocentric/sociocentric worldview differences well. The director of the program informed me that several of the female students complained that their Chinese roommates were being dishonest and duplicitous because they "refused to tell us what they were really feeling." Rather than seeing this as a cultural difference, the American students interpreted it in an individualistic way and took it quite personally. So, though reflexivity is one of the hallmarks of an anthropological perspective, it does not necessarily come natural or easy, which emphasizes the need for pre-departure and re-entry training. For students to get the most out of their experiences, they need to be able to anticipate where cultural differences might lead to misunderstandings, and they need assistance in making sense out of their experiences once they return.

Conclusion

Throughout this chapter I have given examples, both my own and those of others, that largely reflect the damage that can be done by short-term missionaries being unaware of the local culture they are going to and focusing too much on doing rather than learning. Let me close with a more positive example. Megan was a student I had the pleasure of working with during her undergraduate years. In the fall of her sophomore year she took an anthropology course that focused on interacting with an ethnic or racial community different from her own. Megan did her project among Sudanese refugees at the Lutheran Social Services in Des Moines, IA. This was her first exposure to refugees from the Sudan. The next semester she took a course entitled "Ethnicity and Nationalism" in which she studied the civil war in the Sudan for her final project. She also took "Ethnographic Field Methods" that semester which allowed her to interview Sudanese refugees she previously had met in Des Moines. Megan had also decided she was going to participate on a summer mission project in Cairo sponsored by InterVarsity. I recall how excited she was when she found that a number of Sudanese she was working with and interviewing in Des Moines had actually spent time at the refugee camp she would be working at in just a few months. In a presentation she gave the following fall regarding her Cairo experience, Megan talked about how the academic work she had done prior to the experience had prepared her to work among the refugees. One thing that was especially helpful to her was knowing about the different ethnic groups from the Sudan that were represented at the refugee camp. She was aware of how important their local languages and cultures were to them; in other words, they did not necessarily see themselves as Sudanese, but as Dinka, Nuer, etc. However, the common suffering, and their fighting a common enemy, had drawn these various groups closer together. From her Cairo experience she came to see that not only does God have a "heart for the world," but He is also concerned about injustice. She said that her definition of joy had been redefined through the experience. That same fall Megan once again worked with Sudanese refugees in Des Moines, and was able to use the little Arabic she had learned in Cairo to communicate with new arrivals who spoke very little English. When asked about her future plans, Megan said that she now wanted to work with refugees, but probably outside the United States. Currently she is working with international students on an American university campus with InterVarsity, and loving the experience.

Applying an anthropological perspective to the missionary task is not new in missiology; indeed, it was twenty-six years ago that I was first exposed to this application at the U.S. Center for World Mission. However, in my experience with missionaries in the field, and in working with short-termers at a liberal arts college, I still find this perspective to be largely lacking. Whatever the reasons for this, I believe the conceptual tools of cultural anthropology discussed in this presentation—holism, the natives' point of view, and reflexivity--can help equip our students to more fully appreciate the role that local culture plays in how people understand everything around them, including foreign missionaries. It can also help them understand the role their own culture plays in how *they* give meaning to the world around them—including the world of Christianity. In this way, short-term mission projects have a much greater chance of being successful, as the participants are able to make the Gospel "Good News" both to those they are going to, as well as themselves. After all, in order to contextualize the Gospel, you must first have an understanding of the cultural context from which you come, and the one to which you are going.

References Cited

Axtel, Roger, ed. 1993. *Do's and taboos around the world.* New York: John Wiley & Sons, Inc.

Dealy, Glen Caudill. 1992. Homo Políticus. In *The Latin Americans: Spirit and Ethos.* Boulder, CO: Westview Press, pp. 53-95.

Douglass, William A. 2000. In Search of Juan de Oñate: Confessions of a Cryptoessentialist. In *Journal of Anthropological Research* 56: 137-162.

Geertz, Clifford. 1973. Thick description: Toward an interpretive theory of culture. In *The interpretation of cultures.* New York: Basic Books, pp. 3-30.

Geertz, Clifford. 1983. "From the native's point of view": On the nature of anthropological understanding. In *Local knowledge: Further essays in interpretive anthropology.* New York: Basic Books, pp. 55-70.

Kraft, Charles. 1996. *Anthropology for Christian witness.* Maryknoll, NY: Orbis Books.

Livermore, David A. 2006. *Serving with eyes wide open: Doing short-term missions with cultural intelligence.* Grand Rapids, MI: Baker Books.

Loewen, Jacob A. 1976. Evangelism and culture. In *The new face of evangelicalism,* C. Rene Padilla, ed. London: Hodder and Stoughton, pp. 177-189.

Loewen, Jacob A. 1979. The Gospel—Its content and communication: An anthropological perspective. In *The gospel and culture,* John Stott and Robert Coote, eds. Pasadena: William Carey Library, pp. 154-174.

Noll, Mark A. 1994. *The scandal of the evangelical mind.* Grand Rapids, MI: Eerdmans Publishing Company.

Priest, Robert, Terry Dischinger, Steve Rasmussen, and C. M. Brown. 2006. Researching the short-term mission movement. *Missiology* 34: 431-450.

Wuthnow, Robert and Stephen Offutt. 2008. Transnational religious connections. *Sociology of Religion: A Quarterly Review* 69: 209-233.

CHAPTER 5

THE MYTH OF THE
BLANK SLATE:

A CHECK LIST FOR SHORT-TERM MISSIONS

Imagine this. You are part of a 150-member church which runs an Alpha course and several seeker Bible studies in homes scattered throughout the community. The church also contributes support to six international missionaries, a downtown rescue mission, and a home for runaway teens.

Your pastor receives a letter (in Spanish) from a Mexican lay leader. He wants to bring an intergenerational team of twenty-five Mexicans to minister alongside your church for two weeks. They don't speak English, but they will have English printed materials to distribute in your Alpha course and seeker groups and city missions, as well as an English gospel video to show. They are eager to preach in your church services if someone will translate from Spanish. Of course they will be happy to serve in physical projects, receiving direction in Spanish.

They have heard that there are a number of serious deficiencies in the American way of life, and they hope to address these in word and deed, although they will need translation.

They have a little money to spend on housing, but would appreciate your finding low cost or even free accommodations. Simple is fine, but they will need hot showers daily. They hope you can arrange transport to and from the airport, and even around the city.

Long before the Mexicans arrive, your church will need to spend thirty hours on emails and phone calls with them and in making local arrangements for their translation and housing and transport and ministry. During their stay it is likely that two will get sick and will need to be taken to a doctor, one will lose his passport, and another will be hassled on the street, requiring some intervention and counseling. Although you don't know it yet, there will be an internal dispute on the team which will consume most of their emotional energy for several days.

They are tentatively scheduled to arrive five months from now.

Do you want them to come?

How does a short term mission look from the receiving end?

On the sending end, it begins nobly. The Lord touches hearts. He opens eyes to see the peoples of his world. Church leaders want members to grow as Christ's disciples, relationships to be strengthened, hearts to be softened, vision to be expanded, and wallets unzipped, all for the glory of God. They know a short term mission can help accomplish these goals.

So a team is sent. (Actually this happens over and over. It is estimated that half a million North Americans each year do STM in Latin America alone.) There is one problem. The destination is not a blank slate. Christians probably exist there. Cultures certainly exist there. And—of importance for American teams—perceptions of Americans exist there.

For maximum success, these three realities must be faced.

"Welcome to Our Home": Christians Are Already There

In nearly every nation, there are people who follow Jesus. Philip Jenkin's book, *The Next Christendom,* shows that most Christians now live in Asia, Africa, and Latin America. While Jenkins includes Catholics and Orthodox, evangelicals also praise God all around the globe. One hundred twenty countries have national evangelical fellowships which are members of The World Evangelical Alliance. Reportedly ten thousand Spanish and Portuguese speaking missionaries share the good news globally.

What about "unreached peoples"? This term refers to ethnic groups, a more focused category than nations. Some of these groups do lack Christians. Others contain Christians but not enough to make an impact. However, many of these people participate in the larger world. They watch television, follow national or international sports events, attend schools taught in the national language, and conduct market business in that language. Though racism builds barriers, many "unreached peoples" are not completely cut off from their neighbors.

Some "unreached" peoples have churches. Sometimes there are dozens of congregations. Yet because of the size of the population in relation to the number of Christians, they still are categorized as unreached in mission tables.

"May We Come In?"

Our help is needed. Yet when we arrive in a place, courtesy demands that we ask, "May we come in?" It requires us to behave like good guests. How much more this is the case when we are entering the home of brothers and sisters in Christ who are trying to apply the Word and the Spirit to their time and place.

Consider Arabs, for example. Consider Lebanon. This nation was once known as the pearl of the Middle East, an oasis where

Christians and Muslims lived together in peace. Today violence threatens to explode the society. Yet Christians continue to live out their faith. When Israel invaded in late 2006, Lebanese sympathetic to the violent Hezbollah fled north. Evangelicals welcomed them into their homes and onto the grounds of their Christian institutions. One evangelical leader housed fifty refugees in his house. The main Bible school drilled a well on its property to provide water for the hundreds who were camping on its grounds. Evangelicals went out to the refugee camps, bringing food and medicine. They helped pregnant women who were about to give birth. They organized children's games. "The miracle was that God put love in our hearts for the Hezbollah," one testified.

Of the three hundred million Arabs in the world, five per cent are Christian. Lebanese Arab evangelicals have accepted their responsibility to reach out to both Christians and nonChristians. In the first months of 2007 they distributed 40,000 Arabic picture Bibles in hospitals in Iraq. They have sent trainers to Sudan to train 950 Sunday School teachers to whom they are providing Arabic Sunday School curriculum.

Does the Arab world need foreign missionaries? Does Lebanon? Of course. But neither Lebanon nor the Arab world are blank slates.

"Always Go Through the Church"

What are the implications for STM teams? "Always go through the church. Don't sidestep it." These are the words of the pastor of a large Arab congregation outside Lebanon. So many Muslim inquirers come to this church that they have set up two offices "like dentist offices" with a steady stream of appointments. Satellite evangelism has caused this influx. "Missionaries <u>must</u> come under the advisement of a church," this pastor says. "Without the local church, there is no way that new believers will have enough support."

When you arrive in a country, you may not find any evangelicals on the street where you live, or even in that town. Check with the World Evangelical Alliance. Check with the various student ministries like International Fellowship of Evangelical Students or Campus Crusade for Christ. They work with the future leaders of the country, and will know some evangelicals among these potential leaders.

The believers you find may not be easy to understand. They may not even like you very much. Certainly they will not be perfect Christians. Some will be embroiled in turf wars with each other. Some will be mired in church traditions. It will take time to discover your colleagues.

Don't settle for those who are most like you. Look for those who want to grow in the Word and the Spirit, and who have their people in their heart. The more representative they are of their people, the less comprehensible and comfortable they may be to Americans. Still, these are the ones with long term leadership potential. Profound friendship can grow between you over time. In the end, you may agree to disagree on some strategies. You may be called to plant churches in groups and communities they have not reached, rather than simply joining them in their existing projects. However, courtesy demands that you talk with and listen to them first.

"So if Christians are all over, why do they need _me_?" a student asked recently. The answer is not hard to find. Half the world lives on two dollars a day or less. More than three billion people do not know Jesus as Lord. The world needs us. However, it needs us to be team players. "Plays well with others" is a criterion for success in kindergarten. It also applies to mission. Do we take our toys and go home if we can't control the sandbox? The last section of this paper will give practical alternatives.

Would Jesus Kill That Fly?
Cultures Are Already There

A missionary was studying the Tibetan language with a Buddhist monk. One day as they conjugated verbs, a fly dive-bombed them. Absentmindedly the missionary reached out to swat it.

"Stop!" The monk protested. "Would Jesus have killed that fly?"

What a difference a culture makes. How differently people in various cultures see the world around them, even something as simple as a fly. Therefore mission teams must adapt to cultures.

This is old news. Short termers can repeat it like a mantra. What does it mean?

It means systematic, empathetic, and theological approaches to culture.

Systematic Approach to Culture

A culture is a system with parts, like a body or a motor. To understand your new friends, you need to study the system that frames their lives. The *Cultural Research Questions* in the Appendix list six parts: Family, Social Structure, Communication Patterns, Economy, Religion, and Values.

How do you use these research questions? They can guide your observations on the field, as well as your reading before you go. On the field, you can skim through all the questions once a week. Choose one question. Look for answers to that question while carrying out your regular activities. At the end of the week, review what you observed. Then choose another question from another category. At the end of six weeks, you will have begun to learn in all of the categories with minimal effort.

Within any culture there will be variations. There will be subgroups, depending on education, wealth, tribal affiliation, religious training and commitment, political passions, etc. People will differ according to their role in the life cycle, their unique life experiences, and their personalities. Every man is an exception, as Kierkegaard noted.

Other factors will impinge on the culture from *outside*. International business, migrant labor pools, global political or religious movements, consumer advertising, world soccer and missionary evangelism all change cultures from outside. You must ask: What are the structures of domination and influence, whether within the society or pushing in from outside? What large scale changes can you anticipate in the next ten years?

Theological Approach to Culture

Aren't cultures sinful? Isn't that why we do mission? Yes, we often encounter fragmentation, generation gaps, alienation, lust, hate, corruption, selfishness, injustice, laziness, disorder, and violence systematically patterned throughout a culture. No part remains pure. Science tends to serve militarism or hedonism, ignoring morals. Art often becomes worship without God. Mass media is full of verbal prostitutes. Advertisers exploit sex. Businessmen pull shady deals whenever they can. Politicians fill their own pockets with the people's money. Teachers don't bother about scholarship after a few years in the profession. Workers do shoddy work. Husbands deceive their wives. Wives manipulate their husbands. Parents neglect their children, or dominate them. Children ignore their parents as persons.

All this is true. But it is true of our own culture too. And it is not the whole truth. We are sinners. We are also created in God's image. God endowed us with creativity and set us in a world of possibilities. Using his gifts, we have developed the cultures of the world. As A.A. Stockdale says,

> When God made the earth, he could have finished it. But he didn't.

He left it as a raw material—to tease us, to
tantalize us, to set us thinking, and experimenting,
and risking, and adventuring. And therein we find
our supreme interest in living.

He gave us the challenge of raw materials, not the
satisfaction of perfect, finished things.

He left the music unsung, and the dramas
unplayed.

He left the poetry undreamed, in order than men
and women might not become bored, but engaged
in stimulating, exciting, creative activities that
keep them thinking, working, experimenting,
and experiencing all the joys and satisfactions of
achievement (1964:20).

When I lived for several years in the Philippines, I saw strong families, warm hospitality, lots of time lavished on children, enduring friendships, a heritage of economic freedom for women, the ability to live graciously on little money, sauces that extended a small amount of meat to many people, a delight in sharing, skill in the art of relaxation, lithe, limber bodies, and the ability to enjoy being with a large number of people continuously. I could not look at these traits as though they were merely the products of nature. Every good gift is from above (James 1:17) and all wisdom and knowledge come from Jesus Christ (Colossians 2:3). These beautiful qualities in Filipino culture were gifts of the God who loves diversity—billions of unique snowflakes, personalities, smells, colors, even tropical fish. Does God look for a beige uniformity around his throne at the end of time? No, he welcomes a kaleidoscope of peoples and tribes and kindreds and nations. Is it any surprise that he programs us with the capacity to enrich his world with an amazing array of cultures?

Cultures contain sin, and must be judged. But taking joy in our culture is not sin. It is like the joy a father or mother feels at their child's graduation. Your child marches across the platform. Your chest hammers with pride. This is not pride at the expense of your neighbor, whose face also glows as his child graduates. No, you are proud simply because you know your child's stories, the sorrows he has suffered, and the gifts that have blossomed like flowers opening to the sun. You yourself have cried and laughed and given away years of your life in the shaping of some of those stories. At its best, joy in culture is an expansion of this good family pride. It is a sense of identity, a birthright.

Human beings were created to live in community. "Even when our material needs are met, still our motivation…emotional resilience… and moral strength…must come from somewhere, from some vision of public purpose anchored in a compelling image of social reality," according to anthropologist Clifford Geertz (1964:70). Being a world citizen is too vague to provide this, says Geertz. It makes the common person feel insignificant. Even national citizenship may breed apathy. But when you are a member of a cultural group, you have celebrations which give zest, values which give a cognitive framework, action patterns which give direction to your days, and associational ties which root you in a human context. You have a place in time in the universe, a base for the conviction that you are part of the continuity of life flowing from the past and pulsing on into the future. You are in the story.

Short term teams must honor that heritage.

Empathetic Approach to Culture

If people were simply objects, studying them by means of cultural or theological categories might be enough. But people also are subjects. To understand them, then, we must live alongside them, laugh with them, cry with them, and plod through boring days with them. In this way we begin to know them as we ourselves want to be known, in ways that transcend words and categories. We develop empathy.

As a team heads for the field, it needs to study its destination culture systematically, theologically, and empathetically.

"Dumb Things Done in Jesus' Name": Ideas About Americans Are Already There

"Dumb Things Done in Jesus' Name" is a talk that Fred Bailey delivers on university campuses around the country. Fred is an Intervarsity staff worker. Christians have done some bad things, he admits--from bombing abortion clinics to apartheid. Christians aren't perfect, although the more we learn to follow Jesus the better neighbors we become. On the other hand, not all the "dumb things" Christians are accused of are true. Some are caricatures, stereotypes, ignorant generalizations. Fred tackles those because he knows that people cannot trust you when your faults are in their face. You have to get past those barriers in order to earn a hearing.

Rick Richardson, professor of evangelism at Wheaton College, makes the same point in his recent book *Reimagining Evangelism.* He tells about a Christian named Daniel who went to work in a Starbucks coffee shop, expecting opportunities to share his faith.

> One surprise was that all twenty-one people he worked with believed in God. Not one was an atheist. Their lives and attitudes and his impression of the broader culture had led him to expect many more people to be anti-God. But they were all very positive toward God and spirituality.
>
> A second surprise was that all were very interested in spiritual things but not in Christians,

Christianity, or the church. No one wanted to hear Daniel's proofs for God or invitations to come to church or ideas about salvation. Almost everyone thought they knew what Christianity was about and had decided they didn't want it. They were post-Christian. At some point along the way, each of them had experienced a breach in trust related to Christianity. Maybe a Christian friend had been hypocritical or pushy. Maybe when they were young they had attended church and found it boring and irrelevant. Maybe they had watched TV preachers and been turned off. Or maybe they had experienced a tragedy—death or sexual abuse or some other trauma—and felt that God had been distant and uncaring.

Richardson comments:

> Daniel wasn't starting at ground zero, but rather at minus three or four. He would have to pierce through their stereotypes and rebuild broken trust before they would even listen to what he had to say…The biggest thing Daniel learned is that people in this generation have a prior question of trust that must be addressed before he can have meaningful spiritual conversations with them (2006: 65-66).

How crucial this is in intercultural mission work. The "ugly American" stereotype is alive and well. When I was in West Africa several years ago, the African director of a Christian NGO said, "Would you like to know what it is like to do mission with Americans? Let me tell you a story."

In this story, Elephant and Mouse were best friends. One day Elephant said, "Mouse, lets have a party!"

Animals gathered from far and near. They ate, and drank, and sang, and danced. And nobody celebrated more exuberantly than the Elephant.

After it was over, Elephant exclaimed, "Mouse, did you ever go to a better party? What a celebration!"

But Mouse didn't answer.

"Where are you?" Elephant called. Then he shrank back in horror. There at his feet lay the Mouse, his body ground into the dirt—smashed by the exuberance of his friend, the Elephant.

"Sometimes that is what it is like to do mission with you Westerners," the African storyteller commented. "It is like dancing with an elephant."

Missiologist Andrew Walls has reflected on "elephants" in mission:

> In some broken-backed nations, those marked
> out by poverty of resources, technological
> breakdown, political instability, or economic
> disaster, the missionary bodies, often working
> in concert (Missions Incorporated, as one may
> say) now have the most flexible, powerful, and
> efficient organization in the country. They can
> fly people around the country and in and out of
> it; they can bring in machinery and service ailing
> plants; they have radio telephones that work;
> they can arrange currency, get foreign exchange,
> and send an international message quickly. They
> can sometimes do things that the government
> itself cannot do. And the local church, however
> independent or indigenous, can do none of these
> things, except insofar as it can act as a link to

an outside mission. In the end, what will be the implications of all this power held by Mission Incorporated? (1990:22).

Missiologist Charles Taber has observed similarly:

> Is the task medical care? We think of doctors and nurses. Is the task education? We visualize expensive buildings, equipment, and professional staff. We quite literally lack the capacity to imagine doing things other than this capital-intensive, technology-intensive way.

> And we bring these ideas along wherever we do the Lord's work. Even where technology is inordinately expensive. Even where believers are all but destitute. And even where the most abundant resource is willing minds, willing hands. Soon it becomes apparent that local Christians can't pick up the tab. And because they also lack the know-how to operate the system, we end up taking over.

Such "managerial missiology" frequently comes under fire from Latin Americans. Samuel Escobar has warned about

> "the effort to reduce Christian mission to a manageable enterprise…to project missionary action as a response to a problem that has been described in quantitative form…a linear task…with logical steps…management by objective…following marketing principles… giving predominance to that which can be reduced to a statistical chart. ..The pragmatic approach

deemphasizes theological problems, takes for granted the existence of adequate content, and consequently majors in method...The tough questions are not asked because they cannot be reduced to a linear management-by-objectives process. ...However, only categories like paradox, mystery, suffering, and failure can help us grasp something of the depth of the spiritual battle involved in mission" (1999: 109-110).

Escobar adds:

The suspicion of some Third World Christians is that they are being used as objects of a missionary action that seems to be directed to the main objective of enhancing the financial, informational, and decision-making power of some centers of mission in the First World (1999:112).

David Zac Niringiye, Assistant Bishop of Kampala in the nation of Uganda, says in a recent article in *Christianity Today*, "Africa's crisis is not poverty. It is not AIDS. Africa's crisis is confidence. What decades of colonialism and missionary enterprise eroded among us is confidence." On the other hand, "one of the gravest threats to the North American church is the deception of power...Those at the center tend to think, 'The future belongs to us. We are the shapers of tomorrow. The process of gospel transmission, the process of mission—all of it is on our terms because we are powerful, because we are established. We have a track record of success, after all" (Crouch 2006:35).

The irony is that we know so little. Many of our short-term "solutions" do not fit. Missiologist David Livermore has taken teams of pastors on teaching trips to Africa. Recently he interviewed both the pastors and the Africans that they taught. The pastors commented:

> The training was outstanding. I think they were hungry, very hungry for more effective ways and tools. They would sit and listen. They wouldn't get up and go to the bathroom every five minutes… They were spellbound…These are the next generation of leaders. They are anxious to apply their learning…It was fresh and new like they had never heard it before (2004:460).

The African pastors viewed the teaching sessions differently. They commented:

> It was a nice day, but I don't think what they taught would ever work here. But if it makes them feel they can help us in ways beyond supporting our ministry financially, we're willing to listen… I'm glad the trainers felt respected. What they need to realize, however, is that we would never think about getting up to leave in the middle of their lecture…I wish we could have shared more about the real challenges we're facing in our ministry. How do I lead a church when most of our godly men have lost their lives in battle? How do I help a parent care for their AIDS baby? Those are my pressing issues, not growing my church bigger or starting a second service (2004:460).

Many of our solutions do not fit, and many are not sufficiently complex. At the 2007 World Economic Forum in Davos, secular young leaders sparkled with plans for creative, complex, carefully-crafted solutions to problems in various poor countries. By contrast, too many mission projects limit their focus to children. Too many send carpenters to places where unemployment runs twenty-five percent. We like these projects because we can control them. We can succeed. But God gave us brains to get to the root of problems, not to dabble on the surface. There is a proverb:

> If you give a man a fish, you feed him for one day.
> If you teach him to fish, you feed him for many days.

John Perkins adds:

> Who owns the pond?

These are systemic questions. They recognize that when problems are big and complex, efforts at solutions also must be big and complex. We are bad stewards if we stick with simple projects when we *can* access the knowledge to do more. This is not an honor to God's name on the world scene.

Admittedly, complex projects will show fewer successes. That is what life is like in the hard places. Real love will mean entering into brokenness. Identifying with the poor and needy will draw us into mourning. This is the opposite of quick positive thinking. It goes beyond cheap cheerfulness and naïve optimism. "Christians in Africa and many other parts of the world have not absorbed the myth that is promoted so pervasively in the United States," writes Lynne Baab in her book on the Christian discipline of fasting. "They do not believe that God will make life easy. They do not believe that suffering is a sign that God has abandoned us. They understand that suffering shapes our character" (2006:128). They know that this life yields only partial successes. Some longings will only be satisfied when we reach heaven. They welcome practical help, but they also want true brothers and sisters who can cry with them, and laugh with them, and carry them in their hearts.

"Have you noticed that Westerners only support successes?" one Asian mused as he walked beside a lake at a Christian conference. He had supervised a highly praised socioeconomic program. U.S. and European Christians had lionized him. Publications had described his work glowingly. But as he gazed across the lake, he mused to his friend—who reported it to me—"Have you ever noticed that Westerners only support successes? I wonder, would anybody be interested in me if I were to fail?"

All this applies to short-term missions, because they have so little time to accomplish their goals. The temptation to worship American values—efficiency, pragmatic problem-solving, quantification, compartmentalization, speed, and plenty of money—is tremendous. But it may make us appear to be elephants rather than brothers and sisters.

In sum, if your church is considering a short term mission, get to know the Christians where you are going, get to know the culture, and get to know what they really think about Americans. If long term help appears to be what they need most, consider how you can plug into that. This is the focus of the final section.

What Else Can We Do Besides Send Short-Term Mission Teams?: Six Suggestions

Right after Hurricane Mitch devastated Honduras, I spoke all week in a large church on the east coast. After each session, people came to talk with me. Inevitably they exclaimed, "I can't ignore the call of God's world anymore! I'm going to join the short-term team to Honduras!"

Each day I reported the new volunteers to the mission pastor. He got nervous. Some of these members were older, some were in bad health, and the team was getting too big.

Yet what alternative was available to these people whose hearts had been touched? The church *did* sponsor career missionaries, as well as local missions among needy people. Somehow those had not caught the members' imaginations. The true sign of spiritual authenticity was to go on a short term mission.

We must teach alternatives over and over in attractive, reasonable, convincing ways, until church members understand the value of investing prayer and money in long term love. Sometimes we are told that "Americans need to see it to support it." I do not believe that. As a woman, I remember the heritage celebrated in 1910: Forty missions run by American women supporting 2,500 women missionaries, 6,000 indigenous Bible women, 3,263 schools, 80 hospitals, 11 colleges and innumerable orphanages and dispensaries (Robert 1993: 111). Where did the finances come from? Bake sales, chicken and egg money, and second hand thrift stores. These supporters did not need videos of themselves on the field before they could picture the needy. Do we? Surely not.

We *do*, however, need a sense of relationship with those on the field, and a sense that our money is being used in worthwhile projects. Toward that end, here are six suggestions.

Make It Easy to Know a Missionary

When I was ten years old, Don and Faye Smith spoke in the Sunday morning worship service in my church. They had founded Daystar University in Kenya. Studies of communication-in-culture were their passion. Already at age ten, I knew that subject would be an important part of my life. I will never forget the hymns we sang that morning: *All Hail the Power of Jesus' Name* and *O Zion Haste*. And I will never forget Don and Faye's presentation.

Do people today hear such missionaries? Are missionaries allowed an entire Sunday service to share their lives with people like me? Not likely. There are good reasons. Pastors who are preaching series don't want the momentum disrupted. And not all missionaries are articulate. Still, something has been lost. In its absence, we must find other ways for church people to get to know their missionaries. These arrangements will vary from church to church.

Why focus on long term missionaries? Because it takes time to learn a language. It takes time to see how local patterns work. What is the right way to plan a schedule? To expend money and account for it? To exercise authority? To take initiative? To settle quarrels? These patterns are not mastered in the first week off the plane. God in Christ took thirty-three years in one place. It takes time to be a friend, to listen, and to love. Competent long term missionaries should be our focus, as well as indigenous Christian leaders. We must create places where church members can get know them.

Connect With the News

Here is a suggestion: In every church bulletin, publish a question about some nation that has been in the news that week. Post the answer on the church's web site. Make it a friendly contest to see how many people can answer correctly.

Better yet, connect your web answer with what the church is doing in that nation. Ask: In what nation did (this event) happen, and what is happening in the church there? For the answer, write a paragraph with information easily gleaned from *Operation World* (Patrick Johnstone). If your denomination is working in that country, use that information instead. Of course you will change names and locations when you post material on the web if there is any chance of persecution. Think before you post, and omit anything that might cause harm.

End your posting with a prayer for that country. In six months, the "global literacy" of your congregation will grow by leaps and bounds, and some members will have started to form the habit of praying over the nations. There is a Bible school in Nepal where the students sleep nine to a room—a small room. In the student-maintained garden that covers the central courtyard, chickens scratch between the rows. Two weeks out of every month, the school's director plants churches in the mountains, taking students with him. No technology overwhelms this school. But there is a big map hanging on the wall which is put to use in their all-night prayer sessions twice a month. The school is praying through the nations, learning the names and locations as they pray. Can we do less? We who have *Wikipedia?*

Show What a Good Mission Does

Americans like to start new things. I myself have an anti-institutional bias. "Why bother with a mission?" many of us wonder. A mission skims off administrative costs. Maybe it straitjackets its members into lockstep strategies. Why not just gather a few supporters, a church or two, and head out to implement the vision God has laid on our hearts?

Sometimes that is the right thing to do. In other cases, it makes more sense to go with a mission. David is a friend who directs a 500-member mission focusing on Muslims in sixteen countries. What did the mission do this past year? David reports:

- Six underground churches planted by tentmaker-missionaries, and twenty planted by indigenous leaders nurtured by such missionaries.
- Individuals coming to faith in all sixteen countries, especially through dreams and visions, and some of these leading numbers of others to Jesus.
- Ten percent increase in numbers of missionaries, in spite of a very difficult political context.

- Multimedia ministry, including an evangelistic website. On average, 230 quality email contacts are harvested from the website each month. Contacts are followed up in person in a seamless web integrating media and real live followers of Christ.
- Eleven partner mission agencies, mostly nonwestern. In 2005 this included the first collaboration with historic Arab churches in the Middle East that are missional.

Sometimes there are advantages to being part of a community like David's mission. Beyond shared long-term strategies and economies of scale, such missions can provide practical services like language training, political and legal advocacy, health care, schooling for children, refresher courses and in-service training, spiritual renewal conferences, and technology upgrading. American church members need a more comprehensive and more positive understanding of what missions do. Going out on our own may feel empowering, but it also may mean "reinventing the wheel." It may divert energy to building new structures when that energy otherwise could have been devoted to loving people.

Connect With Internationals Locally

God has brought the nations to America. We no longer have a choice between going on a short term mission or going to the mall, because when we go to the mall we ride past global mission fields. We pass by Iranians and Arabs who have never heard that the Word became flesh and lived among us. We pass by Asian Indians who do not know that He was wounded for our transgressions, bruised for our iniquities, that the chastisement of our sins was upon him, and that by his stripes we are healed. We pass by Ethiopians and Sudanese and Somalis who have yet to hear that we can have peace with God through our Lord Jesus Christ, that if anybody is in Christ he or she is a new creation, that we can be born again. On the way to the mall, we pass by the original owners of this land, Indian people who need to experience the hope of Christ. All sorts of "unreached peoples" are one bus ride away.

This is not glamorous. We would prefer to serve exotic people and places. How much more exciting—and containable—than befriending people across town who might show up on our doorstep with awkward needs and time-consuming requests.

Yet when these friends travel back to their home nations, they will take us along gladly if we indicate that we would like to visit their country. Their families and communities will welcome us. We will have an open door to share the good news. Beginning locally does not mean stopping there. It provides an excellent foundation for global mission that is rooted in relationships.

Advocate for a People.

A U.S. congregation can develop a focused relationship with a specific ethnic group overseas. This means returning repeatedly to visit specific communities. If there are Christians, it means relating to specific churches. While it is not always the same individuals who go, people on both ends feel they know each other because their friends have gone before, or they have received representatives from this church before.

The long-term connection means you can celebrate with those who are growing up, graduating, taking significant steps. You can cry with those who have suffered tragedies. You can see how projects are developing, or not. A certain accountability occurs naturally.

You can sponsor a delegation to visit your church in the U.S. Or sponsor a young adult or two for university or seminary study, or as an intern in your church. Or sponsor a hardworking pastor and spouse for a two-month sabbatical.

A church in Singapore has connected with a village in Thailand. This was initiated by a Thai Christian worker with relatives in Singapore. Many short term teams have come. Youth were the first.

Eventually elders from the Singapore church wanted to see what was going on. Various individuals have visited repeatedly, both younger and older. The Buddhist village now looks forward to the teams because they teach English and computer skills and enliven the ordinary routine. The teams also lead worship events. Language skills are developing in both directions: Singaporeans are leaning some Thai, and Thai are learning some Singaporean English. There are Thai studying in Bible College in Singapore, sponsored by the Singapore church. One of them is being prepared to be a pastor. The mission site will turn into a church when he graduates. Even some intercultural marriages are on the horizon as a result of this partnership.

One danger is elevating a single church/community above those around them. You should keep in touch with the larger community of churches in that country, and with other agencies. Keep reaching out. Teach that we are blessed to be a blessing. Show that this is a natural step.

A second caution: Don't get so locked in to "your people" that you have no room to maneuver, to link up with those whom God may bring to you unexpectedly from other places. Although building strong relationships with one culture is good, you should always keep some time and money available for "angels" who may connect with you "out of the blue."

Teach Kingdom Stewardship

> Mobilization should include less of "our favorite mission-trip" stories and more of God's One Story…The biblical theology of God's purpose for the nations and every believer's responsibility to live a strategic "world-Christian" lifestyle can be the "magnetic north" that this generation needs…to raise up world-Christians who are praying, giving, going, welcoming internationals

> and mobilizing others…strategic lifestyle choices
> that can keep them involved during the seasons
> they are not overseas (Hickman 2006).

We Americans tend to view people in other countries in three categories. They are exotic. They are problems to solve. Or they are good business contacts.

We bring these views into the way we promote mission. Exotic? We make other peoples into an adventure. But they are not exotic, they are sinners, just like us.

Problems? We present internationals as spiritually, physically, and socially needy. But they are not only needy. They are also made in the image of God, with a great deal to give as well as receive.

Business contacts? Internationals are not machines to be treated pragmatically. They are whole persons, as complex and common as we are. Even after decades of friendship, they will continue to boggle us.

In the end, it is likely that American church members will lose interest in internationals if we see these people merely as exotic, problems, or business contacts. Our country is big and isolated. We have not had to learn how to relate well to other peoples. We like clear goals. Uncertainty, paradox, and ambiguity seem like a waste of time. After a while, these factors will outweigh the positive aspects of our foreign involvements, and our mission efforts will not seem worth the bother. In the end, only biblical teaching will keep us caring. Only the compelling love of Christ will turn us into ambassadors of reconciliation. So we must teach, and teach, and teach again the biblical basis of mission.

Appendix: Cultural Research Questions

General

Briefly describe the people's physical environment; demographic statistics; political environment.

Family

1. What is the role of each member of the family?
2. How companionable is the husband-wife relationship? How much trust, respect, and understanding are there? How much disrespect, deception, or tension?
3. How much freedom does the woman have? How much authority? Give examples. How much education has she had? What is her economic role?
4. How are the children taught? How are they disciplined? How important are other adults in socializing the child? How important is the child's peer group? How much does the father play with the child? How long do the parents control the child's choices? Is there a generation gap? How do people try to bridge it?
5. What do the old people do? How do other family members treat them?
6. How does the family make decisions? Who takes the lead? Are there discussions? How does the family settle quarrels? Describe some quarrels you have seen or have been told about. Who are the most loyal family members? Who are the least loyal? Are there some marginal members?
7. How is the family related to other structures in society: to the neighborhood? to the kin? to the community organizations?

Social Structure

8. Who are the community opinion leaders? (Include media and national as well as local figures.)

9. What is the community decision-making unit? What is the process?

10. How does the community settle quarrels?

11. What are the natural lines of affiliation? (These may tie individuals to several networks.)

12. In their most common group, what are: the rights and obligations of members; any distinctive roles; special rituals or celebrations; myths or special reputation of the group; models; villains; other techniques of boundary maintenance; any distinctions between formal and informal behaviors.

Communication

13. What are their: topics of conversation; joys; achievements (from their point of view); failures, heroes? What are they reading? Listening to? Where are they traveling? What questions are they asking?

14. Do they have any in-group language, codes, or symbols?

15. Do they have any distinct kinds of humor?

16. What kinds of media do they prefer: books, magazines, newspapers, leaflets, comics, radio, TV, tapes, drama, music, demonstrations, posters?

17. What style of verbal arrangement do they prefer: nonfiction, narrative, poetry, myth, proverbs, comics, debates, frankness or subtlety; abstractions or references to tangible things; induction or deduction; lectures or case studies; memorization or problem-centered learning; enthusiasm or formal presentations?

18. What are the main themes of columnists in national newspapers and magazines?

Economy

19. What are the local natural resources?
20. What are the common local products made for home use or for sale?
21. What is the spread of occupations?
22. What percent are rich, comfortable, subsistence level, or destitute? Do these economic class lines coincide with other classifications (i.e., kin, caste, etc.) or do they cut across these divisions, tying people together?
23. What is the average daily diet?
24. Do they consider themselves impoverished, or not?
25. What kinds of expenditure do they delight in? (clothes, parties, insurance policies, investments, labor-saving gadgets...)
26. What kinds of expenditure do they consider extravagant?
27. What do economists think are the country's chief economic problems? Its assets? Its economic opportunities?
28. What do neighbors think the country's chief economic problems are? How do they experience these?
29. Is there a Marxist movement among university students? What are their specific complaints?
30. Is there economic tension between ethnic groups?
31. What percent own their own land and/or business?
32. What are some of the most powerful political and economic entities in the environment of these people? How do they feel about these?
33. In the main, what social class in the national system do these people occupy? What are the functions or potential functions of this class in the total system?

34. How are large political and economic entities likely to affect these people over the next ten years? Hypothesize various alternative scenarios.

Religion
35. What do they turn to in a time of crisis?
36. What do they think is man's destiny? Man's origin?
37. What do they think will provide a full and meaningful life?
38. Do they think there is any transcendent power in the universe? Do they think they can relate to it? How?
39. What are their ideas of the supernatural? God? Christ? man? sin? Christians?
40. What moral system do they actually try to live by?
41. Do they participate in more than one religion? If so, when, where, and concerning what do they express each faith?

Values
42. What are their distinct felt needs?
43. What are their distinct values? (Contributing to needs/values may be: economic problems; ethnic history; social tensions; marital or generational conflicts; problems in housing, schooling, medicine, legal justice; recreation; technology; child raising patterns; art; vocational aspirations; modernization or obsolescence; attitudinal emphases such as romantic love, loneliness, pleasure, family pride, friendliness, achievement, communal solidarity).
44. What do these people consider to be the significant events of the last 30 years? of the last 500 years? How have they reacted to these events?

Social Extension Network
45. What internal variations do these people exhibit: in language and dialect; in social class; in national citizenship; in geographic distribution, and in differing ecological

milieus; in degree of modernization (including education, urbanization, types of jobs, desired family pattern and size, spending habits, etc.)

46. What various networks tie members of this people to other people outside the group? What are the strongest externalizing networks?

47. Are a significant part of these people functioning customarily in terms of two (or more) cultural codes? Beyond the mother-tongue-and-culture, do the other codes come from: near neighboring people; early foreign colonizers/immigrants that helped form the nation? recent foreign colonizers/traders?

48. Given multiple codes, do these people seem to evidence code integration or code switching? Is the code switching direct and cumulative? i.e., are the people gradually changing from one ethnic identity to another over time? How do they feel about having multiple codes?

49. How do the people identify themselves? With what specific traits would they identify someone who is a _____ (member of their group)?

50. How do their near neighbors identify them - i.e., with what specific traits?

51. How do they feel about their identity and ethnicity?

52. Is their ethnic affirmation maintained more because of a sense of satisfaction in their primordial roots, or because their ethnic identity gives them economic/political advantage?

53. If a church exists among this people, in what ways has Christianity enhanced their sense of their heritage?

54. In what ways has Christianity facilitated national integration? Has this eroded ethnic distinctives?

55. In what ways could Christianity enhance this people's ethnic distinctives?

References

Baab, Lynne. 2006. *Fasting.* Downers Grove, Illinois: InterVarsity Press.

Crouch, Andy. 2006. Experiencing life at the margins: Interview with David Zac Niringiye. *Christianity Today* (July 2006): 32-35.

Escobar, Samuel. 2000. Evangelical missiology: Peering into the future at the turn of the century. In *Global missiology for the twenty-first century: The Iguassu dialogue,* ed. William Taylor. Grand Rapids, MI: Baker Book House, 101-122.

Geertz, Clifford. 1964. Ideology as a culture system. In *Ideology and discontent,* ed. David Apter. New York: Macmillan Publishing Company.

Hickman, Claude. 2006. Compass, telescope and tour guide: Lessons learned in mobilizing students for missions. *Missions Frontiers* (May-June 2006): 21-24.

Livermore, David. 2004. AmeriCAN or AmeriCAN'T: A critical analysis of western training to the world. In *Evangelical Missions Quarterly* 40:458-466.

Richardson, Rick. 2006. *Reimagining evangelism.* Downers Grove, IL: InterVarsity Press.

Robert, Dana. 1993. Revisioning the women's missionary movement. In *The good news of the kingdom: Mission theology for the third millenium* eds. Charles Van Engen, Dean Gilliland, and Paul Pierson. Maryknoll, New York: Orbis Books.

Stockdale, A.A. 1964. God left the challenge in the Earth. *His* (December 1964): 20.

Walls, Andrew. 1990. The American dimension in the missionary movement. In *Earthen vessels: American evangelicals and foreign missions 1880-1980* eds. Joel Carpenter and Wilbert Shenk. Grand Rapids, MI: William B. Eerdmans Publishing Co.

CHAPTER 6

THE MINDFUL MISSIONER

A youth pastor in a rural Pennsylvania church leads a group of high schoolers in a weekend "plunge" into a Philadelphia housing project where they distribute food and form interracial prayer groups with residents. Seventeen hundred miles to the south, a Christian college in Texas organizes its annual spring break "mission trip" to Mexico. Thirty undergraduates caravan across the border and then travel three hours to a ranch community where they perform skits, play with the children, and share testimonies in a Pentecostal church. These participants may be among the hundreds of collegians that mission organizations recruit each summer for internship programs in Asia, Africa, and Latin America. The hope is that some will choose to serve as either career missionaries or financial supporters for various fields of service.

These snapshots of short-term mission (STM) experiences point to the burgeoning number of U.S. adolescents and adults involved in religiously-inspired excursions across cultural and geographic borders. Most of these trips are relatively brief (between six days and six weeks)[1] and service-oriented. While actual participation figures are imprecise, it is estimated that across Christian (including Catholic) denominations alone, upwards of one and a half million Americans are involved in international short-term mission trips each year (Priest, Dischinger, Rasmussin, and Brown 2006, 432). This number does not include mission-type ventures carried out *within* U.S. borders, or volunteers mobilized through non-U.S. congregations. It also excludes the thousands of U.S.-based non-Christian congregations (mosques, temples, synagogues, and benevolence societies) sponsoring short-term philanthropic work throughout the world.

In this paper, an attempt is made to subject this movement to ethical examination. Specifically, we inquire how short-term missioners might travel in ways that honor God's redemptive purpose in the creation. "Mindful" missioners are conceived as ones who participate in STM for reasons that reach beyond themselves. They exercise a clear, intentional awareness of the motivations and expectations that underlie their activities, as well as of the often unintended effects upon the social and natural environments they enter and act upon. They distinguish themselves from both the carefree drifter and the rigid religionist in allowing a vision of God's peaceable reign (shalom) to guide their mission in the world.

The Great Dream

One quality seems to mark those who live from something and exist for something that's extraordinary: vision. They have been able to connect their personal interests to a future expectation of a more just, humane, and life-affirming world. Vision is an act of seeing, an imaginative perception of what *should* and *could* be. It begins with dissatisfaction—even indignation—over the status quo and it grows into an earnest quest for an alternative. Mission as an act of love faces the world as it is and declares, "This is unacceptable… the nihilism, the dispossession, the exploitation, the contempt for human dignity… there must be another way." Then it dares to dream. "Nothing much happens without a dream," declares Robert Greenleaf. "And for something great to happen, there must be a great dream. Behind every great achievement is a dreamer of great dreams" (2002, 16). So we begin with the question: Is there a great dream or story that is capable of giving ultimate meaning and purpose to the short-term mission movement? If there is, how might we internalize that vision in such a way to better grasp it, affirm it, and struggle for its realization?

Questions like these tend to elicit a strange silence from our intellectual traditions. Most have chosen to either ignore or devalue regions of experience penetrable only through faith, consciousness, and spirit. That leaves us to draw upon our Judeo-Christian heritage as a critical source for the story we need. Ancient Israel spoke of this vision or "great dream" as *shalom*. Jesus taught it as the *kingdom of God*. Both terms capture a vision *of* and *for* a world "made right." A world where all individuals and institutions, families and peoples, the natural world in all its richness, and the divine powers that provide ultimate explanation for existence are knit together and fulfilled in mutual respect and delight. Alienation and exclusion, domination and subjection, oppression and exploitation are finally overcome by the One who gathers up all things in Christ and makes them new (Eph. 1:10; Rev. 22:5).

Shalom captures the dream of our innumerable life-relations restored to how they ought to be. Especially in the minds of the Old Testament poetic and prophetic writers, the meaning of shalom encompasses much more than what we call peace, be it peace of mind or an end of hostilities between enemies. It is best understood as that state of affairs in which intimacy and mutuality, unending variety, fairness and freedom, wholeness and delight reign supreme

(Plantinga 1995; Wolterstorff 2004). An impressive array of biblical narratives and metaphors reveal for us the contours of this state of universal flourishing.[2] For example:

- A new heaven and new earth (renewal) where the past is erased, and where all peoples and the entire material universe are energized by the divine presence and restored to their fullness

- A new era of harmony (peace) where instruments of brutality and war are transformed into implements of mutual caring; where nothing threatens the weakest segments of society— particularly the children and elderly—and where the age-old enmities in nature will cease

- A new order of plenty (prosperity) in which people voluntarily share of their wealth and power with each other, and the basic needs required for life are provided for all

- A new order of liberation (freedom) from every form of alienation, servitude, and oppression; where the least will be first and the first last; and where individuals and nations enjoy a sense of worth and self-respect

- A new era of righteousness (justice) in which the lives of the poor and the powerful are changed, and where all individual and institutional evil is put away

- A new world of compassion and restoration (healing) in which the blind see, the deaf hear, the lame walk, and everything that is partial is made whole

- A new realm of joy (delight), where all the causes of pain and suffering are done away with; where children live and learn without fear of death or exploitation; where the elderly live out full lives; and where all enjoy the fruits of their labors

- A jubilant wedding feast (community) on the holy mountain where communion with the Eternal, fellowship with each other, and respect for the land is celebrated with the full diversity of transformed humanity — sisters and brothers from "every nation and tribe and tongue and people"

It is impossible to overstate the indispensability of this vision to the way in which short-term missioners frame their actions. In it the core affirmation of Christian faith is made manifest: that God is love and all of creation—human others, other species, and their habitats—are products of love. As such, everything in the entire created order deserves to be esteemed as ends in themselves, not merely as means to another's ends. This radical affirmation of love compels missioners to be "mindful," to continually ask how we might minimize the harm and maximize the good as we seek to manifest God's grace to the world through service and proclamation. Love strengthens our resolve to arrest those practices that undermine shalom and to labor for the kind of transformation that shalom anticipates.

Travel Worlds

Perhaps nothing expresses our relation to the world better than our journeys. Travel of all types has become the planet's largest truly transnational industry, generating more than twelve percent of global GNP. It encircles the globe through an astonishing integration of sectors, from resort construction and travel tours to guidebook and suntan lotion production. In fact, it employs one out of every fifteen workers across the planet -- transporting, feeding, housing, and indulging the estimated *billion* people traveling abroad each year. By 2020, that number is expected to top 1.6 billion (World Tourism Organization 2001). Experts estimate that travel now occupies forty percent of available free time in the United States, and it consistently tops the list of leisure activities throughout the industrialized world.

A thirst for change and a more satisfying life underlies much of the travel that has occurred throughout history. During the medieval period, pilgrims endured hardship for months and even years on journeys they hoped would end in spiritual enlightenment. Religious scholars crossed national and cultural borders in search of new knowledge or to spread their faith. They were followed by the young elites who undertook "Grand Tours" through Europe starting in the 17th century. Following established trade routes, they would dedicate two or three years to expanding their intellectual and cultural horizons through travel-study. Then there were the real explorers and adventurers—from Marco Polo and David Livingstone to contemporaries like Freya Stark and Sir Wilfred Thesiger—who pioneered routes in uncharted lands. All that was left was for an eclectic and far more civilized swarm of colonists, merchants, and missioners to fill in the details and beat down tracks that would eventually appear in guidebooks to virtually every country on earth.

St. Augustine of Hippo once wrote, "The world is a book, and those who do not travel, read only one page." Travel is a school for life, one that generates fresh insights and unforgettable memories. Nevertheless, it primarily enrolls a class of wandering elites. The explorer of the Amazon, the collegian studying abroad in Spain, and the religiously-inspired volunteer to Haiti may each bring different personal backgrounds and goals to their travel. What they all share in common, however, is the expectation that travel will confer a certain social status while satisfying an existential need for life meaning. Peak experiences are accumulated and rehearsed in conversation or on a resume for years to come. Each trip also offers, in the here and now, a release from the alienation and regimentation of bourgeois life. Chris Huertz, leader of the mission organization Word Made Flesh, characterizes the twenty-somethings that volunteer to work within the world's poorest communities: "[They] are intelligent but doctrinally confused, lonely but community-resistant, cause-driven yet commitment-averse, idealistic yet cynical, magnanimous yet suspicious" (2007, 92). For young adults like these, mission trips are a means of filling an "existential vacuum" and creating meaning in life through fresh encounters and good works.

We might like to think that short-term missions are a special case, immune to this self-actualizing orientation. However, it probably has more in common with other "enlightened" forms of travel—like adventure travel, study abroad, and pro-poor travel—than we would like to think. This is evident both in the type of participants and in their travel expectations and consumption practices.

Most short-term mission trips involve transporting rich, white meaning-seekers into societies where the majority are poor and dark-skinned. In common with others from their ethno-class, missioners learn to distinguish themselves from others, not just by their education, income and place of residence, but by the objects and experiences (what Pierre Bordieu called "cultural capital") they accumulate. Missioners often emerge from their ventures as figures of admiration, earning a certain cachet from having braved two or three weeks amidst resource-poor people in an exotic locale.

The mission traveler, then, sets out to do good in the world. As an expression of sincere desire or obligation, there's nothing wrong and everything right about holding Vacation Bible Schools, feeding the hungry, or building shelters for the homeless. "The problem," contends John Hutnyk (1996, 219), "is that the technical apparatus and the conventional possibilities that are currently established for such expression tend easily towards servicing a grossly unequal exploitative system which affects us at every turn." In other words, the collection of service experiences can be just one more consumer form where the volunteer "takes," actively. While this comes as no surprise in a world market where virtually everything is for sale, it is still important to stand back and consider what it actually means. What are the links between the global economic system and "working for the poor"? To what extent do short-term missions reinforce the view that poor people need to be looked after and protected, not the least from themselves? In what ways does consuming charity redeem the giver?

By 2015 the world's population is expected to swell to 7.2 billion, with ninety-five percent of the new growth taking place in the cities of the South. Not surprisingly, mission travel from the so-called "developed" world to the "developing" world has also expanded. Many missioners are unprepared for what they see: a brutal level of poverty and inequality rooted in poor soil, land shortage, primitive technologies, population growth, violent exploitation, and despotic leadership (Diamond 1999). Lacking productive industrial capacity, various forms of tourism increasingly define and confine their economies. Nations like Thailand, Guatemala, and Nepal hope that their stunning landscape, distinctive culture, and low labor costs will attract a new generation of traveler, turning tourism into their "passport for development."

North to south educational travel tends to highlight these harsh economic imbalances. This is especially evident as collegians from the West use their surplus time and cash to travel to destinations where just the plane fare alone is more than most of their hosts will earn in an entire year. Australian priest Ron O'Grady (1982, 1), who has lived much of his life among Asia's poor, asks us to ponder their reality:

> They are people who will never be tourists. When they speak of travel they mean going on foot, or in a crowded bus, to the next village or town.... Family incomes are barely sufficient for survival and there is no extra money available for luxury travel. Indeed, when they think of luxury, their minds cannot stretch far beyond a bottle of soft drink or a better meal. The concept of a paid holiday or expenditure on leisure travel or visiting

a foreign culture is totally outside their conceptual framework.

Ironically, the gross disparity in the worlds of the poor and the non-poor underlies much of the allure of Third World destinations. The inexpensive and unspoiled places that missioners search out and appropriate into their personal worlds reflect, to a great extent, political and economic imbalances that originated under colonial rule. "Imperialism has left its edifices and markers of itself the world over," notes Caren Kaplan (1996, 63), "and tourism seeks these markers out, whether they consist of actual monuments to field marshals or the altered economies of former colonies. Tourism arises out of the economic disasters of other countries that make them 'affordable.'" Not only can affluent missioners to the Third World live "on the cheap," as noted earlier the experience itself is also seen as a form of liberation from the shallow and sometimes smothering "overdevelopment" of modern life. Authentic experience is thought to lie elsewhere, in simple and spontaneous relationship with natural environments and purer cultures. The thought of roughing it for six weeks in a "primitive" village amongst "traditional" peoples reflects this nostalgic search for a freedom and authenticity that the West lost centuries ago. Of course, the very act of traveling to whatever remote and unusual cultures remain ensures that they, too, will eventually lose *their* simplicity.

All About Me?

It is often said that what we're attracted to in other people and places are those qualities we miss in ourselves or our homeland. If this is true, travel allows us to escape the banality of our own lives in order to seek satisfying experiences among those who can't escape the reality of their lives. Even when STMs successfully distance themselves from the four widely-mocked S's of tourism—sun, sea, sand, and sex—they still are powerless to completely extricate themselves from the subordination and subservience that defines the basic commercial character of guest-host relations.

Karl Marx reminds us in his analysis of historical materialism that it is in the nature of commodities to veil the social relations embodied in their production. When we eat a piece of fruit, buy an article of clothing, or participate in a short-term mission project, the economic conditions and social relationships of the many people responsible for producing that particular commodity or service are typically hidden from our view. We simply consume the product without giving the larger context a second thought.

Professor Ben Feinberg (2002) of Warren Wilson College was curious to know what "second thoughts" study abroad participants had after spending months in another culture.

> Doubting that a professor could elicit sincere responses from students, I invited one of my favorite undergraduates to work as my research assistant, interviewing thirty or so of her peers who had recently returned from courses in Central America, Europe, and Africa. The responses from Peter, who had spent ten weeks studying and working on service projects with a group in South Africa, Zimbabwe, and Lesotho, were representative. When asked what he had learned from his African experience, Peter used the first-person pronoun seven times, eliminating Africans: "I learned that I'm a risk taker, um, that I don't put up with people's bull, uh, what else? That I can do anything that I put my mind to. I can do anything I want. You know, it's just—life is what you make of it."

The term abroad became all about them.

Feinberg goes on to suggest that a generation raised on reality shows like *Survivor* and *The Amazing Race* come to see exotic locations as personal playgrounds sealed off from real people in real places producing real goods under real conditions with real effects. Even the inequalities and injustices that travelers experience in some parts of the Third World become commodities to be voyeuristically "consumed" as part of the overall experience. Colorful street scenes of modern skyscrapers towering over teeming shantytowns and scruffy street peddlers are transformed into aesthetic images of "nativeness" to be discovered, sighted and "shot." Few stop to consider that heterogeneous conditions like these reveal, above all, the persistent gap between extreme wealth and dreadful poverty. The vast majority will simply observe the cruel hardship of others' lives and come away feeling "blessed" or "lucky" that divine providence or fate has permitted them to be born in privileged circumstances and not as one of those "made to suffer."

The gratitude expressed through this sense of one's fortune may be profound and heartfelt, and contain important personal lessons. But as a form of closure to an STM it can easily become a self-serving way to assuage guilt or manage poorly understood realities. Interpreting complex situations through this kind of "lotto logic" evades any serious analysis of the geographic conditions, historical relations, and real abuses (social, economic, political, and environmental) that explain the disparities they observe. It can also allow an ignited sense of social responsibility to be extinguished by a naïve faith in the justice of fate. In either case, the structural relationships between communities of the First and Third worlds are side-stepped in favor of an exclusive focus on the individual.

This may help to explain why the growth of STMs has not been met with a corresponding increase in longer-term cross-cultural engagement, whether at home or abroad. It is hard to call people to radical responses to a world that has only served as backdrop for ephemeral episodes consumed purely for personal enrichment. The challenge for STM leaders is to help move participant thinking beyond "luck" explanations of inequality by exploring *why* these conditions exist and *how* their lives intersect with the lives of residents.

As a step towards thinking in non-fatalistic, non-individualistic ways, we can begin to consider the various unintended consequences of the mission trip on host peoples and places. Too often the effects of travel are studied in bits and pieces: missiologists focusing on the impact of STMs on the recruitment of career missionaries, economists focused on basic finance and employment issues, anthropologists on culture change, and environmentalists on how tourism development impacts natural resources. Missioners who truly cherish God's shalom in the creation are uniquely positioned to appraise how well love-as-justice is being expressed through their short-term mission policies and practices.

At the same time, many mission leaders are sounding the called for a higher degree of "quality control." Some have even begun to question the moral propriety of sending unprepared First World youth for "vacations with a purpose" among Third World peoples. They raise a number of uneasy questions: In what ways do ethnocentrism, racism, nationalism, and exoticism subtly operate within cross-cultural sojourns? How do mission trips tend to feed off of and service gross political and economic inequalities? Is it even possible for non-poor students to "encounter" resource-poor residents in anything other than a paternal and intrusive mode? What, after all, can they realistically expect to "export" abroad?

The Journey Towards Shalom

Challenges of this kind are on the increase and missions administrators do well to think long and hard on them. For now, what we can all agree on is the moral and ethical duty for missioners to be agents of shalom in every place, doing everything in their power to promote harmony, justice, community, reconciliation, and communion through their journeys abroad. This kind of "mindful" travel is perhaps most visible among a new breed of young, independent, and ethically-conscious traveler. Though largely white and middle-class, more and more of them are seeking out culturally-sensitive and "low-impact" styles of travel.

Some elect to backpack their way through regional circuits, *Lonely Planet* or *Moon* travel guide in hand, as a latter-day equivalent of the Grand Tour. Others pre-arrange volunteer service placements through organizations like Action Without Borders (*www.idealist.org*) and Volunteer Abroad (*www.volunteerabroad.com*). Still others enroll in programs that feature locally-sponsored homestays and service projects organized around issues of conservation, human rights, and community education. What they all share in common is an awareness of the downside of conventional tourism and a desire to make responsible choices about where, how, and even whether to travel.

This welcome trend in the larger culture may actually help to "raise the bar" for missional travel. For decades, many youth pastors and mission directors would enlist anyone to an STM project who had spare time, extra money, and a thirst for adventure. The larger ethical question of how the trip might carry both positive and negative effects was either submerged under all the excitement and planning details, or regarded as too complex to venture into. The *personal* "benefits" seemed obvious enough: roughing it with friends, discovering new places, meeting new people, putting one's faith into action, building more self-confidence. But careful consideration of the potential pro's and con's in relation to the *host community* weren't so obvious.

The STM movement is increasingly being asked to think in ways that bridge the interests of both guests and hosts. The basic question might be framed as follows: *Are there ways in which short-*

term mission travel can be managed so that it broadens the spiritual and cultural horizons of participants while also improving the quality of human and earth communities?

This inquiry may lie at the heart of ethical travel, but it eludes easy answers. At one level it is clear that travel potentially carries both positive and negative effects for host communities. On another level, however, a careful accounting of the complex pattern of gains and losses is difficult to arrive at, for both technical and ideological reasons. One person might deem a given activity to be "just" and "beneficial" to a given community if it involves only X amount of disturbance to traditional lands and lifeways. Another person may define it as involving Y number of new jobs and infrastructural improvements. A third may define it as involving all of these, as well as the cultivation of certain types of relationships between missioners and hosts.

Instead of offering technical cost-benefit calculations, our focus is on practical strategies that might enable mission travel to maximize the benefit and minimize the harm to communities. There are some who argue that an immediate moratorium be placed on First World travel to the Third World until the most deleterious environmental and social effects are reversed. One can't help being sympathetic with the sense of urgency behind this call. But is it realistic to expect that cross-cultural travel can *ever* be totally freed of any undesirable effects? As Deborah McLaren (2003) reminds us,

> For a tourist to have truly minimal impact, she would have to walk to the destination, use no natural resources, and bring her own food that she grew and harvested. She would also have to carry along her own low-impact accommodations (a tent) or stay in a place that is locally-owned and uses alternative technologies and waste treatment. Of course, she would also leave the destination

in no worse and perhaps in even better condition than she found it and contribute funds to local environmental protection and community development (93).

The missioner—like the trader, student-traveler, or soldier—is unavoidably an agent of cultural change. And particularly so in those regions where the sociocultural gap is greatest. Because culture is never static, the question is not whether they will introduce change but *in what direction?* How might missioners journey in ways that strengthen rather than undermine the goals of economic development, cultural preservation, social harmony, environmental protection, and spiritual flourishing?

Economic Shalom

Third World tourism has become one of the world's most rapidly expanding economic sectors. One in every five international tourists now travels from a "developed" country to a "developing" one. This has allowed tourism to become the leading service export sector in twenty-four of the least-developed countries and the first source of foreign exchange earnings in seven. These countries promote tourist activity as a means of generating new jobs and services, earning foreign exchange, and alleviating poverty. Tourist demand creates much-needed jobs in construction, light manufacturing, transportation, telecommunications, and financial services. Locals can then use their wages to buy food, farm machinery, pharmaceuticals, and other items needed to improve their lives. New economic enterprises can even be established in isolated locations, stimulating much-needed infrastructural improvements.

However, these potential benefits are not automatically fulfilled. Third World economies drawn to tourism as a way of earning foreign exchange soon discover that a relatively small amount of the non-wage revenues generated actually enters their national economy.

Much of it ends up being repatriated ("leaked") to First World investment firms that own and operate the airlines, hotels, car rental agencies, and food services that foreign travelers, missioners included, depend upon. In fact, it is possible for a team of American church members or college students to book round-trip flights on a United airliner (with commissions paid to a U.S. based travel agency), enjoy a variety of on-board meals provided through a U.S. catering company, and then, following touch down, rent a Ford or Toyota van that transports them to a hotel owned by a French transnational before making their way to a local McDonald's or Pizza Hut for dinner. During their brief sojourn, the group is likely to shop at foreign-funded mega-malls before boarding the plane and returning home to tell how "awesome" a place the Third World is.

This example may be generalized, but it highlights the money-power held by foreign interests compared with local communities and national governments. In fact, the United Nations Environmental Programme (UNEP) estimates that an average of fifty-five percent of gross tourism revenues to the developing world actually leak back to developed countries. What does stay in the country is typically captured by relatively affluent groups, with very little actually benefiting the poor. That's not all. To attract foreign exchange, governments market their beaches and wildernesses, as well as the customs and festivals of their people, to the rich world. In the process they seldom hesitate to evict existing communities from prized properties earmarked for tourist development. Real estate prices then soar, requiring local families to spend a larger share of their income to meet their housing needs. Once expropriated from their natal lands, subsistence farmers and fisher folk often have little choice but to re-invent themselves as seasonal tour guides or low-paying security guards for vacation homes locked up for most of the year. Women are especially vulnerable to having to find alternative ways of generating income, whether as pick pockets, barmaids, or beggars.

Economic shalom compels missioners to remain ever mindful of who actually gains and loses financially from their presence. Some may decide to stay in locally-owned and operated guest houses, youth hostels, eco-lodges or—better yet—in the homes of those who typically find themselves left out of tourism development. Transportation may be chosen that employs poorer members of the community and maximizes opportunities for interaction. When essential goods and services are needed, mindful travelers opt to patronize locally-owned eateries and other businesses. They also learn to pay a fair price to vendors operating within the "informal" sector. In these and other ways, local residents come to share in the generation and control of tourism revenues – a first step toward creating a more economically just world.

Cultural Shalom

Besides bringing into the local community money to purchase goods and services, missioners also introduce a new cultural reality. The languages they speak, the clothes they wear, the electronic gadgets they carry along, the consumption habits they prefer -- all of these carry an impact. That impact can be overwhelming, especially in traditional societies unaccustomed to foreign forms. This is not to say that societies can—or should—exist completely independent of outside influences. The free exchange of ideas and practices can be mutually enriching, and can act to challenge and correct aspects of the local culture that undermine shalom. Many of the world's most vulnerable populations are protected today as a result of transnational movements that continue to address cultural practices like child slavery and domestic violence that deserve to go.

Third World entrepreneurs have also learned to reach beyond their own societies, effectively marketing aspects of their way of life to a new wave of "culture vultures." In some cases, this has helped revitalize traditional folk arts and instill a fresh sense of cultural pride. Miriam Adeney (2006) reminds us that, "With government or private grants, traditional houses and community centers may be built. Local music and dance and storytelling may be valued and practiced. People may weave and throw pots and dive and trek and climb who otherwise would have become plantation or urban laborers. 'Lost' stories may be recovered and brought back into public discourse" (467). Local traditions and material heritage is important for anyone wanting to gain a deeper appreciation for another culture, and mission travel can help keep them both alive.

There is a fine line, however, between the revitalization of culture and its "trinkitization." Virtually all travelers, missioners among them, find themselves inescapably complicit in the process of commercializing Third World "otherness" within a global market economy. Witness the spectacle of indigenous community members-turned-actors in embalmed cultural rituals or artificially-staged festivals. Tourism prioritizes remote, exotic areas of the world, placing on them an almost irresistible pressure to modernize. Helena Norberg-Hodge (1996) documents how this happened in the Himalayan province of Ladakh (Kashmir) as a result of tourist "development." Within two decades, the traditional culture became a negative reference group, held up to scorn and ridicule by youth who began to see themselves as ugly, poor, and backward compared to the beautiful, rich, and culturally advanced foreigners. Is it any wonder that missioners often encounter a perplexing mixture of love and loathing for things western from older members of their host community?

Ventures by First World persons into the Third World inevitably entail unequal cultural encounters. Aware of this fact, mindful travelers do all they can to communicate respect for distinguishing elements of the regional culture. Leading up to the trip, they take it upon themselves to learn about the area's political history, current events, religions, and customs. They also make sincere efforts to "unpack" and "claim" the cultural "baggage" of myths they inevitably carry to the field (see Hughes 2004). During their field stay, they forsake the tourist bubble in favor of becoming accepted outsiders within local neighborhoods. Neighbors come to admire, not only their eagerness to adopt native ways without demanding Western amenities, but also their willingness to speak, however haltingly, in the local language. Foreign guests who move towards the local culture in these ways will also tend to refrain from offensive cultural practices, whether it is stealth photography or condescending treatment of service workers. This not only helps to dismantle "ugly American" stereotypes; it also opens up local hearts to receive the best of Western virtues and values.

Social Shalom

One of the primary goals of shalom is to produce greater understanding and respect between strangers. Every missioner is potentially a cultural bridge between peoples, enabling a two-way learning process that is deeply rewarding for host and guest alike. Especially in the context of collaborative service or research projects, foreign missioners and local residents have the rare opportunity to form cross-cultural relationships based on a common commitment to community improvement.

Most of the harmful social effects are due to the large numbers of westerners introducing a foreign sociocultural reality into a weaker, receiving culture. It often happens that, as soon as tourists "discover" an unspoiled destination, governments and multinationals rush in to build roads, hotels, restaurants, souvenir shops, and golf courses—special enclaves that enable temporarily leisured foreigners to enjoy a privileged separation from the mainstream culture. These social divisions can also reach far beyond guest and native. The presence of large numbers of outsiders may exacerbate already-existing tensions felt between the young and the old, the traditional and the modern, the beneficiaries of tourism and those marginalized by it. Given the disparity in economic and cultural power, it is the native peoples and social system—not the foreigners—that are expected to adapt.

Little wonder European American missioners often experience an unexpected guardedness from non-white community members. Real or perceived oppression breeds a group defensiveness that many cultural outsiders are oblivious to. This is especially the case with American white males raised in suburban communities insulated from people of color. But Abraham Citron's (1969) observation is repeated in white-dominant societies across the world: "The white ghetto creates exactly the kinds of beings who act as if they are on the other side of a thick pane of glass, not only from Negroes, but from the real world. They are blandly unconcerned, unaware, operating in an aura of assumed rightness and unconscious superiority." I can testify how hard it is for someone who is white, affluent and educated to just make contact with—not to mention form an enduring bond with—someone who labors in a local factory or lives on the streets. Mere physical proximity in no way guarantees personal proximity; "natural" divisions of race, social class, and culture keep us worlds apart. When I then decide to venture abroad, what will keep me from exporting a mindset that fears the unknown, minimizes differences, and safeguards privileges? Any social gap that already existed between foreigners and locals is likely to only widen.

Under these circumstances it behooves Euro-American missioners—and especially men—to come to terms with what Peggy McIntosh (1992) calls "white privilege." This refers to the largely unconscious prerogatives and unearned assets that whites can count on cashing in on each day, whether at home or abroad. These privileges operate to nourish notions of male dominance, national pride, racial purity, and cultural supremacy. Consider the following selection from McIntosh's list:

- The day I move into new housing, I can be pretty sure that my new neighbors will be either neutral or pleasant to me.
- I can go shopping alone most of the time, pretty well assured that I will not be followed or eyed as a potential shoplifter.

- I can swear, or dress in second-hand clothes, or not answer letters, without having people attribute these choices to the bad morals, the poverty, or the illiteracy of my race.
- I can walk down the street, especially at night, without being perceived as a threat.
- I can remain oblivious of the language and customs of persons of color who constitute the world's majority without feeling in my culture any penalty for such oblivion.

The first step toward social shalom, then, is for missioners to acknowledge the privileges that they take for granted but that are often denied to their hosts. Hosts don't expect guests to stop being what they are, or to individually "take responsibility" for historical injustices. But they do expect them to think and behave in non-ethnocentric ways. What's obvious to them, but largely oblivious to guests, is that being rich and white in the contemporary world is to be "associated with" and "benefited by" a global social hierarchy that places rich white males at the top and poor females of color at the bottom. Resources and power—economic, intellectual, and emotional—are largely distributed according to this hierarchy. The wealthy, whites, and males, as groups, consistently reap more benefits than people of color, the poor, and females.

Aware of the vast social chasm needing to be bridged, mindful missioners will actually begin their "going" in their own backyard. In virtually every U.S. community, the complex interplay of race, class, language, religion, and immigrant status are highlighted by those living and working, schooling and worshipping, right next to us. Choosing to enter the social worlds of our near-neighbors, we learn to confront our stereotypes and false assumptions. We recognize our tendency to romanticize, rather than love, the stranger. But if we can somehow sustain difficult conversations in the face of emotion-laden and sometimes unpleasant differences, we can come to see the world from a radically different perspective. The result is a fresh appreciation for how power and privilege is distributed in the modern world.

These local outcomes then become the cognitive "hooks" upon which we hang our experiences abroad. Conditions of poverty, oppression, inter-group conflict, and social exclusion no longer are innocently identified with a distant world alone. Instead, we learn to compare realities abroad with everyday realities back home. Intercultural trainers have long wondered why "tourists withdraw from social others in their own suburbs, but pay to engage social others abroad" (Priest et al., 443). Perhaps international travel allows us to neatly "bracket" experiences accumulated abroad from the next-door realities that can potentially unsettle our protected sense of self. Seneca, the ancient Roman philosopher, once queried: "Why do you wonder that globe-trotting does not help you, seeing that you always take yourself with you?" If what we gain from our international sojourns largely depends on the kind of person we've become prior to departure, the best route to global competence may actually run through the lives of strangers around us.

Ecological Shalom

Until recently, one of the most neglected areas of Christian ethical reflection has been the relation of humans to the ecosphere. The natural world was generally perceived as theologically trivial, having no intrinsic relationship to the Creator and little or no redemptive significance. Its primary value was as a storehouse of raw materials to supply the needs of people. Consequently, the environmental impacts from human activity presented missioners with no particular moral questions or obligations. In fact, as the popular chorus goes, "the things of this earth" were expected to "grow strangely dim" as missioners grew in their intimacy to Jesus.

Thankfully, this general disposition is beginning to change. After nearly three decades of eco-theologizing, and with the release of Al Gore's absorbing documentary, *An Inconvenient Truth,* a growing number of eco-sensitive missioners have begun to re-assess their historical indifference towards the ecological consequences of their actions.[3] One of the "inconvenient truths" that seems to be getting increased attention is that global travel is closely linked with climate change, with international mission flights playing a contributing role. Airplanes travel in the sensitive upper troposphere and lower stratosphere where they release a cocktail of greenhouse gas emissions which currently accounts for about 13 percent of total transportation sector emissions of carbon dioxide (CO_2). A single trip from Toronto to Tokyo produces over one ton of CO_2 per passenger. This does not include the emissions from energy used in airport buildings, facilities, baggage systems, airport service vehicles, concession facilities, aircraft fueling, airport construction, and air navigation and safety operations. "Fortunately for the climate," writes Ian Jack (2006), "a lot of the world's population is too poor to do much traveling at all."

As the situation with atmospheric CO_2 worsens, it is likely that national governments will be pressed to impose some form of carbon tax or greenhouse gas "allowance" in order to meet legally-binding carbon emissions reduction targets. Until they do, respect for the aggregate rights of fragile ecosystems calls mission travelers to embody personal lifestyles of restraint and frugality. "Love entails giving up at least some of our own interests and benefits for the sake of the well-being of others in communal relationships," notes Christian ethicist James Nash (1991). Yielding at least some of our rights to safeguard the well-being of others— particularly earth others—is not what most of us are accustomed to doing. Especially when it comes to making travel decisions, our primary consideration is whether or not we have the time and money to make it happen.

An ethic of ecological shalom begins with our willingness to "look not only to our own interests, but to the interests of others" (Phil. 2:4). It calls us to weigh the missional benefits of our travel against the real harm done to the biosphere. Here we ask, without denial or rationalization, *Is this travel really necessary? Do the benefits justify the costs?* If we truly believe that mission trips should not just be "about us," we should at least be willing to ask: Is a greater good achieved by sending a team of fifteen North Americans to Ghana for three weeks of service at a local orphanage at a combined cost of $35,000 and forty tons of CO_2 when that money could support six full-time nationals for an entire year without damaging the environment? Mindfulness invites us to reflect upon our own rights to discovery and learning alongside the economic and ecological rights of human and earth others.[4]

At the point that missioners do take up residence abroad, mindfulness requires that we retain our eco-sense. Tourism development is notorious for thoughtlessly "paving over paradise" and overusing scarce resources to meet the heavy water and energy demands of its patrons. It is said that in Phuket (Thailand) the fresh water needed for showers, toilets, baths, swimming pools, and golf courses at the ten largest hotels equals the water used by the entire local population of 250,000. Mindful missioners can help reverse this trend by opting for accommodations—like local families or neighborhood hostels—that don't disturb natural living patterns. There they consciously adjust their level of water and power consumption toward the local standard by learning to turn off lights, take short or "bucket" showers, and sparingly use air conditioning and heating. They are attentive to the fact that their service destination is someone else's home, and that they share with their hosts a finite planet with exhaustible resources. They choose to cultivate habits of thrift and restrained consumption as a primary expression of ecological love, integral to the hope of a fully healed and redeemed creation (Ro. 8:19-23; Rev. 21-22).

Spiritual Shalom

Every mission trip brings us to a forking of paths: it can be yet one more "been-there-done-that" venture that pampers a spirit of pleasure and conquest; or it can be something of a love story that romances the other with the blessings of the Kingdom. Spiritual shalom follows the latter path, inviting missioners and community members, together, to pursue community transformation through the works of the kingdom: peacemaking, healing of infectious disease, repentance and the forgiveness of sins, political advocacy, women's education, economic development, discipleship, cultural revitalization, and environmental protection. It is this kingdom that Jesus said was causing people to climb over each other and gladly sacrifice everything just to get in (Matthew 13:44-46).

This is quite different from the all-too-familiar image of manic youth descending on a forgotten place of the world to conduct evangelistic raids of "enemy territory." Mission practices are always rooted in certain ideas about the character of God and salvation, and the sight of wild-eyed young people seeking to "get people saved" independent of reciprocal relationships runs the risk of distorting both. The cultural harm that has resulted from such mis-evangelism is inestimable, although missioners are usually the last to know. They are often too hived off from locals to even realize their untoward effects. Unwittingly, they repeat the imperial error of a previous generation of Christian workers. According to David Bosch (1993),

> They were predisposed not to appreciate the
> cultures of the people to whom they went — the
> unity of living and learning; the interdependence
> between individual, community, culture, and
> industry; the profundity of folk wisdom; the
> proprieties of traditional societies — all these

> were swept aside by a mentality shaped by the
> Enlightenment which tended to turn people into
> objects, reshaping the entire world into the image
> of the West, separating humans from nature
> and from one another, and "developing" them
> according to Western standards and suppositions.
> (294)

In a post-9/11 world, the margin for such error has narrowed significantly. American missioners in particular often report being perceived as cultural imperialists interested only in extracting personal satisfactions from Third World miseries. This is all the more reason why short-term missions must be an affair of love. It must dispose us, first of all, to seek out and to welcome all reflections of truth, goodness, and beauty in the lives of those we meet. This reverses our natural tendency to denounce lifeways poorly understood or to dole out pre-packaged answers to questions that are not being asked. Instead, we choose to see and be impacted by the "holy" in even the most wretched places and the most tragic persons (Matt. 25:40).

Imagine entering any of the *favelas* of Brazil, *bustees* of Kolkata, or *umjondolos* of Durban as part of a service-learning project. Immediately we would be immersed in a wider world of physical and social realities unaffected by fantasy and illusion. At that point our impulse might be to treat the slum as simply a spectacle: a personal theme park of poverty that does little more than feed an appetite for the bizarre. Alternatively, we could choose to enter into the resilience, ingenuity, communal bonds, and spiritual vitality of those struggling to improve their lives. "In the slums of Dhaka," reports Jeremy Seabrook (1995) "there is an attempt to teach literacy to 60,000 adults. In the late evening, by the smoky flare of kerosene lamps, rag-pickers, brick workers, domestic servants, child laborers, and rickshaw-pullers meet to learn and to share their lives. They are delighted when others try to understand what motivates them" (23).

Mindful missioners carry a desire to become a sympathetic, contributing part of their host communities. They generously serve alongside people of different faiths but like passion in the difficult task of making the world a better place to live. They share the conviction of theologian and martyr Dietrich Bonhoeffer: that everything moving forward towards the overcoming of disintegration, distress, and disease at the same time moves backward to the "reconciliation of all things in Jesus Christ." This doesn't signify individual salvation, per se, but it does mean that nobody and nothing is beyond the reach of Christ. It is precisely this confidence that provides the context for true dialogue about real issues and ultimate life meanings. One of the diaries of Catholic theologian Henri Nouwen is illustrative:

> More and more, the desire grows in me simply
> to walk around, greet people, enter their homes,
> sit on their doorsteps, play ball, throw water, and
> be known as someone who wants to live with
> them… I wonder more and more if the first thing
> shouldn't be to know people by name, to eat and
> drink with them, to listen to their stories and
> tell your own, and to let them know with words,
> handshakes, and hugs that you do not simply like
> them, but truly love them.

Story telling plays an important part in ravishing people with the beauty of the gospel. This doesn't mean, however, that our primary role is to speak and the others to listen. "The dialogue," suggests Lesslie Newbigin (1989, 181), "will be initiated by our partners, not by ourselves" as they observe that "our action is set in a different context from theirs. It has a different motivation. It looks to a different goal." In promoting spiritual shalom, demonstration precedes declaration. Our words must refer to a transcendent reality embodied in our corporate lives or they ring hollow. Too often our "evangelism" consists of giving answers to questions our hearers are not yet asking. Our lives must provoke the questions as it engages with the real problems of people living in the real world. If our intentions and behavior can easily be explained in natural terms (e.g. the desire to get away, experience adventure, assuage guilt through service, etc.), is it any wonder why we're not being asked to "give a reason for the hope that lies within us" (I Peter 3:15-16)?

In the end, we may find that the work of redemption to be much less "cut and dried" than we ever imagined. Many of the forces shaping the life of local communities lie outside anyone's direct control, frustrating our best efforts to do be a redemptive influence. That very frustration may actually prove to be a defining mark of mindfulness as it reveals a willingness to stay ever self-conscious about the connection between how we travel, the impacts of that style on our host community, and the structurally unequal context in which short-term missions exist. Expect the path toward greater love and justice in the full spectrum of our relationships to be grassroots and risky. That must not prevent us, however, from doing all we can to re-balance relations of power as we struggle for a nearer realization of shalom.

References

Adeney, Miriam Adeney. 2006. Shalom tourist: Loving your neighbor while using her." *Missiology: An International Review.* 34 (4): 463-476.

Bosch, David. 1993. *Transforming mission.* Maryknoll, NY: Orbis Books.

Citron, Abraham. 1969. *The rightness of whiteness: World of the white child in a segregated society (pamphlet).* Michigan-Ohio Regional Educational Laboratory

Diamond, Jared. 1999. *Guns, germs and steel: The fate of human societies.* New York: W. W. Norton & Company.

Feinberg, Ben. 2002. Point of view: What students don't learn abroad. *Chronicle of Higher Education* (May 3: B20).

Greenleaf, Robert. 2002. *Servant leadership.* Mahwah, NJ: Paulist Press.

Huertz, Christopher. 2007. Community of the broken. *Christianity Today* (February).

Hughes, Richard. 2004. *Myths America lives by.* Chicago, IL: University of Illinois Press.

Hutnyk, John. 1996. *The rumour of Calcutta: Tourism, charity and the poverty of representation.* Zed Books.

Jack, Ian. 2006. Introduction. Granta. 94: On the Road Again.

Kaplan, Caren. 1996. *Questions of travel: Postmodern discourses of displacement.* Durham, NC: Duke University Press.

Lapp, John A. 1972. *The Mennonite Church in India, 1897-1962.* Scottdale, PA: Herald Press.

McIntosh, Peggy. 1992. White Privilege and Male Privilege: A Personal Account of Coming to See Correspondences through Work in Women's Studies. *Race, class, and gender: An anthology.* Ed. M.L. Anderson and P.H. Collins, 70-82. Belmont, CA: Wadsworth.

McLaren, Deborah. 2003. *Rethinking tourism and ecotravel.* Sterling, VA: Kumarian Press.

Nash, James. 1991. *Loving nature: Ecological integrity and Christian responsibility.* Nashville, TN: Abingdon Press.

Newbigin, Lesslie. 1989. *The gospel in a pluralist society.* Grand Rapids, MI: Eerdmans.

Norberg-Hodge, Helena. 1996. The pressure to modernize and globalize. In Jerry Mander & Edward Goldsmith, Eds. *The case against the global cconomy.* San Francisco, CA: Sierra Club Books.

O'Grady, Ron. 1982. *Tourism in the third world.* Maryknoll, NY: Orbis Books.

Plantinga, Cornelius. 1995. *Not the way it's supposed to be.* Grand Rapids, MI: Eerdmans.

Priest, Robert, Terry Dischinger, Steve Rasmussen, C. M. Brown. 2006. Researching the short-term mission movement. *Missiology: An International Review*. 34 (4): 431-450.

Said, Edward. 2003. *Orientalism*. New York, NY: Penguin Books.

Seabrook, Jeremy. 1995. Far horizons, *New Statesman & Society*, 8(365).

United Nations Environmental Programme. (n.d.). Economic impacts of tourism. Retrieved on February 19, 2007 from: *http://www.uneptie.org/pc/tourism/sust-tourism/economic.htm*

World Tourism Organization. 2001. *Tourism 2020 vision*. World Tourism Organization.

Wolterstorff, Nicholas. 2004. *Educating for shalom*. Grand Rapids, MI: Eerdmans.

Endnotes

[1] There doesn't seem to be a consensus within the STM movement as to what constitutes "short-term." In the field of international education, Sarah Spencer and Kathy Tuma report that "the definition of short-term programs abroad has changed significantly over the last 50 years. First considered as year-long, and then as semester, they are now considered one- to-eight-week programs (less than a term), usually faculty-directed and sponsored by a home institution or consortium." See The Guide to Short-Term Programs Abroad (NAFSA, 2002), xv.

[2] See, for example: Gen 12: 1-3; Deut 8:7-10; Isa 2: 1-5, 12-22; Isa 9:2-7; Isa 11: 3-9; Isa 25:6-9; Isa 35:1-10; Isa 58:5-7; Isa 65:17-25; Isa 66: 18-24; Zech. 8:4-5, 20-3; Zech. 9:9-10; Psalm 72:1-7, 12-14; Mt 2:1-12; Mt 11:2ff; 12:18-21, 28-9; Mt 13:43; Mt 22:2-10; Lk 1:46-55, 68-79; Lk 4:17-21; Lk 7:18-23; Acts 3:21; Rom. 8:19-23; I Cor 1: 26-28; II Cor. 5: 16-17; Col 1:19-22; Col. 3: 9-11 with Gal. 3: 27-8; Eph 1: 7, 9-10, 20-21; Eph. 2: 13-17; Phil 2:9-11; I Pet 3:10-13; 2 Pet 3:13; Rev 5:1-10; Rev 7:15-17; Rev. 21: 1-5, 23-27.

[3] In 2006 a group of more than 85 Christian leaders—which included over 30 college president—signed a controversial statement on climate change (available at: *http://www.christiansandclimate.org*). This statement dramatically reversed the "global warning as hoax" position that characterized evangelical attitudes toward the environment, and prompted Bill Moyers to produce a PBS special ("Is God

Green?") that explores the potential split among evangelicals over environmental concerns.

[4] A number of travel companies now offer conscientious travelers "carbon-neutral" or "carbon offset" plane tickets. For example, Expedia partners with TerraPass (*www.terrapass.com*) to enable companies and individual travelers to sponsor measured reductions in greenhouse gas emissions directly proportional to the emissions created by their airline flights. Travelers buy "passes" (also called "green tags" or "offsets") for a small fraction of the average cost of their airline ticket. These revenues are then invested in projects—like wind farms and biomass energy—that are certified to either avoid or reduce CO_2 emissions. To calculate the environmental cost of specific flights see *http://www.chooseclimate. org/flying/mf.html*

CHAPTER 7

ON THE
RHETORIC OF SHORT-TERM
WITH SOME PRACTICAL

MISSIONS APPEALS, SUGGESTIONS FOR TEAM LEADERS

EDWIN ZEHNER

Trends in missions—including short-term missions—are often driven as much by ideological trends in the sending community as by needs expressed by the recipients. Yet the recent growth of STM provides an opportunity to move toward more meaningful cross-border engagements, by taking advantage of the multi-stranded cross-cultural interactions necessary for the planning and management of these efforts. Doing so may require attention to the rhetoric of missions appeals. With special attention to missions of North American origin, while drawing on recent fieldwork in Thailand, the article notes shifts in evangelical mission ideologies associated with the development of STM and recently increased interest—especially among young evangelicals—in addressing socio-humanitarian concerns through cross-cultural service. The article goes on to suggest some practical means of working toward better cross-boundary understandings, including attention to the scriptural rhetoric underlying short-term efforts.[1]

Changes in Mode, Changes in Rhetoric

Short-term Missions as a New Paradigm of Cross-cultural Relations

Evangelical missions have undergone tremendous changes in the past few decades. By the early twenty-first century, even the definition of what constitutes a mission had become open to debate, as the notions of service-learning, study abroad, humanitarian aid, STM, and career missions had come to overlap in complex ways. The motivation and practice of evangelical missions had become far more complex than earlier efforts focused primarily on evangelism. This is especially evident in STM, which has flourished despite the skepticism and criticisms of some observers (for example, Adeney 2006, Johnson 2003, Livermore 2004, Montgomery 1993, Shepherd 2005, Slimbach 2000, Van Engen 2000). It is appropriate to ask what are the new motivations for mission; how well they fit the increasingly multicultural and non-Caucasian global Christian community (see Jenkins 2006); and how better cross-cultural and multi-social-class partnerships can be fostered in and through the practice of STM (a concern also voiced or implicit in Adeney 2003, Birth 2006, Priest 2006, Shepherd 2005, and Zehner 2006).

From their beginnings in the 1960s, STM has grown rapidly, especially recently. The number of trips through North American organizations registered in the *Mission Handbook* grew from 21,000 in 1985 to 64,000 in 1996 and 346,000 in 2001 (see Moreau and O'Rear 2004, Pelt 1992, and Slimbach 2000:441). There may have been more than a million a year by the early 21st century (see Peterson, Aeschliman, and Sneed 2003:243, 255; Priest et al. 2006:432). In addition, increasing numbers of short-termers have been flowing from countries like Korea, the Philippines, and Singapore, and even from relatively small Christian communities like the ones in Japan and Thailand. Anthropologist Arjun Appadurai (1996, 2006; also see Ong 1999, Tsing 2005, Yanagisako 2006) has suggested the increased flows of people around the world have implications for the ways that polities, peoples, and cultures relate to each other. This is potentially the case for STM as well.

The growth of STM parallels broader developments in North America, including the growth of international tourism, high school community service, college study abroad and service-learning programs, and humanitarian volunteer programs (for example, Wuthnow 2004). Among evangelicals, motives for mission have likewise shifted. Though most still focus on evangelism or evangelistic support, many evangelicals have adopted a broader definition of mission that includes humanitarian concerns. This shift is amply expressed in STM.

One of the issues in STM is how to manage relations between host churches and the visiting teams. Though they share a religious tradition, their perspectives only partially overlap, and this can be as true of humanitarian missions as for evangelistic ones. A key question is how to make the short-term encounter a positive learning experience for both parties while embodying the cross-cultural respect that many short-termers desire to exhibit. For this reason, the essay closes with some practical suggestions for better encounters.

The Old Focus – Evangelism Only

As recently as the 1960s and 1970s, evangelical missions focused almost solely on saving souls, making disciples, and establishing churches, referring to the Great Commission of Matthew 28:19-20 and to Jesus' predictive commissioning (Acts 1:8) that "you will receive power . . . and you will be my witnesses." This emphasis on evangelism was in conscious opposition to the "social gospel" thought to be associated with non-evangelical missions. Evangelicals also pursued humanitarian efforts, but those efforts were often meant to aid directly the communication of the gospel.

This emphasis on evangelism was supported by popular hymns and gospel songs, many from the turn of the twentieth century. Songs like "We've a Story to Tell to the Nations" (composed 1896), "Go Ye Into All the World" (composed 1886), "Go and Tell Them," and "Send the Light, the Blessed Gospel Light" focused on spreading the message as story. Fanny Crosby's (1901) *Go Forth* called to "spread the news afar" and "gather all the lost ones to his fold." James McGranahan's (1886) *Go Ye Into All the World* urged going to the people "Far, far away, in heathen darkness dwelling" (alternatively, "Far, far away, in death and darkness dwelling"). H. Ernest Nichols's (1896) *We've a Story to Tell to the Nations* called to tell "a story of truth and mercy, a story of peace and light" that will "turn their hearts to the right."

Songs like these were still in place as the STM movement began in the 1960s, and accordingly, many of the earliest short-term missions focused on evangelism or on recruiting future missionaries. There were also short-term missions focused on humanitarian efforts like school and home building, but those were minor efforts compared to the evangelistic thrust. Over the years, however, short-term missions have expanded into a more diverse set of goals, including themes of helping others and of self-transformation.

Broadened Foci – Humanitarian Aid, Self-Transformation

When visiting Thailand in the summer of 2007 I found that evangelism remains the primary concern of both host churches and many visiting short-termers. Yet overall by 2007, especially in North America, there had been a subtle shift to new rhetoric and expectations, including greater interest in practical action and more realistic notions of what short-term efforts can accomplish. Though many short-termers retain the hope of promoting conversion, much practical action tends to be invested in such things as building houses, painting rooms, providing medical services, conducting summer youth camps, and teaching English—in effect, on humanitarian aid.

Sometimes the broadened focus is explicit. At Rick Warren's Saddleback Church, for example, the purpose of missions is said to be not only "to share the good news of Jesus Christ" but also to "care for the hopeless and hurting" (see purpose statement at *http:// www.saddlebackfamily.com/peace/*, viewed January 29, 2007). The website of an STM organization says it focuses on "evangelism and development that honors Jesus" (Sharing International, viewed on *www.missionfinder.org*). Another large evangelical church describes its short-term efforts interchangeably as "mission trips," "work trips," and "short-term mission projects and trips," reflecting their work-oriented nature (*http://www.trcpella.com/pages/page.asp?page_id=13616*, viewed January 29, 2007).

The increased emphasis on hands-on involvement dovetails with the concerns and needs of the people who go on these trips, both young people and older adults. David Kirkpatrick has written in the *New York Times* (2007) that young evangelicals have recently been taking more liberal stands on issues of social import. Similarly, an Intervarsity staff member recently told me that whereas young people had once been attracted to the engaging music of contemporary worship services, they now preferred to engage in life-changing activities for self and others. Another person, in an unrelated context, suggested that Christian young people in North America have recently come to perceive a "darker world," a perception that may be paralleled by the increased popularity of "songs of lament" in contemporary Christian worship and radio airplay.

Many who send or train short-termers have also developed the hope that the trips will transform those who go. Some hope the trips can contribute to college students' faith development (Beers 2001, Meier 2001, Tuttle 2000). Others seek ways to make the trips "a more significant educational experience" (e.g., Johnstone 2006:523).

Others hope the trips will help recruit the short-termers as career missionaries, increase giving to missions, reduce ethnocentrism, or improve relationships across ethnic lines back at home (see discussions in Robert Priest et al., 2006). Such desires are expressed by scholars and practitioners alike.

Some pastors and youth workers leading teams from their own congregations have also come to see intra-team bonding as a major benefit of the trips. One pastor told me he insists that his team members travel to distant sites together, so that the trip can help build community, thereby making the congregation more the "people of God." Another said he hoped that his group's trips to assist ministries in urban neighborhoods could foster spiritual growth, personal change, and greater empathy for relatively "marginal" people back home. However, he realized that one of the trips' most significant effects was actually to increase participants' bonding with the youth group, the home church, and the adult sponsors, opening additional counseling opportunities in the process. In this way, short-term trips function much like religious pilgrimages, in that they can have intense though often temporary community-building effects as people move outside the norms of daily life (compare with Turner 1969; also Myerhoff 1974, and Coleman 2002).

The traditional mixing of evangelism and humanitarianism has not gone away. In Thailand, for example, short-termers are often asked to teach English. The efforts are often (but not always) openly evangelistic, with groups sometimes even teaching from the Bible, yet they were also conceived, especially by the host churches, as social outreach, a way of building relationships with surrounding communities, and the use of native speakers could make them especially appreciated. Thus one missionary provided short-termers to local schools as a way of expressing friendship with their staff. Another did so as a way of thanking a local school principal for admitting HIV-positive children from their orphanage. A Thai church said it placed short-termers in local schools as a way of building positive community visibility, and another arranged teachers for government offices as a way of gaining assistance for government visas and other paperwork. In such cases, it is not clear the extent to which English teaching was evangelism, humanitarian effort, or something else altogether.

Some Criticisms

Though STM's increasingly humanitarian efforts have been praised, they have also been criticized. The more holistic focus presumably entails greater cooperation with local churches and communities, which often happens, yet such efforts can be problematic when combined with a propensity to "rush in and help" (see Zehner 2006). They can also "leave a large footprint" by erecting buildings that are overly large or that require maintenance expertise that local communities lack. The missionaries' funds and efforts can encourage dependency (e.g., Adeney 2003; Johnson 2003; Montgomery 1993; Schwartz 2004; Slimbach 2000:431). And some critics suggest that the missions tend to be overly goal-focused, overriding local cultural priorities.

Some are also concerned about power imbalances between helpers and recipients. Teenagers from the USA may be ascribed higher status than the elders in the places they are visiting. Short-termers may also displace local laborers and professionals (Montgomery 1993; Van Engen 2000:21). They also invoke hospitality costs while potentially disrupting local work routines. Even the ability to travel far for mission marks a power differential, and short-term organizers also have the upper hand in deciding who to help and how to help them. Overall, there has been concern that visiting teams are relatively free of local strictures and that they could take a superior attitude, violate cultural norms, or assume they are doing more good than they are. Many of these criticisms apply to both evangelistic and humanitarian missions.

Even *promoters* of STM note potential for misuse. One American pastor suggested that adults who go on repeated humanitarian missions may "need to be needed." Another noted the possibility of "reverse exploitation," saying he was never sure if he was helping the greatest local need or if his teams were simply being used by one or another local faction.

Supporters counter the above criticisms by noting that in many cases the work would not be done without short-termers, due to host groups' lack of time and funds. In Thailand, people seemed willing to overlook cultural missteps as long as they were not too serious, as long as local hospitality was not overly taxed, and as long as visitors focused on locally-identified needs. Many in Thailand seemed to feel, however, that better advance communication between visiting teams and local recipients or organizers could reduce some of the most serious problems by helping to calibrate mutual expectations.

Regardless of the above, however, there may also be a need to address some aspects of missions at a deeper level. For STM, this can be addressed by: (a) considering the potentials of partnerships, (b) reconsidering the rhetorical appeals to mission, (c) addressing the qualities of the team leaders, and (d) planning practical steps for engaging short-term team members with the field context.

The Potentials of Partnership

In the United States, it has become common to voice themes of "listening," "relationships," and "partnerships" as ideas that could frame STM. These terms imply that the missions can foster intercultural exchange and learning, and even suggest potential for the receiving churches and organizations to provide some of the practical direction once given by overseas missions. Robert Priest (2006) indicates that such shifts of authority and mutuality are already present in Peru. The same is true in some parts of Thailand. When I talked with church leaders there in 2007, I encountered a variety of supervisory models at work. Some churches expected foreign missions to do the recruitment, supervision, and training of short-termers, while others eagerly handled most of those arrangements themselves, usually in liaison with missionaries or former missionaries who helped recruit short-termers from home. While short-termers were not universally desired, most Thai church leaders claimed to find them useful. One church welcomed periodic evangelistic teams from abroad as part of the means of inviting the sending church's input into its cell-group ministries. Several churches, including this one, suggested that foreign missions and groups were getting better at asking what was needed, where to place teams, and what work they should do.

But just how useful is cultural exchange as a model for STM? Many Thai leaders seemed less interested in cultural exchange, as an ideal, than in such practical matters as clear advance communications and the willingness of visiting teams and leaders to take correction when needed. A couple also requested that short-term teams partner with the larger urban churches in directing help to smaller churches elsewhere in the country. Enduring cultural exchanges or personal relationships were not expected, at least not from the brief trips that are most common. Indeed, many said most of their congregations' members had little significant contact with the short-term visitors, though a few members might have intense and mutually beneficial (though brief) relationships with the visitors. As for "cultural" issues arising from short-term teams, most focused on a desire that short-termers have good personal interaction skills (fitting Thai patterns of conviviality), and that they be relatively conservative in dress and self-decoration.

Attention to cultural matters can still be useful, though. It is particularly important that short-termers be equipped for taking the views and religiosity of their hosts seriously (see the later section on practical tips). And this, too, is a form of partnership. However, even in 2007, this style of partnership was not yet consistently articulated among evangelicals in ways perceived as arising from scripture and wedded to notions of mission. Several who heard an earlier draft of this article asked how to change the theology of mission so that the "going," which they agreed was important, could entail less of an emphasis on "doing," allowing more sensitive adjustment to host Christian communities (also see Birth 2006). Several suggested we may need to look to scripture for new models that would be more empowering to the hosts of STM. Below are a couple of suggestions.

New Models of Mission?

The Incarnational Nature of Mission

A theological student from Asia who heard an earlier draft of this article suggested thinking about cross-border missions—especially STM—in light of the two natures of the incarnated Christ. In a way, Christ's human nature resembles the "insider" perspective developed through engagement with the culture(s) of the field, while his divine nature might represent the outsider culture brought to the field. While there are issues with the analogy (e.g., potentially implying that the "outsider" nature is superior), the orthodox notion that the two natures are equally important might encourage short-termers to consider adaptation as a major element in the cross-cultural task, entailing a willingness to be enculturated by others just as Christ's human nature enabled his own enculturation. The idea of mission as modeled on Christ's incarnation is not entirely new, and some have pointed out the limitations of going too far in the "insider" direction (e.g., Hill 1990; Kraft 1973). Furthermore, interviews with church leaders in Thailand gave me the impression that few, if any, expected visitors to "become Thai." Nevertheless, as was pointed out by my interlocutor at the conference, in STM it is easy for "teachability" to be overlooked, as the contacts are brief and the short-termer is often placed in the role of teacher, not learner.

The Body of Christ

We could also draw on Paul's notion of the church as the body of Christ (I Corinthians 12), but with the "body" metaphor indicating the global church rather than the local congregation. Each contributes differently, and those who go on missions are not the head, hands, and feet all by themselves. As Paul notes in Colossians 1:18, *none* of us is the head, a role reserved for Christ. Christians must work out their roles in relationship to each other, including the development over time of mutually supportive cross-cultural competencies, thus enabling local hosts to have a greater say in the mission. Furthermore, if those who go are the "feet," as suggested in the well-known passage "How beautiful are the feet of those who bring good news" (Romans 10:15, TNIV, alluding to Isaiah 52:7), then maybe it is the local hosts, rather than the "feet" arriving from abroad, who deserve the greater honor.

Paul's discussion of the body of Christ leads into the I Corinthians 13 discussion of love, whose first characteristic is said to be patience, and which is presented as the opposite of pride (I Cor. 13:4). Again, the church's ministry is grounded in a deeply relational give and take across cultures. Since short-termers are culture-bearers even in their styles of ministry, religiosity, and scripture-reading, interaction with others abroad should lead them to see their own styles as but one, and not necessarily the "best," aspect of the global community.

Antioch as Model for the Home Base

Additional grounds for such thinking might be found in Paul's missionary practice, which exemplified respect for the culture of the groups receiving his message, a stance perhaps rooted in his being raised in Tarsus and sent from Antioch, both of them cosmopolitan cities. It was common in the late nineteenth and early twentieth centuries to conceive of Europe and North America as the "Jerusalem" out of which missions were to proceed to the rest of the world, thus the oft-heard references to Acts 1:8 ("You will receive power when the Holy Spirit comes on you, and will be my witnesses first in Jerusalem, and in all Samaria, and to the ends of the earth"). This metaphor may have been appropriate when the church was mostly confined to Europe and North America. However, many of the places missionaries go today (especially short-term missionaries) already have Christian communities, so the missionaries are not working in isolation. Too much of a focus on Acts 1:8 can foster cultural imperialism, just as it did for many of the early Jewish Christians, because it is easy to assume that anything done in "Jerusalem" (the sending church) may be communicated as part of the message.

Today, it may be more appropriate to focus on Antioch, the starting point of Paul's missionary journeys (Acts 13:1-3), whose itineraries and methods are the only ones described in detail in the New Testament. The church in Antioch was multicultural (see Acts 11:19-21; Galatians 2: 11-14), and there Paul and others worked to distinguish gospel essentials from Jewish culture and laws (Galatians 2: 11-14). Over time, it was the Antioch model (allowing cultural diversity), not the Jerusalem one (culturally centric) that became dominant, as non-Jewish Christians were allowed to retain more of their customs than many in Jerusalem thought appropriate.

Thus, in the New Testament it was the *receiving* culture, not the sending one, that provided cultural templates for Christianity's future. A similar process may be underway today, with the Global South creating templates that will shape Christianities of the future. On a global scale, the religious styles of the African minority groups of North America may already be one of the majority Christian spiritualities (see Jenkins 2006:12-13). Churches outside Europe and North America have appropriated scriptures in ways that highlight preoccupation with justice, demonstrative worship, and a more vivid sense of the spiritual realm than is common in most white

North American churches. Those going abroad need to recognize that God may be teaching the global church through these relative latecomers (one might cite Matthew 19:30, "But many who are first will be last, and many who are last will be first," with parallels in Matthew 20:16, Mark 10:31, and Luke 13:30). Short-term contacts are therefore an opportunity not just to help others but to learn what God is doing in his church abroad.

Stepping to the Foot of the Table

Finally, we might remind those who go that they represent a relatively powerful culture and society as they travel far to do God's work. We can point to New Testament calls for humility, as when Jesus says to sit in the lowest place (Luke 14:8-10), and when James (2:1-4) warns against distinguishing people on the basis of outward appearance. We must be careful lest differential access to resources shapes differential roles in ministry, in effect elevating short-termers to the head of the table simply because of where they come from.

Some Positive Examples

In some places, the potentials for partnership are taken very seriously. One congregational missions organizer told me that his group's partners in Africa had started a women's clinic and left it unfinished. Though the American partners thought this sent a message that the church does not finish what it starts, they considered it important to support the locals' new priority of building an orphanage for children of AIDS victims.

Elsewhere, some short-termers seek to compensate for their power by contributing to the local economy. One congregation's teams buy their building materials locally, and also hire at least one worker from a local church. Another pairs with a local parish in hopes of achieving longer-lasting ministry. The host church provides the primary contacts, while the Americans provide some of the labor, much like a Habitat for Humanity project in the USA, in which a third party pairs workers with needs. Though even these arrangements can dampen local initiative, it has been suggested that in some cases the work might not have been done at all without direct foreign involvement, as the local people lack resources, and the foreigners might not contribute financially if not going themselves.

The Importance of Appropriate Leadership

In the summer of 2007, several church and mission leaders in Thailand suggested that the team leader's character is a major influence on the practical outcomes of STM. As a group of church leaders told me, if the leader is good, the team turns out well, regardless of the team's makeup otherwise. So important is the leader, they said, that attempts to fix leadership problems by working directly with the team members tend to backfire.

People were vague on the specific qualities needed in a leader, other than adaptability and an ability to get team members to follow their lead. Nevertheless, certain kinds of backgrounds seemed to be associated with the qualities people were seeking. For example, in Thailand I heard positive mentions of pastor-led teams, due to their general understanding of congregational needs and dynamics, and to the tendency for their leadership to be accepted naturally by the team. Also praised were youth leaders (if they had significant experience, preferably in the same congregation as the team members), church elders and board members, experienced cell group leaders and administrators (if from a church organized around cells), and other leaders experienced in the team's church of origin. (For parachurch organizations like Intervarsity, the equivalent would be experienced staff members.) Such people presumably have the ear and cooperation of the people they lead. In addition, I'm told such teams, especially congregationally based ones, were relatively likely to understand the daily dynamics of congregations and eager to match team skills to receptor needs (though sometimes doing so better on later trips than on the first ones). Pastor-led teams might also be able to lay the groundwork for longer-term cooperation between congregations.

Often criticized, on the other hand, were teams headed by inexperienced people struggling to develop their legitimacy as leaders; in addition to issues of leadership style, some were also slow to recognize where help was really needed. Also problematic were teams lacking prior ministry experience in relevant settings, such as teams that knew music performance but did not know how to apply it in children's or youth ministry. Such teams could still do good work, especially if the members had a humble spirit, were interpersonally engaging, and sufficiently patient and other-directed. But the likelihood of problems was significantly increased, as was the likelihood of ministerial irrelevance.

At least half the specific complaints I heard in Thailand involved concerns about music and worship training teams. Most Thai churches are eager to appropriate western styles of "contemporary worship" performance. However, there were complaints of "culturally inappropriate" (i.e., insufficiently conservative) dress, hairstyles, and tattoos, and a tendency to argue rather than adapt when Thai or mission leaders requested changes. Also sometimes mentioned was preoccupation with the team's interests rather than the local church's needs (for example when professional musicians were asked to train children's workers rather than doing performances for somewhat older audiences). Music and worship education were appreciated when integral to the team's overall service to a Thai congregation. However, the individuality, creativity, and cultural iconoclasm sometimes associated with contemporary worship leadership translated poorly to Thai expectations of group cooperation, negotiation, and respect for elders. Since music teams were still being welcomed, it was hard to know the extent to which the complaints may simply have been iconic of other issues. Nevertheless, several Thai informants suggested that music teams function best when accompanied by pastoral leaders from the home congregation or organization.

Some Practical Suggestions for Leaders of Short-Term Mission Trips

Many reading this article will identify readily with its sentiments. Short-term missions are almost always well intended. The question is how to improve their value for all concerned while reducing the negatives. Metaphors relating STM to Christ's incarnational nature, the diversity in Christ's body, and the multicultural nature of Antioch may suggest that one of the most valuable outcomes of mission trips could be the relational and instructional effect on the missionary, while highlighting, on the congregational level, the value of becoming longer-term co-participants. As people increasingly engage in STM on their own, this attention to rhetoric is sometimes the only influence formal Christian organizations can have on the in-field activities of short-term missions and missionaries. Nevertheless, there are several practical things that can be done to encourage sensitivity to and cooperation with hosts, while enhancing learning by team members. Below are some suggestions I have heard from various sources, geared to specific age groups.[2]

For Youth Missions

- Include some advance readings on communities being served. If the area is overseas, include readings on the area's culture and history. If the community is poor, include readings on the structure of poverty. Also useful may be first-person accounts in the voices of the hosts and those who serve them.
- Remind team members that they are not the ministers, but are simply helping those who serve, while also having a rare opportunity to learn about themselves and others. The mission

is a chance to learn about the ministry being helped and about the people who live in the area it serves.

- Be sure to invite local ministers and community leaders to talk with the team in both formal and informal settings. If the short-term mission is primarily helping by painting walls or folding boxes, sessions may need to be arranged formally. In cases of more direct engagement with the main ministry, exchanges like these may emerge naturally.

- Assign journaling tasks in which team members reflect on things learned from the ministry or members of the host community. The journals should include not just the missionaries' reactions to local conditions, but also things learned from the locals or the ministry intermediaries. Use the journals to get youth interested in learning what's important to the locals, how the people think about God and life, where they live, what life experiences they have had, what they seem to think of the visitors, and so on.

- Use periodic group discussions to encourage the youth to think about what they have learned from the journals and their experiences. Even half an hour a day could be useful, especially when people are still in the field and the experiences are new and fresh.

- After returning home, refer back to some of these themes in youth meetings. Also encourage youth to share the things learned with the home congregation.

- A few weeks after the trip, invite the youth to reflect again on what they have learned in the field, especially from the people visited. This might be done in a final journal entry, a group-constructed bulletin board, team-constructed art projects, or a public testimonial.

- If you return to the same place in later trips, have members of earlier teams share with those who are planning to go. Again, encourage reflection on what was learned from people in the field.

College Teams

Many of the above approaches may be even more effective with college students than with teenagers, as collegians may be naturally curious about "different others." They are also used to settings asking them to reflect through discussion and reflective journaling. Collegians may have limited time for pre-trip preparation and post-trip processing. Nevertheless, journaling, discussions, and guided reflections during the trip are reportedly effective with this group. This material may need to emerge informally; after all, the students are going on a mission, not attending a class. Yet leaders can still be intentional about encouraging these activities. In addition, as with the younger group, use readings, recordings, and video. Also use programmed discussions to normalize the notion of learning from the people being served. If you organize repeat trips to the same area, and if the host communities have the capabilities and interests, consider working with the local hosts to create digital home-made video and sound files for the team—simply ask local communities and ministry members what they would like the visitors to know, and then post the results (this may, of course, require the help of local cultural and administrative mediators to encourage, gather, and/or translate the materials).

Adult Teams

Adults are more likely than the other groups (with the exception of some book-oriented college students) to learn from readings. Adults involved in planning the trip may also be encouraged to conduct pre-trip research on the area, focusing both on needs and on what some have called "cultural resources" being used to address those needs. Potential issues include: What enables people to survive financially? Where do they go for medical help? What are their primary values? What has been their history as a church, community, or cultural group? What are likely to be their primary day-to-day issues? Adults may be less inclined than youth to write about these things formally (though there are always exceptions), but many may be very happy to participate in discussions before, during, and after the trips. So encourage participation in group sessions, journaling, web blogs, informal discussions while working or relaxing, and whatever else engages that person's learning style.

Final Note for Anthropologically Trained Short-termers

Becoming cross-culturally sensitive and supportive partners can be as difficult for those trained in cross-cultural awareness as for those lacking formal training. The traditional divide between Christians and anthropology (discussed for example in Howell 2007) is easily reproduced on a smaller scale within Christian communities, especially if and when the local Christians seem theologically less sophisticated, more simplistic in their rhetoric, or less concerned with issues of importance to educated people back home. If they are not careful, anthropologically sensitized North American evangelicals can easily find themselves struggling to fully accept local Christians as brothers and sisters in Christ (as one such person put it to me recently). Such differences may be aggravated if the short-termer encounters in the local churches some religious practices or rhetoric that he or she may have been fleeing back home. Training in anthropology or cross-cultural ministry is not an inoculation against ethnocentrism. Rather, it raises new issues, while hopefully also supplying tools for self-awareness and self-critique. For brief short-termers, regardless of background, it is important to direct that critique toward the self, not toward the churches being served. Overall, it is important to remember that short-termers are there to help the church, not remake it in one's own image. Regardless of the local community's style, it is useful to observe what is important to its members and consider how the material relates to, and can even inform, one's own style of Christianity.

References Cited

Adeney, Miriam. 2003. When the elephant dances, the mouse may die. In *Short-term missions today,* edited by Bill Berry, pp. 86-89. Pasadena, California: Into All the World Magazine.

_____. 2006. Shalom tourist: Loving your neighbor while using her. *Missiology: An International Review* 34 (4): 463-476.

Appadurai, Arjun. 1996. *Modernity at large: Cultural dimensions of globalization.* Minneapolis: University of Minnesota Press.

_____. 2006. *Fear of small numbers: An essay on the geography of anger.* Durham, NC: Duke University Press.

Beers, Steve. 2001. The effects of study abroad/mission trips on the faith development of college students. *Growth: The Journal of the Association for Christians in Student Development* 1: 83-107.

Birth, Kevin. 2006. What is your mission here? A Trinidadian perspective on visits from the "Church of Disneyland." *Missiology: An International Review* 34 (4): 497-508.

Coleman, Simon. 2002. Do you believe in pilgrimage? *Communitas,* contestation and beyond. *Anthropological Theory* 2 (3): 355-368.

Hill, Harriet. 1990. Incarnational ministry: A critical examination. *Evangelical Missions Quarterly* 26 (2): 196-201.

Howell, Brian. 2007. The repugnant cultural other speaks back: Christian identity as ethnographic "standpoint." *Anthropological Theory* 7 (4): 371-391.

Jenkins, Philip. 2006. *The new faces of Christendom: Believing the Bible in the Global South.* New York: Oxford University Press.

Johnson, Rick. 2003. Case study 1: Going south of the border. In *Short-term missions today,* edited by Bill Berry, pp. 100-103, 127-128. Pasadena, California: Into All the World Magazine.

Johnstone, David. 2006. Closing the loop: Debriefing and the short-term college missions team. *Missiology: An International Review* 34 (4): 523-529.

Kirkpatrick, David D. 2007. The Evangelical crackup. *The New York Times,* October 28 (online edition).

Kraft, Charles H. 1973. God's model for cross-cultural communication—the incarnation. *Evangelical Missions Quarterly* 9 (4): 205-216.

Livermore, David. 2004. AmeriCAN or AmeriCAN'T: A critical analysis of Western training to the world. *Evangelical Missions Quarterly* 40: 458-466.

Meier, Scott. 2001. Missionary, minister to thyself: The real reason behind mission work. *Youthworker* 17 (5): 24-28.

Montgomery, Laura. 1993. Short-term medical missions: Enhancing or eroding health? *Missiology* 21 (3): 333-341.

Moreau, A. Scott, and Mike O'Rear. 2004. All you ever wanted on short-term missions. *Evangelical Missions Quarterly* 40 (1): 100-105.

Myerhoff, Barbara. 1974. *Peyote hunt: The sacred journey of the Huichol Indians.* Ithaca, NY: Cornell University Press.

Ong, Aihwa. 1999. *Flexible citizenship: The cultural logics of transnationality.* Durham: Duke University Press.

Pelt, Leslie. 1992. What's behind the wave of short-termers? *Evangelical Missions Quarterly* 28: 384-388.

Peterson, Roger, Gordon Aeschliman, and R. Wayne Sneed. 2003. *Maximum impact short-term mission: The God-commanded, repetitive deployment of swift, temporary, non-professional missionaries.* Minneapolis, MN: STEMPress.

Priest, Robert J. 2006. Peruvian Protestant churches find "linking" social capital through partnerships with visiting short-term mission groups. Paper delivered at the 105th annual meeting of the American Anthropological Association, San Jose, CA.

Priest, Robert J., Terry Dischinger, Steve Rasmussen, and C. M. Brown. 2006. Researching the short-term mission movement. *Missiology: An International Review* 34 (4): 431-450.

Schwartz, Glenn. 2004. How short-term missions can go wrong. *International Journal of Frontier Missions* 21 (1): 27-34.

Shepherd, Nick. 2005. Soul in the city — mission as package holiday: The potential implications of a "tourist" paradigm in youth mission. IASYM Conference 2005 Elective Paper, High Lea, Hertfordshire.

Slimbach, Richard. 2000. First, do no harm. *Evangelical Missions Quarterly* 36: 428-441.

Tsing, Anna Lowenhaupt. 2005. *Friction: An ethnography of global connection.* Princeton: Princeton University Press.

Turner, Victor. 1969. *The ritual process: Structure and anti-structure.* Chicago, Aldine.

Tuttle, Kathryn A. 2000. The effects of short-term mission experiences on college students' spiritual growth and maturity. *Christian Education Quarterly* 4 (2): 123-140.

Van Engen, Jo Ann. 2000. The cost of short-term missions. *Other Side* 36: 20-23.

Wuthnow, Robert. 2004. *Saving America? Faith-based services and the future of civil society.* Princeton: Princeton University Press.

Yanagisako, Sylvia. 2006. Producing "Made in Italy" in China: Revaluing commodities and labor in transnational capitalism. Paper presented at the annual meeting of the Society for Cultural Anthropology, Milwaukee, WI, May 2006.

Zehner, Edwin. 2006. Short-term missions: Toward a more field-oriented model. *Missiology: An International Review* 34 (4): 509-521.

Endnotes

[1] Earlier versions of this paper were presented at the North Central Regional conference of the Evangelical Missiological Society, Deerfield, Illinois, on February 3, 2007, and at the Department of Sociology, Calvin College on February 26, 2007. Thanks especially to Noel Bechetti, David Ngaruiya, and several others for

comments on earlier versions. Also to my various interviewees (whom I have left anonymous) and to the participants in a March 2007 research workshop on short-term missions for sharing their experiences organizing, leading, and observing short-term trips and participants. A summer of research on STM in Thailand (2007) was made possible, in part, through funding from the Carl F. H. Henry Center for Theological Understanding, at Trinity Evangelical Divinity School.

[2] Thanks especially to Noel Bechetti for suggestions, some of which are incorporated into this section.

CHAPTER 8

FRIENDSHIP IS FOREVER: CONGREGATION-TO-

CONGREGATION RELATIONSHIPS

C. M. BROWN

We are living in an era of global Christianity, with a majority of the world's Christians now living outside North America and Western Europe (Jenkins 2003, 37; Barrett, Johnson and Crossing 2007, 37; Walls 2002, 85; Sanneh 2004). New patterns of globalization bring "Christians around the world together in new ways" (Ott 2006, 312), with short-term missions being one of the new patterns. Furthermore, short-term mission trips are increasingly structured in terms of congregation-to-congregation or sister-church relationships. With about 350,000 congregations in the United States and about 2.6 million Trinitarian congregations throughout the world (Brierley 1997) the potential impact of this trend is great.

Intercultural congregation-to-congregation partnerships potentially can result in many beneficial outcomes. "Ideally, all will reflect together the glory of God and realize the mission of God in ways greater, clearer, and brighter than possible from merely a single cultural reference point" (Ott 2006, 325). Such intercultural relationships provide opportunities for meaningful interaction resulting in new understandings and ministries. Yet, misunderstandings, invalid power dynamics, and conflicts occur.

Globalization and Mediation

In spite of the ways that many congregations benefit from globalizing forces and international visitors, mediation is needed (Hiebert 2006, 288). According to Hiebert, "mediators must be bicultural or transcultural people who are able to live in different worlds" (301). Accordingly, bicultural missionaries and bicultural national leaders can function as mediators guarding against misunderstandings, missed opportunities, or worse. David Hesselgrave (2005, 232) is concerned, however, that American Christians, while confessing the equality of all "members of the body of Christ," will struggle to relate with believers from other nations and cultures as equals.

> All the seminars in the world on "servant leadership" will not help until leaders from the East, and especially from the West, understand why it is that Americans do not hesitate to "take front seats" while Easterners wait to be "urged forward" (Hesselgrave 2006, 232).

Non-Western church and mission leaders can teach Western Christians about suffering, sharing, true worship, Christian lifestyle issues, patience, and about the negative influence of secularization on Western Christians (Hesselgrave 2005, 232). Walls contends that "shared reading of the Scriptures and shared theological reflection will be to the benefit of all, but the oxygen-starved Christianity of the West will have most to gain" (Walls 2001, 25). Given these contemporary realities, what is the way forward?

Congregation-To-Congregation Partnership Literature

Congregation-to-congregation partnership literature is limited. Prior to my own research (Brown 2007), four people had written Doctor of Ministry projects on the topic, which I summarize below. Steven Chambers (1993) describes understandings gained through a partnership between mainline congregations in Ontario, Canada and in Kingston, Jamaica. The partnership initially formed to enhance the local cross-cultural outreach to Caribbean farm workers in Ontario. STM teams were exchanged. Based upon interviews of focus groups and individuals, Chambers concludes (1993, 10), "Despite the difficulties, cross-cultural partnership between two congregations enables a lively opportunity for understanding what mission might mean today."

David Keyes (1999) describes the benefits of congregation-to-congregation partnerships between Unitarian congregations in the United States and in Romania. By June 2006, over 200 such international partnerships had formed between Unitarian congregations (UUPCC 2006). Typical Unitarian partnerships include STM trips, financial assistance for water resources, and educational scholarships.

Samuel Reeves (2004) conducted a case study of an on-going relationship between a Reformed congregation in Michigan and a Baptist congregation in Liberia. Reeves had been in ministry in Liberia, and later joined the staff of the congregation in Michigan. The partnership formed in part because of his connections with both congregations. STM teams and pastoral staff traveled from each congregation to the other. Reeves concluded that the congregations were positively impacted in terms of cross-cultural learning (57). The partnership "led participants to increased cultural awareness and a more culturally cosmopolitan outlook on life, the ministry of the church and the kingdom of God" (76).

Dean Ahlberg (2005) describes a partnership between congregational churches in Connecticut and Boscobel, Jamaica. Ahlberg tracked his congregation's self-understanding and their mission and relationship to other congregations in this "changing global environment," and noted that after people from each congregation visited the other enthusiasm increased (20). Ahlberg writes, "integral to our identity as a church of Jesus Christ is our connectedness to the global body of Christ" (155). He concludes that "in today's world, it is irresponsible and increasingly impossible for congregations to live in virtual isolation from the global community" (163).

A Golden Magic Wand?

Sociologists have stressed that the well-being of individuals and groups is dependent on positive social ties with others--ties of reciprocity, of trust, and of commitment. Such social ties can be thought of as a kind of "capital," a capital which sociologists increasingly research under the rubric of "social capital." Furthermore, as communities characterized by trust, mutual assistance, and norms of reciprocity (Putnam, Feldstein, and Cohen 2003, 2), congregations have "an important strategic significance for a social capital formation agenda" (Swart 2006, 346). "Bonding" social capital involves networks that link similar people together. The problem with bonding social capital is that it tends to create strong in-group solidarity combined sometimes with strong out-group antagonism. "Bridging" social capital, on the other hand, involves networks between people that differ in terms of ethnicity or culture. "The problem is that bridging social capital is harder to create than bonding social capital" (Putnam, Feldstein, and Cohen 2003, 3). And yet such "bridging" social ties are extremely important in the world today. So Putnam writes, "If we possessed a golden magic wand that could create more 'bridging' social capital that crossed racial and other social cleavages, we would certainly use it" (Putnam 2001, 86). Though not a golden magic wand to be wielded in the absence of sustained, thoughtful effort, the potential of intercultural congregation-to-congregation partnerships to create bridging social capital is great.

Bridging social capital can be either *identity-bridging* spanning "culturally defined differences" such as ethnicity, religious tradition, or national origin, or *status-bridging,* spanning "vertical arrangements of power, influence, wealth, and prestige" (Wuthnow 2002, 670). Writing from the perspective of economic development, Michael Woolcock (1998) developed his social capital framework based upon the value of both horizontal "integration" and vertical "linkage." Because "bridging" is generally a "horizontal" concept, status-bridging social capital is more frequently referred to by scholars as "linking social capital," a phrase first developed by Woolcock (1998; 2001, 72; Szreter and Woolcock 2004, 655).

Congregations are uniquely positioned to make positive contributions both toward creation of bonding social capital and, through intercultural congregation-to-congregation interactions, bridging and linking social capital. That is, these partnerships help construct forms of social capital that cross cultural and ethnic lines and that also cross major divides of wealth and power.

Robert Wuthnow analyzed religion and politics survey data and concluded that "people who belong to congregations are more likely than those who do not belong to congregations to say that they have friends who are political leaders, business executives, or persons of wealth" (2002, 682). Wuthnow (2003, 204) suggests that "the role of religion in generating social capital is, in one sense, relatively incontestable: people who participate actively in congregations make friends with other congregants and are often more likely to interact with neighbors and hold memberships in other civic organizations." Members of congregations tend to be given ample opportunities to volunteer in various ministries. "Volunteering is a way of bridging the gap that may exist between congregations and the needs of the wider society" (Wuthnow 2004, 100), and volunteers that are members of congregations gain motivation through congregational values and "opportunities to tell their stories" (132). Similarly, Corwin Smidt (2003, 217) says that religion is of great importance in generating social capital because, in addition to the fact that social capital generated through religious means far exceeds social capital produced through other means; "religion often seeks to give 'voice to the voiceless,' to speak on behalf of others when other voices are silent, and to express values that cannot always be reduced to logic or simple calculations of self-interest."

As congregations from differing cultural backgrounds, and from differing socio-economic strata begin partnering together, the possibilities for bridging and linking social capital formation, in terms of quantity, quality, and variety of networking relationships merits research attention. Samuel Reeves concluded that cross-cultural congregation-to-congregation partnerships "inspire faith across boundaries, faith that bridges gaps and reconciles differences" (2004, 77). Miroslav Volf explains that congregations are prepared to partner cross-culturally with other congregations because "openness is a formal identifying feature of the nature of the local church" (1998, 260).

Although some researchers are concerned that "the relative homogeneity of congregations and the close interpersonal ties among members may lead to isolation" (Foley 2005, 238; Beyerlein and Hipp 2005), as we will see in this research, evangelical congregations do engage in bridging and linking activities. Furthermore, in their research on social capital and diversity within the Girl Scouts, Judith Weisinger and Paul Salipante (2005) developed a grounded theory for building "ethnically bridging social capital" that suggests that voluntary organizations should promote the creation of "bonding social capital" first. They argue that "sufficient opportunity and mission-based motivation" are inadequate, but well-bonded "troops" of various ethnicities can create bridging social capital through "intertroop" activities (48).

Healthy congregations are rich in bonding social capital. Intercultural congregation-to-congregation partnerships create bridging and linking social capital. Thus, research on intercultural congregation-to-congregation partnerships should be attentive to all three kinds of social capital and to attendant outcomes.

The Research Approach

The purpose of this exploratory study was: 1) to explore the nature of a grassroots, populist movement through three case studies of intercultural congregation-to-congregation relationships, and 2) to attempt, using an inductive, multi-case analysis approach, to develop a theory which can be utilized for optimal design of future intercultural congregation-to-congregation relationships. The primary research question was: What factors and dynamics enhance or hinder intercultural congregation-to-congregation partnerships in achieving their expectations for ministry and in developing relationships?

From June 2005 through February 2006, I made site visits to congregations involved in three separate intercultural congregation-to-congregation relationships. I conducted semi-structured interviews and focus group interviews with about 100 people, including 89 people directly connected with three specific cases plus others with general understandings of the research topic. Focus groups included an average of eight people. About half of the interviews were conducted outside of the United States and thirty-four of them were conducted in Russian. I also observed worship services, Sunday school classes, small groups, and STM activities. Two of my site visits coincided with STM team visits and activities. Pseudonyms are used for the names and locations of all persons and congregations described below.

The interviews and focus group interviews were recorded and later transcribed. Russian-language data was transcribed and coded for qualitative analysis in Russian.[1] All translations of Russian-language data are my own. After data for a single partnership was gathered, coded and analyzed, an initial report of that case was written. This process was repeated for three cases, and then multi-case analysis was conducted. The multi-case analysis resulted in the generation of a theory.

Case Study 1: "We Tried to Help Them"

The intercultural congregation-to-congregation partnership in case study one was between Vineyard Evangelical Free Church (VEFC), a congregation of about 650 people in California, and Crimea Free Evangelical Church (CFEC), a young congregation of about 30 people in Ukraine. It was proposed in 2000 and then ran for five years, from 2001 through 2006. Unfortunately, the congregations involved were not very healthy—one was losing members and the other was young and under-developed. Both congregations were enduring leadership transitions.

CFEC was started in 1999 by a missionary couple, Matt and Joanna, and by three Ukrainians. The church plant started well, but growth slowed when one of the Ukrainian team-members, an evangelist, left the team for a career in Christian broadcasting—a career path which took him back to Kiev and then to the United States for training. Matt assumed that an American congregation could serve as a resource to help the new Ukrainian congregation grow and mature. His agency promoted "church planting partnerships," partnerships that were to result in new church plants. Because CFEC was already forming, this was to be a variation of the concept. Matt asked Jon, the senior pastor of VEFC, to visit Crimea, Fall 2000. He became enthusiastic about forming a partnership between the congregations. Unfortunately, just weeks after the 2001 Easter service was attended by 1000 people, Jon resigned due to moral failure.

Though people began leaving VEFC in the wake of the scandal, an STM team of twelve that had been meeting for orientation and training prior to Jon's resignation still went to Ukraine to conduct a family camp for new believers and seekers, and to give further consideration towards forming a partnership.

The Americans, excited that 60 Ukrainians had attended the July 2001 family camp, returned home and drafted a partnership agreement. The primary expectation of the American congregation, based upon input from Matt and mission leadership, was that the American congregation would serve the Ukrainian congregation to help it grow and mature. The partnership agreement was signed early in 2002 by Matt and by a VEFC congregational leader, but it wasn't signed by a Ukrainian. Still led by an American missionary, the Ukrainian congregational identity was still forming. Though Ukrainian congregation expectations changed over the years, by 2005, many were discouraged that financial assistance hadn't been greater and that they hadn't had opportunity to contribute toward their partner. Lena, a Ukrainian member and translator, said, "I expected that we would also give to them, and perhaps even that someone from our church would travel there to help them do something."

Although this case included bicultural mediators, the mediation-style did not adequately empower the Ukrainian leadership and it did not facilitate bridging and linking social capital creation. Both the Americans and the Ukrainians spoke respectfully of Matt regarding his Russian language skills and his cross-cultural experience. But just as a bridge across a wide river may actually be constructed as two bridges, one from each bank to an island in the middle, the primary relationships in this case seemed to be congregation-to-missionary, not congregation-to-congregation. Ideal mediation results in empowerment of others, especially of the congregational leadership that would otherwise have less power in the relationship. Typically, the leaders of the congregation with the weaker material-resource base enter into the partnership with less power. In this case, the American missionary retained significant power even after he attempted to reduce his own level of leadership and control.

Healthy congregations with ample bonding social capital are more readily able to create bridging and linking social capital through partnerships. In this case, bridging social capital creation was limited. The congregation of VEFC did not rally behind the partnership. By 2005, VEFC participants were discouraged. They reported that their new senior pastor was only mildly interested in the partnership. Although congregational prayer requests were exchanged each month, VEFC participants felt like they hadn't "lived up to their end of the bargain." They worried that others thought the partnership was "tainted" since Jon had promoted it just before resigning.

The partnership agreement included monthly support for the Ukrainian pastor based upon a declining scale over a five-year duration. The Ukrainians would have preferred to re-negotiate this arrangement. The intended idea was that as CFEC grew and became capable of supporting a pastor, VEFC would contribute less and CFEC would become self-supporting. Instead, because CFEC did not grow, as support from VEFC decreased, the Ukrainian pastor and his wife took jobs outside of the church. The Ukrainian leadership struggled to negotiate STM plans and arrangements without help from the American missionaries. Even in 2005, the STM visitors were met, housed and fed primarily by the missionaries. Some Ukrainian congregation members did not even know they were coming until after they arrived.

Some individual relationships between Americans and Ukrainians did develop. Linking social capital was created through the strength of these relationships and resulted in some serendipitous benefits for individuals: improved English abilities, access to medical textbooks from America, financial help for medical emergencies, and financial assistance for those between jobs, or for widows and orphans. The most significant financial assistance was given, outside of the partnership agreement, by generous individuals, and it was utilized to acquire a church facility.

Because congregation-to-congregation bridging social capital creation was limited, congregational learning was limited, especially for the American congregation. Many in VEFC did not know about the partnership. Yet, some of the American participants spoke about being impacted by the partnership, impacted by the opportunity to personally engage in mission activities, or by the opportunity to meet "another part of the family," Christian brothers and sisters from Ukraine. Though most comments were abstract, some participants, both Americans and Ukrainians, hoped to launch new ministry endeavors for children or for socially marginal people.

Although the partnership was designed to help CFEC grow and mature, it had about the same number of members in 2005 that it had in 2002. STM teams were sent once or twice per year, but the ministry results were not great. Each year, it became increasingly difficult to find members of VEFC to send.

Many partnerships are designed around ministry objectives. Yet, early emphasis on ministry impeded the formation of relationships. Is it right to expect a congregation, regardless of the size, to submit to being another congregation's project? Because a deep relationship did not form between the congregations, and because the Ukrainians remained unempowered, opportunities for learning were limited and ministry results were poor. Rather than growing, CFEC actually lost members in 2006, and the partnership was terminated.

Case Study 2: "We Learned So Much"

The intercultural congregation-to-congregation partnership in case two, which began in 2000 and continues still, was between Plaines

Evangelical Free Church (PEFC), a healthy, growing congregation in Nebraska, and New Hope Church (NHC), also a healthy, growing, though younger congregation in Pavlovsk, Ukraine. From 2000 to 2005, PEFC grew from about 150 to 375 and NHC grew from about 60 to 300 or more people.

The congregation-to-congregation relationship was originally proposed as part of a network of relationships between a Ukrainian association of independent churches, an American mission agency and its missionaries, and American and Ukrainian congregations. It was assumed that such networking together would facilitate legal registrations, visas, material-resource needs, and mutual encouragement. Ukrainian leaders assumed that American partner congregations would help Ukrainian church plants succeed during the economic crises that occurred as the new millennium began.

The economy was so bad in Ukraine, that the congregation of sixty could not even purchase an electronic keyboard for their worship services, even though music and worship was greatly valued by the congregation. Pastor Maxime had studied at a conservatory. He could improvise professionally on a violin and his verbal aptitude was equally impressive. He speaks English and was one of two or three people within NHC that could translate during STM projects. In spite of the overwhelming financial needs and the incredible ministry opportunities before NHC, direct appeals for financial help weren't made to PEFC by Pastor Maxime. Because of his ideals regarding Jesus' divine leadership over congregations, he felt he should not make such a direct appeal.

The Ukrainian congregation primarily expected to form a deep, lasting relationship with the American congregation, but they initially hoped that such a relationship would include financial assistance. PEFC members believed that they needed to be more directly involved in missions, and if they entered into an intercultural congregation-to-congregation relationship, they would learn much and their own congregation would be positively impacted. Like the participants in case one, having been coached by denominational mission leaders, they sought opportunity to plant a new church, an expectation inadequately or unclearly disclosed to the Ukrainian leaders.

The American missionary leader, due to life-threatening illness, ceased to be involved after initially brokering the formation of the partnership. His replacement never visited NHC in Pavlovsk and did not tend to be overly involved as a mediator. The Ukrainian association leaders were also minimally involved after the partnership began. So it developed without outside mediation. Translation during STM trips was conducted by the Ukrainian pastor, a congregation member, and sometimes by translators from Kiev. The Ukrainian pastor was quite involved in the relationship, but he tended to wait for the Americans to write or call. He was reluctant to initiate communication, though it could be done via e-mail relatively cheaply. Once the American congregation proposed an STM trip, he would facilitate the trip and propose an extremely aggressive ministry schedule filled with orphanage visits, ministry projects, small group meetings, prayer meetings and worship services. While teaching or preaching, Maxime's influence was profound—as stated below, he even influenced the American pastor to change some of his theological positions.

The American pastor and the congregation leaders tended to speak about serving the Ukrainian congregation. Like the other American congregations in this research, they understood that STM should be field driven. Yet, the Americans decided when to conduct STM trips and whether material-resource transfers occurred.

Bonding social capital was strong within both congregations. Substantial bridging and linking social capital was created at both individual and congregational levels. Relationships formed. E-mails were regularly exchanged. When one of the STM teams departed from Pavlovsk, eighty people accompanied them to the train station. As the train departed, the American team and many of the Ukrainians, including some of the men, shed tears. As a Ukrainian member pointed out, "Tears are not something you can easily fabricate." Yet, in spite of the warm personal relationships formed, Pastor Maxime was realistic about the nature of the congregation-to-congregation relationship. "If they want to come, they come. If they don't, they don't," he noted. He also was mildly offended that PEFC had sent dozens of people to Ukraine, but they hadn't invited even one person to Plaines.

Linking social capital benefits were relatively limited. American participants believed that they should attempt to de-emphasize their own material-resource abundance, not wanting the partnership "to be about money." They worried that if they gave financial assistance, "it would spoil the relationship." Yet, in many of their narrative discourses, they tended to mention the Ukrainian lack of material resources. "They have so little, but they trust in the Lord." PEFC did give some financial gifts to NHC. NHC was able to purchase a five-room church office after PEFC gave $2000, and a property for a drug and alcohol rehabilitation center after PEFC gave another $2000 gift.

In 2005, during the focus group interview, PEFC participants utilized 13.5 feet of freezer paper to document the impact that the congregation-to-congregation relationship had on their own congregation. PEFC participants said their congregation had deepened in terms of worship, gained a vision for small groups, for outreach, for prayer, and for the importance of relationships. The senior pastor of PEFC said that he had changed his preaching style and even his position on miraculous gifts because of his interactions with Pastor Maxime and with another leader Dimitry. Pastor Maxime and his wife also influenced PEFC participants to make major life-decisions. In spite of their meager income, Pastor Maxime and his wife had become legal guardians for two teenage orphan girls. Their example influenced a couple from PEFC to adopted two teenage girls from Ukraine. The senior pastor of PEFC and his wife adopted a baby girl. Although she was from China, they attributed the idea to their exposure to orphans and street children in Ukraine.

Though intentions were good, the system for partnership decision-making was inadequate. A recent high school graduate of PEFC, discovered through his personal research that the Crimean Tatars of Ukraine comprise one of the world's unreached ethnic groups (groups with very few followers of Jesus). He proposed that a member of NHC should be sent to Crimea to reach Tatars. One of the leaders, Dimitry, though he never knew his father, was actually part Tatar. Dimitry had told STM participants that when he repented and became a follower of Jesus, his addiction to heroine had been miraculously removed. STM participants from PEFC, impressed with his evangelistic fervor, were delighted when he agreed to relocate to Crimea. Unfortunately, they did not initially speak with Maxime or other NHC church leaders about this plan. After he attended a short training program, PEFC began directly sending $250 per month to Dimitry and his family through Western Union. NHC also sent financial support to Dimitry. Within six months, a congregation of 20 began meeting in a predominately Tatar region of Crimea.

Maxime and Dimitry, through an inexpensive mobile telephone plan, remained in regular contact. Maxime was pleased that Dimitry's ministry was progressing well. Yet, PEFC hadn't allowed NHC to be the primary decision-making body in the venture of sending their member to start a new church.

The Ukrainian congregation considered the congregation-to-congregation relationship to be a *friendship*. Prior to an STM trip, they would say, "Our American *friends* are coming." The American congregation had been coached to commit to a five-year partnership and then to find a new partner. When they mentioned this, the Ukrainians were offended and perplexed. For to the Ukrainian participants, "Friendship is forever."

Case Study 3: "We Met the Mayor First"

The sister-church relationship in case three, 1991 to present, is between Central Evangelical Free Church (CEFC), a church attended by about 2500 people in Central, Illinois, and Central Baptist Church (CBC), a congregation in Zainsk, Ukraine that grew from about 40 people in 1990 to over 200 people. Although occasional statements are made from CEFC's pulpit about CBC or the Ukrainian pastor, Ivan, the American participants did not tend to assume that most of CEFC even knew the partnership existed. Samuel, the sister-church champion, said, "You can't say that it is CEFC, you would have to say that it is individuals, because being a church this size, probably half of the people don't even know where Ukraine is."

This congregation-to-congregation relationship started through the initiative of a prominent businessman that attended CEFC. Bobby Gustafson was a member of the city council of Central, Illinois, and he was also on the board of an evangelism organization that became active in Ukraine in 1990. Bobby traveled to Ukraine to help plan a large evangelism project and then he invited the Ukrainian counterparts to Central. When they heard of Bobby's interest in forming a sister-city relationship, one of the Ukrainians suggested that Central become a sister-city with Zainsk, Ukraine. On his next visit to Ukraine, Bobby hired a taxi driver to take him and the former senior pastor of CEFC, to meet the mayor of Zainsk, to discuss the idea of forming a sister-city relationship. After discussing the sister-city relationship, the pastor asked if they could visit a church in Zainsk. The mayor took them to an orthodox church, but no one was there. So the pastor asked, "Do you have an evangelical church in town?" The translator suggested they visit CBC. The group went to the Baptist church, rang the bell, and finally, the deacon came out, opened the gate, kissed the American men on their lips and said, "We have been praying." Both a sister-church relationship and a sister-city relationship formed.

The American businessmen used their financial and social status to facilitate ministry in another part of the world. They understood that ministry requires financial support and they were willing to personally support legitimate ministry ventures. Ivan, pastor of CBC, was highly motivated to do ministry in Ukraine. He was pleased that ministry opportunities abounded since the Soviet Union had disbanded. He quickly realized that partnerships were advantageous. His proposals for cooperative ministry projects were met with positive response and financial support, as necessary.

Over the next fourteen years, businessmen continued to be the primary people involved from CEFC. Bobby was joined by Samuel who became the sister-church champion for CEFC. Pastor Ivan was the primary Ukrainian involved. In one sense, outside mediation was lacking, yet, through the establishment of on-going relationships with the American businessmen, Pastor Ivan was empowered. Mediation, such as it was, was accomplished through the contact maintained between these key individuals. Soon, Pastor Ivan's daughters were able to serve as translators who facilitated both verbal and written communication between the sister churches. CEFC pastors eventually also became involved. They communicated through Pastor Ivan's daughters. Samuel continued serving as the champion of the sister-church relationship.

The American businessmen continued to build social capital. They invited the mayor, the chief of police, and the school superintendent to Illinois, and after they observed the prominence and value of churches in Central, Bobby challenged the mayor of Zainsk to treat the churches in Zainsk well. Bobby and the City Council of Central gave an expensive, modern playground to the city of Zainsk. The playground was so greatly valued, that when CEFC promised to give a second playground, they were permitted to distribute 14,000 Bibles throughout Zainsk, in the schools, hospitals and other places. The second playground for Zainsk was erected by a large STM team and contains a plaque stating that it was a gift from CEFC,

Central, Illinois. Pastor Ivan was initially shocked that Bobby and others from CEFC were eager to establish relations with the mayor and other city officials—he thought to himself, "They were godless communists!" Yet, eventually he developed his own relationship with the mayor. The present mayor calls him "brother" and asks him to pray at city functions.

In addition to bridging and linking social capital created through this sister-city relationship and through this sister-church relationship, additional social capital was created through four more sister-church relationships brokered by Bobby and Samuel. The four other sister-church relationships include churches from three other denominations in the United States and with churches planted by Pastor Ivan, daughter churches of CBC.

The system for decision-making was simple but functioning. Samuel said that Ivan proposes an idea, usually a church planting venture, or construction or renovation of a facility for a new church plant. Samuel would find out the costs involved and would report the proposal to the CEFC mission team or to individuals or groups of Christians. CEFC expected to see local involvement, and so it would not fund 100 percent of any proposal. Eventually, nine churches were planted. The largest funding amount went toward the interior finish costs of a new educational wing for CBC.

Linking social capital was created and resulted in significant benefits. Each year, with the approval of the city administration, a small team from CEFC would travel to Zainsk and join Ivan and his wife visiting schools and giving Christmas gifts to orphans and impoverished people. Pastor Ivan's daughter was invited to study in a private Christian high school in Central, Illinois. Her English skills, university and career options improved through that opportunity. Though Pastor Ivan's visa applications had twice been rejected, once his daughter was studying in a US high school, he too could travel to Central, Illinois where he spoke at CEFC and at the 10-year anniversary of Bobby's mission organization. During another visit to the United States, a Christian surgeon conducted surgery on Pastor Ivan free-of-charge.

CEFC continued to be active in Zainsk and the senior pastor preached at the 25th anniversary of CBC. CEFC also has a partnership in Slovakia. In July 2005, a youth team from CEFC combined with a youth team from Slovakia and members of CBC to conduct a children's camp near Zainsk for Ukrainian children. In spite of pre-trip communication problems and a financial disagreement, the kids described the camp as "Super."

Bridging and linking social capital was created in abundance. Upon the relational foundation, ministry was conducted. The ministry results were greater than anyone would have anticipated when Bobby was first startled by a Baptist deacon's brotherly kiss. Theological perspectives and minor divisions were challenged as social capital networks branched out to include participants and sister-churches from multiple denominations.

Multi-Case Analysis

The congregations and the partnerships described above differed significantly. Although each case was unique, similar causal processes were found in each case. In conducting the multi-case analysis, two challenges were faced: the challenge of underdetermination, "too many variables, too few cases," and the problem of equifinality, "the fact that different causal patterns can lead to similar outcomes" (George and Bennett 2004, 156-57).

Each case included about thirty factors, some positive and some negative, that influenced the partnership. Case study research that merely generates lists of factors is incomplete and potentially misleading. Thus, in this research, factors, both positive and negative, were grouped into five primary dynamic process categories that included: Empowering mediation, Existence of bonding social capital, Creation of bridging social capital, Creation of linking social capital, and Development of a system for decision-making. After factors were grouped into dynamic process categories, process-tracing analysis was conducted.

Mediation differed in the three cases, yet the value of empowering mediation is evident. In case one, the mediation style did not tend to empower the Ukrainian congregation and its leaders. In case two, the Ukrainian pastor was able to speak English. He was a competent preacher and teacher, but he was reluctant to set the agenda for the partnership. The American congregation, though desiring to serve and support the Ukrainian congregation, retained the power in the relationship and set the agenda. In the third case, though bicultural mediators were scarce during the early stages of the partnership, the mediation offered through the personal relationships formed between the Ukrainian pastor and his family and the American businessmen resulted in significant empowerment of the Ukrainian pastor.

Empowering mediation, in combination with bonding social capital, promotes and facilitates the creation of bridging and linking social capital creation. In case one, the general lack of congregation health and support for the partnership were negative factors, and bridging social capital creation was also impeded because congregation-to-missionary relationships formed more readily than did a strong congregation-to-congregation relationship. Of course some relationships did form between individual Americans and Ukrainians, but the general lack of bridging and linking social capital at the congregation-to-congregation level further disempowered the Ukrainian leadership, which impeded decision-making, learning, and ministry outcomes.

In case two, substantial bridging and linking social capital formed between the congregations. The social capital resulted in serendipitous benefits, empowerment of Dimitry who was then sent to begin a new ministry in Crimea, and some new understandings. If additional outside mediation had been available, the American congregation might have learned how to understand the Ukrainian pastor's indirect speech and how to allow the Ukrainian congregation to take the lead in sending Dimitry. The American congregation might have also developed deeper understandings regarding compassion and social ministries.

In case three, substantial bridging and linking social capital were continually created. The American businessmen seemed to instinctively understand the value of networking and of developing relationships, even relationships with city officials. The Ukrainian pastor benefited from the social capital creation and eventually became a sort of unofficial spokesman for the Evangelical and Pentecostal churches of the region. Although much of the Ukrainian pastor's sense of empowerment was due to his personality and the supportive denominational structure, because he was so empowered, and because the businessmen were willing to assist in a fund-raising capacity, significant ministry objectives were accomplished. Yet, learning objectives were muted. To the Ukrainian pastor and to the American businessmen, ministry objectives were primary. The Americans overlooked the denominationalism of the Ukrainian pastor, even though his denominationalism sometimes was at odds with the distinctives of some of the American sister-churches.

Mediation and empowerment, especially of the leadership of the congregation with the lesser material-resource base, are necessary for development of a suitable system for decision-making. Systems for decision-making will vary from partnership to partnership. Some partnerships will include minimal material-resource transfers, whereas other partnerships will include substantial on-going material-resource transfers. In case one, the system was developed by the Americans and was written into a partnership agreement that no Ukrainian signed, but that the American congregation followed throughout the five-year duration of the partnership.

In case two, the system was inadequate. Because some STM teams raised more support than required, the American congregation gave some financial gifts. Then when the American congregation decided that a Ukrainian congregation member should be sent to Crimea, they took action to approach someone and then to directly support him circumventing local accountability structures.

In case three, the system wasn't elegant, but it was efficient. Sometimes American businessmen would just immediately fund a ministry themselves, other times they would raise most of the financial support needed. The Ukrainian pastor learned which kinds of proposals were more likely to be received positively. Though he sometimes disagreed with the American perspective—for example, he believed the priority should be funding for church facilities—he accepted these limitations in the system.

Initially participants in congregation-to-congregation relationships should engage bicultural mediators, focus upon empowerment, and involve those most likely to promote social capital creation. Ministry objectives, and even learning objectives, should not receive exclusive emphasis in the early stages of developing a partnership. In case one, the American participants entered the relationship primarily with ministry objectives and secondarily with learning objectives. Their expectations were largely unmet. In case two, the American participants expected to learn and be impacted. They learned much, but mostly they learned that which they themselves anticipated learning (c.f. Linhart 2005). They did not develop deep understandings informed by Ukrainian cultural perspectives. They also missed opportunities to assist the Ukrainians in ministry to orphans. During the early stages of a partnership, once mediators have been identified, emphasis should be upon bridging and linking social capital creation and upon empowerment. As the relationship develops, other objectives can be appropriately pursued.

A Theory for Congregation-to-Congregation Relationships

As a result of this research, a theory for optimal intercultural congregation-to-congregation relationships emerged. The theory states that such relationships develop with the greatest benefits and fewest weaknesses and misunderstanding when:

(a) Empowering bicultural mediators are engaged
(b) Bridging and linking social capital are deliberately created
(c) An appropriate, empowering system is developed for decision-making regarding partnership activities and material resource transfers

The outcomes associated with optimal congregation-to-congregation relationships should include numerous, valid, new understandings; on-going benefits from the creation of bridging and linking social capital, including both serendipitous and strategically planned benefits; and increasingly strategic partnership ministry accomplishments. Pursuit of these outcomes in the absence of empowering mediation, deliberate social capital creation, and an appropriate, empowering system for decision-making will likely result in unmet expectations and frustrations.

This theory does not attempt to direct congregations regarding proper use of material resources. It does suggest, however, that 1) there must be a system that allows the partner with the deepest understandings of the proposed ministry context to play the central role in decision-making, and 2) the partner with the greater material-resource base should clarify its criteria and priorities for material-resource transfers. Decision-making regarding partnership activities and funding should be conducted in a manner with allows partners to maintain dignity in the process.

In personal conversation Robert Priest suggested to me one example of such a system. Well-endowed research foundations announce their own priorities, solicit and receive research proposals, and then provide funds according to established criteria. Researchers submitting proposals seeking funding prepare proposals grounded in their own expert knowledge and which fit their own situation and research goals. Foundations offer grants to those researchers whose proposals exemplify promise of success and whose intentions align with foundation interests. Grant recipients maintain their dignity throughout the process, and in fact, those frequently awarded grants gain prestige and effectiveness.

Typically, the congregation with the lesser material-resource base has less power in a partnership. The leadership of the congregation with the greater material-resource base sometimes is unaware of the power imbalance in the relationship. Mediation is needed that can research and explain the power dynamics and empower those with less power, facilitate communication, promote social capital creation, and help the congregations develop an appropriate, empowering system for decision-making.

Conclusions and Practical Implications

Intercultural congregation-to-congregation participant expectations are not likely to be met if the relationship lacks empowering mediation, ample social capital creation, or an appropriate acceptable system for decision-making. An optimal intercultural congregation-to-congregation partnership, that includes emphasis on these causal mechanisms, should result in on-going ministry results, deepening understandings of God, the Church and the mission task, and other serendipitous benefits.

The theory proposed above requires testing, refinement and verification. If it proves to be valid with minimal refinement, or valid for most types of intercultural congregation-to-congregation relationships, then specific implications follow:

1. Empowering mediation is needed:
   - Some of the people involved in the mediation should be bi-cultural and bi-lingual.
   - Mediators should promote bridging and linking social capital creation.
   - Mediators should investigate and clarify power dynamics and facilitate the empowerment of the congregation with the lesser material-resource base.
   - Mediators should facilitate the development of an appropriate, empowering system for partnership decision-making.

2. The partnership should be formed in a manner that deliberately accelerates the creation of bridging and linking social capital.
   - Initial STM team staffing decisions should be made based upon social capital creation objectives.
   - Communication systems between the congregations should be developed, implemented, and maintained.

3. The congregations should develop a system for decision-making regarding partnership activities and material resource transfers.
   - Those with the deepest contextual knowledge of the proposed ministry should exercise primary decision-making authority.
   - The congregation with the greater material-resource base should make explicit any existing criteria or priorities regarding material-resource transfers.

- The system for decision-making should include a culturally informed method for proposing ministry projects and funding requirements for the proposed projects.
- Both congregations should be able to maintain dignity throughout the process.

4. Participants should patiently await the outcomes of the partnership.
   - Participants should celebrate the serendipitous linking social capital benefits.
   - Participants should listen without trying to teach, while seeking to understand their partner's perspectives, to gain deep new theological and human understandings.
   - When decisions can be made appropriately, partnership ministry projects should be conducted.

References Cited

Ahlberg, Dean C. 2005. Our identity: The story that gathers us in, sends us out. D.Min. project, Hartford Theological Seminary.

Barrett, David B., Todd M. Johnson, and Peter F. Crossing. 2007. Missiometrics 2007: Creating your own analysis of global data. *International Bulletin of Missionary Research* 31: 25-32.

Beyerlein, Kraig, and John R. Hipp. 2005. Social capital, too much of a good thing? American religious traditions and community crime. *Social Forces* 84: 995-1013.

Brierley, Peter. 1997. *World churches handbook*. London: Christian Research Association, BPC Wheaton Ltd.

Brown, C. M. 2007. Exploratory case studies and analyses of three intercultural congregation-to-congregation partnerships. Ph.D. diss., Trinity International University.

Chambers, Steven J. 1993. The partnership conversation: The contribution of cross-cultural experience to contemporary mission understandings. D.Min. project, Toronto School of Theology.

EFCM. *n.d.* EFCM church planting partnerships: Using church planting partnerships in church planting, a guide for missionary field staff. Evangelical Free Church Mission.

Foley, Michael W., John D. McCarthy, and Mark Chaves. 2005. Social capital, religious institutions, and poor communities. In *Social capital and poor communities*, ed. Susan Saegert, J. Phillip Thompson and Mark R. Warren, 215-45. New York: Russell Sage Foundation.

George, Alexander L., and Andrew Bennett. 2004. *Case studies and theory development in the social sciences.* Cambridge, Mass.: MIT Press.

Hesselgrave, David. 2005. *Paradigms in conflict: 10 key questions in Christian missions today.* Grand Rapids, Mich.: Kregel.

Hiebert, Paul. 2006. The missionary as mediator of global theologizing. In *Globalizing theology: Belief and practice in an era of world Christianity*, ed. Craig Ott and Harold A. Netland, 288-308. Grand Rapids, Mich.: Baker.

Howell, Brian M. 2006. Globalization, ethnicity, and cultural authenticity: Implications for theological education. *Christian Scholars Review* 35: 303-23.

Jenkins, Phillip. 2002. *Next Christendom: The coming of global Christianity.* New York: Oxford University Press.

Keyes, David. 1999. *Most like an arch: Building global church partnerships.* Chico, Calif.: Center for Free Religion.

Linhart, Terence David. 2005. Planting seeds: The curricular hope of short-term mission experiences in youth ministry. *Christian Education Journal*, series 3, 2: 256-71.

Ott, Craig. 2006. Conclusion. In *Globalizing theology: Belief and practice in an era of world Christianity*, ed. Craig Ott and Harold A. Netland, 309-36. Grand Rapids, Mich.: Baker.

Priest, Robert J., Terry Dischinger, Steve Rasmussen, and C.M. Brown. 2006. Researching the short-term mission movement. *Missiology* 34: 431-50.

Putnam, Robert D. 2001. Community-based social capital and educational performance. In *Making good citizens: Education and civil society,* ed. Diane Ravitch and Joseph P. Viteritti, 58-95. New Haven: Yale University Press.

Putnam, Robert D., Lewis M. Feldstein, and Don Cohen. 2003. *Better together: Restoring the American community.* New York: Simon & Schuster.

Reeves, Samuel Broomfield. 2004. *Congregation-to-congregation relationship: A case study of the partnership between a Liberian Church and a North American Church.* Lanham, Md.: University Press of America.

Sanneh, Lamin. 2003. *Whose religion is Christianity? The gospel beyond the West.* Grand Rapids, Mich.: Eerdmans.

Smidt, Corwin, ed. 2003. *Religion as social capital: Producing the common good.* Waco, Tex.: Baylor University Press.

Swart, Ignatius. 2006. Churches as stock of social capital for promoting social development in western cape communities. *Journal of Religion in Africa* 36: 346-71.

Szreter, Simon and Michael Woolcock. 2004. Health by association? Social capital, social theory, and the political economy of public health. In *International Journal of Epidemiology* 33: 650-667.

Unitarian Universalist Partner Church Council. 2006. UUPCC international partnership handbook. Bedford, MA: UUPCC. Accessed February 6, 2007. Available from http://www.uupcc. org/docs/2006UUPCCHandbook.pdf; Internet.

Volf, Miroslav. 1998. *After our likeness: The Church as the image of the Trinity.* Grand Rapids, Mich.: Eerdmans.

Walls, Andrew F. 2002. *The cross-cultural process in Christian history.* Maryknoll, N.Y.: Orbis.

_____. 2001. *The missionary movement in Christian history: Studies in the transmission of faith.* Maryknoll, N.Y.: Orbis.

Weinstein, Matthew. 2005. *TAMS Analyzer 3.1 User Guide.* Accessed October 2005. Available from at http://tamsys.sourceforge.net/; Internet.

Weisinger, Judith Y, and Paul F. Salipante. 2005. Grounded theory for building ethnically bridging social capital in voluntary organizations. *Nonprofit and Voluntary Sector Quarterly* 34: 29-55. Accessed March 15, 2007. Available from http://nvs.sagepub.com/cgi/content/abstract/34/1/29; Internet.

Woolcock, M. 2001. The place of social capital in understanding social and economic outcomes. In *ISUMA: Canadian Journal of Policy Research* 2: 1-17.

_____. 1998. Social capital and economic development: Toward a theoretical synthesis and policy framework. In *Theory and Society* 27: 151-208.

Wuthnow, Robert. 2004. *Saving America? Faith-based services and the future of civil society.* Princeton, N.J.: Princeton University Press.

_____. 2003. Can religion revitalize civil society? An institutional perspective. In *Religion as social capital: Producing the common good*, ed. Corwin Smidt, 191-210. Waco, Tex.: Baylor University Press.

_____. 2002. Religious involvement and status-bridging social capital. *Journal for the Scientific Study of Religion* 41: 669-84.

Endnotes

[1] Because Russian-language texts are written with Unicode fonts, I utilized TAMS Analyzer 3.1 (Weinstein 2005) on a MacBook Pro computer for coding, searching and sorting data in the original languages.

CHAPTER 9

URBAN CHURCH RESOURCES

FOR SHORT-TERM MISSION

CHIN T. WANG (JOHN)

Short-term mission (STM) as a grassroots missionary movement is a recent phenomenon. The rapid growth in the number of people involved in these trips, the large financial commitment from the Christian community, and the lack of academic research make the study of these trips increasingly urgent and necessary. Although many people have conducted studies on STM trips organized by youth groups, college students, and suburban white churches (Linhart 2006; Birth 2006; Tuttle 2000), few studies have related to the experience of urban churches in multiethnic immigrant communities. This paper reports the experience of an STM trip to Ecuador organized by an urban church in New York City. The 33-member team was diverse in language, nationality, ethnic background, age, and class. The receiving church was a minority Quichua congregation in the rural mountain region of Ecuador with transnational ties to New York City. The focus of this paper is on the cultural, financial, and transnational resources the urban church drew upon in the STM trip experience. It also provides insights for urban churches in developing their own STM programs.

Short-Term Mission Trip to Ecuador

First Baptist Church of Flushing (FBC) is an urban church in New York City. Founded in 1856, it has a history of ministering to the surrounding neighborhood in Flushing, New York. Like many parts of New York City, Flushing welcomed the arrival of many immigrants from around the world after the passing of the 1965 Immigration Act. The majority of these new residents followed the flow of the contemporary South-to-North global migration movement. Driven by economic needs, many of them came from the developing nations in Asia, Africa, and Latin America (Hanciles 2003). The steady population growth of Flushing in the past 40 years has created a vibrant economy and a multiethnic community (Smith 1995, Bonney 2003, NYS Report 2006). As Flushing became increasingly Asian and Hispanic, some Christian immigrants planted new ethnic churches. Others decided to join existing local congregations (Travis 1989, Ortiz 1996, McKenzie 1996, Rosser 1999). In 1979, after fourteen years of pioneering ethnic outreach, FBC was formally reorganized into a three-language ministry. The church is led by a multiethnic and multilingual pastoral team and currently there are worship services conducted in English, Spanish, and Chinese (Cantonese/Mandarin). Although the church maintains a dual focus on traditional long-term mission in foreign countries and on local cross-cultural evangelism among the Asian and Hispanic immigrants, STM is equally emphasized in the mission program. In the past many individual members took STM trips to many parts of the world. The church established a special fund in the year 2000 to provide some financial resources for STM trip participants. However, FBC did not begin sponsoring its own STM program until 2002.

After a few years of going to countries in different continents, the church decided to focus on some of the areas where its members have stronger transnational ties in Asia and Latin America.

About this time, a group of Ecuadorian Quichua immigrants began to join the Spanish service at FBC. More than half of all the Ecuadorian immigrants in the United States live in the New York metropolitan region (NYC DCP 2004). Among them there is a minority Quichua community. In the case of FBC, many of the Quichua believers were related and were all from the same town of El Tambo, Ecuador. In 2003 FBC received an invitation to visit and support their home church in El Tambo. In the following year, the FBC pastor for the Spanish congregation and two other members flew to Ecuador in an exploratory trip to study the needs of the local Quichua church. Encouraged by the potential ministry opportunities, the first FBC STM group trip to El Tambo was launched in 2005 with sixteen members. In 2006 a Spanish Bible teacher and his wife were sent to support the Quichua church in teaching and training ministries. This year a team of thirty-three members traveled to continue ministries among the indigenous believers in El Tambo, Ecuador.

The main foci of the 2007 Ecuador STM ministry were a medical clinic, vacation Bible school, teaching, and preaching. In addition, FBC cosponsored a local soccer tournament and a Christian music competition by providing the necessary funds and judges. The team also joined the food fair during the local church anniversary celebration by sponsoring a booth to introduce some foreign flavors. In the course of the STM trip preparation and the time spent in El Tambo, the team took advantage of the available cultural, financial, and transnational resources to meet the ministry demand. They proved to be vital in the success of the mission trip.

Cultural Resources

The diversity of the STM team is the major cultural resource of FBC. Participants in the STM trip came from all three language groups of the church. Each congregation provided approximately one third of the team members. About half of the team was fluent in Spanish and the majority of the team used English as a second language. In addition, one participant fluently spoke the local Quichua language.

The team was diverse in many other aspects. The members came from twelve countries representing Asia, North America, and Latin America. They reflected ethnic backgrounds of Caucasian, Caribbean, Indian, Chinese, and Latino origins. There was also an age gap between the youngest (six years old) and the oldest participant (seventy-two years old) because the team allowed families to bring their children on the trip. Socially the team came from a variety of professions: retirees, medical professionals, students, computer programmers, public school teachers, pastors, bankers, musicians, housewives, construction workers, and unemployed people. In reality, it was a very diverse group by all criteria. Such a multicultural team presents a difficult challenge to group dynamics and team spirit. Potential for conflict was high. Fortunately, for most, the diversity was simply an extension of their daily social life and weekly church experience.

This team, an urban and diverse group from NYC arrived to El Tambo, Ecuador to visit a rural, homogeneous, minority church. The hosting church was founded in 1978 (Muyulema 2003). Some considered it the first Quichua Baptist church of its province. The growth and development of the church coincided with the struggle of indigenous people to gain recognition in social and political life (Drange 1997).

Many immediate consequences in the life of FBC became apparent following the STM trip. This encounter permitted many

FBC members to understand a specific group of people who were visible in the Spanish congregation of their own church. They were accustomed to witnessing the ethnic diversity of NYC, but were in some respects less sensitive to the deeper needs of an individual people group. According to Christerson and Emerson (2003), a minority group in a multiethnic religious community normally bears a disproportionably higher cost of belonging. It is often difficult for the majority group to recognize the challenges and struggles of smaller subgroups. Because of cultural and language barriers, people from the English and Chinese congregations had little knowledge about the immigrant experience of the small Quichua community in NYC. Through the STM trip, many people began to understand the painful reality of the migration pattern of the southern Ecuadorian Quichua people. Many of them, driven by local poverty, decided to have the male adults of their family migrate to North America to provide for their financial needs at home (Kyle and Liang 2001). This practice reflects the global pattern of the multi-billion dollar market of economic remittance among the immigrant communities (World Bank 2006). The STM trip helped the FBC members understand the real faces of their own church members, as sometimes they were unable to see beyond their respective language circle.

In addition, people of other language groups began to visit the Spanish services before and after the trip. Currently there are attempts to develop an exchange of musical talents among different congregations. The participants also talked about carrying out joint ministries for a health fair and for future fundraising concerts. On the individual level, some participants began to explore ministry opportunities in multiethnic activities among the church's youth group and children's outreach programs. The deepening of cross-congregational relationships helped to ease tensions among different language groups.

As for the local Quichua church, the visit of the STM team provided exposure to the diversity of the Body of Christ. Because of the historical marginalization of the indigenous community, the local believers tend to be suspicious of outsiders. Instead of sending their children to the Spanish-Quichua bilingual Christian school run by the Ecuadorians, many believers prefer to send their children to secular schools run by indigenous educators. Although Caucasian missionaries and tourists are often seen in town, other ethnic groups like Chinese, Caribbean, and even Indian believers made lasting impressions on the Quichua believers. The presence of the multiethnic STM team gave a vivid reflection of the diversity in NYC often described by their relatives living in North America, thus helping them improve mutual understanding in their long-distance conversations. One of the local church pastors, who has years of ministry interaction with foreign missionaries in Bible translation, and has himself visited NYC and Europe, encouraged the congregation in one joint meeting, "¡Qué seamos todos internacionales esta semana!" (Let's all be internationals this week!). For the Quichua church it was an important step in recognizing the diversity of the Body of Christ.

Financial Resources

Among the many practical issues urban churches face, Roger S. Greenway (1999) pointed out the challenges of poverty and the higher financial cost of urban work. FBC was no exception, and needed to find innovative mechanisms to raise financial supports for STM trips. FBC is not a wealthy church as its members struggle with the income level of the surrounding immigrant community. For the Ecuador trip, the lead pastors divided the STM budget into two categories: individual cost and collective ministry cost. Individual costs consisted of personal airfare, room and board, and local transportation. The ministry costs covered expenses for vacation Bible school, the medical clinic, the soccer tournament, facility rental for music competition, and other ministries like the local church anniversary food fair.

The funding mechanisms were further divided into three areas: personal responsibility, church STM budget support, and collective fundraising events. At the beginning, the church required the payment of a $250 registration fee. This down payment guaranteed the space, and it was applied to the cost of airfare. A person was responsible for the total cost of his/her trip which included the individual cost and a fair share of the ministry cost. The budgeted cost for a participant in the case of Ecuador trip was $1020 (See Table 1). Fortunately, with the church support and the collective fundraising it was possible to reduce this amount to the individual airfare of $573 only (See Table 2). This personal share was paid by individual savings, family and friends' support or donations from outside of the church. One sister testified that she experienced God's timely provision in this area:

> … The most wonderful experience was raising
> the funds for myself. Near the end I needed to
> complete my funds to go to the mission trip so I
> decided to talk to some friends at work and God
> again showed me that we should talk to everyone
> about his work because I was touched when one
> of my closest friends (a guy raised in a military
> family with high moral values, but a non-believer)
> came to me and gave me a donation saying that he
> really wanted me to go on this trip and saying that
> he was going to pray for me.

FBC did not permit team members to solicit donations within the church. Instead it designed two other ways for church member to support the participants. For one month the church collected special offerings dedicated to all the 2007 STM trips. Together with the STM fund from the church's regular budget, FBC mission committee decided to support twenty percent of the total cost per person for every STM participant. In the particular case of the Ecuador trip everyone received $200 from the church support funds.

The third way to meet the financial needs was through collective fundraising events at FBC. While the church provided the space and facilitated the promotion of these events, they were planned and organized solely by the STM participants. The team organized two flea market sales and a whole church BBQ luncheon in the spring. For the flea market, the team received donations from church members. The team members then priced all items accordingly. Both flea market sales were well attended by church members and people outside of FBC. The BBQ luncheon was provided on a Sunday after worship services by team members with assistance from people of all three congregations. It not only raised some income for the trip, but also provided an opportunity for people to stay at the church and fellowship across congregations. In the early summer a Christian music concert was organized under the leadership of the Spanish music director who was also a participant in the Ecuador trip. He contacted professional musicians who were willing to donate their talents and time to perform. In order to reflect the church's ethnic diversity, he included artists of Asian, Latin American, African American and Caucasian backgrounds. On the evening of the concert, not only the STM team but also many other FBC members were mobilized to serve in different responsibilities. Together, the team raised more than $8,000 (Table 3) for the STM trip.

Individual Cost (33 members)		
Air Transportation		$19,800
Ground Transportation		$500
Airport Expenses incl. Tax.		$1,350
Travel Insurance		$1,320
Food and Lodging		$3,800
Subtotal		**$26,770**
Total Cost	(Team)	$33,670
	(Per Person)	$1,020

Ministry Operation Cost	
VBS Materials	$500
Medical Clinic	$5,000
Facility Rental	$200
Sport Ministry	$700
Miscellaneous	$500
Subtotal	**$6,900**

Table 1: Short-Term Mission Budget

Total Cost Per Person = $1,020		
Personal Responsibility (56%)		$573
STM Fund from FBC	(20%)	$200
Fundraising Income	(24%)	$247
Total Per Person		$1,020

Table 2: Funding Mechanism for Individual Member

Fundraising Income	
Flea Market 1	$1,075
Flea Market 2	$1,568
BBQ Luncheon	$1,126
Christina Music Concert	$4,366
Total	**$8,135**
Total Per Person	$247

Table 3: Fundraising Income

According to many participants the fundraising events before the trip were the best opportunity for preparation of the team spirit. Although the pastors organized several STM training sessions, it was the time of planning and working together for the fundraising events that allowed everyone to bond. As one of the members said, "I think the fundraising has been a great instrument to integrate the team together to achieve a common goal. It helped build up the team dynamics before the trip."

This three-part funding plan provided multiple advantages for FBC. First the individual responsibility provided an opportunity to exercise personal faith and a responsible attitude recognizing that money must come from the individual whether through earning, savings, or donations. Second, the collective fundraising cultivated team spirit as well as the unity of FBC. It also proved to be an important financial income source for the Ecuador trip. Lastly, the mission budget allocation and the congregational collection of special offerings provided a substantial support for the team members. In addition, it helped avoid multiple solicitations to the church members, and still permitted them to contribute to the STM ministry.

Transnational Resources

Many sociologists have noted the rich input transnationalism offers to studies of immigration and religion (Levitt 2004, Ebaugh and Chafetz 2002). As more immigrants engage in the social, economic, political and even religious activities of their home countries, traditional assimilation theories became increasingly inadequate to explain their behavior (Foner 2000). Most of the Quichua believers involved in this trip were connected to the town of El Tambo and the surrounding villages in the same province. They belonged to the few evangelical Quichua churches in the same association. They grew up knowing each other, and now also experience immigrant life in NYC together. They support each other, and their family members back home also support each other. Indeed, the transnational community of the Quichua believers engaged in this Ecuador STM trip reflects the characteristics of a "transnational village" as described by Peggy Levitt (Levitt 2001). In addition, the larger Ecuadorian immigrant community in NYC also provided important resources for the ministry. Some members in the Spanish congregation of FBC own properties in both the United States and Ecuador. They continue to return every year and celebrate holidays with their relatives in South America. These immigrants live in two worlds, NYC and Ecuador. In clarifying the concept of transnational communities, Alejandro Portes says (1997):

> Transnational communities are dense networks across political borders created by immigrants in their quest for economic advancement and social recognition. Through these networks, an increasing number of people are able to lead dual lives. Participants are often bilingual, move easily between different cultures, frequently maintain homes in two countries, and pursue economic, political and cultural interests that require their presence in both.

The relationship between FBC and the Quichua church centered around one brother, who entered the United States in 1990. He was one of the first people in El Tambo who left for America seeking a better life. After settling in NYC, he began to attend the Spanish service at FBC. As the first indigenous Quichua member in FBC, he later introduced the Spanish congregation of FBC to other immigrants from his home town. He was instrumental in organizing two local Quichua churches in NYC, one in Brooklyn and another in the Bronx. Eventually he became the liaison between the NYC Quichua churches and the Spanish congregation of FBC. Today, the Quichua churches in NYC form part of a fellowship of Ecuadorian Quichua churches in America. Regular gatherings, like Christian music/choir competitions, are celebrated annually. It has become one of the most important diaspora networks among the southern Ecuadorian Quichua believers in the United States. Their frequent communication and visits to Ecuador have created an important transnational community that provided financial support to their homes and home churches. It is through this transnational tie that FBC was able to develop a relationship with the El Tambo Quichua church and consequently embarked on the series of missionary activities.

The transnational ties are also present in the social mechanisms of the immigrant community. Living in New York City, there are very large service demands from the many different immigrant communities. From international telephone calls to airline tickets to Latin America, all means of communication have become increasingly affordable. However the most salient demonstration of transnational ties is the services provided by a Latino travel agency located two blocks from FBC in downtown Flushing. This travel agency dedicates its business to Latin America not only by providing travel services, but also phone service, money transfer, and courier services. In one instance, when money needed to be sent to El Tambo, the agency offered same-day service with a fee substantially lower than regular commercial banks. The only information needed for a fund transfer was the name, address (street corner), and a cell phone number of the recipient. Later the team was surprised to discover a branch office of the same travel agency in El Tambo, a town of merely 10,000 inhabitants (Muyulema 2003)! This further demonstrates the intense impact of the Ecuadorian transnational community in North America. The STM team was able to take advantage of this advanced technology and convenient services in its preparation for the trip (Johnson 2003).

In addition to the Quichua community, there are other transnational ties that cannot be ignored. Because of the potential language barrier and the reciprocity issue of professional licensing, the STM team decided to seek medical expertise from the local Ecuadorian community. Through a member in the team, who is an Ecuadorian immigrant originally from Guayaquil, they were able to contract her niece, a gynecologist, and her coworker, a dentist, for the medical work. She went ahead of the team to secure the doctors' availability and to purchase medical supplies from local pharmaceutical companies in Guayaquil. This connection enhanced the quality of the medical ministry as the doctors with local expertise were able to make adequate preparation for the common diseases in the mountain regions. Their knowledge of health conditions and connection with the pharmaceutical companies also helped to lower the cost of medicines. Together with another doctor of general practice from the region (known by the local church), they saw more than 820 patients in five days.

The transnational communities of both Quichua and Ecuadorian believers in NYC became a powerful resource in planning STM trips. They helped to establish contact among FBC, Quichua churches in NYC, and the hosting Quichua church in El Tambo, Ecuador. This knowledge of the people and culture allowed for better planning and preparation for the trips. When the team returned from Ecuador with a desire to serve the Quichua people, the relation with the Quichua churches in NYC and the presence of the Quichua believers in the Spanish congregation of FBC provided new opportunities for follow-up ministries. It helped to avoid an abrupt discontinuity in ministry many STM participants faced when they returned to their home country. In addition, the infrastructure of tourist and immigrant services like the Latino travel agency made the operation of the trip efficient and cost effective. Finally the transnational ties that led to the Ecuadorian doctors provided much-needed professional and language expertise to the medical ministry.

Conclusion: Practical Implications for Urban Churches in STM Trips

Urban churches are usually characterized by a lack of financial resources combined with strong exposure to immigrant communities.

Are there resources these urban churches can use in order to prepare for the STM trips? Based on the recent El Tambo trip organized by FBC, an urban church can benefit from its cultural, financial, and transnational resources. Challenged by the complexity of a diverse team with potential cross-cultural conflicts, the group was strengthened by the leadership of its multicultural pastors and the collective fundraising events before the trip. A multiethnic team working together in unity can be a blessing to the hosting church as it demonstrates the diversity of the Body of Christ. A minority church which has been suspicious about the dominant group in a local society now has a chance to see that not everyone of a different ethnic group is hostile to them. Experience with multiethnic STM teams further enhances the unity of the sending church as it provides opportunities for the participants to minister under close contact. The three-part approach to financing an STM trip can help to cultivate personal responsibility, team spirit, and congregational participation, as well as to avoid multiple solicitations of donations to individual members. Lastly, the transnational resources may be the most useful asset for an urban multiethnic church. They not only provide ties to the hosting church but also logistic and technical support in the actual ministry.

Many urban churches with a large immigrant presence tend to go back to their own country in their STM efforts. However, organizing a multiethnic team can be of great value to both sending and hosting churches. The experience of FBC's STM trip to El Tambo, Ecuador is a demonstration of the potential use of some of these resources. A balanced use of financial resources demonstrated prudent stewardship. The full use of the multiethnic assets of an urban church helped to give new understanding of the Body of Christ. The wise use of transnational ties not only enhanced the STM experience but also provided incentives and connections to follow up after the trip.

In describing the paradigm shifts among the different roles the local church plays, Camp (1994) pointed out a transition from supporting and sending to the latest synergetic (owning) paradigm. There are more local churches bypassing mission agencies and directly partnering with foreign congregations in STM. For an urban immigrant church with limited means, a deeper look into its cultural, financial, and transnational assets may provide surprising resources for future STM trips.

References Cited

Birth, Kevin. 2006. What is your mission here? A Trinidadian perspective on visits from the "Church of Disneyworld." *Missiology* 34: 497-508.

Bonney, Richard. 2003. Understanding and celebrating religious diversity in Britain. *Encounters* 9(2): 123-151.

Camp, Bruce K. 1994. Major paradigm shifts in world evangelization. *International Journal of Frontier Missions* 11(3): 133-138.

Christerson, Brad and Michael Emerson. 2003. The cost of diversity in religious organizations: An in-depth case study. *Sociology of Religion* 64(2): 163-181.

Drange, Live Danbolt. 1997. *Encuentro de cosmovisiones: El encuentro entre la cultura y la religión de los autóctonos de Cañar y el evangelio*. Quito, Ecuador: Abya-Yala.

Ebaugh, Helen Rose and Janet Saltzman Chafetz. 2002. *Religion across borders*. Walnut Creek, CA: Altamira Press.

Foner, Nancy. 2000. Beyond the melting pot three decades later: Recent immigrants and New York's new ethnic mixture. *International Migration Review* 34(1): 255-262

Greenway, S. Roger. 1999. The challenge of the cities. In *Perspectives on the World Christian Movement*, ed. Ralph D. Winter and Steven C. Hawthorne. Pasadena, CA: William Carey Library.

Hanciles, Jehu J. 2003. Migration and mission: Some implications for the twenty-first century church. *International Bulletin of Missionary Research* 27(4): 146-153.

Johnson, Ros. 2003. Cutting out the middleman: Mission and the local church in a globalised postmodern world. In *One world or many? The impact of globalization on mission.* Richard Tiplady ed. Pasadena, CA: William Carey Library.

Kyle, David and Zai Liang. 2001. Migrant merchants: Human smuggling from Ecuador and China. Center for Comparative Immigration Studies, Working Paper No. 43, University of California – San Diego. La Jolla, CA.

Levitt, Peggy. 2001. *Transnational villagers.* Berkeley, CA: University of California Press

_____ 2004. Redefining the boundaries of belonging: The institutional character of transnational religious life. *Sociology of Religion* 65 (1): 1-18.

Linhart, Terence D. 2006. They were so alive!: The spectacle self and youth group short-term mission trips. *Missiology* 34 (4): 451-462.

Muyulema, Manuel. 2003. "Revista – Bodas de plata de la Incorporación Primera Iglesia Bautista Quichua 2003."

NYC DCP 2004. The newest New Yorkers 2000. *NYC DCP #04-10,* NYC Department of City Planning.

NYS Report. 2006. Economic Development and the Economy of Flushing, Queens. *Report 4-2007,* NYS Office of the State Comptroller.

Ortiz, Manuel. 1996. *One new people.* Downer Grove, IL: Intervarsity.

Pier, McKenzie. 1996. Case study: First Baptist Church: Heaven's mirror in Flushing, NY. *Urban Mission* 13(4): 48-56.

Portes, Alejandro. 1997. Immigration theory for a new century: Some problems and opportunities. *International Migration Review* 31(4): 799-825.

Rosser, Russell C. 1998. A multiethnic model of the church. *Direction* 27 (2): 189-192.

Smith, Christopher. 1995. Asian New York: The geography and politics of diversity. *International Migration Review* 24 (1): 59-84.

Travis, William. 1989. His Word to His world. *Urban Mission* 6 (3): 37-41.

Tuttle, Kathryn A. 2003. Effect of short-term mission experiences on college students' spiritual growth and maturity. *Christian Education Journal* 42 (1): 17-30.

World Bank. 2006. Global economic prospects 2006: Economic implications of remittances and migration. International Bank for Reconstruction and Development, Washington DC.

CHAPTER 10

WOMEN AS RESOURCE BROKERS: STM TRIPS, TIES, AND MUTUAL

SOCIAL AND ORGANIZATIONAL RESOURCE BENEFITS

KERSTEN BAYT PRIEST

Introduction

The exploding, but understudied, phenomenon of short-term mission trips is a religious and largely lay movement. It is based on voluntary, unpaid labor, aimed at perceived human need. Contemporary youth, "retired finishers," and middle-aged women and men go on such trips. Clearly these trips are important to those who participate, often framed as peak personal and religious experiences. As a woman sociologist (a wife and mother), I was fascinated to sit in my church's mixed-gender adult Sunday School class a few years ago and hear a "report" from a fellow woman congregant about her STM trip undertaken to address issues of poverty and AIDS in Africa. A nurse, she spoke eloquently and persuasively about the "tsunami" of death sweeping the continent. The visual images she used featured faces of school children staring through broken glass window panes and bars. Various women hearing her report wiped their eyes in response and, with new awareness, asked aloud if they could help. I witnessed an immediate activation of a social network for transfer of resources that Sunday morning. While prior research has focused on the STM involvements of high schoolers, college students, young adults, mixed groups, and men's groups, I am not aware of any research focused on the activities of women in STM. Assuming that all knowledge is located and interested, such a gender gap in our understanding of new trends in global religious connectedness needs to be addressed (cf Mary Jo Neitz on a rationale for engaging feminist inquiry in the sociology of religion, 2003). In this chapter I will examine how STM women become motivated "resource brokers"—activating dense social and organizational ties through their involvements in STM which mutually benefit themselves and the people they travel to serve.

Methodology

Three years ago I began interviewing women in the U.S. about their involvement in STM. Since then I have spent three months in Peru interviewing travelers and their facilitators (i.e. missionaries, hosts, translators), traveled as a participant-observer with a group to South Africa on a two week trip, and visited a successful network of orphanages and a U.S. "sister-church" in the Dominican Republic which hosted short-term missionaries. My collected data includes nearly fifty interviews and transcribed field notes of fund-raisers and other pre and post-trip meetings, supplemented with additional visual and printed materials used by STMers and the organizations with whom they network. In this chapter I will primarily focus on the story and activities of three nurses and their traveling network of women friends who are involved in ongoing STM.

Theoretical Considerations

The vast majority of STM teams go to regions of the world which already have numerically strong churches (Robert Priest and J. P. Priest 2008, 63-67), rather than to regions where the church is absent or numerically weak. What distinguishes the senders from the receivers is less a spiritual divide than a socio-economic divide. That is, the majority of STM teams go to regions characterized by relative poverty (by comparison with the home communities and churches of the STM travelers). STM as a movement is predominantly organized around Christian travelers going *from* highly resourced countries *to* countries and/or destinations with less resources. Robert Priest (2007) examines this relational dynamic in a case study of STM in Peru using the conceptual framework of social capital. Social capital refers to the social networks and accompanying patterns of trust, interpersonal commitment, and reciprocity which are thought of as essential to the good society, and which are important to personal success and community strength. Robert Putnam, in *Bowling Alone* (2000) famously used the concept to warn Americans that volunteerism and dense social ties are waning precipitously in the U.S.—excepting that found in faith communities. Two types of social capital can be contrasted: *bonding* versus *bridging. Bonding social capital* refers to social ties between people who are demographically similar to each other, ties which often foster in-group loyalties and out-group antagonism. *Bridging social capital*, by contrast, establishes ties with those who are unlike the self culturally, linguistically or racially. STM groups tend to foster both types of social capital because individuals from the sending community grow *closer* to one another through the shared travel experience, thus bonding, and they also *connect* at some level with people across cultural/racial barriers, thus bridging. Robert Wuthnow (2002) distinguishes one more dimension—vertical social capital—which "links" persons of higher and lower social status, economic level and/or resources to power. Wuthnow argues that individuals and communities which are socially subordinate and economically poor need not only horizontal social ties, but vertical ties, ties to those with access to resources and power. Robert Priest argues that Peruvian churches acquire this sort of "linking social capital" through Protestant STM partnerships because traveling groups provide: 1) financial assistance as part of the built-in funds each traveler brings to a destination; and 2) status (white Americans) which opens many doors for Peruvian Christians which otherwise would be shut—such as welcome into neighborhood homes for evangelism or entre to institutions such as prisons and hospitals normally only accessible to Catholic clergy (Priest, 2007).

Poverty scholars in the United States are also interested in how resources are accessed by the poor. While the poor may have plenty of social relationships among peers (bonding social capital), their difficulty arises from not having "linking social capital" which would tie them into relations with more resources. Using social network analysis, Mario Luis Small (2006) examines how organizations— neighborhood institutions such as churches, day cares, hair salons, etc.—can function as "resource brokers" for needy clients and neighbors, linking them to additional organizational resources beyond the immediate broker. Small (2006) found that the better an institution was linked to *other* organizations, the more likely a poor person walking in their doors would get access to those resources otherwise unknown or inaccessible. I would suggest that the STM women I observed and interviewed are adept at creating both bridging and linking social capital for those they serve. Furthermore, they activate multiple social networks which extend to diverse organizations. When these women travel, they do so as global "resource brokers" on behalf of those they deem needy.

A weakness of macro economic assumptions behind social capital theory is the tendency to turn micro interactions into "measures" and "trends" or "flows" which render individuals' voices and motives invisible—particularly those of ordinary women. In this chapter I will show how ordinary American women decide to "bridge" or "link" with people outside their national borders, and will explore the strategies they use to "broker resources" globally. If indeed globalization takes place in "nodes" of interconnectedness (Appadurai, 2002), and is not just a "flow" or a "trend" from the top down, women's STM may well be instructive.

The Decision to Link

The women most invested in STM consistently communicate a compelling desire to help those in need, often told in stories of personal transformation. Tina, a middle-aged nurse who works in a cardiologist's office, and also works with an AIDS support group, told how a South African woman visited her church and shared about the devastation of AIDS and HIV in South Africa's capitol—and how homeless people die regularly in the park across the street from one of the largest churches in the city. Tina said:

> "That just blew me away, and I was just so moved by what she was saying, I was just moved to a point where I knew that I couldn't not do something about it. So after the service I went to her and I said: "I would really like to come to South Africa and see what I can do to help." …And it just, it was like a flame I couldn't extinguish. You know, it just kept gnawing at me." (Tina, mother & wife)

One year later, after persistently "pestering" her pastor and convincing fellow friends, Tina went to South Africa with six other people. Four were nurses.

An ER nurse and friend of Tina who went on the same trip explained her awakening obligation to the poor as follows:

> "I'm just kind of like—I need to *fix* something. So we all decided that if we went back [to the U.S.] and pretended like we never saw this, that you know, it would be worse than [if] we had never come. You know, we came, we met these people, we knew their names, we knew these kids by name and by face. We knew their stories." (Jen, mother & wife)

A third friend and nurse also said:

> "…my experience in Africa has just been one of the pivotal moments in my life. The first time I came to Africa I felt strongly called to have a long-term relationship with the children of Africa and do what I could to help the orphans affected by the AIDS pandemic. So that started in 2004. . . . I just hope I [go] to Africa at least once a year for the rest of my life." (Betty, mother & wife)

To go on one STM trip can establish a "bridge." However, to continue developing relationships and building stronger "linking capital"—requires strategic activation of many social networks. These busy women's social networks (church, para-church, kinship, work place, civic clubs) needed to be tapped to support their new activities in behalf of Africa's poor. One woman went for special training to learn how to set up a not-for-profit organization with a 501c3 status. Once incorporated, the women could receive and channel much larger donations under the new tax-exempt status. A website was created and their STM story became public, along with compelling pictures and information for how to send donations. The womens' emerging role as institutionalized "resource brokers" positioned them to be globalizing agents, "nodes" by which Africa's needy can access resources otherwise unknown, and/or unavailable, linked through the STM women to many American organizations.

Global Resource Brokers

Mario Luis Small (2006) points out that key questions to ask about the process of resource brokering are: First, what resources do institutions—in this case, a caring short-term women's group—broker? Second, how are these resources brokered? And, third, why are the resources distributed this way?

By way of definition, resources can be defined as "any symbolic or material good beneficial to an individual" (Small 2006, 276). This includes economic or social capital, information, a credential, a material good or a service. In the case of STM, an often spiritually inspired activity, I would include "spiritual benefit."

What resources do women STMers broker?

The women's STM Africa group acquired large-scale donations of drugs and medical supplies from hospitals and companies connected to various STM group members' workplace networks. One of the members is a researcher at a prominent pharmaceutical company. She also has networks to Catholic charities who donated thousands of dollars in supplies. The combined supply was so large that the group used warehouses for storage. One nurse works for a hospital that actively supports her involvement in STM. They donate supplies, allow her to publish regularly about her trips in their hospital newsletter, and encourage their nurses to participate. Since the hospital is applying for coveted "magnet status" from the Joint Commission of Accreditation of Hospitals, Betty explained:

"...magnet quality hospitals are hospitals that
have the kind of nurses that go the extra mile, and
[STM] is definitely going the extra mile: sitting
on an airplane for eighteen hours to [go] to South
Africa to take care of poor, dirty little children
with very few resources. It's very emotionally
stressful. And the hospital just really applauds that
and they do whatever they can to support us. They
actually even usually give us a check every year
towards the mission team pot."

Each woman is also networked to a local church and she uses those connections to raise awareness and funds for Africa, AIDS and poverty. One nurse returned home and immediately began speaking in every context possible: adult Sunday school, youth group, and in-home adult fellowship groups. Her networks extended to large and diverse community Christian organizations such as Bible Study Fellowship, two other nearby community Bible studies, and Moms in Touch (a local as well as national prayer group for mothers of public school children)—in which she had formerly held a state-level administrative position.

One woman is a triathlon athlete, and therefore has regional ties to running organizations and their runner's publication. She organized and advertised a 5K Fund Raiser through her networks. Groups that do volunteer work, such as an area high school club for the Future Business Leaders of America, were tapped as another set of runners and helpers for the 5K Fund Raiser. The high schoolers, a cheerful multi-ethnic bunch, were the largest organization represented at the early morning race. One nurse's husband participates in various musical bands and a group of his buddies showed up to do drumming for the event. Another friend and small business entrepreneur set up a stand giving away the company's novelty caffeine beverages. Staff and doctors from one nurse's clinic showed up with their families and snapped pictures of the office group with the STM women standing behind a large banner celebrating their support for Africa's poor. The event drew over 200 people, a good showing for a first-time event.

The STM women are also active volunteers in their communities. One was on the board of directors of a local domestic violence shelter for 3 years. She is known and respected. When people hear she is going on a trip, they give. Her husband threw her a birthday party and, at his request, friends gave toward the finances of her trip. She received what she needed. Each woman is also connected to highly supportive nuclear and extended families who support them and their aid organization's work. One father, an engineer of medical equipment, donated generously and supported his brother, sister and daughter to travel to Africa—"a dream come true" for the daughter who hopes to emulate Angelina Jolie's international humanitarian commitments.

Before going on a trip travelers are encouraged to write "support letters" which must be "well written" to represent their mission work in Africa. These are sent out to family as well as professional and friendship networks to collect the necessary funds. One woman was amazed when a former professor sent her money. The women reason that many are glad to give money because although they may not be able to go, they are supportive of someone else going to help and vicariously enjoy participating by way of their donation. Travelers are also instructed in ways to raise money through bake sales and garage sales. The financial resources do indeed flow in to the "brokers."

I attended an impressive annual fund-raising event billed as a formal dinner/dance at a country club. Through yet another social connection, the owner of the club donated the party rooms for their use. Attendees donated $100 per person for an elegant candle-lit meal with live music, performance by a regional African ethnic dance troupe, a highly entertaining auction, an opportunity to purchase T-shirts, framed photos from Africa (taken by a gifted STM photographer), and artifacts from Africa. A full presentation of the needs in Africa was made through power point presentation with "inspiring testimonies." Just over $34,000.00 was raised. The resource gathering in such an event is only possible through multiple connections to other organizations, such as the regional sporting goods manager who reserved a rare signed professional basketball on the day of release for an STM woman to bring to the auction. Most surprising in this event was a video-recorded greeting and endorsement from Senator Barack Obama for the work of the organization. This important symbolic resource was made possible through yet another social connection—an STM friend's nephew who was the right-hand scheduling person for the senator in Washington, D.C.

The work place of each nurse/professional also allocates resources—allowing extra time for several who need additional vacation leave—and also donates generous financial and material resources (i.e. medicines, first aid kits and hospital blankets). One creative nurse uses a DVD about Africa's poor and the work of her STM organization to give patients a distraction during their cardio stress-test. One gentleman, a shoe company sales person, donated dozens of brand new brand-name tennis shoes.

Community youth clubs are also approached with the message of Africa's poor. The STM woman who spoke to one group described their response and involvement as follows:

> The kids immediately said: "what can we do
> to help?" So they jumped onboard and they've
> helped us in a couple fundraisers. And actually,
> they put together an incredible project that won
> them third place in the nation in competition
> for the best Future Business Leaders of America
> programs. So it was held in Chicago this year and

they won third place nationally with their project
for [our Africa STM organization].

An elite charter high school for the arts does an annual show for three days and chose to designate all funds raised from their production of *Fame* to go for Africa's poor. The STM woman I interviewed explained: "And I just got a call out of the clear blue sky from them because the doctor that worked with us last year knew a parent of those students, and so they wanted to do a fundraiser…"

The networks of women's friends are another avenue by which resources are acquired. When one woman's distant friend in another state heard about the Africa trip, she sent dozens of crayon boxes, construction paper and school supplies through the mail. Her Lutheran Sunday School children made simple beaded wrist bands and necklaces with personal notes of encouragement attached. Another STM woman, encouraged by others' efforts, contacted a local specialty fabric store to request a donation of "throw away" end pieces for use in an African women's cottage industry. The African American business woman at the store disappeared in the back for some time and returned with a large heavy box. She found the story compelling, kept the STM woman's business card, and handed over the heavy quality fabrics for the cause of Africa's poor.

Tina's AIDS support group wrote personal letters to HIV/AIDS patients in South Africa and included photographs to encourage black Africans that white suburban Americans also have AIDS and care about their "friends" on the other side of the world. When Tina arrived in the rural community, read the letters and showed the pictures to the gaunt, hollow-eyed group gathered, they were amazed that encouraging messages had been sent personally to them. Before Tina left for the U.S., South African AIDS patients told their stories on film and some dictated letters for delivery to her AIDS support group. The symbolic affirmation through an American "friend's" letter was a powerful affective resource for the stigmatized ill who were waiting to die. The AIDS group also enjoyed the donation of extra groceries with which to cook and share meals during the two weeks the STM group visited. Tina wept when they sang their worship songs in beautiful indigenous harmonies and held hands in a circle of prayer.

One child in Africa that was severely burned was singled out by the STM women on one trip to receive extra medical care. The nurses had connections to the Shriner's Hospital which arranged for his multiple surgeries. The women call him their "poster child" because he is so cheerful and hopeful. His name is Justice—the perfect name for a recipient of resources from organizations in the U.S. that care about global care and social justice. And those resources are accessible to someone like Justice because the STM women were the crucial connection.

The sheer amount of resources and diversity of resources amassed are a reflection of the extensive social ties these STM women have. They are linked to multiple organizations: family and extended family, local churches, community Christian groups, community clubs, small businesses, corporations, hospitals, schools, government—as well as many many friends.

How are these resources brokered or distributed?

Most importantly, the resources are delivered by way of STM travelers themselves. They go to where the needy are and deliver material resources which have been packed in suitcases and 50 pound lockers specially designed to travel, year after year, to Africa. An interesting quandary is experienced when the trip members gather the week before departure and the "gifts" and "donations" far exceed the space and weight restrictions available. Then members must make decisions and reduce the amount to match the most pressing needs as perceived by the travelers (children's clothes, shoes, teddy bears, school supplies, personal crafts made by Sunday school children, first aid supplies, sewing materials for cottage industries and first aid kits and medicines for HIV/AIDS patients). The bags of left-over donated goods are divided and designated for recycling into other community organizations that also care for the needy: the homeless shelter, the community center for immigrants, the local Jewish community center, etc.

When "on site" in Africa, the resources are taken by short-term missionaries—in their host missionary's vehicles—to partners that the short-termers feel are most deserving: i.e. the Methodist mission church school in Pretoria, the home for children affected by AIDS, a rural preschool and AIDS support group which meets in a middle-class family's compound, a home cottage industry carried on by three Christian single mothers who live in a poor tribal area, a local tribal school with whom the short-term missionaries have a "bridge person" on the faculty—a black woman from the Pretoria mission church. Medicines are dispensed by STM nurses to HIV/AIDS patients with instructions on how to use them. In smaller-scaled settings this has a personal dimension that is more intimate and can be accompanied with a testimony by the short-term woman. In larger-scale settings dispensing items and giving physical exams takes on more of a "mob" dynamic and can feel rather frightening, but is always viewed as deeply rewarding.

The sewing items were delivered by the three STM women—all nurses—who lived with the single seamstresses and their children for two weeks. Because the home was close to the rural school, the nurses could also walk to the school and do physical exams and teach AIDS/HIV awareness classes. Together the women sewed during the day, slowly amassing a stack of sewn articles which were carefully packed in lockers for return to the United States. Back home one of the STM women is a "resource broker" for African handicraft items to be displayed and sold in a fair-trade shop located in a desirable vacation spot. She personally negotiates a fair price with the shop owner who allows a placard to be displayed about the African women, with pictures of them at work. Funds from sales are channeled through the STM "resource broker" back to the women.

In some instances women make an effort to create a symbolic aspect to the gift delivery. For example, one nurse planned a foot-washing ceremony for the young people who were to receive shoes. She explained to the African English speakers the meaning of this practice, and proceeded to use a basin with soapy water and a towel to wash and dry their feet, in an inversion of status, emulating Christ's servant-hood. The children ranged in age from elementary school to high school and their foot sizes were all different. There were not enough shoes, and some did not fit. However, each family unit received a large plastic bag which included school supplies and highly valued groceries. One STM woman gathered a group to instruct those interested in sewing, using the new sewing kits which each received. The children made a stretch headband with a decorative flower attached by a button—sewed on using their new skills. It was not enough to just give a sewing kit. The STM woman knew that the children needed to also learn how to thread a needle, knot the thread, run a stitch, sew a button securely, and restore the needle in the pin cushion so it would not be lost—all skills that an AIDS-affected child without adults in their life benefits by knowing.

Eighty-plus fluffy textured bears in pastel colors were distributed in the rural preschool to the eighty-five children who attend—along with the beaded crafts and notes made by the Sunday School children in America. Each child was given their bear by one of the women and their picture was taken. The goal was to get "good" pictures (i.e. children being hugged and smiling with their new toy) to show funders back in the United States. The woman distributing the teddy bears explained that their organization's publicity person had given clear instructions on why these pictures mattered. Resource brokering involves strategizing effectively through media. And while it was an odd experience to the children unfamiliar with such a gift-exchange ritual, it was deeply meaningful for the STM woman who hugged almost every single child as she gave them their fluffy bear.

All the short-term women contributed money to the central Pretoria mission church which disbursed amounts for African hosts to house and feed the guests. A bit of a disagreement arose between what some of the women thought should have been given to the local hosts and what the central church deemed an adequate amount. Some women felt compelled to give more of their personal money toward rural African family funds for food.

When the women are not in Africa their funds are delivered by MoneyGram for projects such as major building initiatives (i.e. drilling a well - $6500, monthly payment for eighty-five preschoolers to receive two school lunches per day). African partner organizations such as churches or hospitals are often the conduits for funds when the women go back to the United States. Sometimes the money is sent with a trusted African go-between. However, when funds go missing or there are claims that "money was stolen," it is hard for the women to know what to believe. Their unfamiliarity with respective national and regional contexts and reliance on short-term visits alone can be frustrating in their efforts to help the "most needy" most effectively.

Why are the resources distributed this way?

Funds could be sent via MoneyGram, emissaries, or intermediary organizations. However, for these women, the actual delivery of care in embodied ways is crucial. They have a sense that they have expertise in nursing and leadership in general. And in fact, their presence does carry clout. When they traveled to the national Minister of Education's office, and requested better school facilities for rural black children whose old school was called "The Whip," politicians got moving and built a beautiful new school. When AIDS awareness classes were initiated in a rural school, concerned South African AIDS educators wanted the Americans along because the principal was more likely to allow access and welcome the foreigners. However, the need for STM travel was captured in the words of one nurse: "I live 354 days of the year for the two weeks I'm in Africa." The intense fundraising and resource gathering pays off for these resource brokers—who work hard in every way when they are at home in the US—when they can see the good accomplished (i.e. healthier kids than they saw 2 years earlier, a new school, youth supported at university). They are also the recipients of appreciation when they travel. African hosts are usually extremely generous and endeavor to put on lavish meals. School children put on elaborate, creative and enthusiastic presentations with faculty adding their own honorific speeches to honor the women—and lots of hugs, all the time. Pictures and more pictures are taken. Such memories will be cherished, put in specially crafted "my trip to Africa" albums, or framed and placed in prominent places at home or the office to remind them of how their hard work was appreciated and made a difference.

Many of these women explain that most Americans are spoiled, happy to keep resources for themselves, and unaware of the world's needy. They are often concerned that fellow Christians are not more aware and involved. They seek to make their faith matter beyond mere Bible study and church attendance. Active faith is seen in its most clarified essence when "making a difference" under extreme conditions, even when facing resistance:

> …and there's a whole real like a dirty aspect of AIDS that I think most conservative evangelicals don't want to deal with. AIDS is a dirty, sinful disease that they don't want to get their hands dirty with. And they really quite frankly don't want to hear about the little dirty orphans. And that's made me a little bit cynical, but it's also caused me to do a check on my heart and wonder where my positive vibes come from. And really they need

to just come from Jesus. It doesn't matter if my church understands or not… (Betty)

I have had the occasional comment like you know, there's enough poor people over here. You know or you don't have to go all the way to South Africa to help people. And then I was also surprised that my husband chimed in on this one as well as me, he'll say, "well, she does. She helps people here too. But she likes to help people around the world." …But I say there's no comparison between the poverty here in our country and the poverty [there]. Because in our country we have access to all the different social services. (Tina)

I think that people here in the United States have many more resources than the people [in Africa]. Because, how many little children do you find going unclothed wandering around maybe with one meal a day? You don't. And that's because we have resources here….I think that just helping another human being, if it's one person, one time in your life that's something that you want to do. (Gina)

Ultimately, these STM women believe that change depends on them and therefore they must actively and personally deliver care to make a difference.

Conclusion

In this chapter we have examined how STM women entered the social worlds of needy African people and brokered connections for individuals otherwise cut off from many resources. Through their extensive networks to multiple organizations, the STM women enable linking capital to form which is far beyond their immediate means as ordinary busy every day working mothers. Furthermore, just as needy Africans must link to short-termers to obtain resource access—so must short-term women be physically connected to the people they serve. Mothers who care for family and community in America often recognize that their suburban existence is "cushioned" and potentially "numbing." They and those they love and care for are caught in an affluent suburban system that requires and expects lifestyle patterns built on materialism. A "good" Christian mother must buy into values that do not necessarily resonate with Scripture. In his book, *Death by Suburb: How to Keep the Suburbs from killing your soul,* David Goetz prophetically writes of the dilemma:

> Too much of the good life ends up being toxic,
> deforming us spiritually. The drive to succeed,
> and to make one's children succeed, overpowers
> the best of intentions to live more reflectively, no
> matter the piety. Should it be any surprise that the
> true life in Christ never germinates? (2006:9)

Involvement in STM nurtures the soul, pries away suburban "blinders" and allows women to care in contexts which obviously need resources. They are conversely rewarded with the deep satisfaction of seeing the poor fed and material items distributed to people who need them much more than those who attend their fundraisers. Material inequalities and medical service inequalities must be rectified. And crucially the deprivation of spiritual capital in suburbia must be rectified. Many of the women bring their daughters, relatives, friends and co-workers along with them on trips. They desire that their loved ones and anyone who will listen will see the world's needy as they have come to see them—deserving of care. The women in this chapter are a case in point of how the globalization of empathy has emerged in new patterns of STM "resource brokering" across international borders.

References Cited

Appadurai, Arjun. 2002. Disjuncture and difference in the global cultural economy. *The anthropology of globalization: A reader* (eds.) Jonathan Xavier Inda and Renato Rosaldo. Malden, MA: Blackwell Publishers, Inc., 46-62.

Goetz, David L. 2006. *Death by suburb: How to keep the suburbs from killing your soul.* San Francisco, CA: HarperCollins.

Neitz, Mary Jo. 2003. Dis/location: Engaging feminist inquiry in the sociology of religion. *Handbook of the Sociology of Religion* (ed.) Michele Dillon. Oxford, MA: Oxford University Press. 276-293.

Priest, Robert J. 2007. Peruvian churches acquire "linking social capital" through STM partnerships. *Journal of Latin American theology: Christian Reflections From the Latino South -- Special Issue on Short-Term Missions in Latin America* 2(2):175-189.

Priest, Robert J. and Joseph Paul Priest. 2008. "They see everything, and understand nothing": Short-term mission and service learning. *Missiology: An International Review* 36: 53-73.

Putnam, Robert. 2000. *Bowling alone: The collapse and revival of American community.* New York: Simon and Schuster.

Small, Mario Luis. 2006. Neighborhood institutions as resource brokers: Childcare centers, interorganizational ties, and resource access among the poor. *Social Problems* 53(2):274-292.

Wuthnow, Robert. 2002. Religious involvement and status-bridging social capital. *Journal for the Social Scientific Study of Religion* 41:669-684.

CHAPTER 11

SHORT-TERM MISSIONS ARE BIGGER THAN YOU THINK

MISSIOLOGICAL IMPLICATIONS FOR THE GLOCAL CHURCH

ROLANDO W. CUELLAR

Introduction

The last two decades have witnessed great growth in the number of short-term missions (STM), particularly in trips going from North America to Third-World countries. This is especially true with regard to Latin America. Driven by "American voluntarism," this type of missions has been a dynamic force adaptive to the changes of globalization. Despite its popularity and contribution to the renewal of the missionary task, STM has received little attention in three primary areas: STM's lack of a formal definition, its biblical and theological framework, and a critical analysis of its contribution to the mission of the church.

In this brief presentation, I will critically work through these three areas with the purpose of offering an appreciation for this modern phenomenon from the perspective of someone who has been the object of mission in Latin America and currently is a subject of mission from North America.

Toward a Definition of Short-Term Missions

In an attempt to define STM, we must be conscious of the ambiguities surrounding the task. One is the danger of exclusively defining STM as cross-cultural experiences that happen only outside of the United States. Another danger is that definitions tend to give too much emphasis to the missional practices of the North American Church, and thereby place God, the protagonist of mission, in a secondary role. STM has greater potential of being a significant instrument of God's mission, if we can place it into the larger agenda of the *glocal* church.

By definition, STM is the mobilization of the church in the power of the Holy Spirit to join in God's action in the world. Its purpose is to announce God's kingdom through brief trips with specific ministerial activities. In an interview on January 27, 2007, Philos Molina, a Methodist Pastor from El Salvador, said, "STM is directed toward the lay men and women who are interested in contributing their talents, time, and resources to other countries or cultures through brief trips and commitments of limited work." This aspect of STM differentiates it from long-term missions, which requires a commitment of extended periods of time and more restrictive ministerial qualifications.

Biblical and Theological Framework

The participation of the church emerges as the result of God's initiative to express God's grace for the redemption of humanity in Jesus Christ. Biblical examples illustrate this important characteristic of mission. Paul, for example, was chosen by God to be involved in the noble task of carrying the Gospel to the Gentiles (Acts 18:5-7).

As he responded to God's call, Paul developed a passion for people of the big cities and a burden to pray and intercede for them. He participated in short-term missions, often visiting the same cities (Acts 15:36), and seldom staying for more than five months in any given location (with the exception of his stay in Corinth, which lasted 18 months). Paul never returned to Antioch thinking that his missionary work was finished. On the contrary, Paul was in constant contact with the men and women who he guided to Jesus. He was involved in evangelism and church planting, but was also interested in the holistic welfare of these new believers as evidenced in his epistles. Therefore, before returning to the Antioch Church which commissioned him for his missional tasks, Paul would ensure he invested his talent and energy in the training of local leaders in each city he visited. These leaders would be in charge of giving continuity to God's mission in their city of service after Paul's departure (Acts 20:27-38). Undoubtedly, Paul is a fine subject of mission because he participates in God's mission, yet he is not the originator of mission. Only God is the initiator, protagonist, and sustainer of mission.

Next, the church, as the body of Christ, participates in God's mission as an inclusive community. Men and women, both young and old, as well as boys and girls together respond to and participate in God's activity in human history. God has been purposefully involved long before long-term and short-term missionaries arrive on the mission field. God's mission from this perspective avoids the common idea among North American Christians that "nothing would have happened here if we would not have come." The effort is cooperative: God acts and God's people respond. God's people are inclusively defined as those who are called and sent, whether full- or part-time ministers in the vocational sense. Therefore, we must emphasize that STM is helping the church to realize the important role of lay people in God's mission. This aspect is what Rene Padilla calls the "declericalization" of the ministries and the "laicization" of the clergy (Padilla, 2003). In other words, due to our identity as disciples of Jesus, all of us can and must participate in God's activity in the world. STM as a missional activity provides an opportunity for the laity to contribute in the extension of God's kingdom. In the process, they, along with their respective congregations, receive more benefits than the receptors of mission.

Third, the participation of God's people is carried out in many unique ways. Orlando Costas has challenged us to think that although every believer is called to be a witness, not all of us can or should fulfill our task in the same way (Costas, 1979). We must remember, however, that these approaches must always serve to promote God's kingdom that is present in history through Jesus Christ in the concrete contexts of suffering and hope in which marginalized people live (Padilla, 2003; Rey, 2002). For these reasons, STM is taking on a variety of styles and purposes.

Finally, the participation of God's people in mission work must be done in the power of the Holy Spirit. According to the missiologist David Bosch, the evangelists Matthew and Mark relate the Holy Spirit with mission on just a few occasions (Matt. 3:11-17; 10:20; 12:18, 28; 28:19; Mk 1:8; 13:11). In Luke and Acts, however, the disciples of Jesus are individuals motivated, inspired, and confirmed by the Holy Spirit to fulfill God's mission (Luke 3:21-22; 4:14; 24:13-35, 49; Acts 1:5, 8; 4:13-29-31; 8:29; 10:44-48; 11:12; 13:1-4, 46; 14:3; 15:8, 28; 16:6-9) (Bosch, 2000). Luke also unfolds Jesus' agenda for mission at his inaugural service in Nazareth:

> The Spirit of the Lord is on me,
> because he has anointed me
> to preach good news to the poor.
> He has sent me to proclaim freedom for the prisoners
> and recovery of sight for the blind,
> to release the oppressed,
> to proclaim the year of the Lord's favor (4:18-19)

If the agenda of Jesus was so missional, the agenda of the church in the twenty-first century should follow suit. In this agenda, faith and action complement each other to overcome injustice and oppression (Engel and Dyrness, 2000). Unfortunately, North American missional activity, with its enormous capacity for creativity and organization, its financial and human resources, and its technology, often tends to undermine the role of the Holy Spirit in mission. These strategic times for the mission of the church challenge us to be open in new ways to the work of the Holy Spirit in the church and the world (Escobar, 2003).

Critical Analysis of the Contribution to the Mission of the Church

Facing the challenges of both the North American and Latin American contexts, I wish to focus our attention on both the duration of STM and its nature as *glocal* mission.

Duration of STM

There is a clear tendency in North American churches to reflect a pragmatism oriented toward instant results. This tendency is dangerous for the missional work. Let us take, for example, the duration of STM. Some missiologists argue that STM can last from one week to two years (Moreau, Corwin, and McGee, 2004). Others think that it should not be longer than three years. These positions demonstrate the ambiguity of this phenomenon. It seems that no one knows how long this missionary activity should last or how to differentiate, for definition's sake, the limits or parameters for short- or long-term missions.

Further, we question what can be achieved in such a brief period of time, whether these trips last a few weeks or three years. The truth of the matter is that there is nothing short-term about God's mission because it is as complex and profound as the needs and challenges that human beings face (Bosch, 2000). STM must take place in connection with God's mission which is much broader in its approach (Friesen, 2004). This concern has been already pointed out by missiologists John Nyquist and Paul Hiebert, who argue that the duration of STM does not allow the participants to be involved in learning the culture and the language of the local people; unfortunately, they come back to the United States still in the "tourist stage" (Nyquist and Hiebert, 1995). They go on to say that those who come back after staying two years return in the second stage known as "disenchantment," characterized by criticism toward the local church, language, and culture. Few participants, if any, experience the final stages of bonding and adjustments in the new culture in such a brief time.

Another of my concerns about the brevity of STM is that discipleship and commitment to Christ and his church are pushed aside. Many STM groups return to the United States with reports of how many people received Christ, but unfortunately the story ends here. STM's brief commitments contribute to the idea that discipleship and mission may be isolated from one another. Victor Rey insists that when discipleship is not oriented toward mission, it results in deification of the self-centered individual (Rey, 2002). We might say the same about the mission that keeps evangelism isolated from discipleship. Christopher Little points out that one of the tendencies of the North American mission movement is the McDonaldization of mission, in which the gospel is presented as attractive merchandise to a large number of people looking for fast and bigger results (Little, 2006)—a perspective Little says is open to serious challenges. Despite the apparent success of the missional task in terms of numerical growth, large budgets, buildings and programs, these is little evidence that this approach is supported biblically or that it works to form genuine disciples of Jesus. Donald Bowdle expresses similar concern by observing that "the secularization of holiness has become the spiritual "Achilles' heel" of the current

Pentecostal denominationalism" (Bowdle, 1999). Undoubtedly, this issue could also affect the Protestant Churches of North America that organize STM trips. I am not suggesting that the name STM is not correct, but it must take shape within the biblical and missiological frameworks described above.

Glocal Mission

Many churches in North America struggle to decide between local or global missions, as though the choice is either/or. By contrast, I strongly support the integration of both. When we are involved in STM, we cannot ignore the challenges and benefits of urbanization and immigration. These trends are essential components to the revitalization of the churches in North America. Our problem in North America is not a lack of resources for participation in God's mission, whether it be local or global, but it is a lack of obedience to join God's action in the world (Cuellar, 2002).

Missio Dei must be carried out with a genuine commitment toward the inner-cities of North America as well as with those cities in Latin America, Africa, and Asia. The explosive growth of the Hispanic population in the United States must be a challenge for North American Christians to be involved in a holistic ministry in the inner cities or *barrios* where many people live in the midst of poverty, violence, oppression, hunger, pollution, and in overcrowded apartments or trailers which are cold in the winter and hot in the summer. In other words, STM must take place simultaneously in local and global contexts. The need here locally is as urgent as the overseas setting on any continent. Charles Van Engen argues that the church of the twenty-first century is *glocal*, in which God's local and global missions are closely interconnected (Van Engen, 2006). Van Engen finds support in a close reading of Acts 1:8 when Jesus promises his disciples the coming of the Holy Spirit so they might become "witnesses in Jerusalem, and in all Judea and Samaria, and to the ends of the earth." It is clear in Jesus' words that mission must be constantly and simultaneously done in our immediate communities as well as in other nations.

An interesting exercise has stayed with me from my time serving as Pastor of Emmanuel Presbyterian Church in Chicago. One of the Sunday school teachers posed the following question to her young adult class, most of whom were second generation Hispanics born in the United States: how many would like to become missionaries somewhere around the world? Most of them raised their hands. Then, she changed the focus of her question: how many would like to be missionaries in Pilsen? Pilsen was our neighborhood full of all kinds of needs and challenges. To her surprise, none of them raised their hands. Many of its inhabitants were undocumented, unemployed, school dropouts, lacking decent housing; there were gang members in each corner fighting every day to expand their territory to sell drugs. Pilsen was really a mission field, and I believe still is despite the changes in the last few years.

For many missiologists, STM is a contradiction in terms (Terry, 2004). Our young people and laity are willing to travel thousands of miles in airplanes to other countries around the world, but are not willing to walk or drive to the poor *barrios* of our inner-cities of North America where many people live under inhumane conditions; they are suffering and in need of hope found only in Jesus Christ. In the words of Eldin Villafane, "too often church programs and worship are geared to the entertainment and "event-full" gratification of its membership, while the preaching of the cross and the call for radical discipleship, incarnation, and justice are absent" (Villafane, 2006). In some instances, this could be applied to STM as we observe its selfishness, inconsistencies, and failures to meet God's expectations.

Shane Clairborne (a North American who worked with Mother Teresa in Calcutta among the poorest of the poor and currently is working in the inner-city of Philadelphia) has observed that "the tithes, tax-exempt donations, and short-term mission trips, while they accomplish some good, can also function as outlets that allow us to appease our consciences and still remain in safe distance from the poor" (Claiborne, 2006). If STM is to have a more powerful impact it will have to be involved in *glocal* mission.

STM should not only focus on the "remote areas in the world." The poor and marginalized are everywhere; we must be engaged in ministry among them to demonstrate the love of Christ in Latin America, Africa, and Asia but simultaneously in our local communities. Such an understanding of mission will allow the church to discover its authentic missionary nature.

Missiological Implications

By way of conclusion, I would like to suggest some recommendations of how we can reverse the evident inconsistencies and failures of STM and how STM can more effectively function in light of the changes we are experiencing.

If there is one aspect of STM that should never change, it is its dynamic missionary force directed to the lay people. This element will break the trap that only professional clergy can lead in the ministry. Terry Cross has pointed out that "this mentality of professional clergy is one torpedo that has sunk the ship of mainline denominations in the United States. It has not been a part of Pentecostal churches in the [United States] until the last 30 years. And now I fear it is weighing us down as well" (Cross, 2006).

The combination of the "North American voluntarism" and the missionary passion of the Latin American Church could create bilateral partnerships of mission to respond creatively to the demands of our culture and to epistemological shifts. This partnership must and should be done on the basis of mutual benefit. I am not proposing a relationship of dependency. On the contrary, I propose an interdependent partnership where North American Christians recognize that the missional task must take place in humility, realizing that the majority of the missionaries serving around the world now come from outside Europe and North America. Engel and Dyrness argue that this must be a reason to celebrate because the "baby has now become a vigorous, maturing and responsible adult in many parts of Africa, Asia and South America" (Engel and Dyrness 2000). Both Engel and Dyrness use the baby as a metaphor to speak about the shift of the center of God's mission from the West to the East and from North to South. These developments of the Church in the Two-Thirds World encourage us to work together like never before, leaving aside the ethnocentrism and paternalism that have characterized the North American missional task. The Gospel of Luke 12:48 tells us that, " ...from everyone who has been given much, much will be demanded; and from the one who has been entrusted with much, much will be asked." God has blessed North America with technological, financial and literary resources while God has given to the Protestants in Latin America an attitude of what we might call "being in a state of mission" (Escobar, 2005). A partnership of interdependency between the churches of both contexts is possible through an incarnational ministry following the example of Jesus. Sherwood G. Lingenfelter and Marvin K. Mayers (1986) remind us that one of the meanings of the incarnation is that Jesus was a student of the language and culture of the Jews because he was not born with the knowledge of both. Before entering into his public ministry, Jesus spent thirty years studying and listening in the temple about the real needs and cruel realities that people from his time faced under the Roman oppression.

Unfortunately, the ministry of STM on many occasions is characterized by a search for answers and immediate solutions to difficult circumstances in the context of mission (Cardoza-Orlandi, 2003). North American Christians must also be willing to reject this tendency to solve complex problems simply with proclamation (Breckenridge, 1995; Engel and Dyrness, 2000). Instead of pretending to have all the answers for the problems of Latin America, North

Americans participating in STM should demonstrate a willingness to live among the local people rather than simply being among them speaking English, staying and eating in hotels and places where the local people cannot afford to visit (Van Engen, 2000).

In this partnership of genuine commitment, participants in STM from North America should consider the Latin American people or Hispanics living in the United States as equals without a sense of superiority. Following the example of Paul, participants of STM must be willing to establish relationship with the local people not only during their visit to Latin America but after their return to the United States. To undermine this kind of partnership will lead the missional task to failure in responding to the needs of the Latin American people and those who live in the poor *barrios* of North America.

I was born and raised in Peru, a land where the gospel of salvation in Christ was brought by European and North American missionaries whose sacrifice and commitment have left extraordinary missionary legacies. This does not mean that they have not made mistakes in their missional task. Reports of abuse of authority, ethnocentrism, lack of sensitivity to people's needs and history are documented. But I agree with Samuel Escobar as he presents his assessment of the twenty century: "Christian mission has advanced in this century, and the balance is positive for the cause of God's kingdom" (Escobar, 2000). But we must continue to critically analyze the long-term missionary enterprise as well as STM trips to avoid the pitfalls of the past. May God allow STM trips to continue in Latin America but also to the least evangelized areas of the world. May God also allow that people from those continents continue to come to North America to contribute in the much needed revitalization of the churches of North America.

References Cited

Bosch, David J. 2000. *Misión en transformación: Cambios de paradigma en la teología de la mision.* Grand Rapids, MI: Libros Desafio.

Bowdle, Donald. 1999. Holiness in the highlands: A profile of the Church of God. In *Christianity in Appalachia: Profiles in regional pluralism.* Edited by Bill J. Leonard. Knoxville, TN: The University of Tennessee Press.

Breckenridge, James and Lillian. 1995. *What color is your God: Multicultural education in the Church.* Grand Rapids, MI.: Baker Books.

Cardoza-Orlandi, Carlos F. 2002. *Mission: An essential guide.* Nashville, TN: Abingdon Press.

Clairborne, Shane. 2006. *The irresistible revolution: Living as an ordinary radical.* Grand Rapids, MI.: Zondervan.

Costas, Orlando E. 1979. *The integrity of mission: The inner life and outreach of the Church.* San Francisco: Harper & Row Publishers.

Cross, Terry. *Implications of theological education for ministry and vocation in Latin America.* Presented at the Latin American Education Leadership Consultation at SEMISUD, Quito, Ecuador on March 2006.

Cuellar, Rolando. 2002. *The influence of spiritual and educational formation on the missionary vision and programs of four hispanic churches in the United States.* Ph.D. diss., Trinity Evangelical Divinity School.

Escobar, Samuel. 2003. *The new global mission: The gospel from everywhere to everyone.* Downers Grove, Ill.: InterVarsity Press.

_____. 2000. The global scenario at the turn of the century. In *Global missiology for The 21st century.* Edited by William D. Taylor. Grand Rapids, MI.: Baker Academic.

Engel, James E. and William A. Dyrness. 2000. *Changing the mind of missions: Where have we gone wrong?* Downers Grove, IL.: InterVarsity Press.

Friesen, Randall Gary. 2004. *Improving the long-term impact of short-term missions on the beliefs, attitudes and behaviors of young adults.* Ph.D. diss. University of South Africa.

Lingenfelter, Sherwood G. and Marvin K. Mayers. 1986. *Ministering cross-culturally: An incarnational model for personal relationships.* Grand Rapids, MI.: Baker Academic.

Little, Christopher. 2006. A new agenda: De-Americanization." *Evangelical Missions Quarterly* 42: 496-505.

Mack J. and Leeann Stiles. 2000. *Mack & Leeann's guide to short-term missions.* Downers Grove, IL.: InterVarsity Press.

Molina, Philos. 2007. Methodist pastor from El Salvador. Interviewed by the author. 27 January.

Moreau, Scott A., Gary R. Corwin and Gary B. McGee. 2004. *Introducing world missions: A biblical, historical, and practical survey.* Grand Rapids, MI.: Baker Academic.

Nyquist, John and Paul Hiebert. 1995. Short-term missions?" *Trinity World Forum* (Spring): 1-4.

Padilla, Rene. 2004. Introduction: An ecclesiology for integral mission. In *The local church, agent of transformation: An ecclesiology for integral mission.* Edited by Tetsunao Yamamori and Rene Padilla. Buenos Aires: Ediciones Kairos.

Rey, Victor. 2002. *Misión y vida en América Latina hoy.* Santiago, Chile: World Vision.

Terry, Douglas W. 2004. Assessing missional effectiveness of midterm missionaries. *Missiology* 32: 173-186.

Van Engen, Charles E. 2006. The glocal church: Locality and catholicity in a globalizing world. In *Globalizing theology: Belief and practice in an era of world christianity.* Edited by Craig Ott and Harold A. Netland. Grand Rapids, MI.: Baker Academic.

Van Engen, Jo Ann. 2000. The cost of short-term missions." *The Other Side* 36. 1 (January): 1-5.

Villafane, Eldin. 2006. *Beyond cheap grace: A call to radical discipleship, incarnation, and justice.* Grand Rapids, MI.: William B. Eerdmans Publishing Company.

CHAPTER 12

SHORT-TERM MEDICAL
A PRACTITIONER'S PERSPECTIVE

MISSIONS: ON EFFECTIVE STRATEGIES

DANIEL W. O'NEILL, MD

The number of health care workers going to serve short-term in developing countries has increased in proportion to the burgeoning growth of short-term mission. This paper seeks to emphasize the beneficial role short-term medical missions (STMM) can play in an effective overall mission strategy. The purpose is to give a theological basis for STMM, review STMM history and philosophy, reveal motivations, summarize problems and lessons learned, analyze physical and spiritual effectiveness, emphasize effective strategies, and offer suggestions for greater impact and further research. The author draws from the mission and medical literature, and from his personal experience with a broad cross-section of STMM endeavors. When done well, these STMM efforts will bless host peoples, those who serve on the team, and the God who calls us to the task.

Theological Basis

Medical missions in general has a theological basis rooted in the concern God expresses in the Bible about healing, salvation, and *shalom* for the whole person. Jesus' compassion toward the crowds resulted in his healing the sick (Matt 14:14), and should be a motivation for involvement in delivering medical care to those in need. Like the parable of the Good Samaritan, there is a moral imperative to help the wounded person across the cultural/religious divide (Luke 10:33-35). As Sydney Hodge (1913) states, medical missions "bring[s] home to this severed and disjointed age the existence of a common humanity." Healing, along with the preaching of the gospel to the poor, was a sign of the advent of the Kingdom of God (Matt 11:5), the borders of which Christians are called to expand by demonstrating God's will for all peoples concerning human life in community. Jesus sent out the twelve disciples and the (short-term) seventy-two to heal diseases, a task inextricably tied with the proclamation of the Kingdom of God to the nations (Luke 9:2 and 10:9). Jesus' concern for the health of *individuals* was more pronounced than his concern for the health of populations (Luke 8:43-44, Mark 6:5). He promised reward for those disciples who give a cup of cold water to "*one* of these little ones" (Mark 10:42), and he likened serving "*one* of the least of these" to serving Jesus himself (Matt 25:40). His concern for expanding the Kingdom in the hearts of his hearers was preeminent (Luke 9:11), and Christ-centered worship was to be promoted beyond helping the poor (Matt 26:6-13). Scripture calls both for evangelism and for service to the needs of the poor (Nelson 2007, Strauss 2007).

According to Scripture, the source of poverty may come from personal laziness or sin (Prov 13:18; 20:13), but it *often* results from unjust oppression by the powerful, or other social factors that make self-sufficiency impossible (Prov 13:23). God's heart for the poor is expressed in Old Testament teachings of the harvest gleanings, the year of Jubilee, and empowerment through promoting social justice (Lev 25:35, Isaiah 58:6). The sins of Sodom and her daughters can be pitfalls for many health care professionals in developed countries: They were, "arrogant, overfed and unconcerned" and did not help (literally, empower) the poor and needy (Ezek 16:46). For the author, short term medical service gives opportunity to live out the call to help the global poor and to put faith and love into practice, cooperating with the wider church in using healing gifts for advancing the kingdom through service, while preparing the heart for potential full time missionary service or enhanced connection with, and support of, missions.

Biblically informed medical mission efforts should ideally seek to encompass physical healing ministry, help for the poor through empowerment, and the proclamation of the gospel in fulfilling their part in God's global redemptive purposes. Clarifying theological views for the agencies and participants is important in order to ground these efforts in purposefulness and effectiveness.

History and Philosophy

There is a long history of effectiveness both for church growth, medical education and cultural transformation in global mission through long-term health care, especially in India, China, and Sub-Sahara Africa from the mid 19th to the mid 20th century (Grundmann 2005). The history of medical missions since the middle of the 20th Century has revealed a trend toward deinstitutionalization, and a stronger emphasis on delivery at the local level, with Kingdom-building a primary goal (Berends 1998). Harold P. Adolph (1981), a long-term missionary surgeon summarized the approach to medical missions that also characterizes short-term service: "They're coming to us with their recognized need; we're taking care of that and pointing out other needs." This necessitates an accurate knowledge of, and capacity to address, their felt health needs. It also requires an understanding of a culturally relevant way to meet their spiritual needs, namely the need to know the transforming power of the gospel. At the Global Missions Health Conference, November 2006, there was a strong call by medical mission leaders to emphasize transformational, holistic care, treating the sick out of love, and proclaiming Jesus out of love (www.medicalmissions.com).

STMM makes up about ten percent of those involved in all short-term missions (Guthrie 2001). There are dozens of Christian organizations which host short-term medical teams, each with a unique focus.[1] Christian organizations make up the vast majority of agencies which are listed regularly in the Journal of the American Medical Association as Physician Service Opportunities Abroad (Mitka 1999), but there are also non-Christian organizations that participate in similar medical work for other philanthropic reasons.

There are some distinguishing features to medical missions. Many participants use their own vacation time and self-fund their projects, which reduces the cost to the local church compared to non-medical short-term mission trips where participants often raise funds from others. This may help reduce the overall cost burden that has been criticized in short-term mission endeavors. Pharmaceuticals and surgical equipment are frequently donated or purchased at reduced cost, some purchased within the host country. Some organizations charge a nominal fee for medical services, helping offset the operational costs, but also providing some dignity and enhanced responsibility among the population served, since it has been shown that free care is potentially less valued and adhered-to.

Short-term medical teams can attract large crowds, enhancing the exposure to a Christian testimony of the partnering mission or local churches, and serving as a way to screen and treat medical illness among large populations, provided there is good communication with locally available health care systems. They can also serve in "linking social capital" from the Christian communities of resource-rich to resource-poor countries (Priest 2007).

Motivations

There are various reasons health professionals would participate in STMM. Dr. Bruce and Michelle Steffes (2002) offer the following reasons: Simple obedience to a specific call, service to the missionaries, service to the host people-group, personal spiritual and world-view growth, family growth (when family members also participate), experiencing a challenging new medical care setting, supporting missions and enhanced ministry in the home church, and exploring the possibility of career medical mission work. Each of these purposes can be accomplished to varying degrees, but these can be elusive without a careful selection of field or agency, and without the right preparation. I have personally experienced each of these multi-faceted outcomes in my short-term service. In addition, this has allowed direct participation with missionaries that my church supports, enhancing the focus and accountability of the church's mission program. While the initial intent was for preparation for career medical mission service, I discovered the intrinsic value in training and discipleship among teammates, the benefit to the host missionaries and to observable church growth, and the impact on individuals in the service population, which gave significance beyond this initial purpose.

Lessons Learned

Crossing cultures effectively to minister to the physical and spiritual needs of others is complex. The problems that have been identified with short-term missions in general have also been experienced with medical work. These include a lack of training, cultural insensitivity, language barriers, tourist mentality, patronizing pride (going as teachers not learners), a narrow view of sin and evangelism (as personal, not social), self-centeredness (high comfort zones), need for control, and lack of a holistic theology of the gospel (Slimbach 2000).

There have been legitimate criticisms of some STMM methods from both Christian and secular observers, often citing poor medical training to deal with the prevailing illnesses (e.g. tropical diseases), misuse or overuse of medication or surgery, the "something is better than nothing" fallacy, poor medical history-taking (e.g. excluding allergy history), poor documentation, ignorance of existing healthcare resources, and lack of long-term responsibility for the patient's follow-up and well-being (Roberts 2006, Dohn 2003). Concerns have been raised about the inappropriate use of medical care that may undermine the health or local health care infrastructure because of ethnocentric cultural understandings of the medical systems, beliefs, and practices, and because of a lack of cooperation with existing systems. There is also a legitimate concern that the participant's desire to be needed, or the participant's need to serve, or the mission organization's need to involve constituents will eclipse the health needs of the people and ignore their cultural realities (Montgomery 1993).

The criticism leveled at STMM should be considered in context. Every human endeavor is fraught with difficulties, so criticism of some aspects of the endeavor should not lead to a wholesale rejection. Rather it should lead to a comprehensive analysis and reevaluation of existing practices to maximize the physical and spiritual impact and minimize the cost and damage. Given the various strategic approaches to STMM described below (and there are other approaches as well), critical evaluations need to remain focused and specific. They should lead to solutions which evolve over time to accomplish higher purposes. What has emerged from the experiences of practitioners of STMM is a need for cooperation with host leadership, strategic planning by leaders, and intentional preparation for participants. In trying to address some of these identified shortcomings of previous short-term mission efforts, an analysis of effectiveness in physical and spiritual health is necessary, and a discussion of strategic models of health care delivery in the short-term setting is vital.

Effectiveness in Physical Health

It is difficult to measure or study the effectiveness of short term medical mission work on overall health in community development work, other than to count the numbers of people attended to, or operated on. There is little data on patient-oriented outcomes or public health measures. In each mobile clinic experience which I've had, I attended fifty to one-hundred patients per day, which is two to four times the volume I see in my private practice in the USA. While this may seem more effective, the individual attention is reduced, compounded by the language barrier and need for translation. In Nicaragua, for example, I had a translator interpreting an indigenous Suma dialect into Spanish, my own second language. In West Bengal, India the translators (who were local pastors) had to ask which language the patients spoke before choosing one of four languages to translate into English. This cuts down on time efficiency, and subtleties of language and culture are lost in communicating health needs.

When evaluated from a purely health care delivery model perspective, most STMM teams would fail a cost/benefit efficiency analysis. However, a balanced assessment must include the effects on church growth, discipleship, and host church empowerment. The impact of delivering sporadic curative medicine to underserved populations probably has little effect on overall health conditions of the population. This is because human health is intimately tied in with the complex spiritual, economic, social, educational and geo-political factors of a population. However, they *can* serve individuals' needs. This has its own merit, especially as a part of an overall approach to loving one's neighbor and making disciples within the theological framework described above. When primary health care and surgery is coupled with ongoing community health work and public health measures (i.e. clean water sources, vector control, vaccination, nutrition programs, etc.), as well as other social justice efforts for the poor (education, economic development, etc.), then there will more likely be some widespread measurable improvement in health, a goal of the World Health Organization. The effectiveness of disaster relief work is more quantifiable, especially when these efforts aim to treat disease outbreaks, and fill in gaps in access to needed acute health care (Duininck and Williams 2006).

Effectiveness in Spiritual Health

The spiritual and transformational impact of STMM has been measured in various ways. For example, where the author served near Dajabón, Dominican Republic where Medical Ministry International has sent a medical and surgical team each year for fifteen years, offering some degree of continuity of care (which is felt to be a more effective expression of care than one-time service projects), twenty-three churches have been planted. These medical/dental/surgical missions are hosted by several local pastors and serve villages with little access to medical care, therefore not undermining or interfering with local health care delivery systems. They adopted an integrated health model, teaching preventive health practices. This approach has been recently advocated as more locally sustainable and in keeping with the Primary Health Care objectives endorsed by the World Health Organization (Montgomery 2007). This is felt to have impacted the population favorably over time. Through their experience in Latin America, and adopting the community health evangelism model, they now work in less-evangelized, restricted-access countries, which has been fruitful (Hunter 2007).

Much of the data on spiritual effectiveness comes from the short-term mission agencies themselves. For example, in the Philippines, Christians in Action reported a short-term medical team treating around 8,000 people. The gospel was shared with each person, and a reported 4,700 people made professions of faith in Jesus Christ, with pastors in place for follow-up (www.mnnonline.org/article/2057, 18 May 2001). East-West Ministries reports that in India, Nepal and Bhutan, 705 people were treated in a four-day mobile clinic, 814 were presented with the gospel, and 278 made professions of faith (Nelson 2007). Counting visible "decisions for Christ," of course, may or may not accurately represent long term spiritual transformation.

A well-established Indian church planting movement and college, Hindustan Bible Institute, puts a high value on STMM that serve in several ways, each working alongside indigenous Christian leaders as part of their overall kingdom work. Medical teams from the US have served as guest speakers to local health care institutions to enhance relations with the Christian community, served to meet the needs of disaster victims when local health care is inadequate (like after the tsunami in 2004), served the population around the organization's satellite training centers with poor access to health care for enhanced community relations (like the centers the author served in Siliguri and Bhopal on 2005), and they have come alongside existing churches to express compassionate care and plant other churches, and expand the effectiveness of discipleship efforts (Gupta and Lingenfelter 2006).

In El Salvador in 2002, working with a large team of students and medical residents through Global Health Outreach, I observed the local church being highly effective in planning and participating in the eye, medical, and dental clinics, so that they reported a near doubling of their church attendance following these cooperative efforts. This organization emphasizes national partnerships to avoid dependency, promotes pastors conferences during their medical service projects to empower the host church's leadership for evangelism and discipleship, forms networks with specialists for distance consultation after the team serves in a location, emphasizes community health education, and helps disciple and teach up to 150 health care student participants per year (Molind 2007).

Another organization initiates STMM teams only upon the request of an established missionary team in restricted-access countries, so that the strategic needs are most accurately met. As is typical of medical missions, these mostly primary care teams draw in a large population, whose health needs are attended to and identified. Then the trained community health workers and missionaries in the host country can follow up in various homes, where health care needs are reassessed, and the gospel can be presented privately to those receptive to it (through community health evangelism). Though the process may take several years, it has produced at least one new church plant for each medical mission team, and enhanced the effectiveness of the long-term missionaries (Bivins 2007).

Community health evangelism, developed and promoted by Life Wind International (www.lifewind.org) which also hosts strategic short-term missions, seeks to integrate spiritual and physical ministries to transform individuals, families, and whole communities. They report that since 1989, 170,000 people have come to Christ through the program (www.missionresources.com/medical.html). When short-term medical professionals pass on their skills to indigenous tribal believers, they have been shown to use these skills to open doors for church growth in unreached places (Saint 2007).

To maximize effectiveness, STMM efforts should propel the participant into deeper involvement back home with their local church or community, establish ongoing partnerships with a mission agency or field, or prepare them for full-time missionary service (May 2000). Most career medical missionaries have participated in short-term work as a preparation and introduction to the call. Offering short-term assignments has helped mission organizations recruit health care missionaries. Ten percent of MAP International medical student short-term scholarship recipients ended up as career missionaries (VanReken 1987). One organization has observed that 2 to 3 participants per year give up their practices for full time missionary service (Molind 2007).

Models of Strategic Work

One form of short-term medical work includes working as an individual or small group in an existing mission hospital. World Medical Mission and other agencies seek to staff mission hospitals with short-term doctors to meet staffing shortages. The working visitor program, through which the author works as an interim staff physician at HCJB's Hospital Vozandes del Oriente in Ecuador has been successful in this regard. This mission, and many others, serve as a center for graduate medical education to meet the needs of the health care work force in the host country. This mission hospital itself sends teams of medical personnel to disaster areas such as Indonesia and Lebanon for short-term medical relief work, which serves to mobilize Ecuadorian doctors for global missions, and was reported to be a stimulus for the local Christians to be more mission-minded (www.mnnonline.org/article/9346, 6 Dec 2006). Hospital-based surgical teams that provide anesthesia, general surgery and specialty surgery are particularly effective in meeting needs that would otherwise go uncorrected given limited resources, and serving as training opportunities for surgeons in the host country.

Mobile medical clinics constitute a large portion of short-term work, able to access populations in more remote areas, some by bus, plane, self-contained mobile units, boat, or helicopter. These typically consist of setting up a system of crowd control and flow, registration (with papers for documentation), exam rooms, pharmacy, procedure rooms, and dental area, typically in a school house, tent, or other large building. The volume of patients can be tremendous, and often an equitable triage system is needed. In more open countries, the gospel is shared or a health-education, prayer or counseling station is set up. Simple mobile laboratory devices with or without microscopy enhance the quality of practice.

I have found it extremely valuable to work side-by-side with physicians and nurses from the host country, who can answer questions about local disease incidence and identify the referral networks. This partnership is valuable, and should be arranged before hand. An adequate supply of competent translators is needed, and in the pharmacy workers fluent in the local language(s) are needed to educate the patient, supplemented with clear, written or pictorial directions. Local health workers can participate in preventive health education alongside the team, and local Christian workers can be instrumental in counseling and prayer. These are efforts toward delivery of quality holistic care.

The transformational development approach in health care ministries requires long-term commitment and cooperation on many different levels among the people served, and is necessary to enhance sustainability. Nevertheless, there remains a role for short-term work to supplement these efforts. For example, I treated the sick and performed a Rapid Rural Appraisal of a semi-nomadic unreached Muslim people-group in North India for one week in 2005 that will be used for community health and development projects as part of the overall strategy of a mission agency to minister to their needs, physical and spiritual. The report also serves as an orientation for other health care workers, and as background for other assessment teams. This integration of short-term teams, under the direction of host country health care leadership that uses existing community resources, is a model that has proven effective in enhancing health in Peru and Russia (Berwick 2004).

Another strategy used by short-term medical workers is to send specialist physicians to restricted-access countries to teach at medical institutions, supporting the professional education of national doctors, and providing a forum to interact on spiritual matters as a testimony (e.g. MEI at www.cmda.org).

A Call to Strategic Planning and Preparation

There are standards of excellence in short term mission that can be applied to medical work, and should be referenced by leadership. These include God-centeredness, empowering partnerships, mutual design, comprehensive administration, qualified leadership, appropriate training, and thorough follow-up (www.stmstandards.org). I am currently involved in efforts to formulate "Best Practices for Short-Term Healthcare Missions" among STMM leaders. Preliminary consensus focuses on long-term partnerships and repetitive deployments, pre-field needs assessments, matching expertise with these needs, host-directed follow-up for sustainability, sensitivity to cultural healthcare approaches, a holistic approach, obedience to local laws and health care standards, informed consent, working within level of expertise, use of local or unexpired medications, spiritual self-examination and humility, and a "do no harm" approach (Soderling 2007). Strategic preparation for individual participants in STMMs should include pre-field orientation, on-site training, and follow-up debriefing in order to sustain impact on their lives in mission. Some of the following recommendations for both mission organizations and participants resonate with the wisdom of short-term mission leaders and missiologists (Rutt 2006, Schwartz 2003). Others are unique to medical mission work (Stevens and Rudd 2001, Jorden and Adair 1985: 317).

Going Where the Need Is

There are vast amounts of human disease and misery throughout the earth, but there are areas where the need is greater. STMM efforts should concentrate in these areas. There is an identifiable correlation between degrees of human poverty and disease, and the areas of the earth historically least affected by the power of the gospel. The unreached people groups who have no self-reproducing church should receive highest priority if the goal is global evangelization. Unfortunately, these arenas are more difficult to access safely, and the host missionaries and indigenous church are less capable of coordinating STMMs due to their limited numbers. Areas of the world with the highest poverty rates, or those most affected by natural disasters or political conflict should also receive priority status. The host people's public health authorities can best determine the areas of greatest health care access needs. There are also areas of the world with a significant Christian presence that are affected deeply by poverty, political oppression and pandemics such as HIV/AIDS in which compassionate care for others in the Kingdom may take priority. Both for the author and for several mission agencies, the experience of working in impoverished places in Latin America has been formative in preparation for working among the unreached peoples in Asia.

Practicing Quality of Care

Ensuring adequate training and qualifications in the medical specialty that best serves the health care needs of the population is important to maintain quality of care. The concept of sending non-professional servants on mission has been promoted (Peterson, Aeschliman, and Sneed 2003), but when it comes to competency of professional services like the practice of medicine, the qualifications should be no different than they are in the home country. Though medical and dental students can offer good care, they should be well-supervised and have access to more experienced practitioners. In Nicaragua I served as a medical student with little oversight due to the high volume of patients. This compromised the clinical decision making, and undermined the learning opportunity. Staff of mobile clinics should have a strong working knowledge of primary care, especially for women and children, who make up a high percentage of the population served (35% of the patients in my experience in the Dominican Republic were children). Surgical teams should stick to their area of expertise, even if called upon to perform operations they are ill-equipped to perform, unless there is adequate supervision. The axiom of Hippocrates in medical ethics, "first, do no harm" was also a description of love toward our neighbor in Romans 13:10.

The author found that his extra studies of tropical medicine in Puerto Rico were valuable in understanding and treating diseases in these settings, but not absolutely necessary to deliver quality care. However, a working knowledge of common diseases is important, especially dermatologic and infectious diseases, comprising 30-49% of all out-patient encounters in published studies (Spann 1986, Lesho 1995). There are many good diagnostic and therapeutic resources to be used for preparation and on-site reference such as the Handbook of Medicine in Developing Countries (Palmer and Wolf 2002). The World Health Organization can be consulted for country-specific health data (www.who.int). The practitioner must understand the limits as well as the potential risks of treatment. Long-term treatments should only be initiated if follow-up can be assured by local health care givers. If medications or supplies are left, they must be entrusted to reliable people qualified to dispense them appropriately. Working with limited resources, and a large amount of human need, the care must be delivered quickly and efficiently, using only the medication and laboratory testing that is absolutely necessary.

There are several good informal training opportunities in missionary medicine for the busy health care worker in preparation for short-term service. The yearly three-day Global Missions Health Conference in Kentucky drew 2,400 students, mission workers, agencies, organization representatives and healthcare professionals in 2006 (www.medicalmissions.com). World Medical Mission has a yearly two day missionary medicine seminar as part of its three day physician renewal conference in North Carolina (www.

samaritanspurse.org/PFR). The Institute for International Medicine also holds a two day conference yearly in Kansas City, MO and offers the accredited course on-line (www.inmed.us).

Adjusting the Attitudes and Motives

Preparation of the heart is as important as the technical preparation for a successful outcome. Concentrating on being a Christian should supersede the doing of the service. Assuming a posture of humility is vital, considering oneself more of a learner, rather than a teacher, even if there are technical skills that one can pass along. There will be much cultural and health-related on–the–job learning that will take place; however, preparation by reading beforehand about the people or country to be served is important. Knowing that the work will be hard will be easier to accept with a Christ-like attitude of, "I am here to serve, not to be served" (Mark 10:45). Flexibility and patience are essential character qualities when serving with unpredictable and limited resources. A study of the Biblical basis for world mission and for serving in STMM, like that summarized above, can have strong impact on the participant's world view and motivation, and therefore affect a better attitude toward the work and future ministry. Participants should remember that their actions speak louder than words. In the rigors of a developing-world environment, with limited resources, uncomfortable living conditions and numerous demands, it is a supreme challenge to maintain a good attitude and keep smiling. This takes faith and maturity, with a strong trust in a sovereign God.

It is important to relinquish a Western time, task, and results-orientation, and to be extremely flexible and relationship-oriented. Radical individualism and the desire for a quick fix must give way to cooperation to address culturally-determined long term solutions for community transformation. Concentrating on discipleship and training of local health care workers should exceed the independent doing of the medical services for longer-lasting benefit to the host peoples.

An analysis of motives is a personal exercise that a short-term participant should pursue prior to signing up. The most noble motives are those which seek to glorify God by practicing Godly love as it is expended thoughtfully and selflessly to those in need, and to the missionaries on the field. Seeking glory through being recognized back home or on the field, thirsting only for adventure, escapism from the stresses of medical practice, or wanting to make a tax-deductible contribution to oneself for an exotic working vacation is not practicing the mind of Christ (Phil 2:1-8). Despite the potential impurity of one's motives, the short-term medical worker can still be used as an effective part of global missions.

Understanding the Poor and Training Cross-Culturally

When working with the poor, a short-term worker must seek to preserve and strengthen people's dignity. When people are treated as objects of pity, their dignity is compromised. There must be sensitivity to the disparity in wealth between the team members, indigenous believers and the population served. There is much to learn from those who are poor in the eyes of the world but rich in faith. There must be a concerted effort to work *with* and not *for* the members of the local church in mutual-submission partnerships. This elaborates a strong testimony to the watching world, and facilitates vital spiritual follow-through.

Some basic cross-cultural training prior to the service project is important to prevent culturally insensitive behavior, which has been a problem criticized in the short-term mission movement. This training can be obtained from a DVD series called Go Prepared (www.stemintl.org), a manual (Steffes, 2002), a book (Livermore 2006), or an online course (www.chalmers.org). Culture is complex, and it takes years for a missionary to begin to understand the nuances. There are health practices that are culturally-determined, tied to the world views of the host peoples, and that may or may not be harmful. Understanding and dialoguing with indigenous folk medicine practitioners, whom many rely upon for health care, has been shown to be a helpful strategy, if undertaken with the necessary spiritual discernment (Seale 1993). An interest in, and working understanding of, herbal treatments and alternative practices of the target population should be part of the preparation for at least some members of a team.

Cooperating Broadly

Working in concert with local health care workers and facilities promotes better medical and surgical follow-up. A preliminary site visit and good communication with health workers serves as good preparation toward that end. Documentation of illnesses detected that were beyond the scope of treatment for the team should be passed along to local health authorities, especially if there are national programs targeting certain conditions like tuberculosis, cholera, or malaria. Short-term missions are excellent training and discipleship opportunities for students of health care professions and community health workers. Recognizing that one is a guest in the host country or people group should lead to acting like one with due gratitude and respect, cooperating with whatever community infrastructure is available to meet human needs. These needs are best assessed by the indigenous leadership. Fellowship with indigenous people promotes relationship building, and enhances the experience for everyone, but care must be taken not to boast about one's home country or criticize the host country or mission. Understanding the extra work needed by the host missionaries to lead a team, discerning their needs, deferring to their wisdom and direction, and being a servant to them to support their ongoing work can become a great encouragement. Health care workers often end up channeling their financial resources to the mission with which they serve, but making unfulfilled promises should be avoided.

Conclusions:
For Practitioners, Mission Leaders, and Missiologists

In the search for a way to participate in God's global redemptive purposes, health care workers can find a place to serve alongside the growing body of Christ in a way that is strategic and cost-effective, provided there is adequate leadership, preparation, cooperation and follow-through. Mission leaders can formulate better approaches to meeting of actual health needs while promoting effective church growth, missionary recruitment, and donor development. Efforts to complete a consensus formulation of Best Practices in STMMs can provide a much needed standard of care. Strategies must be developed to communicate these recommendations to every agency involved with this type of work.

Missiologists and public health leaders can reassess what factors are important in effective short-term medical work, and seek to gather much-needed data on outcomes for both physical health and spiritual health, particularly from the perspective of the host leadership. Research tools can be utilized, such as the International Quality of Life Assessment, which has been shown to be effective in assessing interventions on health outcomes in poor populations in developing countries (Ahmed, 2002). There are lessons to be learned from the collective experience of practitioners and scholars alike, so that the effort to serve in this way is redemptive for all parties. When these important factors are considered and practiced, and when more factors are discovered, analyzed and addressed, the participants grow, the poor are blessed, the Kingdom is expanded, the culture is transformed, and most of all, God is glorified.

References Cited

Adolph, Harold. 1981. *Medical missions' African legacy: For generations, missionary doctors have healed body and soul in Africa.* Timothy C. Morgan, posted 07/25/2003 Interviews; Billy Graham Center, Archives, Collection 169 http://www.wheaton.edu/bgc/archives/GUIDES/169.htm#2, accessed 2/10/07.

Ahmed, Sayed Masud, et al. 2002. Measuring perceived health outcomes in non-western culture: Does SF-36 have a place? *Journal of Health Population and Nutrition* 20(4): 334-342. See www.iqola.org for info on SF-36.

Berends, Willem. 1998. Mission and health care. *Reformed Ecumenical Council Mission Bulletin,* ARTICLE 4389. http://www.strategicnetwork.org

Berwick, Donald M. 2004. Lessons from developing nations on improving health care. *British Medical Journal* 328:1124-1129.

Bivins, Daniel, 2007. Medical mission response. www.mmronline.org. Personal correspondence, Feb 14, 2007.

Dohn, Michael N. and Anita L. 2003. Quality of care on short-term medical mission: Experience with a standardized patient record and related issues. *Missiology: An International Review* 31:4 (2003): 416-429.

Duininck, Mitch and Paul Williams. 2006. Disaster relief, our Christian mandate. *Mission Maker Magazine 2007.* Minneapolis, MN: STEM Press. 39-41.

Grundmann, Christopher. 2005. *Sent to heal!: Emergence and development of medical missions.* Lanham, MD: University Press of America.

Gupta, Paul R. and Sherwood Lingenfelter. 2006. *Breaking tradition to accomplish vision: training leaders for a church-planting movement.* Winona Lake, IN: BMH Books. pp.189-203. and personal correspondence with Dr. Gupta, Feb 13, 2007.

Guthrie, Stan. 2001. The Short-term missions explosion. *Missions in the third millennium,* article 8794. from www.strategicnetwork. org.

Hodge, Sydney R. 1913. *The appeal Of medical missions.* http://www. oldandsold.com/articles20/medical-missions-1.shtml, accessed 10 Feb 2007.

Hunter, Willie Jr. 2007. Medical ministry international. www.mmint. org. Personal correspondence, Feb 14, 2007.

Jorden, Paul with James Adair. 1985. *Surgeon on safari.* Wheaton, IL: Tyndale.

Lesho, EL. 1995. Planning a medical relief mission. *Journal of the American Osteopathic Association* 95 (1): 37-44.

Livermore, David. 2006. *Serving with eyes wide open: Doing short-term missions with cultural intelligence.* Grand Rapids, MI: Baker Books.

May, Stan. 2000. Short-term mission trips are great, IF. . . *Evangelical Missions Quarterly* 36: 444-449.

McDonough, Daniel P. and Roger Peterson. 1999. *Can short-term mission really create long-term career missionaries?* Minneapolis, MN: STEM Ministries.

Mitka, Mike. 1999. Advice for aspiring volunteer physicians and physician service Opportunities abroad. *Journal of the American Medical Association* 282: 413 -418.

Molind, Samuel. 2007. Personal Correspondence, March 2, 2007, Director of Global Health Outreach, Christian Medical and Dental Associations.

Montgomery, Laura M. 1993. Short-term medical missions: Enhancing or eroding health? *Missiology: An International Review* 21: 333-341.

Montgomery, Laura M. 2007. Re-inventing short-term medical missions to Latin America. *Journal of Latin American Theology* 2: 84-103.

Nelson, Kurt. 2007. The universal priority of proclamation. *Occasional Bulletin* 20:1: 3-6.

Palmer, Dennis and Catherine Wolf. 2002. *Handbook of medicine in developing countries, 2nd Edition.* Bristol, TN: Palmer and Wolf. (www.shopcmda.org)

Peterson, Roger and Timothy Peterson. 1991. *Is short-term mission really worth the time and money?* Minneapolis, MN: STEMPress.

Peterson, Roger, Gordon Aeschliman and R. Wayne Sneed. 2003. *Maximum impact short-term mission: The God-commanded repetitive deployment of swift, temporary non-professional missionaries.* Minneapolis, MN: STEMPress.

Priest, Robert J. 2007. Peruvian churches acquire "Linking Social Capital" through STM partnerships. *Journal of Latin American Theology* 2: 175-189.

Roberts, Maya. 2006. International volunteer medicine.[Letter]: Duffle bag medicine. *Journal of the American Medical Association* 296: 652-653.

Rutt, Douglas L. *What a mission executive would like those involved in short-term missions to know.* June 2006.

Saint, Steve. 2007. Interview with Steve Saint. *Christian Doctor's Digest* 12: 1. Bristol, TN: Christian Medical and Dental Association.

Schwartz, Glenn. 2003. How short-term missions can go wrong. *International Journal of Frontier Missions* 20 (4): 27-34.

Seale, J. Paul. 1993. Christian missionary medicine and traditional healers: A case study in collaboration from the Philippines. *Missiology: An International Review* 21: 311-320.

Slimbach, Richard. 2000. First, do no harm: Short-term missions at the dawn of a new millennium. *Evangelical Missions Quarterly* 36: 428-441.

Soderling, Michael. 2007. Best practices in short-term medical missions. Personal correspondence.

Spann, S. 1986. Family medicine in the tropics. *Family Medicine* 18 (2): 84-86.

Steffes, Bruce and Michelle. 2002. *Handbook for short-term medical missionaries.* Harrisburg, PA: ABWE Publishing.

Stevens, David and Gene Rudd. 2001. *Mission survival kit: Practical tips for successful short-term mission service.* Global Health Outreach (www.shopcmda.org).

Strauss, Steve. 2007. A single priority or two commands to be obeyed? *Occasional Bulletin* 20 (3): 1-6

VanReken, David. 1987. *Mission and ministry: Christian medical practice in today's changing world cultures.* Wheaton, IL: Billy Graham Center.

Endnotes

[1] www.mislinks.org/practical/shterm.htm, www.missionfinder.org/summer. htm, http://www.missionresources.com/medical.html, http://www.healthenations. com/links.html.edu/bgc/archives/GUIDES/169.htm#2, accessed 2/10/07.

CHAPTER 13

CHILDREN AT RISK IN SHORT-TERM

MISSIONAL ENGAGEMENT

GREG W. BURCH

Mission to the Piaröas

"It is going to be a long night," I whispered to myself as I lay back in my seat and prepared for our thirteen-hour bus ride to the town of Puerto Ayacucho near the Colombian border. I had lived in Venezuela for six years, primarily working with the ministry Niños de la Luz (Children of the Light), but life and ministry in Caracas in no way prepared me for this mission trip into the estado Amazona (Amazon state). On this trip I was joined by several team members and a group of boys living at the Lighthouse Ranch Boys Home, outside of Caracas.

It was early morning when I was awoken by the boy sitting next to me. "Hemos llegado al Orinonco" (we've arrived at the Orinoco), he told me. The famous Orinoco river was something I was looking forward to seeing, just not at 5:30am! Soon we pulled into Puerto Ayacucho. From there we hailed a pickup and made our way towards the community where we had been invited to minister. Upon entering the indigenous community we were immediately greeted by children of the village. It was obvious that the urban world had made its inroads into this village, for many of the people were dressed in non-traditional wear, and some lived in small concrete homes.

The children and youth who had joined us on this trip immediately re-connected with young people they already knew from a previous trip. We made our way over to where we would be staying for the next few days, set up our hammocks and organized ourselves. Over the next few days we helped with church services in the evening, and work projects and games during the day. The community leaders praised the young men for their hard work in the fields during the day. The boys that joined us on this trip played a central role in the ministry assignment.

Each morning, prior to leaving for ministry, the boys would gather together for a team devotional where they would ask God for guidance in their activities. Following prayer, the youth would begin their time of service in the indigenous community, painting, clearing land, and tending to other construction needs like electricity work; some were even involved in cooking. Everything was done in service to the local community where they were ministering. Each evening, after finishing the service projects and cool baths in a local river, the youth were given opportunities to teach about Jesus with local youth through games and movies.

Perhaps the most powerful aspect of this trip consisted of watching God use these boys to minister to the children and adults in the community. Upon our return trip to Caracas, as I sat in the dark bus preparing to fall asleep, one of the boys sat next to me and asked me to tell him my testimony. As I began to share my journey with him, it suddenly occurred to me that the dramatic transformation point in my life occurred when I was sixteen going on a short-term mission trip. It was at that point where God turned my life around. Marcos himself was sixteen and it was evident that God was working powerfully in his life as well. I found it to be no coincidence that we were able to share this adventure together.

Ministry to Street Children[1]

For several years now groups of young people from the ministry *Niños de la Luz* have been ministering to indigenous peoples in the interior of the country. The team prepares for such trips through prayer and fasting, raising funds, collecting clothes, toys, medicine and cross-cultural training. The youth and leaders seek to involve the local church community and others involved in the ministry in Caracas, Venezuela. While short-term mission projects have become commonplace for many youth groups and churches in North America, this group is different. *Niños de la Luz* is a ministry dedicated to reaching out to street-living and working children in the capital city, Caracas. As part of their ministry strategy, the mission team responds to the needs of children living under bridges and in dark alleys, shining light where there is only darkness. It is not uncommon for children to have drug addictions, and violence is a common survival technique. As part of the ministry's multi-faceted outreach program, *Niños de la Luz* runs a program called the Lighthouse Ranch which is located on a twelve-acre ranch nearly an hour outside Caracas. On the ranch are three homes where children live with house parents who care for them as if they were their own children. Some of the children leave the ranch within days after arriving, having been drawn back to the streets, while others stay for years, making the Lighthouse Ranch community their family. Each year, several staff members of *Niños de la Luz* invite a group of interested boys from the ranch to participate in short-term outreaches, mainly among indigenous groups in the Amazon basin. Over the past five years, the boys have ministered primarily among the *Piaröa* and *Warao* indigenous communities. Some young people have traveled internationally to attend mission conferences and have become involved in cross-cultural ministry in neighboring nations.

Understanding God's Heart for Children

As we have seen in the story of the young missionaries, God desires to use young people to extend his kingdom. In September of 2004, an international dialogue began about the importance of children in the kingdom of God.[2] What began in 2004 became more fully developed through the Viva Network's Cutting Edge Conference in September, 2005 in Cirencester, UK. A Biblical framework document, along with a variety of papers and articles, and a book scheduled for publication in late 2007 have resulted from this discussion, further helping us to understand God's heart for children.[3] The framework is made up of seven key principles. They are:

1. *God creates every unique person as a child with dignity.*
2. *Children need parental love in a broken world.*
3. *God gives children as a gift to welcome and nurture.*
4. *Society has a God-given responsibility for the well-being of children and families.*
5. *Children are a promise of hope for every generation.*
6. *God welcomes children fully into the family of faith.*
7. *Children are essential to the mission of God.*

Each principle represents a biblical understanding of God's heart for children. While all of the statements deserve to be touched upon and are critical to understanding the place of children in the mission of God, my focus throughout this paper will be primarily on principle number seven: *Children are Essential to the Mission of God.*

There are two possible ways to understand the place of children in the Community of God: (1) Children are essential in that the Church will never be what God intends for it to be until children become our emphasis in missional engagement and are invited into the Christian community; and (2) Children are essential in that their active participation is required in fulfilling the mission of God to reconcile humanity to himself. That is, we ought to view the mission of God both from a 'centripetal' and a 'centrifugal' perspective. As children and youth are invited into the Church, active participation in missional engagement should be both encouraged and result as a natural occurrence of their relationship with Christ. Historically, the Christian community has focused on children only as recipients of mission, that is, it is our role, as adults, to reach out to children. We are now beginning to recognize that such children are created with a potential for being agents of transformation.

What does it mean that *children are essential to the mission of God*? Like we have seen in the story of the young people participating in short-term mission projects in Venezuela, children and young people have an ability to not only participate with adults, but to be the central actors in spreading the Good News, crossing barriers and borders from church to non-church and distinct cultures to regions where the Gospel has not yet been presented and where the seeds of the Gospel have yet to sprout.

Historical Perspective

Children at risk[4] have an enormous potential to be used by God in his mission of reconciliation. Many of those who have been touched and transformed from horrendous situations of street life and abuse are being used by God to participate in global mission outreach today. Beyond the polarizing question: Should we do short-term mission? I am proposing an alternative approach that assumes the place of short-term cross-cultural mission today and encourages the active participation of those normally considered 'children at risk.'[5] There are few historical evidences of such practices to look at; however, some examples of children involved in mission do exist. At least some of these examples could be described as 'short-term,' although I am hesitant to include the term *mission* due to some of the violent approaches. Authentic mission is neither violent nor coercive.

The Children's Crusade of 1212 A.D. is one example of the efforts of young people to carry out missional engagement.[6] Initiated by a young boy named *Nicholas* from *Cologne*, the movement attracted thousands of children from Germany and France who responded to what they felt was God's call for them to deliver Jerusalem from the Muslims. While on their way to the holy city, many died of hunger and exposure while some were sold into slavery and faced a life of abuse (Sexton 2006). Their mission ultimately failed.

Another example comes to us from colonial Latin America. The friar, Toribio de Motolinía,[7] writing from New Spain during the 16th century, describes young indigenous people engaged in missional activities to reach other natives who had yet to convert to Christianity:

> Two years after the death of the child Cristóbal[8], there came here to Tlaxacallan a Dominican friar named Fray Bernardino Minaya, with a companion, on their way to the province of Oaxyecac. At that time the guardian of the monastery here in Tlaxacallan was our father Fray Martín de Valencia, of glorious memory, whom the Dominican fathers asked to give them some of the boys whom we had taught to help them in the matter of teaching the elements of the faith, if there was anyone who would, for God's sake, be willing to go to do that work. When the boys

were asked, two volunteered, both were very handsome children and sons of very important personages. One was called Antonio. He had with him a servant of his own age named Juan. The other was called Diego. At the time that they were about to start out, Father Martín de Valencia said to them: 'My sons, consider that you are to go away from your own land and that you are going among people who do not yet know God, and I believe that you will encounter many hardships. I feel your troubles as if you were my own sons and I am even afraid that they may kill you on your journeys (1950, 250-251).

These young missioners are said to be of similar age to that of Cristóbal, who earlier in Motolinía's writings is described as twelve or thirteen years of age. The boys bravely volunteer to go with the visiting friars to evangelize others who have not yet been told of Christ. Upon hearing of their possible death for volunteering for such a work, in unison, the boys replied,

We are ready to go with the fathers and to accept willingly any hardships for God's sake, and if He should be pleased to take our lives, why should we not give them for Him? Did they not kill Saint Peter by crucifying him and did they not behead Saint Paul and was not Saint Bartholomew flayed in God's service? Why, then, should we not die for Him, if that be His pleasure (1950, 251).

The boldness and bravery of these young people certainly deserves our respect and underscores their commitment to missional engagement during this time period in early Mexico.[9]

Another example, in more recent history, is that of Emma Whittmore. Whittmore founded the Door of Hope mission to street girls. Her first home was established in 1890 in New York City, but by the time of her death in 1931, she had nearly one hundred homes in cities around the world. Many of the girls whom Whittmore helped, later went on to become missionaries themselves, reaching people in the New York City slums and beyond (Tucker 1988). In this case we sense an intrinsic desire by the girls to reach out to young women in similar circumstances.

> In contemporary history there are other examples as well. Recent reports from Mozambique tell of thousands of children being equipped to care for the sick and to preach the Gospel, with a number of people coming to faith and being healed. We are also told of a children's congregation in Argentina and their ministry among business people during lunch time. They often go into the parks to pray for those so desiring. As a result of this ministry, the adult congregation has also begun to grow (Glanville 2007, 275-276.).

Children as Co-Participants in the Mission of God

It should not be too surprising for us to see God use children and youth that come out of disadvantaged backgrounds as central players in his mission. Several biblical characters surely convince us of God's power to work in surprising ways. Some of those whom God used mightily were: Joseph (Genesis 37); Mary (Matt. 1:18ff.); The Leper (Mark 1:40-45); The Good Samaritan (Luke 10:25-37); and The Samaritan Woman (John 4:1-42).

As is commonly practiced, it is one thing to participate in short-term mission work focused on reaching children, but it is another thing altogether to participate in short-term mission *with* children and youth who come out of at-risk circumstances. Most consider street children and other at-risk children to be victims of dire circumstances in need of service. While this is often true, I believe it is time that we consider, given their background, inviting them to participate in cross-cultural mission projects. Many believe that children must be given the opportunity to respond to the message of Jesus Christ, and I certainly concur with this belief, but I also believe we need to think about this from a different angle as children begin to integrate into the Church. One theory of participation that can assist us in our desire to involve children in missional engagement is the ladder of participation by Roger Hart (1992). Hart uses a ladder illustration to describe the importance of participation in responding to needs of children at risk, but I would like to apply the theory to the subject at hand, focusing on children as co-participants in short-term missional engagement (See Figure 1).

The steps of the ladder of participation develop a progressive approach towards full participation and child-centered action. The ladder progresses as participation moves from tokenism to an authentic child-centered participation. The lower half of the ladder includes *Manipulation, Decoration* and *Tokenism.* None of these developments would be considered authentic participation, but rather lead us to the use, and in some cases exploitation of children and youth as puppets of mission. Spiritual abuse can occur by coercing children and youth to be part of something that does not truly resonate with who they are as individuals. Care should be taken that children and youth are in no way manipulated or coerced into active participation in caring for others. This must be an authentic and compassionate response on their behalf. There are many churches and organizations that invite children to engage in short-term mission, but there are few that truly acknowledge the importance of a co-participatory action of engagement. Many prefer to allow children to participate to a certain level without granting a central role in mission involvement. Moving up the ladder of participation we find what we can refer to as areas of child-centered degrees of participation. These next areas consist of *Assigned but Informed, Consulted and Informed, Adult-Initiated Shared Decisions with Youth* and finally we encounter high participatory involvement through *Youth-Initiated and Directed* and *Youth-Initiated Shared Decisions with Adults* steps. These areas focus on a progressive approach to child and youth control over the actions and processes. As children and youth progress in their knowledge of God's mission, their active participation should be encouraged from passive participation to energetic involvement and leadership. In applying Hart's participatory theory to mission, it would be advisable to consider a progressive approach, one in which children and youth are mentored and guided into the later stages of full-participation. A mission project should not arrive at this point without leadership training and organizational skills development, but there should come a time when the children or adolescents are ready to lead a short-term project. Increased participation, such as *Child-Initiated and Directed* or, ultimately, *Child-Initiated Shared Decisions with Adults,* should be our goal for children coming out of at-risk situations. In fact, I believe this is a key issue for transformation in the lives of children coming out of high risk situations. *'To love thy neighbor' is probably one of the greatest restorative strategies we can offer these children.* Like we have seen with the participation of young people from *Niños de la Luz* in Venezuela, a progressive development of participation is needed in order to be fair to the young person involved. In Venezuela, the youth leadership has not yet arrived at a place where they are ready to take on the *Child-Initiated Shared Decisions with Adults* step in participation, but their increased involvement in short-term missional engagement has encouraged their place as agents of mission and empowerment, creating ownership of a very important ministry to people in need.[10]

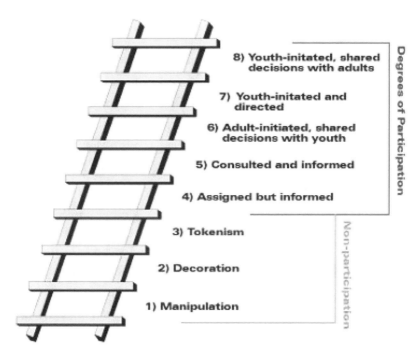

Figure 1: Adapted by Covenant House Vancouver (Hart 1992)

The ministry *Niños de la Luz* is progressively moving toward a higher youth participatory-action response in cross-cultural mission projects and stands as an example for creative solutions by encouraging children at risk to begin applying the biblical principle of caring for their 'neighbor.' One young man, after participating in a short-term outreach, said, "It was great to be able to cut the hair of the children and sense all that God was doing in their lives through me." Perhaps the key in this new understanding of child-led missional engagement is the place of empowerment through service.

Empowerment for Mission

The issue of empowerment is complex. Empowerment is regularly referred to in minority movements and political discourse, and has frequently been linked to people like John Locke, Karl Marx, Susan B. Anthony, Martin Luther King and Paulo Freire (Weissberg 1999). Empowerment is normally viewed as a top-down approach for enabling those who are considered powerless to increase their authority and power in any given area.

However, I believe that empowerment must be an internal choice; it cannot be forced upon someone. Kassey Garba (1999), in her article entitled "An Endogenous Empowerment Strategy: a case-study of Nigerian Women," calls for an *endogenous* empowerment that should be viewed as opposed to the typical *exogenous* approach too often employed by non-governmental organizations (NGOs), Christian agencies and churches. An endogenous empowerment perspective is a bottom-up approach that encourages the agent (protagonist) to bring about change; it is something that is acquired internally, something that the subject seeks out. *Exogenous* empowerment is a top-down approach, originating with the external agent, not from within the individual or group that has been excluded and disempowered (Garba 1999). By calling for an *endogenous* approach to empowerment, I am not saying that there is no place for external animation. That is, Christian leaders and community organizers can and should play a role in helping those in positions of powerlessness to discover their self-dignity and voice. Those in a place of influence can function as change agents and stimulate the conditions for the empowerment to occur.

Children's worldviews affect how they perceive themselves and others around them. This includes how they perceive their locus of control and assumptions about God.[11] One of the ways to encourage their self-dignity and healthy self-esteem is to encourage empowerment through missional engagement. If we continue to allow children and youth, coming from difficult backgrounds, to conceptualize themselves only as victims and passive recipients, we fail to rightly acknowledge the *Imago Dei* in which they have been created. As external leaders, those in a place of authority over young people, our primary task is to animate, that is, to blow the breath of life into the soul of the child and move them into action (Friedmann 1992).

In borrowing from Paulo Freire's concept of *concientização* (consciousness-raising), there must be an awareness of the social and spiritual conditions at work in any given community. Children and youth, coming from difficult backgrounds, are often force-fed information and rarely given the opportunity to discern what God might be leading them to do in his global mission.

Freire is best known for his revolutionary pedagogy which calls for a conscientization paradigm that encourages the poor and oppressed to be about "learning to perceive, social, political, and economic contradictions, and to take action against the oppressive elements of reality" (1993, 35). My purpose in addressing this ideology is to ask the question: What would happen if we encouraged children and youth to read the Bible with a missional perspective? The Bible is often used to teach children right from wrong; and while I do not deny its place in guiding children and adults in our moral development, I believe we must encourage children and youth to apply all of Scripture to their lives, including the call to mission. My assumption is that within each child that comes to faith in Christ, there is an internal desire to want to missionally engage with others who are in need, regardless of their maturity in Christ.

Contemporary Christian education is missing key ingredients in encouraging empowerment that leads to missional action in the lives of children coming from complex situations. Freire calls traditional education "a banking concept" (1993, 72). This banking concept can also be understood in the context of working with street children and others at risk. We often think of ministry to children as only beneficiaries, that is, they are a type of bank account and have nothing themselves to give. Freirean philosophy interprets human relationships as subject to subject, not subject to object. If we continue to view children and adolescents as only mechanical receptacles, we fall into a belief that children are only passive beings, those that are simply "manageable beings," in using Freirean terminology, and not regarded as people who can participate in transforming their own lives and the lives of others. Christ calls us to be transformers as well as recipients of love. The kingdom-of-God paradigm calls for a radical departure from the victim mentality that so many churches and organizations fall into when it comes to ministering to children at risk. That is, they view these boys and girls as simply victims of their environment and that they are the objects that we should invest into, instead of seeing them as givers as well, people who are just as much agents of transformation as the individuals seeking to care for them. While we cannot deny the fact that street children and others are victims, in the sense that they have been subjected to immoral and dehumanizing acts, we should move beyond viewing them as non-participatory victims. Children should be perceived as protagonists in the drama of life, with agency and ability to bring about hope in the lives of others. Ultimately, this kind of interaction with children and youth will lead into a pedagogical relationship, where both children and adult leaders are educated about the mission of God. My friend Duglas in Venezuela is a good example of this type of relationship

Duglas' Story

One of the first boys I met while on a short-term mission trip to Caracas in 1993 was a boy named Duglas. Since 1993, Duglas has gone through some severe trials in his life. In his younger pre-street life, he lived with his mom and stepfather. They lived in a poor neighborhood on the outskirts of Caracas. Douglas was sent to the streets of this mega-city to beg and if he returned with enough money, he would be patted on the head and be told "good boy." But if he returned with less than the required quota, he would be hit and cursed at.

Duglas made a decision one day to stay on the streets for good, to leave behind his life of abuse and to seek out an existence for himself on the mean streets of Caracas. He spent most of his time high on drugs and stealing food and other things he wanted. On occasion, when he and his friends were desperate for food, they would throw dead mice onto outdoor tables so that dinner goers would abandon their meals quickly, giving the kids time to grab the food and run. One day, while making contact with the boys on the boulevard, a colleague and I noticed him nearby. Duglas immediately showed us some sores he had on his stomach, which later turned out to be scabies. After being taken to see a doctor, Duglas was desperate to leave the street, so we invited him to the Lighthouse Ranch. Over time Duglas healed physically, but the years of abuse and street life made it hard for him to heal emotionally. One evening, while cleaning one of the boys' rooms, I noticed a knife under Duglas' mattress. He had become so accustomed to having to protect himself he still felt the need to have a weapon.

While living at the Lighthouse Ranch, Duglas began to show an interest in God and committed his life to him. He grew in his relationship with the Lord, yet still struggled with obeying the house rules and structure. One day we heard the sad news of the death of one of the boys on the street. Some of us from the ministry made our way over to the funeral home where the boy was being mourned. Hesitantly, I invited Duglas to come with us, knowing that he would want to grieve the loss of his friend's life, yet worried that he would come into contact with his old friends. As was feared, the group of boys with whom Duglas had spent most of his time on the street also came to the funeral. What surprised me was how Duglas responded to them. He powerfully proclaimed the hope and restorative power that is found only in Jesus. He shared what God had done for him and how much the Lord loves each one of them. This was a spontaneous reaction to having encountered God! We adults did not have to guide him through this experience. Through this occurrence I learned a lot about how God moves in the lives of young people who have committed their lives to him. I am grateful for friends like Duglas who have spoken into my life through their example.

Today, as a member of the *Niños de la Luz* staff, Duglas continues to proclaim the love of God to at-risk children. Duglas and his wife, Ismerling, are parents of two precious boys and are committed believers seeking to restore other children who come from at-risk situations (Burch 2005, 153-156).

Beyond Charity

The anthropologist and author, Tobias Hecht (1998), discusses the issue of *asistencialismo* (help-ism) and the tendency, within charities and church-based organizations, to over help the 'victim' in a way that prevents true transformation and creates dependency. Perhaps one of the reasons why we have not considered allowing the involvement of children at risk in missional engagement is because many are poor. Many feel that the poor do not desire to give, but rather only need to receive. This is simply not true.

Jayakumar Christian, in his book, *God of the Empty-Handed: Poverty, Power and the Kingdom of God*, says "Poverty does not . . . mar the potential of the poor to be agents of transformation" (1999, 50). The poor (including children at risk) can be agents of mission, holistically involved in both proclamation and good works. One example of the power of such young people can be seen in the political *Movimento Nacional de Meninos e Meninas de Rua* or National Movement of Street Boys and Girls (MNMMR) in Brazil. In June of 1985, the MNMMR was formed to shape street children educators and the children themselves into a political force that would fight against powerlessness and poverty (Swift 1997). "In May 1986, in the first event of its kind, some 500 street and working children—ranging from the most streetwise from São Paulo to the most unworldly from *Amazonia* [Brazilian State]—bussed with their educators into Brasilia for the meeting" (1997, 106). The youth and leaders went to the Brazilian national congress and protested the needs of poor children everywhere. They sought to bring about change to society. As a result of their annual pressures on the Brazilian congress and the work of child advocates, constitutional rights were awarded to children and now "family, society and the state are required to protect children and adolescents as a matter of absolute priority" (1997, 115).

Children and youth can become agents of transformation in society and in the Church. Padre Bruno Sechi, a Salesian Priest, was fundamental in the beginnings of the MNMMR. Prior to the conception of the national movement, Padre Sechi worked with a young group of Christians. They studied the Bible together and asked the question: What would Jesus do in the midst of such suffering and poverty? As a result of reading Scripture, the young people began to notice the needs of people around them (Swift 1997). It was this very group of young people that began to work with the street-living and working children and eventually formed the MNMMR. This is just one example of what empowering young people can accomplish. Full participation in short-term mission projects is something that can not only impact the lives of the recipients of mission, but the very young people that have been empowered to respond in the task of reconciling people to their Maker.

As we pursue the development of a mission mindedness in young people, biblical resources should be approached as a primary tool for focusing young people toward missional engagement. The Bible has long been a source of motivation for both short-term and career minded missional employment. I contend that children and youth, regardless of their current levels of social risk, should be led to Bible reading as a key resource for developing a missional approach to life. If literacy is a problem, alternative approaches to Bible reading (audio, story telling etc.) should be pursued. The Bible was instrumental in guiding me as a young person as I struggled with a number of potentially very serious issues during my childhood and adolescence. It was the positive influence of a few mentors in my life, and Bible reading, which led me to my first involvement in short-term mission action, which in turn transformed my own life.

One tool that can be employed in developing the idea of missional engagement is the place of a hermeneutical relationship. I believe dialogue or rather 'trialogue' in Bible reading can provide a resource for enabling missional perspectives in young people. As we pursue a 'trialogical' experience in our missiological reading of Scripture (see figure 2), we create a learning experience for both the child and adult alike. This trialogical encounter includes the place of the Bible, child-care worker and young person. Another way of stating this is that we need an integration of three voices; the Bible, the Christian leader and the child. Included in this cooperative encounter is the voice of the Holy Spirit, illuminating the Word of God to us as we read. The Holy Spirit speaks into our lives as we dialogue between Scripture and the context.

In the trialogical process we are seeking a multi-faceted approach to mission on multiple levels. As the Bible speaks to us and into the context, a mutual learning atmosphere develops where both the child and adult leader are internally empowered. The multiple levels in which this happens are: (1) Social realities and (2) Spiritual realities, without fragmenting the two in a dualistic way.

Another important Biblical principle that should be invited to speak into the context is the incarnation. The incarnation should focus our trialogue toward a place of real mission in the world today. David Bosch (1991, 21) wrote: "If we are to take the incarnation seriously, the Word has to become flesh in every new context." It is the incarnation of God that steers mission for both child and adult alike. As we invite God to enter into the mission conversation, we not only invite God to speak to us through the Bible, but rather we invite him to take over the conversation guiding the future direction, plans and strategy for engagement. So in the end, it is God who takes the primary role in the implementation of his mission.

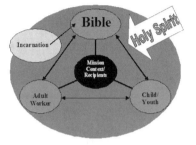

Figure 2: Trialogical Encounter for Mission Engagement

The Bible has a proven track record in guiding young people through their early years and should be our first priority in encouraging young people to connect with God's mission. Charles Van Engen (1996, 37) contends that "we cannot have mission without the Bible, nor can we understand the Bible apart from God's mission." The Bible is the main source for mission and without its voice we will fail to understand God's intent to mobilize wounded children into a mission force. As we encourage young people in Bible reading, we should be careful not to interpret the Bible for them. If it is necessary, basic understanding of culture and context should be explained, but the child and young person should be given the freedom to read the Bible as it is. The Church down through the ages has tended to see young people in Scripture in adult-like scenarios, failing to recognize their youthfulness. My experience leads me to believe that children and youth are not age-biased when it comes to interpreting Scripture. As adults, we often are led to gloss over the age and gender of those in the text. How often have we heard stories of Moses and Joseph without focusing on their age? As we enter into a dialogue with children and an appropriate understanding of the Bible reading, based on gender and age, we will enjoy a new understanding of some familiar passages. As children and young people are permitted to read the Bible for their own sake, they will naturally be encouraged to engage in the mission of God.

Conclusion

The current director of the ministry *Niños de la Luz* in Venezuela remarks about a recent short-term mission trip where she and a group of boys ministered to an indigenous community in the Orinoco river basin of the Venezuelan Amazon:

> "I can remember leaving from Alto Carinagua. José was crying as we boarded the boat that would take us to town. He asked himself: 'why am I crying?' After a few minutes, pondering this question, he said, 'I love doing this—taking the love of God to these people who have so many needs. I want to go to college and study and then go and share the word of God with people.'"

As a result of this short-term mission trip, José was profoundly impacted by the opportunity to participate in this project. This same boy, just years before, could be found sleeping on the streets at night and selling candy and roses during the day. She tells of another boy, Jorge, who had a similar reaction: "Another one of our boys sitting next to me as we left the village was also crying as he told me, 'I feel like I have left part of my heart here!'" She went on to say, "I'll never forget Jorge's first mission trip experience when he said, 'I haven't been able to sleep because I keep thinking how self-centered I have been, thinking only about myself and now I understand that there are other people with even more needs than my own.'"

As children who come from extremely difficult backgrounds involve themselves in mission service projects, they begin to find their true selves in service to others. The "neighbor" begins to become the center of their attention, leaving a deep impact on their own lives as well as those to whom they have been privileged to minister.

Missiological Implications for North American Churches and Agencies

While the primary focus on this chapter is on children at risk engaged in short-term missional activity within a Latin American context, several implications are possible for North American contexts as well. My own experience in leading a youth group to do short-term mission as a teenager myself has led me to believe that this type of mission activity is possible in other cross-cultural relationships as well. North American children and youth, as part of their authentic spiritual journey can and should be permitted to participate in holistic mission ventures that aim to provide a specific service to those in need. Just as there are young people in South America caring for the needs of adults and children alike, so North American young people should be given the opportunity to co-participate and lead mission projects whether in their own city or in neighboring states or nations. By giving young people in North American contexts an opportunity to co-lead and eventually plan and direct mission engagement, we are providing an environment for them to grow in their own faith as full citizens of the kingdom. I believe this kind of involvement will ultimately transform the lives of both the giver and receiver if appropriate engagement occurs.

> *"The wolf will live with the lamb, the leopard will lie down with the goat, the calf and the lion and the yearling together; and a little child will lead them"* (TNIV).
> Isaiah 11:6

References Cited

Bosch, David. 1991. *Transforming mission: Paradigm shifts in theology of mission.* Maryknoll: Orbis Books.

Burch, Greg W. 2005. *Community children: A ministry of hope and restoration for the street dwelling child.* Miami, FL: Latin America Mission.

Christian, Jayakumar. 1999. *God of the empty-handed: Poverty, power and the kingdom of God.* Monrovia, CA: MARC.

Freire, Paulo. 1993. *Pedagogy of the oppressed.* 30th Anniversary Edition ed. New York, NY: Continuum.

Friedmann, John. 1992. *Empowerment: The politics of alternative development.* Cambridge,MA: Blackwell.

Garba, P. Kassey. 1999. An endogenous empowerment strategy: A case-study of Nigerian women. *Development in Practice* 9:130-141.

Glanville, Karissa. 2007. Raising kids of mission in the 21st century." In *Understanding God's heart for children: Toward a biblical framework.* Edited by Douglas McConnell, Jennifer Orona, and Paul Stockley, Monrovia, CA: World Vision-Authentic.

Hart, Roger. 1992. Children's participation: From tokenism to citizenship. Innocenti Essays,Unicef, Florence, Italy.

Hecht, Tobias. 1998. *At home in the streets.* Cambridge: Cambridge University Press.

McDonald, Patrick. 2000. *Reaching children in need.* Eastbourne, UK: Kingsway Publications.

Motolinía, Toribio. 1950. *Motolinía's history of the Indians of New Spain.* Translated by E. A. Foster. Berkeley: The Cortés Society.

Sexton, Andy and Phyllis Kilbourn. 2006. *Offering healing and hope for children in crisis.* Fort Mill, SC: Crisis Care Training International.

Swift, Anthony. 1997. *Children for social change.* Nottingham, UK: Educational Heretics Press.

Trexler, Richard C. 1982. From the mouths of babes: Christianization by children in 16ᵗʰ Century New Spain, in *Religious Organization and Religious Experience.* edited by J. Davis. London: Academic Press.

Tucker, Ruth. 1992. *Guardians of the great commission.* Grand Rapids, MI: Academie Books.

Van Engen, Charles. 1996. *Mission on the way.* Grand Rapids: Baker.

Velazco, Gundelina A. 2002. *The worldviews of street children: Implications for the development of Bible-based resources.* London: SGM International.

Weissberg, Robert. 1999. *The politics of empowerment.* Westport, CT: Praeger.

Endnotes

[1] A familiar term to describe children living and working on the street is 'street children.' In the book *Community Children* (Burch 2005), as the title conveys, I argue that a more appropriate missiological understanding and term is that of 'community children.' In my book I go to great length to discuss why I feel the term street children is *not* the most appropriate wording for these children, however, due to its use in academic literature I will on occasion use it as well.

[2] In reference to 'children' throughout this paper I am assuming the United Nations definition and include anyone under the age of eighteen. I will, on occasion also use the term youth or adolescents as well when making specific reference to young people.

[3] See *Understanding God's Heart for Children: Toward a Biblical Framework.* Edited by Douglas McConnell, Jennifer Orona, and Paul Stockley. Monrovia, CA: World Vision-Authentic, 2007.

[4] In using the term 'children at risk' I am referring to "children in danger of not reaching their God-given potential, physically, environmentally, mentally, socially and spiritually" (McDonald 2000, 16). This term has become a familiar one to refer to children and youth coming from a number of particular areas of risk, such as: street lifestyle, physical, verbal and sexual abuse, malnutrition, extreme poverty, trafficked children, child laborers etc. Some argue that all

children who have not come to faith in Christ should be considered 'at risk.' While this is generally true, given the context of this paper, I am focusing on young people who have come out of one of the many social risk factors that have been mentioned above.

[5] It is assumed that these 'children at risk' that I refer to are children and young people who have come to faith in Christ and have acknowledged their need for the Savior despite on-going social risk factors.

[6] This event has been disputed by some historians. Some suggest that the terminology is not in fact referring to children, but rather to landless peasants. Some aspects of the event are most likely fictional.

[7] Fray Toribio de Motolinía was one of the 'twelve disciples' invited by Father Martín de Valencia to join him on his voyage to preach the gospel to the inhabitants of New Spain. He was also listed sixth on the list of invitees to New Spain in a letter sent to Father Martín de Valencia from the General of the Franciscans. Prior to the adoption of his new world name "Motolinía, he was referred to as Fray Toribio de Benavente. The friar took on the name Motolinía upon learning that it meant "poor" in the Nahuatl language (Motolinína 1950, 1-2).

[8] The child Cristóbal was a young person, reportedly, either twelve or thirteen years of age, who was found to be hidden away from the Friars by his father. The father sent his three other sons, as requested by the Dominican Friars, to the monastery. Upon the eventual conversion of Cristóbal, he began seeking to convert his father and remove the idols he had in his home. This enraged his father and one of his wives and thus they plotted to kill him, eventually succeeding in this (Motolinía 1950, 246-248).

[9] It is important to recognize that Richard C. Trexler (1982) argues that indigenous children were often used and exploited by Church officials in the evangelization of early Mexico. Trexler says, "The strategy of the Christian clergy involved pitting the young people of New Spain against their fathers and elders; in the early Spanish Conquest liminal group of the Indian young crossed, or were carried over, tribal borders and found new fathers among the Priests" (1982, 115). As Catholic Priests began to teach young Indians in the ways of Christianity, children were indoctrinated into thinking radically differently than they had prior to their internships. Many young natives were manipulated into committing violent acts upon Indian Priests and others in the name of Christianity, and they involved themselves in forcing others to convert to the faith.

[10] We must take into account basic child development and maturity levels. I am not suggesting that we expect a very young child to plan and implement a

complex humanitarian project, but rather we move towards the child/youth led mission project in accordance with their level of maturity and development. The adult project leaders are responsible to oversee the selection process of potential child-leaders.

[11] Gundelina Velazco (2002) presents one of the best studies on street children and their worldviews. The report is titled, "The Worldviews of Street Children," and is a research report focused on selected elements of worldviews among street children in Brazil, The Philippines, India and South Africa.

MISSIONAL BUSINESS
THE STRATEGIC AND PRACTICAL
PROFESSIONALS AS

PROFESSIONALS: USE OF BUSINESS EMPOWERED PARTNERS IN SHORT-TERM MISSIONS

MARK RUSSELL

This article is based on over 150 feedback forms and countless interviews of business professionals involved in intercultural volunteer missionary service. I have also conducted interviews with leaders of seven other organizations that are strategically and intentionally using business professionals as short-term volunteers. Among other things this article addresses the need to have a missiological foundation that affirms the contribution of the business professional as a business professional. It discusses strategic models for involving business professionals, such as seminars, on-site consulting, virtual consulting, business development partnerships, and business training for local entrepreneurs, missionaries operating businesses and mission administrators. The paper concludes with practical observations that are gleaned from personal experience, feedback forms and interviews.

Introduction

The Christian church has always used people with unique skills in the advancement of the Gospel in missions. Doctors, nurses, educators, and construction workers along with preachers and teachers have been a formidable group in missions. Like everyone else, business professionals have been given opportunities to participate in missions; however, they have not had much chance to use their unique gifts and skill sets. Tetsunao Yamamori wrote, "If the traditional Western missionary movement had some flaws this last century, surely one of the most obvious, in hindsight, was its failure to mobilize many Christian business professionals (beyond using their money) for the Great Commission. At the start of a new century and millennium, we can no longer afford this oversight" (Yamamori, 2003, 7).

Though it could be argued that the use of business in missions (BAM) dates back to biblical times, the current BAM movement is a very recent phenomenon. The term was coined in 1999 at a meeting at the Oxford Centre for Mission Studies (Johnson and Rundle, 2006, 24). It is a developing movement that is in need of missiological reflection and guidance. When announcing a call for BAM papers for the 2005 annual meeting of the Evangelical Missiological Society, Douglas Pennoyer wrote, "To put it bluntly, business as mission (BAM) is a work in progress. It is a field that needs definition, theological clarity, and missiological focus" (Steffen, 2006, 1).

The development of BAM has been the result of many factors. Increased awareness of global needs and the relative ease of traveling around the world are two primary reasons. These two reasons have also spurred the rapid rise of short-term mission volunteers. There are estimates that one and a half million Christians from the United States travel abroad each year on STM trips (Priest, Dischinger, Rassmussen, and Brown 2006, 432). STM researcher Robert Priest (Priest et. al. 2006, 445) has written, "Short-term missions is a huge phenomenon. It has great potential. But STM does not appear to be realizing this potential. We need to revise and clarify our goals, submit our claims to a process of research and testing, and devise the right sorts of research to help modify our ministry practices in God-honoring ways."

Business professionals as STM volunteers are a conflation of two rapidly accelerating phenomena, BAM and STM. Leith Anderson in his address to the EMS annual meeting on September 27, 2007 said that a plethora of mission agencies will be created in the next generation. Many such mission agencies are already being formed to meet the need of using business professionals in STM and it is my contention that this will be an ever-increasing phenomenon. The intent of this paper is to understand and explore how business professionals are being and can be used in STM. Beginnings are frequently marked by energy and passion but not as much by direction and reflection. We need to give sufficient thought to this important issue.

Four problems are a result of the ineffective use of business professionals in Christian mission. First, we have lost the services of a large percentage of the Christians who could contribute. Second, the business professionals who have engaged in intercultural mission have been forced to work in roles for which they are less gifted and qualified. This has resulted in ineffective ministry and frustrated professionals. Third, many business ministries that have been attempted in the mission field have had minimal results. This is partly because the people running the businesses are not business professionals. The result is frustrated missionaries. Fourth, since we have ministered through a restricted set of professionals (doctors, nurses, and preachers), we have inadvertently limited the groups of people we have served.

By promoting creative uses of business professionals as business professionals in missions, we can provide long-term solutions to these ongoing problems. First, we will provide a greater avenue for participation in missions. We can rightly encourage participation from business professionals on the premise that their unique skills and gifts will not be neglected. They are needed to meet the unique task of advancing the gospel in the current global situation. Second, business ministries throughout the world will reflect a higher quality. Qualified people will be the ones doing the job. Third, we will no longer be limited to using a restricted set of people to reach a reduced group of people. Neal Johnson has pointed out that business has "a remarkable capacity to touch virtually every person on the face of this planet" (Johnson, 2003, 87).

Compare a BAM STM to an STM construction trip. Construction trips are very common for many churches and in one sense do good in some locations. However, in general these trips have three significant problems. First, they often take people out of their skill and knowledge set. Obviously, professional builders and construction workers go on the trips. But more often than not the recruiting call is that anyone who can pick up a hammer can do it. Second, these trips incur tremendous costs, much higher than if done locally. Third, these trips take away jobs from locals who could do them. An alternative would be to bring down a construction "expert" who could share techniques and knowledge with local construction people, and where they could work together on a joint project. This would 1) enable travelers to work within their unique skill sets, 2) lower costs, and 3) empower the local labor force with payable jobs and additional training. These are the types of scenarios that can be and are being realized through BAM STM. But before we delve too deeply in the practical benefits of BAM STM, we should address its missiological foundation.

Missiological Foundation for Business Professionals as Short-Term Volunteers

In past years business professionals have expressed frustration that their role in God's mission was simply to pray, pay and obey. In order to incorporate business professionals meaningfully into our missions' activities, we need to adopt a missiological paradigm that sees their gifts and talents as vital.

The first step toward a firm missiological foundation for business professionals as short-term volunteers is to validate their unique contribution in meeting people's physical needs. Rundle and Steffen make the case that BAM should be done according to a clearly defined concept of holistic mission. They give four assumptions that are the foundation of their concept of holistic mission. The first is that God created us to do good works. The second is that opportunities to share good news are created when we do good works. The third assumption is that holistic mission responds to physical needs but does not stop there. The fourth is that holistic mission strives to bring people into the Christian family but does not stop there (Rundle and Steffen, 2003, 35-36). Broadly speaking, holistic mission is a missiological paradigm that "attempts to bring all aspects of life and godliness into an organic biblical whole" (Tunehag, et. al., 2005, 288-289). This includes business.

The second step toward a firm missiological foundation for business professionals as short-term volunteers is to validate their unique capacities. The biblical concept of corporate mission (1 Cor. 12:12-31) affirms that every part of the body is valuable and should work together. Business professionals need to hear at mission conferences and from church pulpits that their skills and gifts are needed. We need to proclaim clearly and loudly that we reject a hierarchy of holiness that has business people at the bottom and those in remunerated full-time ministry at the top. They are as important as vocational ministers. By affirming the unity of the body of Christ and the importance of the businessperson's contribution, we have constructed a missiological foundation that can support business professionals as short-term volunteers.

There are many ways business professionals can be used on STM trips. A survey of several organizations reveals six strategic models:

1) Seminars, 2) Training 3) Consulting, 4) Virtual Consulting, 5) Business Development Partnerships, and 6) Hybrids.

Seminars

Missionaries using this model host a team of business professionals who present seminars to local people. Generally speaking, the goals of these seminars are 1) generation of local business contacts, 2) stigma alleviation/status elevation, and 3) leadership access.

Cross-cultural missionaries in many countries seek to create awareness of their presence in the country through meeting new people. A business seminar allows missionaries to connect with local business professionals and community leaders who may be strategic for the missionaries' local work and who might also become followers of Christ.

Followers of other religions frequently view Christians suspiciously or negatively. By providing a legitimate service that meets real needs the fog of suspicion can sometimes be removed. Therefore, a second goal of this strategy often is to alleviate the stigma of the missionaries and their Christian co-laborers, and to elevate their status in the eyes of the majority people.

Another goal of such seminars is to gain access to strategic local, regional, or national leaders. By marketing and promoting the upcoming seminars, missionaries are able to meet, get to know, and spend time with prominent citizens and government officials in their regions. Normally it would be difficult to meet these people.

There are some advantages to this approach. First, it is relatively simple to organize. Missionaries who have no previous experience working with business professionals can generally set up a seminar quickly and easily. Second, the seminars can open doors of opportunity for missionaries. Often a missionary needs something to generate movement and action. Seminars have the potential to get things going.

This approach is a popular way to use business professionals because of its simplicity and common sense logic; however, many short-term trip organizers express mixed emotions with this approach. Feedback forms have also indicated that trip participants often have misgivings as well. I have been involved in several trips using this approach, both as a host and a trip leader, and I resonate with some of the concerns.

Case Study in Chile

When I was a missionary in Chile, I hosted a dozen business professionals on an STM trip. Our primary strategy was to have them present seminars at a local university where I was starting an outreach ministry. Through the process of organizing the lectures I was able to meet several deans and professors. The seminars were professionally delivered and well attended. At the end of each seminar, I made a brief presentation as to my purpose in Chile and gave the opportunity for anyone interested in studying the Bible to return a form indicating interest.

By the end of the week, I had received forty-four forms. We immediately considered the trip a success. Team members returned home and announced the good news. I was enthusiastic about the future possibilities. However, as I started to follow up on those forty-four responses, I discovered that many were already active Christians. A few who were not Christians expressed interest in learning more, but at my first meeting only one person showed up. At the second meeting, no one came. I called all forty-four respondents again. In the two months following the seminars I invested many hours of work, but in the end not a single meaningful relationship developed from the experience.

This is not to say that the entire experience was worthless. There were many positive results of a less quantifiable nature. I did have some meaningful spiritual conversations. A year later many students remembered me as the guy who facilitated the seminars. As a result of his experience, one of the trip participants returned to Chile as a career missionary. It is impossible to say how much this trip benefited our ministry in terms of status elevation and recognition. However, it is possible to say that the goal of developing a relationship network that would produce small groups of non-Christian students studying the Bible was not reached. Frequently, people have a tendency to take whatever happens in a ministry setting and reformat it so that we can say it was worthwhile or was a success. This experience was a success only in the sense that it was a learning experience and showed me what I should not do.

There were three primary problems that hindered the effectiveness of this project. First, we invested significant time with minimal measurable results. Due to the size of the group, we spent a lot of time preparing for the trip. Related to the group's size, we had to follow up on a substantial amount of contacts. This could be countered by restricting the number of business professionals that come. Frequently, missionaries and participants measure the success of an endeavor by the amount of people who participate. This is not necessarily true. In this case the size of the group created time requirements that prevented focus on the primary goals. This could be countered by bringing in more locals to help. This was not possible in our situation as this was a pioneer project. However, when possible, bringing in others can benefit in this regard.

Second, we had an inadequate filtering process of the contacts. Due to our desire to work respectfully in the pluralistic environment of the state university, we did not express our desire to reach out to the non-Christian student community. As a result, most of the people who expressed interest were already Christians. In later seminars, we had small break-out groups in which we filtered contacts through personal interaction rather than public announcements. Even though Chile is a religiously open country and there are no legal ramifications for openly expressing one's faith, we found that this more subtle approach was more effective for making the desired contacts.

Third, we also had an inadequate follow-up process with the contacts. Our follow up was hindered because we only had one strategy, namely to group interested people into a Bible study. It was also hindered because I was the only person doing the follow up. One way to solve this problem is to 1) develop a series of seminar-related meetings that will continue in the weeks following the initial seminar, and 2) announce these follow-up meetings during the seminar. The transition from business lecture to bible study is sometimes too big to be jumped immediately. Even though it is a more prolonged approach, it is helpful to have a more highly developed system in place.

Despite the problems we had, the lecture strategy can still be used effectively in certain situations with appropriate planning. However, to be done well it needs to be a significant part of a long-term ongoing strategy to reach the targeted community. Involving other Christians throughout the project can help with the set-up, contact filtering, and follow up. When the lecture model is used in an ad hoc manner to increase contacts, the results generally do not match the energy expended.

Training

Another popular model is the training model. It is distinct from the seminar model in that the teaching is more specific to the local needs and unique business operations. The seminar strategy is typically focused on large groups and the teaching is broader in nature.

When done well this model can serve multiple purposes. For example, a Cairo- based, Egyptian-registered company sells training courses in business skills and management. This company partners with a London-based Christian organization that provides the consultants who teach these courses. Although evangelism is not possible, the trainers clearly communicate biblical concepts and principles. The approach gives security to resident expatriate missionaries, training to aspiring Egyptian Christian entrepreneurs, and a way of developing relationships between non-Egyptian business missionaries, Egyptian Christians, and Egyptian non-Christians and generates revenue for other local ministry needs (Report on the Consultation on Business and Mission, 1997, p. 2). There are several different ways that this model is used. The following three organizations serve as examples for the most common adaptations.

HighMark Inc.

HighMark conducts over sixty short-term business trips per year with the purpose of mobilizing business professionals into "strategic, meaningful roles in world evangelization." HighMark has two goals: 1) transfer meaningful knowledge to local business people so that the local economy can be developed and 2) create a relationship network for local missionaries so that there is a context for effective evangelism.

In order to accomplish these goals HighMark believes that an intimate environment is necessary and, therefore, focuses on smaller groups. They average approximately three business professionals per trip, with one volunteer for every five attendees. They say that large lectures with thirty-five or more participants are essentially "a waste of time."

HighMark has developed packaged curricula for all of their seminars taking on topics such as accounting, finance and marketing. They note that this strategy reduces the workload for the volunteers as well as provides uniformity of services. Other organizations have critiqued the prepared curricula approach saying that it does not sufficiently integrate the personal insight, skills and experiences of the presenters. The critics argue that an interactive, dynamic approach is more valuable for the attendees and the presenters. HighMark seeks to counteract this disadvantage by having business professionals combine their training seminars with on-site consulting. They note that the small number of people involved allows for sufficient interaction and a personal touch.

In order to keep the focus on reaching non-Christians, HighMark does not allow more than 20% of the attendees to be Christians. They have noticed that if there are more than 20% Christians, they start to speak Christianese and the non-Christians leave.

They require participants to pay US$2500. This ensures that the participants are serious and successful. Furthermore, it enables HighMark to fund some of its expenses and ensures that the people in their target group are the ones that attend the seminars.

Consulting

Another strategy is consulting. In this model, business professionals provide consulting services to local business entrepreneurs, missionary-operated business ventures and missionary administrators. Approaches and purposes for the consulting strategy are varied.

In providing consulting to local entrepreneurs there are distinctions between working with Christians and non-Christians. The primary purpose of some organizations is to work with Christians. Generally they have two goals. First, they seek to reduce dependency on foreign church subsidies by strengthening local businesspeople. This enables them to contribute more significantly to the local church through increased profits. The purpose of this goal is to equip the local church to minister effectively within their own country with their own resources.

Second, these Christian-focused organizations seek to develop a venue so that local Christian entrepreneurs can share their faith with non-Christians. Unlike mission strategies in which only the missionary is the evangelist, these organizations show local business leaders how normal business interaction provides natural opportunities for faith sharing.

Other organizations focus their consulting on non-Christian entrepreneurs. Generally they also have two goals. One goal is to make a meaningful social contribution. By equipping local entrepreneurs to be more effective businesspeople, the consultants are building up social capital in the local community. The entrepreneurs hire more people, reducing unemployment. It also limits economic compulsion, the pressures that compel people to engage in socially destructive behaviors like prostitution and other illegal enterprises.

The help provided can often be quite simple but very meaningful. For example, Dr. Sandra Gray, President of Asbury College and professor of business management, regularly leads consulting trips to Central America. She worked with one business that produced t-shirts and had a print and copy center. They were losing money. Dr. Gray looked over their expenses and realized that they were making money on the print and copy center but losing it all on the t-shirts. Due to inexperience and lack of training, the owners did not have an adequate measurement system and had not realized this. As a result they eliminated the t-shirt business and overnight turned a "going into bankruptcy" business into a profitable one.

Another goal is to create a positive atmosphere for relationship development with the goal of gospel proclamation. By helping the people in a personal and significant way, doors are opened and bridges are built through which the good news can be shared. One organization says that approximately 40% of the entrepreneurs became Christians within one year.

The traditional missionary visa has gone the way of the dinosaurs, leaving many missionaries scrambling to find ways to stay in adopted countries or access new ones. A common approach is to start a business. Other missionaries see how economics influences the quality of life for the local people as well as their choices and relationships. Concerned about bettering their lives, combating social ills and creating opportunities for sharing Christ, many of them are also starting new business ventures. Frequently, in both of these scenarios the missionaries operating the new ventures do not have a business background. In these circumstances business professionals can provide invaluable assistance on a short-term volunteer basis.

One team of missionaries in Asia started a ministry focusing on businesspeople in order to reach their targeted people group. Initially, they invited groups of business people to present seminars. But after several trips and lots of work they had nothing to show for it. Eventually, they invited a small group of business professionals to come and help them develop ideas. As a result of these trips, they determined that actually starting a business venture as opposed to simply a ministry was the best approach to reaching out.

The business professionals returned in small groups, helping the missionaries develop a business plan and launch the new venture with minimal funding. The business venture is now successful in terms of the team's spiritual mission and is financially sustainable. This has happened because the missionaries partnered effectively with business professionals. The business professionals' help was more effective because the model was field-driven.

Another missionary in Asia started a business venture to provide alternative employment for sex workers. There was a tremendous response for employment. However, due to lack of experience and time, the project was losing too much money to sustain itself. A Christian businessperson became aware of the needs and developed a system for monitoring inventory, streamlined the supply chain, assisted with product design, trained the missionary team, and enhanced the local employees' basic business skills. They reduced costs, raised prices and increased their profit margin. As a result the missionary team is able to provide more women with dignified employment, and conversations on the gospel flow freely in the workplace.

The third way business professionals use consulting is to assist mission support personnel. Missionaries, whose primary interest is often interpersonal ministry as opposed to office administration, staff many mission offices. Furthermore, many mission support offices cannot keep up with new administration technologies and techniques due to remote locations and/or lack of financial means.

On several short-term trips we sent business professionals into mission support offices for one to two days. The results were almost always transformational. Just a few tips or installed software helped the local administrators dramatically improve operations. This, of course, has an immeasurable impact on the future performance of the support office. This increases efficiency of financial stewardship, saves valuable kingdom time, and has the potential of significantly improving ministry effectiveness of all personnel.

Virtual Consulting

Virtual consulting is a recent development. This strategy harnesses the power of the Internet and other information technology products so that business professionals can provide consulting services from afar. This may or may not be done in conjunction with on-site consulting visits. The primary goal of this approach is to increase effectiveness of operations. Due to distance, the relational dimension is diminished. Like regular consulting this approach can service local entrepreneurs, missionary-operated businesses and mission administrators.

In servicing local entrepreneurs, an on-site consulting visit usually precedes the virtual consulting. Once business professionals are aware of the issues and needs of the project, they are able to provide guidance. Since most business professional trips are short (seven days or less), the on-site interaction tends to be minimal. However, once the business professionals return home, they can continue to monitor and give insights to the local entrepreneur. This can be as simple as exchanging emails or something more complex like graphic design, accounting assistance or technology advice.

In order to support missionary-operated businesses and mission administrators, frequently on-site visits are not needed. Several businesses that I interviewed used business professionals in their home country to develop web pages, establish distribution channels and give strategic insight into the project without ever visiting the business location.

Two difficulties with this approach have emerged. First, due to distance, there is a reduced relational connection. This has been more of a concern in dealings with local entrepreneurs. However, this can be counteracted in two ways. The first and most obvious way is that the local missionary or Christian community should be aware of the exchanges and follow up with on-site visits. These visits do not need to be business oriented in nature. The missionary can simply check in, offer prayer and ensure that everything is going well. A second way is for the virtual business consultant to return to the same location on an annual (or as much as possible) basis. Through his letters the Apostle Paul ministered from afar. With the gift of information technology; business professionals can do so as well.

The second and slightly more complex disadvantage is that some business professionals have not maintained the level of service expected by those receiving the consultation. Due to time commitments in their home country, some business professionals simply drop out of the exchanges. One missionary told me that a project they were doing was held up for six months because the business professional volunteer never completed his expected contribution. This is, unfortunately, a common problem in operations dependent upon volunteers. Many organizational plans are thwarted because the organization has no recourse. Working preventively can counteract this problem. First, one should clearly communicate the expectations beforehand and arrive at a mutually agreed upon understanding. A second way is to affirm the voluntary contribution of the business professional on a regular basis. Many business professionals have testified that they have become frustrated when they felt that their contributions were not helping or were not recognized adequately.

Business Development Partnerships

Another emerging model is the business development partnership model. This is more complex since the relationship is a partnership rather than a consulting support relationship. Generally this involves financial investment in for-profit businesses in the developing world by professionals in a developed country. Local Christian entrepreneurs or expatriate missionaries manage these businesses. Since financial investment is involved, these partnerships may not qualify as a legitimate volunteer endeavor. However, I mention it here because the partnership can be subsidized with volunteer labor. Furthermore, the expected return on investment is frequently lower than normal because the investor is supportive of the social and kingdom purposes of the business. Therefore, there is a volunteer quality to many of these operations.

There are other partnerships that do not provide financial investment. For example, a church can adopt a local entrepreneurial endeavor as a partner. They may have no financial stake in the business but simply desire to see it succeed for kingdom purposes. This goes beyond general consulting as the relationship is long-term, sustained by multiple teams and is integrated into the growth strategy of the business.

From my research it does not appear that this model is widely used. However, it seems to hold much promise. First, focus is good. Instead of sending business professionals far and wide, it is worth concentrating their efforts in a few locations so that their contribution is more long lasting and direct. Second, in a church-business project it is easier to complement the business services with other ministry possibilities. For example, there is one business that primarily employs women. In order to employ women, they provide a day care center for the employees. Through the church partnership, the business receives ongoing consulting from business professionals in the church. However, other people from the church accompany the business professionals and lead activities with the children in the day care such as vacation bible school. This type of synergy creates a dynamic environment for maximum kingdom impact. Another missionary-operated business is itself a day care center for working mothers. Through a church partnership, business professionals provide assistance to the business side of the day care center while other church members help to enhance the ministry interaction with the children.

Hybrids

Many organizations intentionally and strategically use a combination of two or more of the aforementioned models.

Global Business Success Foundation

The purpose of the Global Business Success Foundation (GBSF) is to be relevant to unreached people groups (UPG) through the use of business professionals in cooperation with missionaries. They combine training with seminars. Seminars are offered as university lectures and the training is provided to specifically targeted business people.

GBSF trips have two goals. The first is to train local believers in business skills so that they can create wealth and steward their finances. These local believers, in turn, can develop the local economy and wisely utilize limited resources. The heartbeat of this goal is to reduce dependency on foreign subsidies for ministry and to create locally the finances needed "to fulfill the Great Commission within that country."

A second goal of the training trips is to equip local Christian business owners, marketplace leaders and entrepreneurs to be effective in outreach. The training seminars are not simply about business but also teach Christians how to leverage their marketplace position for evangelistic purposes. The trainers seek to open the Christians' eyes to the possibilities of sharing Christ within their natural business interactions. They also help them develop appropriate methodologies for proclaiming the good news in the marketplace.

Many organizations have complained that missionaries do not adequately follow up with the contacts developed through their presentations. Frequently missionaries agree to host a business professional group but do not have a long-term strategy for ministering to the local business community. In order to avoid this problem GBSF works exclusively with missionaries who are specifically reaching out to business professionals. They estimate that only one in fifteen missionaries is interested in partnering with them. This focus serves as a filter for the organization.

Though they have had opportunities to work directly with local business people instead of in cooperation with local missionaries, GBSF has chosen not to do so. There are several reasons for this. First, missionaries committed to reaching out to the local business community can follow up. Second, missionaries understand both cultures and they can bridge the cultural gap for the visiting volunteers. Third, by working with missionaries, there is a shared understanding of the approach used by the volunteers. This is not only a shared ethical and biblical framework, but also an economical and business one. This shared understanding enhances the partnership and allows them to communicate collaboratively to those who do not understand these issues in the same way. Fourth, missionaries have gone through an extensive application process in order to be accepted by a mission agency. Thus GBSF feels that a relationship with the mission agency not only provides follow up, guidance and shared understanding but also accountability and trust.

GBSF does not have prepared seminars, preferring to leverage business professionals' unique skills and experience in the teaching. They train the volunteers in the local culture and to be a BAM ambassador. GBSF expects the volunteers to be well prepared for their seminars and this has not been a problem.

Their training is provided to large groups of twenty-five to thirty people. On the trips the volunteers also visit local factories and businesses. However, the purpose of these visitations is not to provide consulting or further training, but rather to learn more of the local needs so that they can better serve them in the future.

The GBSF model has four strategic advantages. First, it is a field-driven approach. By partnering with local missionaries who are focused on reaching the local business community, it creates synergistic environments. Second, it is relevant to the local situation. The strong missionary connection enables them to understand the local culture and its needs. Third, the approach empowers the locals. By focusing on encouraging the local believers, it creates a context through which the locals can reach their own. Fourth, the approach empowers the lay volunteers by utilizing the business professionals in their unique skills and expertise.

There are some challenges to the GBSF model. By avoiding pre-packaged materials, they are not able to offer uniformity of services. The quality of the presentations varies considerably, based on the skills of the person presenting and the time they dedicate to preparing. Another trade off is that they have focused on relatively large groups of twenty-five to thirty people. This does not allow much relational intimacy to develop on the trip. Thus the success of the endeavor is largely dependent on the follow-up effectiveness of the local missionaries.

Encourage Inc.: Training + Consulting

Encourage Inc. (pseudonym) provides a unique service that combines consulting and training, working solely with Christian business owners in foreign countries. Their primary goal is to teach the owners how their businesses can bring glory to God. They teach that God values work and that the Bible speaks clearly about business. They instruct owners to view their companies as extensions of the biblical household. The desired result of the training is for the business owners to know how to operate their businesses in an ethical and competitive manner.

On every Encourage trip, ten business professionals travel to a foreign country. These ten foreign consultants are paired with ten local consultants. Each pair of consultants serves a single business owner. Thus each trip involves thirty people focused on ten distinct businesses. All involved are Christians. Encourage Inc has written a pre-trip training curriculum. Every consultant, local and foreign, completes the twelve-week training, approximately a 100-hour commitment. This ensures that the consultants understand and are ready to teach Encourage's view of business. It also means that everyone is trained equally. Encourage Inc. strongly values equality and feels that the shared training experience abolishes hierarchical tendencies and promotes an egalitarian understanding between the consultants and participants.

Pairing foreign consultants with local consultants serves three primary purposes. First, it gives the teaching and the experience a local flavor. This prevents the teaching from being too Western or American. Furthermore, it helps the foreign consultants adapt more easily to the local culture and decrease cross-cultural blunders.

Second, having a local consultant helps the business owners have relationships with other local Christians. As a result they can encourage and hold one another accountable to their newly developed and shared understanding of the high calling of business.

Though the foreign consultants can stay in touch through email and return trips, having a local connection is seen as more meaningful and effective in enacting sustainable, long-term change.

Third, this increases the foreign consultants' understanding of the local needs. The local consultant has been through the same training curriculum. Therefore they have a common language and understanding with the foreign consultant. However, as a local businessperson they have a common language and understanding with the other local business owner. Thus they are able to communicate clearly the needs of the business owners to the foreign consultants. Encourage Inc. believes this dramatically increases the effectiveness of the interactions.

Encourage Inc. charges reasonable fees based on the local market for the services they provide. This serves two purposes. First, the local participants are committed to learning and changing future operations. Second, Encourage Inc. is able to offset some of its expenses through the capital generated from the training and consulting.

A team leader who is not a foreign consultant does all of the training seminars. Like HighMark the training presentations are packaged seminars. In order to offset the perceived staleness of packaged seminars, the presenters integrate their personal stories and life experience with the material. During the presentation the foreign consultant, local consultant and business owner all sit together. Thus they are able to interact with one another as the seminars are presented. Following the seminars the groups of three then go to the local business and consulting services are provided for the rest of the time.

This model has several strengths. First it is very field-driven. The local needs and culture are respected and understood. Second, as a result of a developed training system, the organization can replicate the seminars in various locations. Third, by combining training and consulting, the organization not only provides uniformity of services but also the necessary flexibility to address the unique needs of the local situation.

There are some challenges with the approach. First it is very time consuming. Volunteers have to devote 100 hours to training before the trip. This is by design, as Encourage Inc. only wants to work with business professionals who can make a serious commitment. A second challenge is that thirty people have to conform to the approach of the trip as well as the timing of it. They do not do trips unless all ten foreign consultants are matched with ten local consultants and ten local Christian business owners have paid for the service. Encourage Inc. accepts these challenges as a necessary component for providing high-quality, long-term, sustainable, and transformational services. They generally find that ten businesses directly affect 25,000 people and indirectly impact many more. In a recent venture to Southeast Asia the local businesses served over 30 million customers, more than 10% of the population.

Practical Observations

There are several observations that can be seen from the models and research mentioned above, which highlight principles which contribute to success.

Strategic Alignment

Using business professionals as volunteers is probably not worthwhile unless it aligns with the local strategy. This is probably true for all short-term mission trips (Zehner 2006, 509-521). However, unlike other short-term mission approaches, using business professional generally requires greater focus and long-term follow up in order to be effective. For example, a short-term medical team can treat people and have a long lasting impact in a relatively short time. A construction team can build a church or community center during their stay. However, with the approaches used for business professionals, follow up for evangelistic or sustaining business operations is generally required. Thus it can be said that using business professionals as volunteers is not for everyone. However, if it aligns with the local strategy it can be very effective.

In my research most business professionals expressed frustration about missionaries who 1) host the trip but are not convinced of the concept, 2) do not see the business professionals' contribution as uniquely and genuinely significant, 3) are not committed to follow up and 4) appear threatened by the business professionals. These frustrations are not present when there is strategic alignment. In cases of strategic alignment, missionaries understand the concept, validate the business professionals' contribution, follow up appropriately and are not threatened by the business professionals. This creates a virtuous cycle in which the business professionals' contribution is more effective, the missionaries' ministry is advanced and both parties are encouraged through the experience.

It is worth noting that effective follow up can be done in several ways. Some missionaries use what they call roundtables. These are small groups of local business professionals that meet on a regular basis to discuss issues. These roundtables can be composed of Christians, non-Christians or a mix of both. The missionaries can serve as facilitators for the groups and do not have to be experienced in business.

Missionaries can also network Christian and non-Christian business professionals. This means that they provide a means for them to get to know one another and continue developing the relationship. This can be done through one-time meetings or social gatherings.

Follow up can also be done through subsequent training opportunities or seminars. This is effective when the sending organization can commit periodic volunteers over an extended period of time and the missionaries are still trying to establish themselves in the local situation. Alternatively, the missionaries and/

or local Christian businesspeople can offer the follow up seminars. When possible, follow up should be done in partnership with local Christians.

Positive Environment

In order to use business professionals effectively it is essential to create an environment in which business professionals are able to use their skills, interests and passions. Interviews with business professionals demonstrated that they are frequently disinterested in church mission activities because they feel their gifts are not utilized or that they, themselves, are put in situations in which they are unfamiliar and uncomfortable. Business professionals want to contribute in line with who they are. Therefore, it is important to match their personal contribution with a particular situation. They (and the mission) will benefit more if they are truly meeting a need in their unique way as a business professional. Thus a positive environment for business professionals means that their contribution is authentically integrated into the overall mission and not in a tangential or ad hoc manner. They do not simply need to be involved in mission activities; rather they need to be integrated as business professionals into mission.

Small is Beautiful

Research seems to indicate that small teams of business professionals are more effective than large ones. Missionaries, business professionals and BAM organizational leaders all mentioned this. This is, of course, not an absolute. Encourage Inc. uses rather large groups. However, they have an established preparation process and strict organizational requirements. This enables them to work effectively with large groups. For those who do not want to establish such an organization and desire more fluidity, this is best done with small groups.

Small teams are beneficial for practical reasons. Transportation and other logistical matters are easier and less time consuming. It also enables the small teams to respond dynamically to the local situation.

Short is Sweet

For family and work reasons, business professionals are typically limited in their ability to take extended vacations. Therefore, trips tend to be seven days maximum from departure to return. Longer trips dramatically reduce the pool of available professionals. Priest, et. al. (2006, 432), have noted that two-thirds of short-term trips are for two weeks or less. However, my research indicated that for business professionals, approximately 80% of the trips were six or seven days.

Dynamic Partnerships

Many of the organizations researched do not self-identify as mission agencies and many expressed hesitation and frustration in working with mission agencies and/or missionaries. However, the vital role of the missionary should not be dismissed. Missionaries are valuable because they can provide spiritual direction to business professionals from both countries. They can help incoming business professionals with intercultural insights. They can continue in-country relationships after the trip. Missionaries who understand their unique contribution can dramatically increase the effectiveness of all interactions.

However, mission agencies should not wait for the business professionals to come to them. Entrepreneurial pioneering types are doing much of the current work. Mission agencies should be open to their participation and actively pursue developing partnerships with them. Through dynamic partnerships between local ministers and traveling professionals, we can reach the common goal of loving God and neighbor and transforming society.

Organizational Focus

Organizations that are effectively using business professionals in STM have a very clear focus on their purposes and processes. They have clear structures that are well communicated to all parties. The responsibilities, boundaries and expectations are well understood. There are systems of measurement in place that hold everyone accountable to the mutually agreed upon goals. Everything is done with excellence, exuding professionalism in the smallest detail.

Simplicity is key and missionaries should not rush to use multiple strategies until the foundation is stable and the system is producing results. A strong focus on the unique purpose for using business professionals should be maintained. This focus and purpose should be repeated often to the business professionals, other missionaries, local Christians and other local business professionals as appropriate.

Conclusion

These six strategic models express how business professionals are being used effectively in STM today. As this is a newly developing movement it is very likely that other models will be created in the near future. However, these models can help mission agencies, BAM practitioners and others see what is being done and what lessons have been learned.

Soli Deo Gloria.

References Cited

Johnson, C. Neal. 2003. Toward a marketplace missiology. *Missiology: An International Review* 31: 87-97.

Johnson, Neal and Steve Rundle. 2006. Distinctives and challenges of business as mission. In Tom Steffen and Mike Barnett (eds.), *Business as mission: From impoverished to empowered* (Pasadena, CA: William Carey Library).

Priest, Robert J.; Terry Dischinger; Steve Rasmussen; and C. M. Brown. 2006. Researching the short-term mission movement. *Missiology: An International Review* 34: 431-450.

"Report on the Consultation on Business and Mission," held on Wednesday 19 February 1997 in London, England, p. 2, available from *http://www.globalconnections.co.uk/business.asp*; Internet, accessed on 25 August 2004.

Rundle, Steve and Tom Steffen. 2003. *Great commission companies: The emerging role of business in missions.* Downers Grove, IL: Intervarsity Press.

Steffen, Tom. 2006. Introduction. In Tom Steffen and Mike Barnett (eds.), *Business as mission: From impoverished to empowered.* Pasadena, CA: William Carey Library.

Steffen, Tom and Mike Barnett. 2006. *Business as mission: From impoverished to empowered.* Pasadena, CA: William Carey Library.

Tunehag, Mats; Wayne McGee; and Josie Plummer (eds.). 2005. Business as Mission. In David Claydon, Ed., *A new vision, a new heart, a renewed call: Lausanne occasional papers from the 2004 Forum of World Evangelization hosted by the Lausanne Committee for World Evangelization in Pattaya, Thailand.* Pasadena, CA: William Carey Library.

Whitner, Steve. 2003. The value of short-term missions. In Bill Berry (ed.) *Short-term missions today.* Pasadena, CA: Into all the World Magazine, pp. 54-58.

Yamamori, Tetsunao and Kenneth A. Eldred (eds.). 2003. *On kingdom business: Transforming missions through entrepreneurial strategies.* Wheaton, IL: Crossway Books.

Zehner, Edwin. 2006. Short-term missions: Toward a more field-oriented model. *Missiology: An International Review* 34: 509-521.

CHAPTER 15

SHORT-TERM MISSIONS AND THE LAW

LESSONS FROM CANADA

CHARLES A. COOK

The recent capture and release of a group of short-term mission participants in Afghanistan has, among other things, raised the issue of organizational liability and risk management. Following the release of the nineteen hostages, Taliban spokesman Yousef Ahmadi informed the Associated Press that the Taliban would "...*do the same thing with the other allies in Afghanistan, because we found this way to be successful*" (Shah 2007,1). Ahmadi's cryptic warning suggests that those involved in short-term missions may continue to be the target of various forms of extortion. The ongoing clash between religious ideologies (Barber 1999; Huntington 1998; Jenkins 2002; Klein 2007) and the ever-increasing uneven distribution of the world's wealth (De Soto 1999; Gray 1998; Micklethwait 2000) certainly make further incidents a real possibility. How the marginalized and disenfranchised of the world will respond is unknown.

Missions have always been dangerous. Previous generations had to contend with shipwreck, persecution and disease. Today's global servants deal with home invasion, pollution, kidnapping and terrorism. The reality is that there are relatively few safe places in the world.

Despite such global realities, there is an increasing Canadian interest in voluntourism[1] and church-to-church contact through short-term mission (STM) trips.[2] These grass roots movements have set the stage for a number of interesting intercultural and missiological conundrums. The Afghanistan incident is a reminder that local churches working on the international stage need to be fully aware of risks. The relative safety of the West often blinds Canadians to the inherent risks associated with short-term global engagements. Some have even dismissed concerns regarding liability and risk management as unspiritual; offhandedly insisting that *"God will take care of us."*

While it is true that our times are in God's hands, such convictions should not preclude thoughtful and responsible planning for potential eventualities. "Religious organizations," observes lawyer Terrance Carter, "often function on the mistaken assumption that their dedication to spiritual values elevates them above the need to deal with mundane matters of complying with the laws of the land" (2005, 8). Unfortunately in short-term missions, as in life, *everything changes when something goes wrong.* Consequently, churches must not understate the potential dangers of sponsoring an STM trip and must explicitly recognize that a lack of awareness of the law can lead to litigation. Balance, of course, is critical. Understating the dangers can lull the church into an unhealthy complacency regarding how it carries out the mission of God, while excessive concern over danger and liability can potentially paralyze the church into inaction. Lawyers Cassels, Brock and Blackwell (2004, 1) highlight this tension, acknowledging that:

> While it is … true that many cherished institutions are under attack and that society, in general, has become more litigious, the matter is particularly acute in the charitable and non-profit sector because, for the most part, the law provides no special protection to them with respect to the conduct of those persons through whom they carry on their activities, where such persons are paid or unpaid. Apart from altruism, the value of which should not be underestimated, there is no counter-balance to this exposure to liability. Thus, charities and non-profit organizations find that they are faced with many of the same challenges as for-profit entities, but without the same resources.

Local church inattention to the potential legal exposure associated with short-term missions is highlighted in a 2006 study by Ambrose Seminary (formerly Canadian Theological Seminary) students on "*Researching Canadian Short-Term Missions.*" The students examined the way 146 Canadian evangelical churches defined, used, and implemented short-term mission trips (Berard, Buleron, Lok, and Ragan 2006). Among the various findings, two areas were identified where churches might be susceptible to Canadian legal or regulatory challenges, and where local churches should consider becoming proactive in order to minimize risk.

The first area centers on the way churches *screen, select and prepare participants* for STM trips. It would appear that in the excitement and rush to "*do good*" churches fail to do "*due diligence.*" This section identifies some of the issues and suggests ways in which a church might shore up their short-term missions policies in order to minimize exposure to potential liability.

The second area examines the way in which church-sponsored short-term mission trips *gather, manage and expend tax-receipted monies*. Canada has among the most rigorous regulations governing the use of tax-receipted funds. Understanding the Canadian Revenue Agency's (CRA) requirements for issuing tax receipts for short-term mission can be difficult. This section concludes by suggesting a number of approaches a church might take to ensure they handle tax-receipted funds properly.

These are two significant overarching caveats. First, in addressing these two concerns the author is not in any way advocating the implementation of risk-free STM experiences. Risk is inherent in international engagement. Exposing people of faith to those risks is part of understanding how people express their faith in various corners of the world. Furthermore, STM experiences provide a means by which to learn from each other. Enabling Christians to expand their understanding of "others" and their "otherness" is at the heart of creating greater understanding. What is advocated, however, is that churches become more intentional about putting in place policies that minimize their exposure to litigation as they pursue what they believe God wants.

Second, the issues highlighted herein are addressed from a Canadian perspective. To that end it should be noted that, unlike many countries, the government of Canada has some of the most stringent guidelines on how registered charities manage and disperse their resources. Therefore, an underlying theme throughout this paper is this: *the Canadian experience may be instructive inasmuch as the events of 9/11 have caused many countries to reexamine how registered charities work in and outside their national boundaries.* In recent years, many nations have moved quickly to enact legislation that approximates some of the rigorous parameters set forth by Canadian law.

Socio-Economic Trends Influencing Canadian Short-Term Mission Interest

The short-term mission movement will continue to garner Canadian attention by pushing local churches to develop even more innovative approaches for connecting the person in the pew to the global work of God. Canadians, by and large, are a generous people who support a myriad of activities through charitable and nonprofit giving.

A 2006 Statistics Canada report summarizing a *National Survey of Nonprofit and Voluntary Organizations* reported that approximately 22.2 million Canadians (over the age of fifteen) donated annually an estimated $8.9 billion in charitable giving. During that same period, 11.8 million Canadians (from the same demographic) volunteered their time, contributing an average of 168 hours per person to charity (Hall, Lasby, Gumulka and Tryon 2006, 13).

With nearly half of Canadians predisposed to volunteer, it is not difficult to understand why Canadian Christians are interested in short-term missions. The coupling of this Canadian proclivity to volunteer with an increasingly affluent society is spawning a change in the nature of Canadian involvement in charities. Among a number of socio-economic trends at play, four are summarized here because of their direct influence on the short-term mission movement. Each ultimately impacts the churches' ability to function responsibly within its purview as a registered Canadian charity.

Personal Touch—"Involve me and help me make a difference."

The desire for donor participation is creating significant pressure on Canadian charities. Canadians, for the most part, want to be part of the transformation process and are not content with just cutting checks. An Ipsos Reid survey conducted for BMO Harris found that 72% of British Columbian baby boomers want to know where their funds are going before they are willing to part with their cash (Wilson 2006, 1). Canadian boomers, in particular, understand philanthropy differently and are forcing charities and philanthropic services to engage with them in new and meaningful ways.

Driving this desire for a deeper level of engagement is a significant shift in Canadian social values. *Environics*, a Toronto-based consulting firm, tracked changes in Canadian social values and the effect that they have had on the way people give. "In the 1950s," observes Marvi Ricker, VP and Director of Philanthropic services for the BMO Financial Group, "the social values that characterized Canada were deference to authority, deferred gratification and involvement in organized religion" (Cohen 2005, 6). That all has changed with the baby boom generation that grew up questioning authority and often defying it and doing things their own way. While previous generations may have been content to trust institutions with their resources, Canadian boomers are less inclined to do so without attaching a few stipulations.

Greater Accountability—"Take me and show me what you do."

Shifting Canadian social values have in turn fostered a second pressure point for Canadian charities. Since donors want to understand how their involvement will make a difference, many are requesting more information on the inner workings of the charities they support. Charities are being forced to be more intentional about defining their purpose and strategy in order to be heard and supported. For many charities this trend is reflected in a more personalized approach to would-be donors. Many larger charities, particularly those with deep pockets are providing personalized strategies for donors that help showcase their activities (MacNamara 2002, F3). For many charities the shift has meant the incorporation of some type of exposure trip. Smaller charities find this type of engagement a bit more challenging. Nevertheless, many are working hard to develop dynamic equivalents that showcase their initiatives in order to be heard and supported.

Charitable Donations as an Investment—"Assist me and help me get the best return on my charitable investment."

A third trend shaping Canadian involvement in charities stems from an evolving idea that charitable donations are seen as investments for which the donor would like to see some type of "social return." Jo-Anne Ryan, VP for Philanthropic Advisory Services at TD Waterhouse Canada, observes that to reach, particularly the "boomer market, . . . charities will need to do a lot more reporting to donors on the impact of their donations, and ... understand the broad range of giving techniques ... [requiring charities to] align themselves with 'centers of influence' such as lawyers and accountants" (quoted in Cohen 2005, 6). Ryan insists that charities will need to take on a team approach with their constituents which will require that they "... keep themselves informed on various methods of giving, . . . [on] tax rules, and [that they] have a network of people who can assist them in the process" (Cohen 2005, 6).

A shift in the way donors manage their charitable giving is evident in the surging popularity of community foundations (MacNamara 2002, F3). Craig Alexander, VP and Deputy Chief Economist for the TD Bank Financial Group believes that in the 21st century "... foundations are likely to become more popular vehicles for the distribution of charitable funding" (Alexander 2006,1). Gifting through community foundations is an effective, easy and flexible way for donors to achieve their philanthropic objectives while continuing to have a say in the way funds are dispersed long after the gift is given.

Voluntourism—"Enrich me and enable me to volunteer and have a vacation."

The notion of wanting to make a difference and have a vacation is accentuated in a fourth trend. While many Canadians like to holiday in Mexico because of the hot weather and sandy beaches, an increasing number of them are part of a trend to exchange their beach vacation for a vacation in some "out-of-the-way place" in order to do something to help others. Increasingly Canadians from all walks of life are getting together to make a difference. Today's Canadian volunteer force is made up of a demographic cross-section which includes teenagers, working people, senior citizens and entire families. The trend is increasingly being referred to as voluntourism (Clemons 2007). Simply put, volunteerism is about enriching the soul through a volunteer vacation. It is about mixing a holiday with work; about giving something back to the needy in the world while learning how people live in other places. The movement is bringing together cash-strapped charities and non-governmental organizations with affluent Canadians who want more than a standard vacation.

All four trends coalesce in the church and find expression through the increasing popularity of church-to-church contact. Many local churches (especially the large ones) are bypassing the mission agency and are giving oversight to ministries that heretofore had been the sole purview of the mission agency. In assuming this increased role, many churches are having to navigate through a myriad of regulations and are having to learn how to operate outside of their historic comfort zone. Terms like "care, direction and control" are increasingly being bantered around in church board rooms as they try to figure out how to comply with Canada Revenue Agency regulations. Unaware of the complexities, some churches are simply engaging in church-to-church relationships oblivious of the risks. Many lack the infrastructure or the intercultural competence for nurturing ongoing global partnerships. While we celebrate local churches' renewed desire to engage in the world, many of them are unaware of the risks and accompanying legal implications of their new patterns of global involvement.

Short-Term Missions Practice in Light of the Law and the Revenue Agency

The renewed involvement of the local church in mission and its active participation in sending out short-term mission trips was evident in the Ambrose student project on "*Researching Canadian Short-Term Mission*." It revealed a lack of attentiveness in two significant areas: 1) The screening, selecting and preparing of would-be STM participants and 2) the gathering, managing and expending of tax receipted monies (Diagram 1.1).

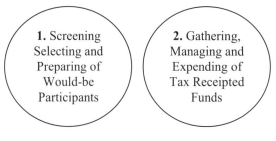

1. Screening Selecting and Preparing of Would-be Participants

2. Gathering, Managing and Expending of Tax Receipted Funds

Diagram 1.1

The research grid (Table 1.1.) provides the parameters for the rest of the paper. The two areas under scrutiny are examined through a three-fold framework. The *discoveries* piece relates the finding from the Ambrose research; the *developments* portion relays the Canadian socio-political, legal and regulatory milieu in which the church operates; and the *demands* segment suggests a number of areas a church might implement policy to minimize potential litigation and comply with Canadian Revenue Agency guidelines.

RESEARCH GRID	1. Screening, Selecting and Preparing of Participants	2. Gathering, Managing and Expending Tax-Receipted Monies
Discovery	Most of the churches in the study had a relaxed approach toward the screening, selecting and preparing participants.	Many of the churches in the study were unclear of the Canadian Revenue Agency's guidelines for the use of tax-receipted funds.
Development	Religious organizations are being held to higher standards of accountability.	The Canadian Revenue Agency (CRA) insists that religious organizations adhere to its guidelines for the use of tax-receipted funds.
Demand	Religious organizations should minimize the potential threat of liability by developing a clearly articulated risk management policy.	Religious organizations issuing CRA-authorized tax credits need to comply with the criterion for expending tax-receipted funds.

Table 1.1

Screening, Selecting and Preparing of Participants

Mission associations and short-term mission networks have long called for intentional and morally responsible ways of screening, selecting and preparing would-be participants. The *Canadian Guide to Best Practice in Short-term Mission*[3] developed by the Evangelical Fellowship of Canada's Global Mission Roundtable was created in 2000, in part, to respond to the lack of rigor being applied to short-term mission trips. The Guide was a call to Canadian STM sponsors to develop well-thought-out selection procedures (EFC 2000, 17) that would raise the security level and effectiveness of many STM experiences. At the time, these factors were particularly important given the numbers of youth and young adults participating in short-term mission trips.

The safety of STM participants is still paramount, and some seven years later youth and young adults account for a large portion of those involved in STM trips. In fact, churches in the Ambrose study reported that 51% of those who went on their STM trips were between the ages of thirteen and thirty. Of these, 29% were teenagers (Berard, Buleron, Lok, and Ragan 2006, 37). This finding correlates with research done by Statistics Canada on Canadian volunteers that identified youth, university students and people of religious organizations as the demographics most likely to volunteer with a charitable organization (Hall, Lasby, Gumulka, Tyron, 2006, 31).

Discovery: A relaxed approach to screening

With a large group of youth participating in STM trips, Ambrose researchers were curious to know how churches selected and trained participants. What they discovered was a fairly relaxed approach to screening. Half of the churches indicated that they did not have an integrated or standardized screening process. Sixty-three percent ranked interviews as their primary means of selecting STM participants. Forty-five percent contacted would-be participant's personal references. Only 15% insisted on a level one police check (local/provincial level), and 5% required a level two police check (national level). Sixteen percent indicated that they did not have any process in place for screening and selecting participants (Berard, Buleron, Lok, and Ragan 2006).

Development: Religious organizations are being held to higher standards of accountability

Given the high percentage of youth and young adults involved in short-term missions, the lack of rigor in screening is potentially problematic. With reported instances of inappropriate behavior and sexual abuse on the rise, churches involved in STM trips need to be intentional about developing a clearly defined process for screening and selecting both its STM leaders and its participants.

The much-publicized abuse cases involving Canadian residential schools and the ensuing litigations have sensitized Canadians to the danger. Increasingly Canadian churches are being held vicariously liable for acts perpetrated by either paid staff or volunteers (Cassels, Brock and Blackwell 2004). Lawyer Terrance Carter notes that progressively more "...organizations operating in good faith and providing valuable services to the community are being held to a high standard of accountability ... even to the point of being 'guarantors' of conduct of volunteers or employees" (Carter 1996b, 6). Vicarious liability as defined by Canadian law includes "... liability attributed to a person who has control over or responsibility for another who negligently causes an injury or otherwise would be liable. Whenever an agency relationship exists, the principal is responsible for the agent's actions" (Cassels, Brock and Blackwell 2004, 2).

Given the potential for various forms of exploitation, molestation, or sexual abuse, churches involved in STM experiences need to be aware of the potential legal exposure to which their organization and personnel may be subject. In the final analysis, a criminal charge of negligence is easy to bring, and one of the most difficult charges to disprove, since ignorance is not a valid defense.

Demand: Reduce liability through risk management

In an increasingly litigious society churches engaged in planning short-term mission trips need to be particularly attuned to the potential legal threats generated from a lack of attention to internal policies (i.e. Application Process; Training and Awareness Program; Abuse and Behavior Policy) and external risks (i.e. illness, robbery, accidents, kidnapping, or terrorism). Risk is inherent in everything that is done. Nevertheless, volunteers, employees of charities and church leaders must be mindful of these risks and regularly reexamine their practice in order to anticipate potential exposure to litigation.

Internal threats minimized by developing application, education, and conduct policies

A church sponsoring an STM trip can minimize potential internal threats by taking a more proactive approach towards screening, selecting and training its participants. While ultimately there is no fool-proof approach to a selection process, a well-developed set of policies, accompanied by intentional education and training can serve to minimize potential threats. Lawyers Cassels, Brock and Blackwell (2004, 23) recommend that as a minimum a good set of screening and selection policies should include the following (see Diagram 1.2):

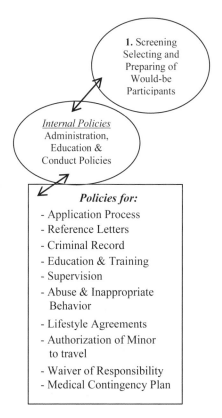

Diagram 1.2

- *An Application Process* that gives a clear statement of who the applicant is and why they want to participate in the church/charities activities (i.e. STM trip).
- *Letters of Reference* requested from a minimum of three people describing how long they have known the person in question and vouching for their character.
- *A Criminal Record Check* that should include Level I Police check (local/provincial); Level II Police Check (National); Interpol Police check (International); and a Social Services Inquiry that identifies if charges or complaints have ever been laid for endangerment, neglect or abuse of children under the age of fifteen.
- *Provide Education and Training* that occurs regularly and in a timely way for the purpose of keeping everyone apprised of any developments.
- *Regular Supervision* that ensures and gives evidence that the sponsoring organization has ongoing direction (care, custody, and control) of the activity they are sponsoring.
- *Conduct Audits* that periodically examine the procedures and practices that undergird the way the organization works.
- *Medical Contingency Plan* that indicates the protocol that would be followed should any participant require medical assistance while in their host country (i.e. where medical assistance is located, who the contact person is and who on the team is responsible to give oversight).

Once participants are selected, churches need to ensure that a reasonable training program is provided that, among other things, apprises them of the risks. Churches should approach the training process for the trip with the same level of intensity it would dedicate to the selection of volunteers that work with the church's children's ministry.[4]

External threats are minimized through crisis and risk management policies to address unforeseen crisis.

Effective STM training programs not only assist participants in becoming more culturally sensitive but also acquaint them with the potential risks or challenges associated with their sojourn. Increased hostility and uncertainty around the world obliges STM sponsors to spend a reasonable amount of time understanding potential external threats and assessing the level of risk that might be encountered. Often overlooked in the anticipation and excitement of the experience is the need to do *"due diligence"* or seek to reasonably anticipate potential risk in order to ensure the relative safety of those involved in the work of the charity.

Churches involved in sponsoring short-term mission trips should ensure that as a minimum they have in place policies and accompanying forms that provide participants with the opportunity to make *an informed decision about their participation.*

Building on the work of *Crisis Counseling International,* Harold Priebe (2007) suggests that STM-sponsoring churches incorporate a basic *Risk Assessment Protocol* for participants of a short-term mission trips. Priebe's three-fold protocol enables the participants to make an informed decision before they eventually sign the obligatory waiver.

Risk Management Core Policies

In this three-fold Risk Assessment Protocol, participants attend a session where they are informed of the church's and/or organization's Risk Management Core Policies. Priebe (2007) suggests that the core policies include a:

- *Risk Assessment Policy* that acknowledges the organization's commitment to conduct adequate and timely risk-assessment reviews.

- *Contingency Plans Policy* that recognizes the importance of preparing and maintaining contingency plans for any and all eventualities.
- *Training Policy* that provides security and crisis-management training for all short-term mission leaders.
- *Evacuation Authority Policy* that develops a decision-making protocol for implementation at the individual, local and national levels.
- *Evacuation Criteria Policy* that describes in detail a plan of action for the evacuation of personnel including when to evacuate, the communications process involved, and the procedure to move evacuees from one place to another.
- *Crisis Management Team Policy* that identifies and authorizes the requisite personnel needed to manage a particular crisis situation.
- *Information Management Policy* that authorizes designated people to collect, manage and disseminate all information, including appropriate intelligence, in a coherent and appropriate manner on behalf of the organization and the families of members of the organization.
- *Payment of Ransom, Yielding to Extortion Policy* that articulates the organization's approach and sets forth guidelines related to kidnapping, hostage taking or other methods of extortion.
- *Kidnapper and Hostage-taking Negotiation Policy* that empowers the leadership to conduct negotiations consistent with the organization's over-all policies in order to achieve the safe return of hostages.
- *Relocation of Hostages' Family Members Policy* that provides the Crisis Management Team with the authority to relocate the affected family members in a timely and appropriate manner.
- *Government Notification of Kidnapping and Hostage Taking Policy* that delineates the cooperative relationships of the

organization with the appropriate and legitimate government agencies that would be deemed helpful and in the best interest of the hostage and the organization.

- *Member Care Policy* that outlines the process whereby affected individuals receive immediate and/or ongoing assistance from qualified Christian mental health professionals.

- *Post-Crisis Evaluation Policy* that delineates a post-crisis evaluative process for assessing and understanding the issues that precipitated the crisis in order to identify best practices for the future.

Geographic Risk Awareness Search

A second stage engages participants in a hands-on *Geographic Risk Awareness Search*. Participants are required to apprise themselves of the inherent risks associated with travel to the particular country or geographic region in which they have expressed interest.

At this stage, would-be participants are encouraged as a minimum to visit their country's *Foreign Affairs and/or International Trade Department* (or dynamic equivalent) website (i.e. *www.voyage. gc.ca/dest/ctry/new-en.asp*) to acquaint themselves of any travel advisories and updates issued by their government. Equally useful is *Crisis Counseling International's* (*http://www.cricon.org/*) "Hotspots" report which highlights issues pertaining to various regions and countries around the world. Similarly, travel health and medical concerns for the location in question can be examined at the *Public Health Agency of Canada* (or dynamic equivalent) website (i.e. *http:// www.phac-aspc.gc.ca/tmp-pmv/index-eng.php*). News reports and magazine articles serve as a secondary means of further information for assessing the level of risk in the country for which they have expressed interest.

Sign a Release or Waiver of Liability Form.

The final step in the *Risk Assessment Protocol* is signing the *Release or Waiver of Liability Form*. Having read, investigated and understood the potential level of risk, the participant is now able to make a more informed decision. A waiver should include, as a minimum, the following statements.

- A statement releasing the sponsoring organization from liability;
- The location and dates of event;
- An acknowledgement of risk;
- Confirmation that they have read and will abide by the risk management policies of the church or organization.
- A signature and witness to that signature.

Enacting policy is not a guarantee against vicarious liability or negligence. Nevertheless, a clearly developed coherent set of risk-management policies is good practice, making the church more defensible and minimizing potential litigation.

Summary: Importance of Screening, Selection and Preparation

As a minimum a church should develop two sets of clearly developed policies (see Diagram 1.3). From an organizational level a church or faith-based organization should have a clearly defined set of *Application, Education and Conduct Policies* that internally govern the way they approach and implement a short-term mission trip. Likewise, in an effort to anticipate and minimize external threats a church or faith-based organization should develop a *Crisis and Risk*

Management System that is able to respond to potentially difficult situations.

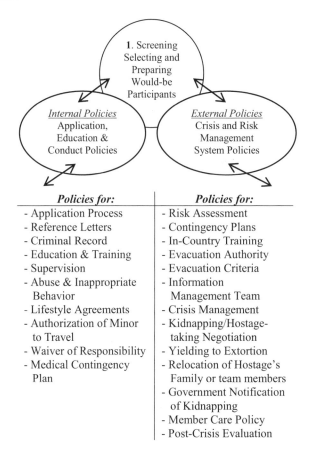

Policies for:
- Application Process
- Reference Letters
- Criminal Record
- Education & Training
- Supervision
- Abuse & Inappropriate Behavior
- Lifestyle Agreements
- Authorization of Minor to Travel
- Waiver of Responsibility
- Medical Contingency Plan

Policies for:
- Risk Assessment
- Contingency Plans
- In-Country Training
- Evacuation Authority
- Evacuation Criteria
- Information Management Team
- Crisis Management
- Kidnapping/Hostage-taking Negotiation
- Yielding to Extortion
- Relocation of Hostage's Family or team members
- Government Notification of Kidnapping
- Member Care Policy
- Post-Crisis Evaluation

Diagram 1.3

The *Application, Education and Conduct Policies* (internal threats) and the *Crisis and Risk Management System Policy* (external threats) enable a sponsoring organization to demonstrate that reasonable care was taken to minimize potential risks. In addition, a church or faith-based organization may want to develop other policies that serve its charitable purpose. Some have required participants to comply with a lifestyle agreement, fill out a battery of health forms and, if applicable, complete a form authorizing minors to leave the country. All STM sponsoring organizations ultimately have a duty to protect, a duty to communicate (warn), and a duty to inform regarding health risks (Walker and Ross, this volume). *In the final analysis, a church minimizes its legal exposure by demonstrating that due diligence was exercised in a reasonable and timely manner to inform participants of the risks.*

Gathering, Managing and Expending Tax-Receipted Monies

The second potential regulatory quagmire with legal implications for many Canadian STM activities, centers on the way in which funds are collected, receipted and then expended. Anytime money is involved there is potential for misuse. The donor-driven trend of managing their donations as an investment and maximizing the use of tax credits puts significant pressure on the church to understand how and what is eligible to be receipted.

Discovery: Some churches may not be as compliant as they think.

Research on the way many Canadian churches use short-term mission trips confirmed that the primary funding source for STM trips comes from family and friends through their local church. Eighty-eight percent of the churches in the study indicated that they did not budget for short-term mission trips. Of those that did, all were churches of over five-hundred people. While sponsoring an STM is well within the purview of a church's mandate, working agreements and disbursement of funds must comply with the Canadian Revenue Agency's (CRA's) guidelines for charities working internationally (Canada Revenue Agency 2004).

Eighty-six percent of respondents to the Ambrose study indicated that their church-sponsored short-term mission trips lasted anywhere between one to three weeks. When churches were asked how much of the STM trip should be dedicated to ministry to qualify as a legitimate ministry trip, forty-six percent indicated that seventy-five to one-hundred percent of the time should to be invested in ministry. Thirty-one percent indicated that fifty to seventy-five percent of the trip's time should be invested in ministry. When asked what the primary benefit of the STM trip was, close to three-quarters of the churches which responded (74%) indicated that it was personal and spiritual growth (Berard, Buleron, Lok, and Ragan 2006, 38).

These cursory findings are informative insofar as they identify how churches view and use STM trips. The critical issue is whether or not all short-term mission trips should qualify for tax credit status under Canadian Revenue Agency (CRA) guidelines. With increasing numbers of STM trips being openly promoted as a means of broadening one's worldview and/or reigniting one's spiritual life, it raises the question as to whether or not some STM trips comply with CRA criterion as described in the following section.

Development: Criterion for use of Canadian Revenue Agency (CRA) Tax-Receipted Funds (Tax Credits)

A church's charitable tax status comes with significant advantages. A primary benefit is their exemption from having to pay tax on income or capital gains. Furthermore, a church's capability to provide tax receipts to donors is particularly helpful since churches, like many charities, rely primarily on the good will of individual donors for their funding.

Where the issues get somewhat murky is in the way in which tax-receipted funds can be spent. While there is some variance in the way various churches and charities understand and apply the CRA guidelines, several guidelines regarding the way in which tax-receipted funds can be used are set forth by the CRA (Canadian Revenue Agency 1997, 3).

First, the *CRA prohibits the issuing of tax receipts for a donation for which a donor may derive a personal benefit.* This guideline raises the delicate question for short-term mission advocates as to whether or not accommodations (either in a hotel or in a host's home) and a plane ticket to some marginalized community of the world constitutes a personal benefit. Many well-funded charities get around the conundrum by simply paying all the expense for their traveling volunteers. Doing so is preferable in that it removes any implication of potential conflict of interest vis-à-vis a personal benefit.

Secondly, the CRA states that *tax receipts can only be issued for gifts (cash, securities and material goods) donated to the charity.* To be considered a gift, there must be a transfer of property. The bottom line is that a volunteer (short-term participant) should not expect to be receipted for contributions of service (their time, skills or effort) because they are not property (Canadian Revenue Agency 2006, 7). A charity can, however, issue a receipt to a volunteer for service if "... *the charity pays for the service, and the person then chooses to return the amount to the charity as a gift*" (Canadian Revenue Agency 2006, 7). Two transactions must occur. First, a provision of service needs to have occurred that is in keeping with the charity's purposes for which they wanted to pay. Second, by returning the check after the service was provided, a transfer of property occurs. The CRA indicates that this type of exchange is permissible and that such an exchange also provides a trail for taxable income given that "... the donor must account for the income, which would be realized either as remuneration or as business income" (Canadian Revenue Agency 2006, 7).

It is worth noting that for every dollar a Canadian donates to a registered Canadian charity, they receive a tax credit of up to forty-five cents on the dollar (depending on the province in which they file their taxes). This means that each donor is essentially contributing fifty-five cents out of pocket every time they give a dollar for a short-term mission trip. Many Canadians mistakenly assume that they are receiving a tax credit for the total amount of the donation.

Thirdly, *receipts cannot be issued if there is some type of verbal or written understanding that volunteers will be reimbursed for expenses incurred if they give a donation to the charity*. The Canadian Revenue Agency (CRA) is primarily concerned that churches do not inadvertently get into the business of generating tax receipts for what could amount to a donor going on a personal holiday. Therefore, any well-intentioned notion of promoting a short-term mission trip as "vacationing with a purpose" would be frowned on by the CRA. With the increasing popularity of voluntourism, the Canadian Government will likely have to clarify their position on this matter.

Fourthly, *a charity that is working outside of Canada cannot be a conduit or simply hand over resources to organizations that are not a qualified donee as designated by the CRA*. A charity that acts in this manner could be de-registered (Canadian Revenue Agency 2004, 4). The basic principle a church or charity needs to adhere to when allocating assets (usually money) outside of Canada, is that the funds can only be used to fulfill the charity's own purpose outside of Canada. The underlying constraint is that the registered Canadian charity or church must demonstrate that the funds are going to an activity that is their own and demonstrate that fact by having direction, control and supervision of that activity. In order to maintain said parameters, a charity must ensure it has put in place one or more of the following means for carrying out its foreign activities. A charity can carry out its purposes by:

1) Hiring or appointing an employee who acts on their behalf;
2) Generating a contract for a specific project or activity;
3) Developing an agency agreement and designating a principal-agent; or
4) Pooling their efforts with another charity in a more complex joint-ministry agreement (Johnson 2006, 3-9).

Churches that seek to engage in church-to-church partnerships need to make certain that they comply with these guidelines. Churches that are part of a denomination with a registered mission agency or have some type of formal relationship with a mission agency, may find it beneficial to work through those existing organizations. As a rule, mission agencies will have one or all of the aforementioned guidelines in place, not to mention a great deal of experience in facilitating international encounters. For a helpful framework for understanding many of the issues associated with church-to-church relationships, see the EFC Global Mission Roundtable, *Guide to Best Practices in Church-to-Church Partnerships* (EFC 2007).

Demand: It requires that churches clearly determine the nature of an STM trip.

All four guidelines have significant regulatory and ultimately legal implications for churches involved in short-term mission trips. The challenge for many sponsoring churches is that these trips often have both a ministry aspect and a personal or "holiday/vacation" component. Where these two elements are involved, and tax receipted monies are concerned, the charities need to tread with caution. Paul Lorimer (2007, 1), with the input of the Council of Canadian Christian Charities (CCCC), developed a helpful approach to allocating tax receipted funds for short-term mission trips.

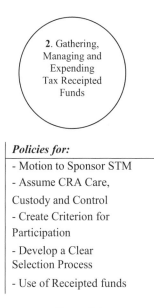

Policies for:
- Motion to Sponsor STM
- Assume CRA Care, Custody and Control
- Create Criterion for Participation
- Develop a Clear Selection Process
- Use of Receipted funds

Diagram 1.4

In order for a local church to receipt monies for a local church-sponsored STM trip, the governing body (in this case the church board) needs to assume responsibility for the trip by ensuring that the following steps are in place (Lorimer 2007, 1).

Motion to Sponsor—First, the board needs to ensure that they register a motion in their minutes stating their intention to approve, support and thereby assume responsibility for the short-term ministry initiative.

Assume Responsibility for Care, Direction and Control—Secondly, in registering the motion the church leadership assumes responsibility for the "care, direction and control" of that particular ministry. Simply put, the church leadership commits to being fully responsible for the actions and activity of those from the congregation who are being sent to carry out the objectives of the charity (their church). As a result, the church leadership is accountable and must be able to demonstrate that the funds they receipted were used in accordance to CRA guidelines governing charities working abroad.

Create a Set of Criteria for Participation—To that end, then, the board (or its designate) should create a set of criteria for participant selection for a short-term missions trip that could incorporate the following elements:

- Be a member or adherent of the local church;
- Be active as a member or adherent of the church;
- Be able to work or contribute resources towards the cost of the trip;
- Demonstrate a desire for Christian service by being involved in a ministry of the church;
- Have the skills commensurate with the specific project.

Develop Clear Selection Process—Fourthly, the board (or its designate) should develop a succinct yet clear process that enables qualified individuals to work through some type of application process. The application process might include conditions such as:

- Filling out an application form;
- Providing references attesting to their suitability to participate;
- Participating in an interview process with church leadership;

Generate Specific Policies Related to the Use of Receipted Funds—Fifthly, the board (or its designate) must be proactive in addressing fiduciary issues related to the oversight of funds they have receipted.

Short-term mission trips often involve personal or non-mission related aspects that need to be distinguished from the ministry component. Individuals will often want to include a segment for a personal vacation. Since funds generating a tax credit cannot be used for personal benefit, the resources used for personal or non-mission activities need to be handled differently. Two approaches may be helpful (Lorimer 2007, 2).

Mission trip that involves a non-mission component—"If the trip includes a non-mission side trip but the dominant purpose of the trip remains missions," writes Lorimer, "all designated gifts for the trip are tax receiptable as long as the church makes sure that any expenses relating to the non-mission component are excluded from what is funded by the local church" (Lorimer 2007, 2).

Non-mission trip that involves a mission (ministry) component— In a scenario where the non-mission component of a trip is larger than the ministry aspect. Lorimer observes that since

> the mission activity is no longer the dominant purpose, the local church's involvement and funding is limited to the missions component only. The local church may not pay for anything more than the expenses of the mission activity involved in the side trip. No part of the airfare can be funded by the local church. The total airfare is a personal expense since the dominant purpose is non-mission in nature (Lorimer 2007, 2).

Determining the Dominant Status of a Trip—All of this raises the critical issue of how one determines the dominant status of a trip. To help distinguish and clarify the nature of the trip, Lorimer (2007) poses a number of useful questions. "To determine the dominant purpose of a trip that has both a mission and a personal component," he writes, "one must look at the underlying reason why the trip is being planned [in the first place]. ... 'Would the trip be canceled if the personal portion is not possible?'" Another way of approaching it, would be to ask; "... would the trip not be made if the missions component is not possible" (Lorimer 2007, 1). In the final analysis, a church's response to these questions will likely give them a clear sense of the dominant purpose.

Status of Surplus Funds—In any case, all donated funds that exceed the stated amount needed for a particular ministry belong to the local church or charity that receipted them. These funds can then be used by a church for subsequent mission-related activities. Likewise, if a person donated funds to the STM fund and was unable to participate; those funds would belong to the church (Lorimer 2007, 2).

The bottom line is this. As a last resort, if the church cannot live within CRA's guidelines, the church should inform the donor that they should send the donation directly overseas without processing the donation through the church. The donor would not receive an income tax receipt, but they would be supporting the work they want to support.

Other Options—If a church is ultimately unprepared to assume the responsibility of sponsoring an STM trip it can opt to either (1) support an STM trip sponsored by another registered Canadian Charity or (2) inform participants of the implications of supporting an STM trip through a foreign charity not registered in Canada (Lorimer 2007, 2).

Summary of the Significance of Gathering, Managing and Expending Tax Receipted Monies

As a minimum, church leaders should be aware of the responsibilities they assume when agreeing to sponsor a short-term mission trip. They must give careful oversight to the way in which the trip is organized to ensure that they have "care, direction and control" at all times. In this, the church leadership commits to being fully responsible for the actions and activity of those from the congregation who are being sent to carry out the objectives of the church. As a result, the church leadership is accountable and must be able to demonstrate that the funds they receipted were used in accordance with CRA guidelines governing charities working abroad.

> In the final analysis, *every church should consult with their own legal council to ensure they comply with Canadian legal and regulatory guidelines. Numerous law firms have developed which specialize in charity law.*

Conclusion

Proponents of short-term mission trips may decry the onerous policy process described in this paper. Many may wonder if participants would be willing to go on an STM if they had to follow the protocols discussed above. The aforementioned is not intended to dissuade people from participating in or planning short-term mission trips. Risk and responsibility are basic facts of life, and every activity we undertake involves a certain amount of risk. Nevertheless, churches and their leaders need to understand the risks involved in sponsoring and leading a short-term mission trip and ensure they have reasonably anticipated potential risks.

The two areas explored in the paper are ongoing challenges for Canadian churches as they seek to understand how they participate in the global work of God. Enacting policy is not a guarantee against vicarious liability. Nevertheless, a clearly developed coherent set of policies is good practice, minimizing vulnerability to litigation. Furthermore, many of the financial polices suggested herein are in keeping with the ethical and theological tenets of Christian faith. It is crucial that the church self-regulate and keep in step with the high standards set forth by the government of Canada.

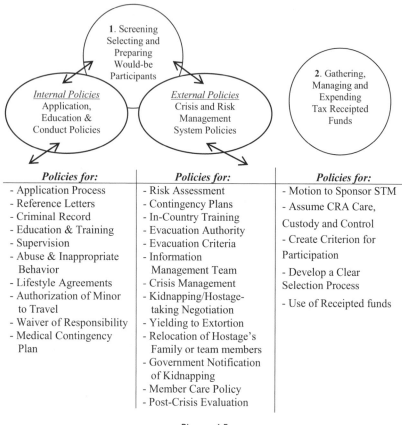

Policies for:	Policies for:	Policies for:
- Application Process	- Risk Assessment	- Motion to Sponsor STM
- Reference Letters	- Contingency Plans	- Assume CRA Care,
- Criminal Record	- In-Country Training	Custody and Control
- Education & Training	- Evacuation Authority	- Create Criterion for
- Supervision	- Evacuation Criteria	Participation
- Abuse & Inappropriate	- Information	- Develop a Clear
Behavior	Management Team	Selection Process
- Lifestyle Agreements	- Crisis Management	- Use of Receipted funds
- Authorization of Minor	- Kidnapping/Hostage-	
to Travel	taking Negotiation	
- Waiver of Responsibility	- Yielding to Extortion	
- Medical Contingency	- Relocation of Hostage's	
Plan	Family or team members	
	- Government Notification	
	of Kidnapping	
	- Member Care Policy	
	- Post-Crisis Evaluation	

Diagram 1.5

Ultimately, this paper is a reminder to STM-sponsoring organizations that it is crucial to approach international engagement sensibly in order to provide morally and legally responsible short-term mission experiences. Of primary concern is the safety and security of the large group of participants, who by participating on a short-term missions trip, may by God's grace, latch hold of some part of God's concern for people somewhere on this globe.

References

Alexander, Craig. 2006. Greying of Canada's population has far-reaching implication for charities. *TD Economics : Topic Paper.* Nov. 22, Toronto: *http://www.td.com/economics/special/ca1106_charity.jsp*

Archbishops' Council. 2004. *Protecting all God's children: The child protection policy for the Church of England.* London: Church House Publishing

Barber, B. R. 1999. *Jihad vs. McWorld: How globalization and tribalism are reshaping the world.* New York: Ballantine Books.

Berard, Lyndsay, Teofila Buleron, Joshua Lok, and Tyler R.Ragan. 2006. *Researching Canadian churches short-term mission experiences.* Canadian Theological Seminary. Unpublished student research project.

Bourgeois, D. 2002. *The law of charitable and not-for-profit organizations.* Third Edition. Markham, Butterworths Canada Ltd.

Broder, Peter et al. 2002. *Primer for directors of not-for-profit corporations.* Industry Canada.

Canada Revenue Agency. 1997. Income Tax Act: Gifts and official donation receipts. *Bulletin IT-110R3.* June 20, Locator Code: 920A

Canada Revenue Agency. 2000. RC4106 registered charities: Operating outside Canada. *Canada Revenue Agency*, October 16. *http://www.cra-arc.gc.ca/E/pub/tg/rc4106/README.html*

Canada Revenue Agency. 2004. Charities working internationally. *Registered Charities Newsletter #20.* Canadian Revenue Agency September.

Canada Revenue Agency. 2006. Receipts—who is the donor? *Registered Charities Newsletter.* No. 27, Fall.

Carter, Terrance S. 1996a. *Charity legal risk management check list*, November, *www.charitylaw.ca*

Carter, Terrance S. 1996b. Church and the law update—No. 8. *Canadian Council of Christian Charities, Bulletin No.2*, 1996.

Carter, Terrance S. 2004 Bill C-45 and its effect on criminal liability and insurance coverage for charities. *Charity Law Bulletin No. 35.* January 30.

Carter, Terrance S. 2005. *Advising the charitable client: Risk management strategies.* Ottawa, ON: Carter and Associates Professional Corporation.

Cassels, Brock and Blackwell. 2004. Vicarious liability in the non-profit sector. *Industry Canada.* Mar. 01 *http://strategis.ic.gc.ca/ epic/site/cilp-dci.nsf/en/h_cl00424e.html*

Clemons, David. 2007. Voluntourism got you curious too? *VolunTourism.org,* September *http://www.voluntourism.org/ resources.html* Chula Vista, CA.

Cohen, Todd. 2005. Learning from Canada's $1 trillion wealth transfer. *Exempt.* Nov-Dec.p.1-8.

De Soto, Hernando. 2000. *The mystery of capital: Why capitalism triumphs in the West and fails everywhere else.* New York: Basic Books.

Douma, Teresa A. 2006. What to consider when sending missionaries outside Canada. *Canadian Council of Christian Charities Webinar,* June 16, *http://www.cccc.org/webinars.*

EFC Global Mission Taskforce. 2000. *A guide to best practice in short-term mission.* Markham: The Task Force for Global Mission.

EFC Global Mission Taskforce. 2007. *A guide to best practice in church-to-church mission.* Markham: EFC Global Mission Roundtable.

Gray, John. 1998. *False dawn: The delusions of global capitalism.* London: Grata Books.

Hall, Michael, David Lasby, Glenn Gumulka and Catherine Tryon. 2006. *Caring Canadians, involved Canadians: Highlights from the 2004 Canada survey of giving, volunteering and participating.*

Statistics Canada, Catalogue no 71-542-XIE, Ottawa, ON: Ministry of Industry.

Jenkins, Philip. 2002. *The next Christendom : The coming of global Christianity*. Oxford: Oxford University Press.

Johnson, David. 2006. Undertaking and funding activities outside of Canada. *Canadian Council of Christian Charities Webinar*, *http://www.cccc.org/webinars*.

Klein, Naomi. 2007. *Shock doctrine: The rise of disaster capitalism*. New York, NY: Henry Holt and Company.

Huntington, Samuel P. 1996. *The clash of civilizations and the remaking of world order*. New York: Simon and Schuster Inc.

Lorimer, Paul. 2007. "Tax-receipting questions relative to short-term mission trips." Unpublished Memo to Church Treasures and Pastors of the Christian and Missionary Alliance in Canada. July.

MacNamara, Kate. 2002. Charities that let donors give where they live. *Financial Post*. Saturday, April 20, p.F3.

Micklethwait, John and Adrian Wooldridge. 2000. *A future perfect : The challenge and hidden promise of globalization*. New York, NY Crown Business.

Priebe, Harold. 2007. "Short-term missions risk management core policies of the Canadian Pacific District of the C&MA." Unpublished District documents.

Shah, Amir. 2007. Taliban free last South Korean hostages. *Guardian Unlimited*. UK: Guardian New and Media Limited. Friday August 31.

Statistics Canada. 2004. Summary of the findings of the National Survey of Nonprofit and Voluntary Organization (NSNVO), *Statistics Canada*, Catalogue no. 61-533-SIE, http://www.statcan.ca/english/freepub/61-533-SIE/61-533-SIE2005001.htm

Wilson, Peter. 2006. Boomer phenom even hits charities. *Vancouver Sun*. Thursday, December 21.

Endnotes

[1] As can be surmised by the etymology of the term, voluntourism incorporates volunteering with vacations and travel. Voluntourists are individuals who seek to combine their desire to explore and travel to new places with their desire to make a difference.

[2] In many respects, short-term missions are a faith-based expression of the much larger societal trend in affluent western societies where people combine travel with volunteering with various ministries.

[3] A copy of the EFC "Code of Best Practice in Short-term Mission" can be downloaded at *www.globalmission.ca*

[4] A number of good church-based resources are available that could easily be adapted for STM use. Three excellent resources include the globally recognized Viva training material (*http://www.viva.org/?page_id=58*), *"Protecting God's People"* resources (Archbishops' Council 2004) and *"Plan to Protect"* (C&MA 2004; *www. winningkidsinc.ca*). All are materials that could easily be adapted as training material for STM events.

CHAPTER 16

SHORT-TERM MISSIONS:

AVOIDING LIABILITY PITFALLS

MICHELLE A. WALKER-ADAMS & SCOTT ROSS

SECTION ONE: Introduction

The dramatic growth of the short-term mission movement throughout North America has raised many new questions for mission leaders, not least questions and issues of tort liability exposure for organizations sponsoring short-term missions.

The focus of this article is the risk a mission organization or church undertakes in sponsoring short-term mission teams. STM members often face the same threats or risks as long-term missionaries, but they are generally less connected with the sending organization and may even be new to their Christian walk. Some of them may be coming from non-Christian homes which will have less understanding of what missions are all about and less loyalty to the sending organization should some unfortunate circumstance occur during the trip.

In this article, we will discuss several theories of liability that may impact an organization or sending church should things go very wrong. The article will begin with a review of common exposures and then cover an organization's duty to protect and warn its employees or participants. Organizational exposure from negligent hiring and the related subject of negligent supervision will then be considered. Finally, there will be a discussion of types of defenses an organization can raise and practical preventative measures that could be effective in avoiding liability.

What is the legal environment if one of the team members were to bring a suit? What if a family member that does not recognize the value of the mission trip were to do so? The organization's good intentions alone cannot shield it from liability when accidents occur. Nor will the volunteer's willing spirit automatically bar his or her recovery. This article will highlight legal scenarios where team members—even willing volunteers—could potentially succeed in bringing action against sending organizations. It will discuss situations where third parties might also bring suit against the organization due to the actions or inaction of the mission team members or leaders.

Although the incidents which could give rise to liability may be occurring outside of the United States, most suits related to those incidents would likely find their way back to the U.S., to be governed by the laws of the jurisdiction of the parties. One needs to remember that American charitable organizations no longer have the protected status they once enjoyed when it comes to negligence liability. Religious organizations may no longer hide behind such status and it is incumbent upon them to become familiar with the present legal landscape if they wish to safeguard themselves against litigation.

When American churches and other non-profit organizations send out STM teams, the thought of one of the team members ever bringing suit against the organization, in the event of an unfortunate injury or disaster, is often not considered. It is normally expected that the individual participating in such trips does so with a servant's heart, in a cooperative spirit of ministry. Most volunteers are willing to participate without compensation of any kind—often even incurring expenses of their own. Unfortunately, the possibility of legal action being brought by team volunteers is all too real.

In keeping with the nature and purpose of mission trips, the locations targeted for such activities are often lacking not only the influence of God's Word, but also laws and a justice system based upon Divine absolutes; the resulting environment is inherently more tenuous and perilous from a legal standpoint.[1] The general lack of desirability of many such locations as vacation sites may be partly due to this uncertain environment. Although natural safety concerns may inspire some precautions and hesitations on the part of sending organizations, the actual risks may be higher than anticipated.

Case law directly bearing upon mission organizations acting in this capacity is lacking in breadth. This paper attempts to summarize pertinent laws and to extract and extend appropriate conclusions from situations that could be considered related in the view of the courts. This article attempts to summarize the most common situations upon which such actions may be based, and to suggest measures that organizations can implement to minimize exposure to findings of liability.

Since the veil of non-profit organizational immunity has been breached, it becomes increasingly important to know and understand the common areas of liability exposure for the mission organization, its directors, officers, and managers.

SECTION TWO: Incident/Liability Exposure

It is difficult to ascertain whether Americans are more in danger of being victims of crimes and accidents when they go abroad. A westerner's intuitive reaction is that this is indeed the case. One source estimates that approximately seventy percent of all road deaths occur in developing countries.[2] The same source estimates that at least two hundred Americans die in auto accidents each year when they travel abroad.[3] Statistics on criminal incidents affecting Americans abroad are not readily obtainable due to reporting inconsistencies.[4]

A second difficulty in gathering statistics on risk is that, generally, issues resolved abroad involving foreign third-parties are not recorded in the U.S. court system. Although legal claims arising abroad between Americans would likely be handled back in the United States,[5] most trial-level court cases are not publicly reported.[6] The bulk of perusable cases exist on the appeals level only, and it is notable that only 15% of civil cases are appealed;[7] thus, the vast majority of cases are never documented in public reports. Most cases in the U.S. are also settled out of court,[8] and consequently are unavailable for collective study.

And yet, incidents forming the potential basis of legal action do occur with some regularity, according to a study conducted by New Tribes Mission. In a survey of STM organizations which reported sending out 24,593 STM team members in 2006, leaders reported that 306 STM participants experienced some level of accident, criminal, political, health, or natural disaster.[9] Thus, on average, 20% of teams experienced an incident of the types described above.[10] In fact, the number and percentage of team members experiencing such incidents in 2006 actually increased by almost 38% over the previous year.[11]

In recent years the number of STM participants has grown rapidly (see Moreau and Priest in this volume), and there is every reason to expect that this trend will continue in the future. These trips tend to attract young participants, whether high-school church groups or college students perhaps obtaining credit at a Christian institution. The younger the participants, however, the more likely they are to be inexperienced travelers, with consequently higher risk.

To varying degrees foreign mission fields will always have inherent exposures. Although reliance on God's sovereignty can be comforting, exercising good judgment is normally appropriate as well; though the cost of some litigation-prevention measures may well outweigh any likely benefit, just *one* successful law-suit could deplete an organization's resources and limit future ministry opportunities. Organizations should attempt to determine what over-protection is and what prudent precautions to be taken are. Significantly, American religious organizations no longer have the protected status they once enjoyed when it comes to negligence liability.[12] Without that historic protection, charitable organizations need to be fully aware of their legal exposures to determine when further precautionary measures may be warranted.

Mission agencies comprised of members or organized as churches are not immune from a lawsuit merely because it was brought by an "insider." Until little over a decade ago, many religious organizations were immune from such actions brought by their members.[13] The courts' thinking was that a church operated like an unincorporated corporation, or a "quasi corporation"—where each member was involved in a joint enterprise with the whole. By that reasoning it would be nonsensical for a member to sue the organization or another member of it; that would be like an entity suing itself. Courts ruled accordingly, disallowing member to member or member to organization suits.[14]

This pattern was broken in 1998 with the Indiana case of *Hanson v. St. Luke's United Methodist Church* when the court overruled the quasi corporation theory and allowed suit by a member.[15] Since *Hanson,* other jurisdictions have followed this pattern.[16] There are consequently now less legal obstacles for mission trip team members today to bring and succeed in suits against their sending organizations.

SECTION THREE: Duty to Protect

3.1 – General Rule

The legally accepted general and natural rule is that people have no duty to protect others from a criminal assault or willful violence by a third-party.[17] It is important to note however that this general rule applies only (1) in the absence of a statute to the contrary, (2) where there is no special relationship existing, and (3) in the absence of special circumstances.[18] In fact, suits for failure to protect against third-party crime is one of the fastest growing areas of tort litigation.[19]

The Restatement Second of Torts (a compilation of common law regarding torts, considered persuasive authority by the courts) includes the following, "It is probably impossible to state any comprehensive rule as to when a defendant will be liable for [an] intervening criminal act of a third person."[20] In other words, there is room for judicial liberty in the law. Although there is a general pattern of rules to follow with regard to the duty to protect and warn, they continue to shift.

3.2 – General Rule Set Aside: Special Circumstances

Volunteering to Protect: Mission organization should be cautious when making general promises of a safe mission trip. A duty to protect can exist when one expressly or implicitly volunteers to protect another under a theory of contract law[21]—a duty which the law will recognize and enforce.[22] In those situations, although the promise to protect must be expressed,[23] it need not be in writing to be binding.[24] For example, if an employer makes a promise to protect an employee, this promise becomes incorporated as part of the employment contract.[25] If a university volunteers to protect students against crimes by third-parties, a duty to exercise due care will accordingly be imposed upon it.[26] In one case a landlord had undertaken a program of security designed to protect tenants in their apartments, yet he failed to prevent one tenant's rape.[27] In another, a mall had arranged for parking lot security, yet this did not prevent an abduction and rape in that lot.[28] In these scenarios entities volunteered to provide protection, consequently giving a sense of security to the victims, and legal liability was subsequently imposed for failure to protect.[29]

The duty to protect is not absolute in these contractual settings; it only exists to the extent of the voluntary undertaking.[30] A duty to protect is not breached if a victim assumes the risk of injury,[31] although it is important to note that the risk assumed by the victim must be the very risk that ultimately caused injury.[32] A promise made not to sue an organization for one type of injury does not protect that organization from every type of injury, particularly if the organization had expressly indicated that the trip would be safe in every other regard. If an STM team member signed a pre-trip release form acknowledging the risks of disease on the trip, and a political riot occurred (a danger not provided for on the liability release form), a court will likely find that the team member did not assume the risk for that variety of danger.

A mission organization which misrepresents its ability to protect team members from a third-party attack can be held liable for misrepresenting the safety of the destination country. Unless an organization is prepared to do so, it should not explicitly state that it will guard the team members from harm.

3.3 – General Rule Set Aside: Special Relationships

Certain types of relationships tend to automatically create a duty to protect. The relationships between employers and their employees,[33] property owners and their invitees,[34] and custodians and their wards exemplify this situation.[35] Case law examples suggest the same duty applies to such relationships as between housing-project owners and delivery men;[36] teachers and students;[37] jailers and prisoners;[38] doctors/hospitals and the nurses and patients;[39] and travel agencies and travelers.[40]

Employers: Even without an express agreement to do so, employers have an understood obligation to provide a safe workplace for their employees.[41] Employers also have the duty to warn their employees of any unusual perils at work which could include an anticipated criminal attack by a third-party.[42] This duty arises when an employer knows or should know of the potential harm and the employee is justifiably ignorant of that harm.[43] (The duty to warn will be examined more extensively below.) A volunteer for an organization is often extended similar rights to that of an employee.[44] So, for example, whether a mission team leader was actually employed by the organization or was just a volunteer, the organization must provide a safe work environment for him. The extent to which a court would apply this principle specifically to mission-field relationships has not yet been tested in case law.

Property Owners: Property owners also have a duty to protect the safety of their patrons—even without an express promise to do so. Property owners are required to exercise reasonable care to keep the premises safe for invitees. This principle has been interpreted by courts as a duty to protect in cases of bowling alleys, restaurants, pool halls, railroad stations, and theaters.[45]

Landlords have also been found liable for crimes by third-parties against their tenants.[46] The landlord in *Doe v. Dominion Bank of*

Washington had a duty to take reasonable measures to safeguard tenants from foreseeable criminal conduct in common areas.[47] A landlord who sets up a security program for tenants may be found negligent upon failure of that security program to protect the tenants.[48] The same reasoning could conceivably be applied to crimes occurring at missionary guest houses or boarding schools where security programs are in place.

Custodians: When one takes custody of another, the custodian could well have a duty to protect the one in custody;[49] this may be particularly relevant to mission trips . The custodian/ward relationship requires that special protective precautions be taken— especially as it relates to children.[50] The courts have applied this principle, for example, to camps and schools, and it could readily apply to others as well. In a case where a camper was sexually assaulted, the camp owner was found liable because, although the camper was at the camp for free, she was in the camp's care and the assault was foreseeable enough to impose a duty to protect her.[51] In another case a school district was found to have breached its duty to protect a twelve-year old student who was raped by one of her peers.[52]

In *District of Columbia v. Doe*, a girl was kidnapped from her school and sexually assaulted.[53] The court recognized that the school was not the absolute insurer of the child's welfare, or strictly liable if harm should befall her, but it had the duty to provide reasonable and ordinary care for the student.[54] The "ordinary care" standard imposes a duty to protect when a third-party criminal act is reasonably foreseeable. The court found that the kidnapping and assault could have been reasonably anticipated and guarded against.[55] Plaintiffs in this situation have to meet a heightened standard of proof, but showing foreseeability of the crime does *not* require the plaintiff to show that the same specific harm had occurred before.[56] In this case, the court examined a variety of factors and concluded that the school had reason to expect the crime. The evidence showed that there were adult males regularly wandering the school halls, that there had been much sexual and violent activity in the surrounding areas, and that school security was deficient.[57]

Another "special relationship" is created when a custodian deprives a ward of the ability of self-protection.[58] In the case of *James v. Meow Media, Inc.*, the court said if one takes another into custody and takes affirmative steps which in turn prevent that person from protecting himself, there is a duty to protect that person.[59] In a scenario where a team leader has taken possession of the belongings, such as passports, keys, and money of the team members, that leader may be acting in a guardian capacity which implies to the member that the leader is responsible for such things as the team's safety. This is affirmed in the Restatement (Second) of Torts: "One who is required by law to take or who voluntarily takes the custody of another under circumstances such as to deprive the other of his normal power of self-protection, or to subject him to association with persons likely to harm him, is under a duty to exercise reasonable care so to control the conduct of third persons as to prevent them from intentionally harming the other or so conducting themselves as to create an unreasonable risk of harm to him, if the actor (1) knows or has reason to know that he has the ability to control the conduct of the third persons, and (2) knows or should know of the necessity and opportunity for exercising such control."[60] An example might be a doctor or nurse who is under a duty to protect patients from attack by another patient or visitor.[61] By analogy, a team leader may have a duty to protect team members under his control from other people who the leader has intentionally placed in contact with the group, or even from other team members themselves. If a team leader brings a dangerous individual along on the team who he should reasonably know to be a threat to the other team members, that leader, and consequently the organization, could be held liable for any resulting crimes committed.[62]

Travel Agents: If a travel agent knows or easily could have learned about the relevant safety exposures in visiting a country, the agent may have a duty to inform the traveler.[63] By extension, if a mission organization sends out a missionary or team and fails to warn them of the risks, a court might impose liability because of similar reliance issues.

3.4 – General Rule Set Aside: Danger Was Foreseeable

More exceptions to the "no duty to protect" general rule can occur when: (1) the crime was foreseeable, (2) the defendant had a duty to take measures to guard against it, and (3) a balance of "fairness," weighing several factors, demands such result.[64] The following is the basic and reoccurring analysis of foreseeability for third-party crime, though some courts vary in their approach.[65]

(1) Foreseeability: If an organization could have anticipated the third-party crime, it is more likely to be found liable for failing to protect.[66] But to show the organization's duty to protect against such crimes, the victim must show that the crimes were *particularly* foreseeable to the organization.[67] For example, knowing a location is generally criminally active is not sufficient proof of foreseeability. Although there must be a logical connection whereby the defendant had an "increased awareness of the danger of a particular criminal act,"[68] the plaintiff is *not* required to show previous occurrences of the same crime.[69] It is insufficient proof, for example, of foreseeability to show that an area was a "high drug area" to suggest that a shooting was likely.[70] Similarly, in a case where presentation of expert evidence that an area was criminally active, based upon police reports, was not enough to show expectancy of shootings—primarily because there were no actual shootings found in those reports.[71]

(2) Victim's Burden to Establish a Duty: A plaintiff's burden to show failure to protect against third-party crimes is greater than for

mere negligence;[72] the plaintiff must show that the criminal act was so foreseeable as to create a duty on the part of the defendant to guard against it.[73] Despite this hurdle, successful suits of this nature have been increasing in the United States.[74]

Mission organizations should take caution from the 2003 case *Workman v. United Methodist Committee* in which a mere technicality kept the plaintiff from succeeding.[75] In *Workman*, a mother sued an organization for the death of her daughter in Somalia. The daughter went to serve with that organization in a volatile area. The mother claimed that the organization had a duty to protect the daughter in that environment from crimes that were foreseeable and which should have been anticipated. Although the plaintiff did not recover damages, the court laid guidelines whereby an organization *may* be found liable for the damage caused by another's crime. Because the victim in *Workman* was regarded by the court as an independent contractor, it was difficult for her estate to prove the organization had a duty to protect; if there were a closer relationship such as employer and employee, proving the duty would perhaps have succeeded.[76] If a mission team is sent to a dangerous region the special relationship that results from children in the care of a team leader may make it easier for an injured plaintiff to prove that a duty to protect was owed and violated.

(3) Balancing "Fairness": Before finding that a defendant breached a duty to protect, courts will usually take a hard look at the relationship between the plaintiff and defendant, the nature of the risk, and the public interest in the proposed solution.[77] Because the abstract idea of foreseeability often cannot be easily solved by factual analysis, there is no cut and dried formula to ensure that one avoids all possible liability. It is helpful, however, to examine the thinking of different courts that have been confronted with the "duty to protect" argument. The range of fairness factors considered (and covered more extensively below) include the defendant's ability to protect himself, the inability of the victim to protect himself,

economic factors, vagueness of obligation, risks involved vs. social value, and utility, or moral quality of defendant's conduct.[78] It should also be observed that, even if a practice is customary in a foreign country, this does not guarantee that the standard of reasonableness has been met.[79]

A few courts focus solely on the reasonableness and fairness of the result,[80] and in reality this may be the underlying theme of the "foreseeability" inquiry, though few courts come out and actually label it as such.[81] Since judges have reserved the right to rule based on their perception of fairness, large organizations may have reason to be apprehensive of adverse rulings from judges that—in the name of public policy—choose to allocate damages to the party that is most able to bear them.

Defendant's Capability to Protect: If an organization is in a better position to protect an individual from harm, the court will often conclude that it should have done so. [82] Case law examples using this line of reasoning include (1) finding a church that should have protected one picnicker from another drunken picnicker[83] compared with (2) finding no duty to protect a guard from an oncoming dangerous intruder because the organization did not have time to warn, and it was therefore not capable of offering protection.[84] Thus, lack of control can be a defense against a duty to protect charge.[85] Another approach to overcoming the charge would be to show that increased precautions would not have prevented a criminal attack.[86] If a political riot, for example, catches a mission team and everybody else off guard, the mission organization could hypothetically argue that not only was it incapable of protecting victims on the team, but also the attack could not have been avoided by any reasonable measures on the part of the organization. This defense will not always be convincing if the region was known to be dangerous and the informed organization chose to send the team despite the risks.

Individual's Self-Defense Ability: One's ability to protect oneself is an important consideration and relevant to the mission field. In a case where the victim actually had a gun in his hand pointed at the perpetrator and could have used it, the court found no duty to protect on the part of the defendant because the victim was able to protect himself.[87] However, in other cases, especially involving women and children, the duty was imposed upon organizations based upon the victims' inability to protect themselves. In a children's camp where a sexual assault occurred, the children's inability to guard themselves contributed to the imposition of a duty on the organization to protect them.[88] Similarly, the owners of bathing pools had the duty to protect women and children patrons who could not easily protect themselves in that environment.[89] The general rule is that an organization's duty is proportionately greater when the victim is young or otherwise helpless, and is proportionately less if a victim is armed or otherwise prepared to defend himself/herself.[90] Short-term mission teams are overwhelmingly composed of young members, frequently under the age of majority. In such cases the scales would be tipped in favor of a finding that the organizations had a duty to protect based upon the injured team members' inability to protect themselves.

Economic Factors: Economic considerations become more evident after examining the special relationships that courts have determined to indicate a duty of protection. Just as property owners owe a higher standard of care to invitees—because of the pecuniary interest in the invitees' presence—employers and proprietors have a pecuniary interest in their relationships with employees and patrons.[91] A camp and camper relationship can also be considered pecuniary even if a camper did not pay to attend; courts consider the camper's presence to have a "commercial angle" because more campers might be encouraged to attend based upon the experience of the first camper. In a case where a camper was assaulted, the pecuniary relationship contributed to the finding of a duty to protect.[92] In a case of a church picnic brawl, the courts saw the relationship between the church and the picnicker as pecuniary because an admission fee was charged; therefore, the duty to protect was heightened.[93]

Another economic consideration is that if providing protection would impose an economic hardship upon an organization, the courts may generally not expect that protection,[94] (although the economic hardship argument is not a carte blanche excuse for non-action when a situation calls for obvious action on the part of an organization). This speaks to the reasonableness and fairness standard.

In summary, a sending organization's potential duty to protect is made more likely if the court finds a pecuniary relationship. Team members, even if volunteers, may be owed the same duties as the mission organization would owe an employee.

Vagueness of Obligation: A fourth consideration is the level of vagueness surrounding the obligation to protect; this amplifies the foreseeability requirement. Unfortunate and unpreventable events do occur. In one case, the court said that finding a duty to protect would require "extraordinary speculation inherent in the subject of deterrence of men bent upon criminal ventures," and that a housing project could not always be responsible for the actions of an "unknown thug."[95] The anticipated criminal act must not be vague.

Social Value of Activity: The last factor may be very relevant to mission organizations as they take risks for causes they consider to be of life and death import. The court will balance the risk involved against the social value, utility, or moral quality of the defendant organization's conduct.[96] In balancing this component, courts will look at whether the social value of the defendant's action is legitimate, whether the action furthers the protection of that value, and the extent to which that value may be furthered by less dangerous means.[97] This is essentially a public policy expression. If the courts do not esteem the Great Commission with the same regard as a mission organization, they may determine that an STM trip to a country that is under a U.S. State Department advisory has unredeeming social value in light of the risk of injury. When a plaintiff was injured while at a defendant's unlawful after-hours bar where prostitutes were working,[98] the court declined to impose a duty to protect upon the defendant, finding no social value in such activities or the victim's presence there. Although that case involved a situation of illegal conduct, it is not inconceivable that courts will begin to extend their judgment on socially redeeming activities of arguably merit in doing their risk assessments. Individuals treading outside the bounds of legality for the sake of a cause (which can occur when man's laws are in conflict with God's laws) can perhaps learn from this case example.

SECTION FOUR: Duty to Communicate

4.1 – Duty to Warn

Closely related to the duty to protect is the duty to warn, which emphasizes communications rather than actions. Travel to foreign countries is a circumstance where this issue arises.[99] Travel agents have a duty to warn travelers of the dangers of a destination when they have knowledge of such dangers or when they could easily obtain such information.[100] Travelers have expectations of worldwide safety or comfort that occasionally are not realized. For that reason mission organizations should be aware of this cause of action and take it seriously since plaintiffs have been successful in such suits. What one person may think to be common-sense travel knowledge, another may find to be a litigable offense.

Superior Knowledge: If one is in a better position than another to know about travel dangers the courts are more likely to insist that the knowledge is disseminated. A travel agent in *Maurer v Cerkvenik-Anderson Travel* was aware that three students had previously died in Mexico due to falls from moving trains, but he did not share that information with a student for whom he arranged a trip.[101] When that student met the same fate, the court found that the agent had breached a duty to warn of the material dangers known to him.[102] A related case, *Loretti v Holiday Inns, Inc.*, produced similar results.[103] After being assured of a beach's safety in the Bahamas, a traveler was raped at gunpoint; she brought suit for failure to warn of the beach's reputation and previous incidences of violence.[104] The court held that if the beach is unsafe, and travel agents know of the danger, they are liable for failure to warn.[105] A court, in *Rookard v. Mexicoach*, agreed with plaintiffs and held an American bus company liable following an accident that resulted in injuries.[106] The American company had transported the plaintiffs part of the way and then turned them over to a Mexican driver. Negligence on the part of the Mexican bus driver caused the accident and the passengers claimed that the American company should have warned them of the inherent dangers known to the American company of bus rides in Mexico.[107]

In another case, the mother of a teenage short-term traveler succeeded in an action against a travel agent because that agent failed to inform the girl that a visa was required to enter France.[108] Her daughter was denied entry and sent home. The court described the travel agent's role as an "expanding" one, saying travel agents "should be expected to provide information which is necessary and of importance to the traveler."[109]

These cases should prompt the following questions before sending a short-term team: How much information do mission agencies currently share regarding previous mishaps experienced in the destination country? When mission agencies are the ones arranging tickets and the itinerary, how likely would a court view that organization as having the same function as a travel agent and hold them equally responsible for the sharing of all pertinent travel information, rather than expecting the individual traveler to take that responsibility?

Closeness of Relationship: The type of relationship or level of reliance between the parties is important in determining one's responsibility to warn the other. As discussed previously, a protective relationship can be formed contractually, either expressly or through implication, such as from the wording of a brochure.[110] In *Stevenson v. Four Winds Travel, Inc.,* a traveler's reliance on a brochure caused her to believe that she would be alerted of all potential perils; she brought suit after she slipped on a pier about which she was not warned.[111] The court said, "In view of the emphasis that the travel agency sponsoring tour put in its brochure on its tour escorts and directors, the tour guest who relied on the brochure had the right to expect that the tour director would warn her of the slippery condition of the pier on which she slipped while alighting from the boat."[112] The court found the tour guide had breached his voluntarily assumed duty to warn and awarded damages accordingly against the travel agency.[113]

In another case, travel agents were invited to visit hotels in Mexico in hopes that the agents would recommend them to clients.[114] When one of the invited agents was killed, a wrongful death claim ensued based on the fact that the corporation which invited the group down was aware that the area was overrun by bands of guerillas, making it dangerous for foreign visitors.[115] The court concluded that there was no duty to warn in this case because the *relationship* between the business invitees and the corporation was not strong enough to create such a duty. The Restatement of Torts Second has an illustrative listing of special relationships that create the duty to protect or warn; yet this court pointed out that the Restatement disclaims itself as an exhaustive list.[116]

Because many travel agencies have been found liable for failure to warn, and the Restatement consciously chose not to limit the possibilities for special relationships, [117] mission organizations should take this issue seriously. In light of the similarities mission agencies have in common with travel agencies, it would be no leap for courts to rule that mission organizations have a duty to warn of dangers known to them, or which could easily be known to them, about STM trip destinations.

4.2 – Avoiding Misrepresentation

Regarding Safety: To avoid claims of misrepresentation, it is advisable for organizations to provide complete safety and warning information to team members; the U.S. State Department's official report is one example of such information.[118] Most agencies appreciate the contents of such warnings but are suspicious of their complete accuracy. Therefore, agencies should consider what kind of exposure they may have, should they ignore such information, and what can be done to avoid such exposure.

It is crucial that an organization not imply that a destination is safer than it really is. Educational institutions occasionally encounter lawsuits for misrepresentation regarding the safety of accommodations to be provided with their study abroad programs.[119] A statement can be considered fraudulent if the maker of the statement lacks confidence or a factual basis for the statement.[120] One approach to avoiding exposure would be for the organization to cite what other reputable sources were used in making the determination, and the logical process the organization went through to come to its conclusion.

Regarding Program Expectations: In the case of *Bird v. Lewis & Clark College*, the institution was instructed to pay $5,000 in damages to a disabled person after it failed to accommodate her special needs on a study abroad program after it had earlier represented that it could do so.[121] The court declared there was a "special relationship" between the student and the college, even a *fiduciary relationship*.[122] The implication of an organization's fiduciary relationship with a participant raises the duty of care in more ways than making accurate representations. This relationship was declared, not because of any titles or expressions, but merely based on an examination of how the parties related to one another.[123]

A mission organization that assures team members of the safety of a region in order to induce participation is liable for fraudulent misrepresentation if there is not a good basis for such assurances.

Susceptibility to Liability: Many states will not bind members of an organization to the liability inflicted upon that organization because of the torts of the other members.[124] On the other hand, states such as California are willing to extend this imputed collateral liability in the name of "fairness" when a third person has been harmed (although they decline to do so if the suit is brought by one of the members instead of a third-party).[125] The appropriate jurisdictional rules should be reviewed to determine if members of a mission team will bear the liability for the negligence of a teammate with whom they are engaged in a common task.

SECTION FIVE: Duties Regarding Health Risks

5.1 – Duty to Protect against Health Risks

In addition to third-party crimes as discussed above, organizations could be liable for directing a team to a region with hazardous health conditions. Special relationships whereby team members rely on the wisdom of a team leader or organization could infer the existence of a duty to warn or protect against the dangers as outlined above.

Non-Delegable Duty: Sending a group to a disease-infested location, or to a known center of an epidemic, might be considered by the courts to be an inherently dangerous activity, and such action could trigger a "non-delegable" duty to protect.[126] In other words, this duty cannot be circumvented through the use of the independent contractor argument. Although the actions of independent contractors cannot normally impose liability on an organization using their services, inherently dangerous activities create an exception to this general rule.[127]

To be "inherently dangerous," the danger could not be removed by simply exercising reasonable care without altering the identity of the activity in some material way.[128] If, for example, the aim of an organization was to send its teams only to locations infected with HIV in an effort to minister to those people, the identity of the activity would be greatly altered if the danger was circumvented by avoiding places infected with the disease. Therefore, a trip might be considered an inherently dangerous activity because the very existence of the disease provides the basis for the organization's activities. Alternately, if an organization used an independent contractor for any of its work, and that contractor's negligence resulted in the spread of a disease, tort liability might be imputed to the organization. Although this scenario has not yet evidenced itself in reported case law, recent cases have shown the courts' acceptance of the general theory.[129]

"Assumption of the risk" (see section 9.1 below) may provide a partial defense for an organization to leverage its non-delegable duty to protect during the "abnormally dangerous"[130] activity. However, case law has shown this argument is not always a complete defense,[131] although it may reduce any damages awarded in a comparative negligence jurisdiction.[132]

Delayed Injury: Mission teams going overseas have been known to bring back diseases. In 2006, a girl who was on a mission trip visiting orphanages in Romania brought back the measles and spread the infection to 34 people in Indiana and Illinois.[133] It is conceivable that the sending organization could be liable for the damages of that infection, if through some negligence on the organization's part the disease was spread, or if a court determined that the risk of infection outweighed any justifying social value that may have been derived from the trip. If a mission team did not observe Department of Health warnings, or take other preventative measures to avoid the spread of disease, the organization might be found negligent.

5.2 – Duty to Give Proper Care in Medical Crisis

If a team member is endangered through the act of another, or even through an illness with no contributing negligence on the part of the sending organization, there is no legal duty to rescue that individual (unless there is an existing separate duty to protect). There may be a duty to exercise reasonable care, however.

In the situation of a medical emergency, unless a special relationship exists one person is not required to come to the rescue or assistance of another,[134] (with the exception of when the danger is actually imposed by the first party).[135] However, if the injured or threatened party is under someone's control, the controlling party must exercise reasonable care as they deal with that person.[136] The following is included in the Restatement (Second) of Torts as just one illustration of when a duty to aid occurs:

> A is a small child sent by his parents for the day to B's kindergarten. In the course of the day A becomes ill with scarlet fever. Although recognizing that A is seriously ill, B does nothing to obtain medical assistance or to take the child home or remove him to a place where help can be obtained. As a result A's illness is aggravated in a manner which proper medical attention would have avoided. B is subject to liability to A for the aggravation of his injuries.[137]

In the case of *McNeil v. Wagner College* a study-abroad student was injured and a professor volunteered to assist her at the hospital.[138]

The student later brought suit for her permanent injuries which she claimed resulted from the professor's failure to interpret the foreign doctor's recommendation for immediate surgery. Only for lack of evidence did the court reject the student's claim.[139] The professor that was helping the injured student at the hospital presumably had no intent of causing her additional harm, and nothing indicates his motives were anything but noble. A similar scenario could easily occur in an STM team setting.

The possibility of liability is not dispelled just because someone assists an injured person, even if the helper is motivated only by a desire to help the injured.[140] Doctors and other medical professionals are protected from liability in this situation through the Good Samaritan statutes in many states;[141] but only a few states extend protection to *anyone* rendering assistance at the scene of an emergency.[142] In some states, this protection from liability is not available, even to doctors, if they had a pre-existing duty to protect the hurt individual.[143] Therefore, if an organization has the duty to protect an injured team member, any negligence of the organization that occurs while providing assistance is not automatically excused by virtue of the emergency situation.

SECTION SIX: Negligent Hiring & Supervision

As the law has dispensed with the doctrine of charitable immunity, there has been an increase in suits against religious bodies under tort theories such as negligent hiring, retention, training, and supervision.[144] Any employment relationship which may exist between a sending organization and the leader of a team opens the organization up to many duties and potential liabilities. The selection of mission trip leadership is extremely important.

Negligent Hiring: Employers can be found liable for negligent hiring of an unfit or incompetent employee.[145] Recently, lawsuits are increasing as the courts are more willing to scrutinize the hiring process in light of recent clergy sexual abuse cases.[146] To succeed in a negligent hiring action, the plaintiff must prove (1) that there is an employment or agency relationship between the tortfeasor and the defendant employer; (2) that at the time of hiring, the employer knew or should have known, through the exercise of ordinary care, of the employee's unfitness or incompetence; and (3) the employee's incompetence, unfitness, or dangerous characteristics proximately caused the plaintiff's injuries.[147] Because this is a negligence standard, unless such inquiry would have had no impact on the result,[148] the court will consider whether the employer took reasonable care throughout the hiring process; this involves making adequate inquiries into the background of the employee, observations of his character, investigation into his work experience, etc.[149] It is important to note that even if the employing organization is not aware of any red flags, if the information indicating the employee's unfitness was available or would have been discovered by exercising reasonable care, the organization is responsible for that knowledge,[150] as in the case in *Evan F. v. Hughson United Methodist Church* where the church failed to investigate a pastor who later abused a 13-year-old boy.[151]

The degree of necessary precautions will depend on the role the employee is to play, the level of contact he will have with others, and consequently, the opportunity he has to imperil others through his position.[152]

A harmed individual has better chances of succeeding in a suit if his relationship to the employer was such that the employer's hiring decisions would affect that individual,[153] creating a duty between the employer and the victim.[154] The employment choices of the organization in commissioning a team leader have a direct impact on team members of a mission trip, as there is heavy reliance upon the team leader for guidance and safety.[155]

Negligent Retention & Supervision: An organization's duty continues beyond the hiring stage; an employer has a continuing obligation to remove an employee from a position of power if that employer knows or should have known that the employee is unfit, incompetent, or dangerous in that role.[156] Doing a thorough investigation when an employee is hired is not adequate protection if the employee later shows signs of unfitness or incompetence. If an employer's failure to take action results in harm to the plaintiff, [157] the employer may be liable for that harm.[158] "Incompetence" includes such things as carelessness, indifference, heedlessness, and recklessness.[159] "Unfitness" may include being accident-prone due to poor eyesight,[160] a propensity towards harmful behavior,[161] having a criminal record,[162] being prone to dishonesty,[163] etc. However, at least one court has carved an exception to liability when the employee's conduct was an isolated and independent act of intentional or criminal misconduct.

A mission agency that provides inadequate leadership training[164] is risking a negligent supervision suit, particularly if the organization retains the leader in his position despite displays of incompetence. Likewise, as discussed further below, if an employee or volunteer for the organization demonstrates a likelihood to be sexually abusive to another team member, the organization must remove that person or incur liability exposure.

6.1 – Duty to Give Proper Instructions

Leaders of mission teams are also in a position to impute negligence to the sending organization by the organization's failure to provide *competent* leadership. The failure to give proper instructions during a construction project, for example, can lead to organizational liability.[165] In *Fernquist v. San Francisco Presbytery*, the fall of a volunteer construction worker was attributed to improperly placed rafters.[166] The court held that whether the organization gave improper instruction, or one of the other workers had improperly performed the work, *in either case*, the organization was negligent.[167]

6.2 – Sexual Assault

If a team leader engages in independent criminal misconduct, such as sexual abuse, an organization may escape liability under the category of negligent supervision if it can be shown that the perpetrator acted independently in a criminal fashion. Similarly, the rules of respondeat superior (which impute liability of an employee onto the employer, discussed in more depth below), may excuse the organization from liability if the employee was not acting within the scope of his employment.[168] The organization still may find itself liable for negligent hiring if the employer knows or should know of the employee's unfitness.[169] In this regard, potential liability under negligent hiring is broader than negligent supervision or respondeat superior.[170] A case example is *Jones v. Trane*, in which a church negligently hired a priest knowing that he had previously abused children with whom he came in contact.[171] Because the priest's behavior was outside the scope of his employment, the respondeat superior argument failed but the negligent hiring theory resulted in a finding of church liability.[172]

Employers have a duty to act reasonably in selecting employees, and this duty may intensify depending on the employee's intended role and the opportunity provided for harm to the public. A leader in charge of an entire team of minors should be thoroughly scrutinized. Sexual abusers tend to continue in their abuse.[173] If a sending organization fails to discover readily available information in an employee's criminal record, it has opened itself up to liability upon the malfeasance of the employee.

6.3 – Ostensible Agency (Apparent Authority)

Normally, an independent contractor's negligence is not imputed to the retaining organization.[174] However, the principle "ostensible agency" (sometimes called "apparent authority")[175] says that if an injured party had reason to believe that an independent contractor was an agent or employee of an organization—and the organization was responsible for that belief and had reason to believe that the injured party would hold such belief,[176] then the organization may be held liable for that injury, as if the negligent person was indeed an agent of the organization.[177]

In an article on liability issues for American students studying abroad, the author of that article used this argument to show how an educational organization might be liable for the negligent actions of someone who is neither an employee nor an agent, if he was placed in charge of the students; tour guides or adjunct teachers with students in their care are examples of this situation.[178] Likewise, if a mission organization obtained the services of a guide or a missionary in such a way that was so seamless to the team members, causing them to believe that the leadership was actually under the authority of the sending organization, that organization may be liable for any injurious negligence of the independent worker. The key is whether the injured party had reason to believe that the agency relationship existed. Imposition of this duty could be dispelled by clearly informing the team members of the distinction.

6.4 – Non-Delegable Duties

As discussed above, hiring a third-party—an independent contractor—to lead an inherently dangerous activity, is not a sure way to avoid liability.[179] Even though that leader is not an employee or agent of the organization, any negligence on his part which results in injury to a team member or an outsider might be imputed to the organization through the doctrine of non-delegable duties.[180] Although available records do not indicate that this legal argument has yet been applied to mission trips, it is a plausible scenario.

SECTION SEVEN: Premises Liability

Premises liability is probably the most common area of exposure for agencies. Churches and mission agencies frequently use volunteer labor for construction projects at home and world-wide, in building churches, schools, airstrips, and medical clinics. That volunteer labor, even when formed from the congregation and in a spirit of collaboration on a religious project, can result in lawsuits when accidents occur. The laws of premises liability may be particularly relevant as STM teams travel to churches and schools in other countries, going either to aid in construction or to help out in some other capacity.

7.1 - Charitable Immunity

Gone are the days of charitable immunity from premises liability.[181] The fact that a charity would be financially destroyed will not prevent a court's finding of liability against it. In the past the "beneficiary theory" has allowed religious organizations, such as churches, to escape liability if the victim was receiving some benefit from his or her presence on the church property, such as maintaining one's membership status or the privilege to worship.[182] There is not much case support for the beneficiary theory due to its weak legal basis and the difficulty in determining the point at which someone becomes a beneficiary.[183] There is even less support for another theory taken from a distortion of English common law, sometimes called the "trust fund" theory.[184] Under that concept churches and other religious organizations were essentially "trustees" for the resources of an organization. Therefore, just as entrusted property is unreachable by suit, similarly the resources of an organization would be untouchable since they were intended only for the use of the organization's beneficiaries.[185] Preservation of the trust was a higher priority than making negligence victims whole.

This view died in England quickly, lingered in the United States a while longer, but is now a highly criticized view, considered to be in derogation of public policy.[186] In accordance with the well accepted principles of *respondeat superior* (further discussed in Section 8.1), charitable organizations are also liable for the negligent acts or omissions of their agents (employees, officer, or members).[187] The non-profit status of an organization does not change the result.

7.2 - Duty to Invitees

There are varying standards of care for property owners, depending upon the relationship between the party entering the property and the property possessor. The obligation accorded to "invitees" means that churches (and others) must adhere to a standard of *ordinary care* in keeping their grounds in a reasonably safe condition.[188] An invitee is anyone who enters the property under the express or implied invitation of the owner for a reason that is mutually advantageous or even *solely* advantageous to the owner.[189] If the individual's presence on the property was for the benefit of that individual alone he would have a much heavier burden of proof in showing liability if he were injured.[190] When a congregant was injured in the slip and fall case of *Sullivan v. First Presbyterian Church*, the court said the church owed the plaintiff the *invitee* standard of care.[191] If the plaintiff had been considered a *licensee*[192] she would have had to show "wanton and willful" misconduct to hold the church liable.

Volunteers: It is important to emphasize that even an organization's volunteers can be considered invitees with a corresponding standard of care. In *Fernquist v. San Francisco Presbytery*, a volunteer suffered a fall while building a dorm for a religious organization.[193] The court pointed out that the volunteer was there for the benefit of the organization, and was therefore owed the invitee duty of ordinary care to keep the premises in reasonably safe condition, or to warn of any dangers.[194] The plaintiff was successful in this case when he showed that the church had failed to do so.[195]

Similarly, the invitee standard would be applicable for teams on an STM trip sent to do construction work; thus the correspondingly higher standard of care would be appropriate.

Open and Obvious Dangers: What condition constitutes "reasonably safe" for purposes of the invitee standard? Some dangers are so "open and obvious" that a property owner will not necessarily be held liable for injuries resulting therefrom. When a volunteer fell from a ladder the court did not hold the landowner liable since the danger of falling is an open and obvious one when one mounts a ladder to a high place.[196] However, the court went on to say that a landowner *may* be held liable for injuries resulting from an open and obvious danger when the landowner knew or reasonably should have known that the individual would become distracted or forget about the danger for a moment.[197]

Ownership Irrelevant: A church's or organization's non-ownership of a construction site does not avoid the duty to provide a proper standard of care. In *Haugen v. Central Lutheran Church* the church was the mere "occupier," and yet, it owed a duty of ordinary care to its construction volunteer, since the volunteer was considered an invitee.[198]

SECTION EIGHT: Liability to Third Persons

Beyond the duties a mission organization may owe to its team members, it might also owe duties to third-parties. Under the doctrine of *respondeat superior*, if a member of a mission team commits a tort against a third-party, the sending organization can be held liable for that tort, even if the team member is a volunteer. Family members of an injured team member can bring wrongful death and loss of consortium suits against the sending organization for any negligence contributing to that injury, even if that team member previously signed a waiver releasing the organization from liability.

8.1 – Respondeat Superior

Like their for-profit counterparts, non-profit organizations can be held liable for the acts or omissions of their officers and employees. [199] As explained earlier, the notion of "charitable immunity" is largely a thing of the past.[200]

Employees/Officers: If a team leader is employed by an organization or can be considered its agent, any negligence on his part can be imputed to the organization if he was acting within the scope of his employment or agency when the negligence occurred.[201]

Volunteers: Employees and officers are not the only ones who can be considered agents of an organization based upon the doctrine of *respondeat superior*; volunteers can also bring liability upon an organization they are serving.[202] In the aforementioned *Fernquist* case the court made it clear that if construction volunteers had been at fault for the personal injury of a colleague, fault would have been imputed to the organization—the principal—for whom they were acting as agents.[203]

For negligence to be imputed to an organization, the volunteer's continuous service is not required, but the consent of the master, or manifestation of such consent, is necessary for the agency relationship to exist.[204] Like all agency law, the most central issue in determining liability is control—more specifically, the right or obligation of the charitable organization to control the activities of the volunteer.[205] A court will look at the following factors in deciding if there was control: (1) the degree to which the charity orders the specific action on the part of the volunteer, (2) the degree of contact between the charity and the volunteer, both before and after the commission of the tort, (3) the structural hierarchy of the charity, and (4) the regularity of volunteering of services to the charity.[206] In a mission trip setting, this agency status would ordinarily exist.

Courts today do not allow churches to successfully argue that their members, while helping with a construction project on the church property, are engaged in a "joint venture" which would bar their recovery against the church.[207] In *Timmons v. Assembly of God Church of Van Nuys* a volunteer's eye was put out when a wire recoiled due to the negligence of another worker. The church argued that it was a joint venture, thereby relieving the organization of a duty of care; the court rejected that argument, imposing liability.[208]

8.2 – Wrongful Death and Loss of Consortium Litigation

In the *Workman* case referred to earlier a mother brought a wrongful death suit after her daughter was killed during a relief mission to Somalia. Despite the mother's non-recovery under that particular argument, the organization was unable to avoid the costs and stresses of the litigation. If negligence had been proven, the organization would have been subjected to several theories of recovery to the girl's family. Note that mission trip team members may willingly sign away all legal rights to recovery in the event of a disaster because they embrace their organization's purpose and goals. There is no guarantee, however, that the deceased's family members will have the same outlook and they may bring a ruinous wrongful death or loss of consortium suit.

8.2(a) – In Case of Death

Wrongful Death: If a mission team member dies due to negligence that can be attributed to the sending organization there are three kinds of losses whereby another party such as a parent might recover for the death in a wrongful death suit: (1) loss of support or services,[209] (2) loss of companionship, society, and affection,[210] and (3) mental anguish suffered.[211] Courts no longer insist that there be a pecuniary loss as a result of the death; emotional losses are also sufficient for recovery in some cases.[212]

8.2(b) – In Case of Injury

Loss of Consortium: If the victim of a disaster is not killed, but rather injured because of the organization's negligence, the organization can still be liable to a third-party on the theory of "loss of consortium."[213] Common law has long recognized a separate cause of action on the part of one spouse when his or her spouse is injured due to an organization's negligence. This action, called "loss of consortium" or "loss of companionship," seeks to address the injury suffered by one spouse due to the injury or death of the other.[214] Damages awarded previously covered only loss of services, such as the domestic services that a wife would provide a husband, but recovery has evolved to include such aspects as love, affection, companionship, and sexual relations.[215]

Parental Consortium: Recently, at least eight jurisdictions have expanded loss of consortium to include losses experienced by children.[216] In those states, a child may succeed in a "loss of parental consortium" suit if a parent has been constructively or actually removed from the child's life.[217] In *Ferriter v. Daniel O'Connell's Sons*, the children of a man paralyzed from the neck down from a negligent injury were permitted to recover for loss of parental consortium.[218]

Child Consortium: Can the parental consortium theory be expanded to allow recovery by parents for the loss of consortium for an injured or killed child? Because the legal theory is no longer limited to marital services but can include sentimental qualities, and because the theory has already been expanded to allow recovery by children for an injured parent, it seems reasonable that courts will allow the reverse for similar reasons. One rationale for expanding the legal theory from spouse to parental consortium in favor of children was highlighted in *Ueland v. Reynolds Metals Co.*[219] It is inconsistent to allow children to recover in the case of a parent's *death* but not if the parent survived but was reduced to a vegetative state.[220] The same issue is present if a child remains in a vegetative state after an injury. If a parent could recover under a "wrongful death" theory for a child's death, the parent could potentially also recover from the child's constructive death if the child was reduced to a vegetative existence.

Inferentially then, if a child is killed or injured on a mission trip, the sending organization could have to defend itself in a wrongful death or loss of consortium lawsuit by the child's parents. An adult injured on a trip may have beneficiaries with similar recourse.

SECTION NINE: Defensive & Preventative Measures

9.1 – Assumption of the Risk

Legally speaking, if an individual has "assumed the risk" of harm, he is barred from recovery for whatever injury results.[221] Assumption of the risk occurs when an individual has (1) actual knowledge of the danger involved, (2) an appreciation for the nature and magnitude of that danger, and (3) there has been an acceptance of the risk involved.[222] In the face of this knowledge, an individual proceeding voluntarily is deemed to have assumed the risk.[223] To voluntarily assume the risk means that an individual has an *actual choice* in the matter, rather than being forced to do something; he must have had legal and moral alternatives prior to choosing the dangerous option before him.[224] This freedom of choice is a fact-intensive determination.

A mission organization may be able to avoid litigation by assuring that its agents have consciously complied with the personal commitments listed above. If a team member was aware of the dangers of a situation, and chose to proceed voluntarily, he cannot later seek to impose liability upon the organization.

Note however, that according to the court in *Bennett v. Gitzen*, children under the age of seven are legally incapable of assuming the risk.[225] Case law shows this to be true even if the child entered into danger and acted with actual knowledge.[226] Other courts could potentially hold that older children, unprepared to make major life-affecting decisions are incapable as well.[227] This is particularly relevant when one considers how many young children are regularly brought along on mission trips with their parents.

Other statutes exist to protect young people, disallowing assumption of the risk defenses. In the case of *Jarrett v. Woodard Bros., Inc.* a nineteen-year old college student drank too much alcohol at a restaurant using a fake ID, was struck by a car as a result, and later died.[228] His parents blamed the restaurant, and were successful, even against the restaurant's defense that the boy assumed the risk by drinking and driving.[229] There was a law imposing strict per se negligence upon restaurant owners for continuing to serve alcohol, *even though* the owner may have been deceived about the student's age, and the student made a choice to continue drinking.[230] Public policy laws often protect young people from their own reckless behavior.

9.2 – Contributory Negligence and Comparative Fault

The states are divided[231] on the issues of contributory negligence and comparative fault.[232] If the mission organization is in a jurisdiction still applying contributory negligence, chances of a successful defense are better. The contributory negligence states disallow recovery for a plaintiff when he was at fault to any degree whatsoever.[233] To determine if a plaintiff contributed in the negligence, the question becomes whether he exercised due care,[234] and whether his conduct contributed to his injury.[235] Unless both elements are satisfied, the plaintiff may not recover even if the defendant was partly to blame.[236]

Comparative fault states, on the other hand, divide up an allocation of damages in accordance with actual portions of fault.[237] If a victim was only 20% at fault (as determined by a jury's examination of the facts), then the organization may still be found liable for 80% of the damages. Comparative negligence states abrogate the common law "all or nothing" approach,[238] and make plaintiff's recovery more likely, since partial recovery is allowed.

9.3 – Releases: Form, Function & Validity

A release can indicate that the participant in an activity is assuming the risk of injury, or is releasing an organization from any future claims of negligence on its part relating to some activity.[239] How effective *are* releases of liability? Can signed forms from an organization's team members shield it from the legal liabilities highlighted above? There is certainly ample case law showing that—in the absence of fraud, duress, or mutual mistake by the parties—releases can be upheld.[240] Although the record varies, some courts have been willing to honor releases, even when they were prepared by the one who was negligent.[241] No magic language is required for a release (such as the word "release") and it need not be done with perfection.[242] Aside from their legal merits, releases may serve as deterrents; people may refrain from filing suit if they have signed a release, either because they incorrectly assume it to be binding, or because of a moral conviction that such promises not to sue should be honored. A sending organization typically attempts to secure a release of liability form from the team members, similar to the practice of recreational organizations.

However, there is adequate case law to place serious doubt upon the reliability of releases to fully protect an organization. They are not the watertight protection that those employing them may believe them to be. A number of cases show a rejection of such liability waivers when used for dangerous recreational sports and outdoor activities.[243] This case law can be instructive to mission organizations because of what both may have in common—dangerous activities. Trips into foreign countries may be perilous undertakings, particularly if the teams are not headed to popular vacation destinations but, rather, to locations with U.S. State Department advisories.

Even though the law generally favors attempts to minimize litigation through settlements and contractual agreements, such as releases,[244] the law also provides for compensation of injured parties when appropriate. Releases are often interpreted in favor of a victim,[245] and there are many circumstances under which a release may be declared "void" or "voidable,"[246] circumstances which could arise in an STM setting as well.

Void Releases: A release is "void"[247] when the one signing has no capacity to sign away the rights in question.[248] A child's age may prevent him from having the legal power to sign a release, therefore rendering his signature ineffective. In a New York case a fourteen year-old child's signed release was not enforceable because of his age.[249] Releases on certain specific activities may be forbidden by statute.[250]

For states that allow "pre-activity" releases, not all have a statute, rule, or decision to allow parents to sign a pre-tort liability release on behalf of their children. In New Jersey, for example, a mother's release of liability on behalf of her son before a skateboarding accident, was held to be void from its inception.[251] In a similar Utah case, the state considered the interest of the child to have priority, and held a release of liability by a mother for her daughter's horse riding to be of no consequence, holding that she had no authority to release liability on the part of her minor daughter before or after an injury occurred.[252]

As a general rule (though a few states have suggested otherwise), willful, wanton, or gross negligence can never be covered by a liability release.[253] Therefore, if a mission trip team leader, acting as an agent of an organization, engaged in gross negligence that resulted in the harm of a team member, a prior release signed by the victim would be of no consequence in protecting the organization from liability.

Voidable Releases: A release may be considered "voidable," which means that it can be voided by the signer, and therefore not enforced (although the presumption of validity works against the signer).[254] When a challenge to a release occurs, the courts consider four main factors: (1) the existence of any duty to the public, (2) the nature of the service performed, (3) whether the contract was entered into fairly, and (4) whether the intention of the parties is expressed in clear and unambiguous language.[255]

(1) Duty to the Public: The duty to the public factor often raises the issue of unequal bargaining power,[256] where a signer is at an obvious disadvantage, placing him at the mercy of the other party's negligence.[257] It was with that reasoning that, in a case where a spelunking participant fell to his death on a guided tour, the court held that to enforce the release would be against public interest.[258]

(2) Nature of Service Provided: Another factor considered by the courts is whether the party seeking exculpation was providing a service of great importance to the public.[259] As mentioned previously, religious organizations may rely less and less on a court's sympathy with missionary causes. This attitude may cause a court to reject the validity of mission trip releases when the court weighs the value of the experience against the risk a team member is assuming by signing away rights to sue.

(3) Fairness: An agreement must be entered into fairly. In recreational activity, setting the sophistication and experience level of the participant is important in determining fairness, based upon his ability to understand what dangers are associated with the activity.[260] Similarly an experienced missionary familiar with a particular region to be visited would be in a better position of anticipating the dangers associated with a trip than a new or younger member.

(4) Clear or Ambiguous Verbiage: The wording of the release must be clear and unambiguous, written in layman's terms, so that both parties understand what is included in the release.[261] Two reasonable people upon viewing a release should be able to agree that the signer knowingly and willingly signed the document, while small print and other deceptive tactics are discouraged, if not rejected outright.[262] The particularity with which the dangers are mentioned will also contribute to its clarity, and thus, its validity. If the word "negligence" is actually used in reference to the conduct of the organization the anticipated dangers may be less particularized; whereas, if no reference to non-liability for the organization's negligence is made, then the dangers for which the team member is assuming the risk must be clearly spelled out.[263] Either the exact dangers must be named, or the exculpatory words for the organization's negligence should be obvious.

In a Wisconsin case, a girl's signed release at a swimming pool did not hold up in a wrongful death suit brought by her family, partly because the term "regardless of fault" was not explained in positive language to include negligence on the part of the establishment.[264] In another case, a horse-riding establishment's release was struck down partly because it was overly broad, including "any injury or damage from any accident, injury, or illness," and partly, because it did not expound on the "unavoidable risks inherent to all horse-related activities."[265] If the victim had been an experienced rider, she might have already had a solid grasp of what risks *are* "inherent" to horse riding.

Finally, releases must be particularly stated; they can cover only that which was consciously and expressly intended to be covered at the time of the signing, and no more.[266] If a scenario arises during a mission trip that was not contemplated at the time a release form was signed, the release is ineffective on that point.

Forum Specification in Releases: To minimize the unknowns of shifting liability law, agreement on a choice of forum for resolution of any disputes is wise, and such an agreement will generally be effective in jurisdictions where releases are permitted.[267] The distinctions between the laws of different states could be crucial to winning or losing a case. When disasters occur abroad, an organization cannot automatically assume that its own state's rules will govern; in fact, courts have been known to decide multiple issues using multiple states' laws.[268] Also, remember that states differ in their acceptances of written releases.[269] When a choice of states is available, an organization should make a strategic selection.

Non-Effect of Releases on Third-party Claims: The signing of a release will not necessarily have any effect on third-party claims in the matter.[270] For example, in some states a release cannot fully guard against loss of consortium claims.[271] In those states, loss of consortium is considered a common law right possessed by the surviving spouse; thus, a prior release by the killed or injured spouse would have no bearing upon a surviving spouse's claim.[272] In an Ohio case, parents were not barred from bringing suit on the "loss of consortium" theory even though their daughter had signed a release on the same matter.[273]

Summary on Releases

An organization should make its release highly inclusive of every type of disaster it anticipates could occur, as releases will often be strictly construed in favor of the signer. Yet it must not be overly broad in describing the exposures; non-obvious terms must be defined and specified risks must clearly relate to the upcoming activity. Lastly, the signer should have a thorough understanding of the document being signed, and every disaster that is covered therein. The more inexperienced or unsophisticated the signer, the more this should to be emphasized. If a serious information session occurs before the release signing, the chances of enforcement will be improved. A signer also must not be pressured in his decision, and if time can be allowed to let the team member take the release home with him and consider the matter before signing, all the better. Inclusion of a "forum selection" clause in the organizational release form is also advisable. If releases of liability are to be used, the sending organization is advised to check its jurisdiction's rules to determine if any minors under consideration for the trip are able to have their parents sign the form or if they are prohibited from doing so by statute. Lastly, the uncertainties of release protection reemphasizes the need for an organization to not fail in any duties to the victim from the onset, such as the duty to protect or warn the victim, if such a duty existed.

9.4 – Additional Measures

Training: One important method in reducing exposure is properly *training* both the team leaders and the participants. Potential liability is reduced as team leaders are educated on appropriate responses in volatile and crisis situations. In addition, participants should be trained in how to respond and defer to team leaders should a crisis situation arise. Going hand in hand with training team leaders and participants is having other personnel in the right positions and properly trained to handle crisis events. Proper and efficient response to crisis events can reduce the emotional and financial costs to all involved. Disaster reaction training is available for organizations that send teams regularly to, or tend to focus their efforts on, disaster-prone regions.

Information: Even before liability is incurred, information may be the biggest asset organizations can wield in a self-protective fashion. Information sessions with the team members, giving them full disclosure on what they are going to be doing, where they are going, who speaks for the organization, and other topics mentioned above would create an early defense against certain claims. Team leaders should be given clear insight into their roles as agents of the organizations, and all that implies. The organization should obtain and disseminate as much public information as they are reasonably able to provide on the safety of the destination and any entry requirements their team members should know. It is incumbent upon an organization sending out a team to know what dangers exist—such as health perils, natural event dangers, criminal activity, and political instability. Does the organization have a system in place to determine these issues? Does the organization have the skill to interpret the information it gathers? Finally, does the organization have in place a system to communicate to employees and volunteers the information? On the other hand, the organization must consider how to communicate the information without scaring away those it is recruiting. There are programs and training that assists sending organizations in guarding against legal liabilities. It is beyond the scope of this article to discuss these additional precautions at length.

Background Checks: It is recommended that those working with young people should go through a background check for the organization to avoid negligent hiring issues; this could also be beneficial in the event that the workers later prove to be unfit or incompetent.

Insurance: There are insurance companies that tailor travel insurance packages to STM trips; the insurance companies will step into a situation when a disaster occurs, covering any liability that might be imposed upon the sending organization.[274] A moderate insurance premium may well be worth the cost if it eliminates the anxiety of risk exposure surrounding a trip.

SECTION TEN: Putting It All Into Perspective

Though the above legal theories expose mission organizations to potentially perilous liabilities, they will not likely freeze the efforts of such organizations. International Justice Mission plainly warns its volunteers that the work can be dangerous. In a recent article, "Dangerous Liaisons," a volunteer for that organization was quoted as saying, "In light of the dangers the victims face each day, we find in most cases that the risk of danger to ourselves is affordable, and a risk we're willing to take."[275] The article goes on to note that International Justice Mission plainly warns its volunteers that the work can be dangerous, which prompted the title for that article containing the quote. Risks are inevitable; yet, higher callings sometimes demand them. Avoidance of unnecessary risks, however, contributes towards good stewardship of an organization's resources. Knowledge of the legal perils potentially impacting an organization's ministry will enable an informed management to most effectively prepare for future ministry.

As illustrated above, Christians may view these legal risks as insignificant when compared to the value of the work being performed. Although God is sovereign, the Christian yet has the responsibility for acting wisely. Should Christians not be responsible with their knowledge of the world around them? If being informed allows one to weigh the benefits of precautionary measures against the encumbrances thereof, Christians should make an effort to obtain such knowledge.

There may be times when the requirements of a legal system do not mesh with the goals that God has laid out for His people. In some countries, it is illegal even to utter the name of Jesus. At those times, it is clear that Christians are expected to obey God's laws rather than man's. Is there any reason why Christians would be less strategic in their fulfillment of the Great Commission than they would be in a secular endeavor?

There are times Christians are called to martyrdom for reasons that may be known only to God. There are times God honors a waste of earthly wealth, such as prize perfume. There are times disasters are permitted to strike, to build faith and endurance. But one is not called to haphazardly take unnecessary risks that could lessen the accomplishment of eternal goals; nor are we called to be loose stewards of the resources that God has given us, and which other believers have entrusted to us. Rather, we are clearly instructed to pursue wisdom[276] while seeking to have something to show for the riches God has bestowed;[277] as sheep in the midst of wolves, Christians are to be wise as serpents and harmless as doves.[278]

The scripture and our own experiences tell us that ministry is not always safe, whether it takes the form of long-term missionary service or STM teams. Because it is known that there is risk in ministry, what we do and why we do it should be solidly rooted in scripture and well thought out. There are many good and exciting things to do, but agencies need to clarify their purpose and ministry, and then focus risk management around them. We must keep in mind that our task is not to make the world a safe place, but to use the tools we are given and trust God for the outcome.

After discussing an organization's exposure when facilitating STM teams, reviewing the actual numbers of incidents, and finally proposing mitigating measures that could be initiated, it is important to examine what could possibly be the ultimate risk to organizations and churches related to STM. It is thought that the ultimate risk faced by organizations is what will be called the "risk unto death." It is possible that organizations and churches could get so caught up in the fear of exposure that they forget the need, the urgency, and the provision.

The first risk would be the risk of forgetting the need. The New Testament tells us that *"all have sinned and come short of the glory of God."*[279] Romans tell us that each man that fails to accept Christ will spend eternity in hell. This knowledge is the need that drives us to do what we do. One of the greatest risks that organizations and churches face is the risk of forgetting that need of every man, woman, and child in the world.

The second great risk facing mission agencies and churches is the risk of forgetting the urgency of the task. II Peter 4:12 tells us, "*Looking for and hasting unto the coming of the day of God.*" Little does unsaved man know that the end times are coming at lightning speed. In addition to the rush of the end times is the fact that thousands are dying each day without a saving knowledge of Christ. Both of these events mean thousands are dying or will be dying without Christ. All of us involved in missions dare not forget the urgency before us to get the message out.

Finally, there is the risk that we get so focused on the exposure and the requirements the law may place on agencies and churches that we forget the provision that has been made for us as we carry out God's will. Paul reminds us in Philippians 4:13, "*I can do all things through Christ which strengtheneth me.*" Yes, the risk may be there to organizations and churches. Yes, the risk may be there for us to possibly lose our lives in getting the message out to unbelievers. But what greater risk is there than forgetting that God has given us all we need to accomplish His task and thus cowering at the task?

"*After this I beheld and, lo, a great multitude, which no man could number, of all nations, and kindreds, and peoples, and tongues, stood before the throne, and before the Lamb, clothed with white robes, and palms in their hand,*

And cried with a loud voice, saying Salvation to our God who sitteth upon the throne, and unto the Lamb."[280]

The content of this article is for informational purposes only and is not meant as legal advice. If you have specific legal questions about this issue, you should talk to a lawyer that specializes in this area, as state to state variations do exist.

Endnotes

[1] *AD2000. The Poor, The Unevangelized, & The 10/40 Window [map], August 1, 1990 edition. Cartography by GMI/GRDB (explaining that* "10/40 Window" as it is termed, containing 2/3 of the earth's population and is believed to be both the poorest region of the earth, as well as the least touched by the Gospel message. Therefore, to the extent that poverty corresponds with crime, this region poses a threat to the missionaries pursuing it.).

[2] Road Safety Overseas, available at http://travel.state.gov/travel/tips/safety/safety_1179.html (last accessed June, 2007).

[3] Id.

[4] Daniel B. Kennedy & Jason R. Sakis, Tourist Industry Liability for Crimes Against International Travelers, 22 TRIAL LAW. 301, 302 (1999).

[5] *See, e.g.* Semmelroth v. American Airlines, 448 F.Supp. 730, 734 (E.D.Ill. 1978) (where appropriate venue for suit was Illinois when death occurred in Mexico, defendant was from Delaware, plaintiff from Illinois, and relationship formed in Illinois); Arno v. Club Med Inc., 22 F.3d 1464 (9th Cir. 1994); McGhee v. Arabian Am. Oil Co., 871 F.2d 1412 (9th Cir. 1989); Filartiga v. Pena-Irala, 630 F.2d 876, 885 (2d Cir. 1980) (stating that "[c]ommon law courts of general jurisdiction regularly adjudicate transitory tort claims between individuals over whom they exercise personal jurisdiction, wherever the tort occurred"); Jurisdiction To Prescribe With Respect To Effect Within Territory, Restatement (Second) of Foreign Relations Law of the United States § 18 (1965).

[6] Robert A. Sachs, Getting a Witness To "Walk the Line": Accident Demonstrations at Videotaped Discovery Depositions, 30 Am. J. Trial Advoc. 487, 516 (Spring 2007) (stating "[O]ne only a small number of trial level opinions outside the federal system are ever published."); See Laurel Currie Oates & Anne Enquist, Just Research § 2.1, 13 (2005); Helene S. Shapo, Marilyn R.Walter, & Elizabeth Fajans, Writing and Analysis in the Law 8 (rev. 4th ed. 2003).

[7] Thomas H. Cohen, Appeals From General Civil Trials in 46 Large Counties, 2001–2005, NCJ-212979, Bureau of Justice Statistics, available at http://www.ojp.usdoj.gov/bjs/abstract/agctlc05.htm (last accessed June 2007).

[8] 36 J. Legal Stud. 171 at 176; 75 UMKC L. Rev. 171 at 171; see also Russell Engler, Out of Sight and Out of Line: The Need for Regulation of Lawyers' Negotiations with Unrepresented Poor Persons, 85 Cal. L. Rev. 79, 108. (1997) (describing how in New York City Housing Court, "most cases are settled with only minimal supervision by the court") (quoting 144 Woodruff Corp v. Lacrete,

585 N.Y.S.2d 956, 960 (Civ. Ct. 1992)); Vincent R. Johnson, Americans Abroad: International Educational Programs and Tort Liability, 32 J.C. & U.L. 309, 314, (stating that "[b]ecause of the tendency of tort cases to be settled, rather than fully tried, the number of unreported cases based on harm to students participating in study abroad programs may be considerably larger than what appears in legal research databases.).

[9] Based upon data from an ongoing survey study initiated in 2007 by Scott Ross of New Tribes Mission and Michelle A. Walker which inquired into the volume of disasters occurring during short-term mission trips organized through mission agencies in the years 2005 and 2006.

[10] Based upon an estimate of 20 people per team.

[11] Based upon data from an ongoing survey study initiated in 2007 by Scott Ross of New Tribes Mission and Michelle A. Walker showing the percent of team members experiencing disaster in 2006 was 1.2%, compared to .87% in 2005.

[12] Abrogation of immunity, 14 C.J.S. Charities § 99 (June 2007) (stating "In many jurisdictions, the doctrine of immunity of a charitable institution for its torts has been abolished or repudiated and is no longer applicable," explaining two-fold reason for change: "it both assures payment of any obligation to the person injured and gives a warning that justice and the law demand the exercise of care."); Tort immunity of nongovernmental charities—modern status, 25 A.L.R.4th 517 (Originally published in 1983).

[13] Hanson v. Saint Luke's United Methodist Church, 704 N.E.2d 1020,1022 (Ind. 1998); Between societies and their members, 77 C.J.S. Religious Societies § 143 (June 2007) (stating "An action may be maintained between a church and its members or officers.").

[14] See, for example Goard v. Branscom, 189 S.E.2d 667, 670 (N.C.App. 1972) (stating "We think, however, that one of the material differences between a church or denomination, religious society or congregation (a Quasi corporation) in North Carolina and a real corporation organized or existing pursuant to statutory law, is that a member of such a Quasi corporation is engaged in a joint enterprise and may not recover from the Quasi corporation damages sustained through the tortious conduct of another member thereof.") and Zehner v. Wilkinson Memorial United Methodist Church, 581 A.2d 1388, 1389 (Pa.Super.,1990) (stating "the members of an unincorporated association are engaged in a joint enterprise, and the negligence of each member in the prosecution of that enterprise is imputable to each and every other member, so that the member who has suffered damages

...through the tortious conduct of another member of the association may not recover from the association for such damages.").

[15] *Hanson*, 704 N.E.2d 1020.

[16] Cox v. Thee Evergreen Church, 836 S.W.2d 167 (Tex. 1992); Crocker v. Barr, 409 S.E.2d 368 (S.C. 1991); Burkhead v. American Legion Post No. 51, Inc., 332 S.E.2d 311 (Ga. App. 1985); Bourgeois v. Jones, 481 So. 2d 145 (La. Ct. App. 5th Cir. 1985), writ denied, 484 So. 2d 136 (La. 1986); Ayash v. Dana-Farber Cancer Institute, 822 N.E.2d 667 (2005), cert. den., 126 S. Ct. 397; Suits by members of unincorporated association against other members allowed by statute: Buteas v. Raritan Lodge No. 61 F. & A.M., 591 A.2d 623 (N.J.Super.A.D. 1991); Tanner v. Columbus Lodge No. 11, Loyal Order of Moose, 337 N.E.2d 625 (Ohio 1975).

[17] Duty to Protect Others from Criminal Attack, 57A Am. Jurisdiction. 2d Negligence § 96 (updated May 2007); Duty To Act For Protection Of Others, Restatement (Second) of Torts § 314 (1965); Toadvine v. Cincinnati, 20 F.Supp. 226 (E.D.Ky.1937); Gilbert v. Gwin-McCollum Funeral Home, Inc., 106 So.2d 646 (Ala. 1958); Louisville & N.R. Co. v. Scruggs & Echols, 49 So. 399 (Ala. 1909); Allen v. Hixon, 36 S.E. 810 (Ga. 1900); Hurley v. Eddingfield, 59 N.E. 1058 (Ind. 1901); Osterlind v. Hill, 160 N.E. 301 (Mass. 1928); O'Keefe v. W.J. Barry Co., 42 N.E.2d 267 (Mass. 1942); Matthews v. Carolina & N.W.R. Co., 94 S.E. 714 (N.C. 1917); Schichowski v. Hoffmann, 185 N.E. 676 (N.Y. 1933); Stager v. Troy Laundry Co., 63 P. 645 (Or. 1901); Prospert v. Rhode Island Suburban R. Co., 67 A. 522, (R.I. 1907); King v. Interstate Consolidated R. Co., 51 A. 301, (R.I. 1902); Riley v. Gulf, C. & S.F.R. Co., 160 S.W. 595 (Tex.Civ.App. 1913); Sidwell v. McVay, 282 P.2d 759 (Okla. 1955); Yania v. Bigan, 155 A.2d 343 (Pa. 1959).

[18] General rule of nonliability, 57A Am. Jur. 2d Negligence § 96 (May 2007) (explaining that "special relationships" refer to situations where the defendant is in a position that implies that he will be looking out for the welfare of the plaintiff, while the "special circumstances" includes times where the defendant created an opportunity and temptation for crime to occur.)

[19] Negligent Hiring and Retention of An Employee, 29 Am. Jur. Trials 267 § 1 Scope (May 2007).

[20] Restatement 2nd of Torts §§ 448-449.

[21] Duty voluntarily assumed or undertaken, 10 A.L.R.3d 619 § 4 (Originally published in 1966).

[22] *Id.*

[23] St. Louis-San Francisco R. Co. v Mills, 271 U.S. 344 (U.S. 1926)

[24] Hansen v Dodwell Dock & Warehouse Co., 170 P 346 (Wash. 1918).

[25] Duty voluntarily assumed or undertaken, 10 A.L.R. 3d 619 § 4 (Originally published in 1966).

[26] Mullins v. Pine Manor College, 449 N.E.2d 331, 336 (Mass. 1983).

[27] Johnson v Goldstein, 864 F Supp 490 (E.D. Pa, 1994).

[28] Jardel Co. v Hughes, 523 A2d 518 (Del Sup. 1987).

[29] Johnson v Goldstein, 864 F Supp 490 (ED Pa. 1994); *Jardel Co. v Hughes*, 523 A2d 518 (Del Sup/ 1987).

[30] Jackson v. Shell Oil Co., 650 N.E.2d 652, 657 (Ill.App. 1 Dist. 1995).

[31] Assumption of Risk; In General, 65 C.J.S. Negligence § 360 (stating "Under the doctrine of assumption of risk or assumed risk, one who voluntarily exposes himself or herself, or his or her property, to a known and appreciated danger due to the negligence of another may not recover for injuries sustained by such exposure."); Lowry v Atlanta Joint Terminals, 89 S.E. 832, 833 (Ga. 1916).

[32] Knowledge And Appreciation Of Risk, Restatement (Second) of Torts § 496D (1965) (stating "Except where he expressly so agrees, a plaintiff does not assume a risk of harm arising from the defendant's conduct unless he then knows of the existence of the risk and appreciates its unreasonable character.").

[33] Employers, 10 A.L.R. 3d 619 § 14 (Originally published in 1966) (stating "Employers have often been subject to claims by their employees for injuries resulting from criminal attacks by third persons.").

[34] Doe v. Dominion Bank of Washington, 963 F.2d 1552 (C.A.D.C. 1992); also see Duty to maintain safe premises, 10 A.L.R. 3d 619 § 5 (Originally published in 1966) (stating that the responsibility to exercise ordinary care in maintaining safe premises "has been held to include an obligation to protect patrons from criminal attacks by third persons.").

[35] Duty of custodian of persons, 10 A.L.R. 3d 619 § 8 (Originally published in 1966) (stating "Persons who become custodians of others, especially of children, thereby place themselves in a special relationship which requires special precautions.").

[36] Goldberg v Housing Authority of Newark, 186 A2d 291 (N.J. 1962).

[37] McLeod v Grant County School Dist., 255 P2d 360 (Wash. 1953).

[38] Special Relations Giving Rise To Duty to Aid or Protect, Restatement (Second) of Torts § 314A (1965), 320; Bloxham v. Glock Inc., 53 P.3d 196, 274 (Ariz. Ct. App. Div. 2 2002).

[39] University of Louisville v Hammock, 106 SW 219 (Ky. 1907); Sylvester v Northwestern Hospital of Minneapolis, 53 N.W.2d 17 (Minn. 1952); Bullock v

Parkchester General Hospital, (N.Y.A.D. 1957) 160 N.Y.S.2d 117, affd 150 N.E.2d 772.

[40] Casey v Sanborn's, Inc. of Texas, 478 S.W.2d 234 (Tex.Civ.App. 1972) (travel agent was liable to a traveler for injuries received in an automobile accident in Mexico because the driver's negligence amounted to a breach of the travel agent's implied agreement to furnish safe, or nonnegligent, passage.)

[41] Duty to maintain safe place to work, 10 A.L.R. 3d 619 § 6 (Originally published in 1966); Am Jur, Master and Servant (1st ed § 183).

[42] Duty to maintain safe place to work, 10 A.L.R. 3d 619 § 6 (Originally published in 1966).

[43] Id.

[44] The volunteer's rights are likened to an employee when he is recognized by the organization as being under its control, and is without personal interest in the matter; see Generally; volunteers and gratuitous employees, 27 Am. Jur. 2d Employment Relationship § 237 (stating "[A] person who might be thought of as a volunteer in the sense of performing work for another without the prospect of compensation may be owed the duties owed to an employee, where he or she is an assistant or substitute procured by an employee with the consent of the employer (which consent may be inferred from the nature of the work to be performed or from the employee's general course of conducting the employer's business), or where he or she is recruited by an employee under the emergency employment doctrine. In addition, it is sometimes said that to be properly termed a volunteer, a person must have no personal interest in the services that he or she performs.").

[45] Duty to maintain safe premises, 10 A.L.R. 3d 619 § 5 (Originally published in 1966); Am Jur, Negligence (1st ed § 131).

[46] Landlord's liability for failure to protect tenant from criminal acts of third person, 43 A.L.R.5th 207 (Originally published in 1996).

[47] Doe v. Dominion Bank of Washington, 963 F.2d 1552 (C.A.D.C. 1992).

[48] Feld v. Merriam, 485 A.2d 742 (Pa. 1984).

[49] Duty of Custodians of Persons, 10 A.L.R. 3d 619 § 8 (Originally published in 1966).

[50] Id.; see also Brown v. Knight, 285 N.E.2d 790, 792 (Mass. 1972).

[51] Wallace v. Der-Ohanian, 199 Cal.App.2d 141 (Cal.App. 1962).

[52] McLeod v. Grant County School Dist. No. 128, 255 P.2d 360 (Wash. 1953).

[53] District of Columbia v. Doe, 524 A.2d 30 (D.C. 1987).

[54] *Id*. at 32.

[55] *District of Columbia*, 524 A.2d 30.

[56] *Id*. at 33.

[57] *Id*. at 35.

[58] Thornton v. City of Flint, 97 N.W.2d 485, 493 (Mich. App. 1972).

[59] James v. Meow Media, Inc. 300 F.3d 683, 694 (Ky. 2002).

[60] Duty Of Person Having Custody Of Another To Control Conduct Of Third Persons, Restatement (Second) of Torts § 320 (1965).

[61] Reasonableness; fairness, 10 A.L.R. 3d 619 § 10 (Originally published in 1966).

[62] Brisbine v. Outside In School of Experiential Education, Inc., 799 A.2d 89, 93 (Pa.Super. 2002) (where court said a duty to control can be imposed on one who is in charge of individuals with dangerous propensities.).

[63] Creteau v. Liberty Travel, Inc., 195 A.D.2d 1012, (N.Y.A.D. 4 Dept. 1993) (stating "where the agent has knowledge of safety factors or where such information is readily available, a travel agent has the duty to inform the customer of those factors."); Wilson v American Trans Air, 874 F.2d 386, 390-391; Fling v Hollywood Travel & Tours, 765 F Supp 1302, 1305, *affd* 933 F.2d. 1008; cf., Levin v Kasmir World Travel, 143 Misc 2d. 245, 247; *see generally*, Dickerson, Travel Law § 5.03 [3]; Annotation, Liability of Travel Publication, Travel Agent, or Similar Party for Personal Injury or Death of Traveler, 2 ALR5th 396).

[64] Duty to Protect Others from Criminal Attack, 57A Am. Jurisdiction. 2d Negligence § 96 (updated May 2007).

[65] Foreseeability, 10 A.L.R. 3d 619 § 11 (Originally published in 1966).

[66] *But see* Foreseeability, 10 A.L.R. 3d 619 § 11 (Originally published in 1966) (explaining that some courts have held that the criminal acts of a third-party can *never* be the logical end to another's actions, thus calling into question the "proximate cause" requirement for tort liability.).

[67] Workman v. United Methodist Committee on Relief of the General Board of Global Ministries of the United Methodist Church, 320 F.3d 259 (C.A.D.C. 2003).

[68] *Id*.

[69] *District of Columbia*, 524 A.2d at 33.

[70] *Workman*, 320 F.3d 259.

[71] Potts v. District of Columbia, 697 A.2d 1249 (D.C.App. 1997).

[72] Bailey v. District of Columbia, 668 A.2d 817 (D.C. 1995).

[73] Clement v. Peoples Drug Store, 634 A.2d 425.

[74] Negligent Hiring and Retention of An Employee, 29 Am. Jur. Trials 267 § 1 (May 2007).

[75] *Workman*, 320 F.3d 259.

[76] *Workman*, 320 F.3d at 264.

[77] Reasonableness; fairness, 10 A.L.R. 3d 619 § 10 (Originally published in 1966).

[78] Reasonableness; fairness, 10 A.L.R. 3d 619 § 10 (Originally published in 1966).

[79] Factors Important In Determination Of Standard Of Reasonable Conduct, Restatement (Second) of Torts § 295A cmt. c (1965) (stating "No group of individuals and no industry or trade can be permitted, by adopting careless and slipshod methods to save time, effort, or money, to set its own uncontrolled standard at the expense of the rest of the community. If the only test is to be what has always been done, no one will ever have any great incentive to make any progress in the direction of safety.") (also stating that "whenever the particular circumstances, the risk, or other elements in the case are such that a reasonable man would not conform to the custom, the actor may be found negligent in conforming to it; and whenever a reasonable man would depart from the custom, the actor may be found not to be negligent in so departing.").

[80] Reasonableness; fairness, 10 A.L.R. 3d 619 § 10 (Originally published in 1966).

[81] Foreseeability, 10 A.L.R. 3d 619 § 11 (Originally published in 1966).

[82] Private person's duty and liability for failure to protect another against criminal attack by third person, 10 A.L.R. 3d 619 (originally published in 1966).

[83] Mastad v. Swedish Brethren, 85 N.W. 913 (Minn. 1901).

[84] 106 SW 2d.

[85] Private person's duty and liability for failure to protect another against criminal attack by third person, 10 A.L.R. 3d 619 (originally published in 1966).

[86] Private person's duty and liability for failure to protect another against criminal attack by third person, 10 A.L.R. 3d 619 (originally published in 1966).

[87] Shane v. Lowden, 106 S.W.2d 956 (Mo.App. 1937).

[88] Wallace v. Der-Ohanian, 199 Cal.App.2d 141, (Cal.App. 1962).

[89] Quinn v. Smith Co., 57 F.2d 784 (C.A.5, 1932).

[90] Private person's duty and liability for failure to protect another against criminal attack by third person, 10 A.L.R. 3d 619 (originally published in 1966).

[91] Private person's duty and liability for failure to protect another against criminal attack by third person, 10 A.L.R. 3d 619 (originally published in 1966).

[92] Wallace v. Der-Ohanian, 199 Cal.App.2d 141 (Cal.App. 1962).

[93] Mastad v. Swedish Brethren, 85 N.W. 913 (Minn. 1901).

[94] Private person's duty and liability for failure to protect another against criminal attack by third person, 10 A.L.R. 3d 619 (originally published in 1966).

[95] Goldberg v. Housing Authority of City of Newark, 186 A.2d 291 (N.J. 1962).

[96] Helms v Harris, 281 S.W.2d 770 (Tex.Civ.App., 1955); Private person's duty and liability for failure to protect another against criminal attack by third person, 10 A.L.R. 3d 619 (originally published in 1966); Genovay v. Fox, 143 A.2d 229 (N.J.Super.A.D. 1958); Factors Considered In Determining Utility Of Actor's Conduct, Restatement 2nd of Torts§ 292 (1965) (current through April 2007).

[97] Factors Considered In Determining Utility Of Actor's Conduct, Restatement 2nd of Torts§ 292 (1965) (current through April 2007).

[98] Lencioni v. Long, 361 P.2d 455 (Mont., 1961).

[99] Special Relations Giving Rise To Duty To Aid Or Protect, Restatement (Second) of Torts § 314A (1965).

[100] Creteau v. Liberty Travel, Inc., 195 A.D.2d 1012 (N.Y.A.D. 4 Dept. 1993) (stating "A travel agent ordinarily is not an insurer or guarantor of its customers' safety and, without a specific request, is not obligated to investigate safety factors of lodging accommodations... Nevertheless, where the agent has knowledge of safety factors or where such information is readily available, a travel agent has the duty to inform the customer of those factors"); Wilson v. American Trans Air, 874 F.2d 386, 390-391 (C.A.7 Ind. 1989); Fling v. Hollywood Travel and Tours, 765 F.Supp. 1302, 1305 (N.D.Ohio 1990) *aff'd*, 933 F.2d 1008; *cf.*, Levin v. Kasmir World Travel, 540 N.Y.S.2d 639 (N.Y.City Civ.Ct. 1989).

[101] Maurer v Cerkvenik-Anderson Travel, 890 P2d 69 (Ariz.App. 1994).

[102] Maurer v Cerkvenik-Anderson Travel, 890 P2d 69 (Ariz.App. 1994).

[103] Loretti v. Holiday Inns, Inc., 1986 U.S. Dist. LEXIS 25871.

[104] *Id.* at *10.

[105] Loretti v. Holiday Inns, Inc., 1986 U.S. Dist. LEXIS 25871 at *10-11.

[106] Rookard v. Mexicoach, 680 F.2d 1257, (C.A.9 1982).

[107] *Id.* at 1260; see also Carlisle v Ulysses Line, Ltd., 475 So 2d 248 (Fla.App. 1985) (applying federal maritime law) (carrier had a continuing obligation of care for its passengers and was not simply engaged for point-to-point transportation, it had a duty to warn its passengers of dangers known to exist in the particular place where the passengers were invited, or reasonably could be expected to visit.); Tradewind Transp. Co. v Taylor, 267 F.2d 185 (C.A.9 Hawaii 1959) cert. den., 361 US 829 (where a common carrier had a continuing obligation for the care of its passengers and a duty to warn of dangers known to the carrier in places where the passengers were invited or could reasonably be expected to visit; this duty extended throughout the length of the voyage, and did not cease at each port of call only to resume when the passengers re-embarked.).

[108] Levin v. Kasmir World Travel, 540 N.Y.S.2d 639 (N.Y.City Civ.Ct. 1989).

[109] *Id.* at 641.

[110] Stevenson v. Four Winds Travel, Inc., 462 F.2d 899, 906 (C.A.5 1972).

[111] Stevenson, 462 F.2d 899.

[112] *Id* at 907.

[113] *Id.*

[114] Semmelroth v. American Airlines, 448 F.Supp. 730, 732-33 (E.D.Ill. 1978).

[115] *Id.*

[116] Duty To Act For Protection Of Others, Restatement (Second) of Torts § 314A (1965) (current through April 2007) (stating "The Institute expresses no opinion as to whether there may not be other relations which impose a similar duty.").

[117] See *Id.*

[118] Found at http:// travel.state.gov/travel/cis_pa_tw/cis/cis_1765.html (last visited June 2007).

[119] Harmon v. Sullivan Univ. Sys., Inc., 2005 WL 1353752 at *3-6 (W.D.Ky., 2005) (holding that a claim was stated with respect to fraud and negligent misrepresentation of the accreditation of the university); Gomes v. Univ. of Me. Sys., 365 F. Supp. 2d 6, 47-48 (D. Me. 2005) (discussing a failed claim relating to a disciplinary hearing); Shelton v. Trs. of Columbia Univ., 2005 WL 2898237 at *5 (S.D.N.Y. 2005) (discussing a failed claim relating to a plagiarism hearing).

[120] Conditions Under Which Misrepresentation Is Fraudulent (Scienter), Restatement (Second) of Torts § 526 (1977).

[121] Bird v. Lewis & Clark College, 303 F.3d 1015 (9th Cir. 2002).

[122] *Id*. at 1023.

[123] *Id*. (stating "What makes a relationship special is not its name, but the roles assumed by the parties.").

[124] *See for example:* Crocker v. Barr, 409 S.E.2d 368, 370 (S.C. 1991); Furek v. University of Delaware, 594 A.2d 506, 513 (Del. 1991); Buteas v. Raritan Lodge, 591 A.2d 623, 625 (N.J.Super.A.D. 1991); Tanner v. Columbus Lodge, 337 N.E.2d 625, 627 (Ohio 1975); Cox v. Thee Evergreen Church, 836 S.W.2d 167, 173 (Tex. 1992).

[125] Roberts v. Craig, 268 P.2d 500, 507 (Cal.App.1.Dist. 1954) (stating "The doctrine of imputed negligence is indulged in to protect third persons from loss caused by the joint enterprise. Liability is imposed on all members engaged in a joint enterprise when the action is brought by a third person because the courts have felt that in such a case fairness requires that the joint enterprise should bear the damages caused by the negligence of any member of the enterprise.").

[126] Work Dangerous In Absence Of Special Precautions, Restatement (Second) of Torts § 416 (1965).

[127] Master; Servant; Independent Contractor, Restatement (Second) of Agency § 2(3) (1958).

[128] Chainani v. Bd. of Educ. of N.Y., 663 N.E.2d 283, 287 (N.Y. 1995) (where court said "This State has long recognized an exception from the general rule [of non-liability for the acts of an independent contractor] where, generically, the activity involved is 'dangerous in spite of all reasonable care.' ... This exception applies when it appears both that 'the work involves a risk of harm inherent in the nature of the work itself [and] that the employer recognizes, or should recognize, that risk in advance of the contract.'").

[129] Many courts that have considered the "inherently dangerous activity" exception have chosen not to apply it. However, several recent cases have applied the exception: McMillian v. United States, 112 F.3d 1040, 1047 (9th Cir. 1997) (activity of felling all of the trees in a right-of-way corridor held inherently dangerous); Maldonado v. Gateway Hotel Holdings, L.L.C., 154 S.W.3d 303, 310 (E.D.Mo. 2003) (boxing match held an inherently dangerous activity, leaving a hotel liable for the negligence of an independent contractor who failed to provide post-fight medical care); Hatch v. V.P. Fair Found., Inc., 990 S.W.2d 126, 135-36 (Mo.Ct.App. 1999) (bungee jumping held inherently dangerous activity); Beckman v. Butte-Silver Bow County, 1 P.3d 348 (Mont. 2000) (trenching held an inherently dangerous activity because the risks of death or serious bodily injury are well recognized and special precautions are required to prevent a cave-in that

could bury a worker); Enriquez v. Cochran, 967 P.2d 1136, 1162 (N.M.Ct.App. 1998) (felling dead trees held an inherently dangerous activity); Pusey v. Bator, 762 N.E.2d 968, 975 (Ohio 2002) (when employer hired independent contractor to provide armed security guards to protect property, the "inherently dangerous work" exception was triggered, and if someone was injured by the weapon as result of a guard's negligence, the employer is vicariously liable even though the guard was an employee of the independent contractor).

[130] Describes activities posing a risk of serious harm which cannot be eliminated by the exercise of the utmost care; See Contrast with abnormally-dangerous-activity test, 57A Am. Jur. 2d Negligence § 387; note that the Restatement of Torts 2d has substituted this phrase in place of "ultrahazardous"; See Saiz v. Belen School Dist., 827 P.2d 102 (1992).

[131] *McMillian*, 112 F.3d at 1047.

[132] *Id.*

[133] *Measles cases linked to Romania trip*, 12/22/06 Balt. Sun 4A, 2006 WLNR 22376080.

[134] Gammill v. U.S., 727 F.2d 950 (10th Cir. 1984).

[135] Jackson v. Tedd-Lait Post No. 75, American Legion, 723 A.2d 1220 (Me. 1999).

[136] Jackson v. City of Joliet, 715 F.2d 1200 (7th Cir. 1983).

[137] Special Relations Giving Rise To Duty To Aid Or Protect, Restatement (Second) of Torts § 314A (1965).

[138] McNeil v. Wagner Coll., 667 N.Y.S.2d 397 (App. Div. 1998).

[139] *Id.* at 398.

[140] Construction and application of "good samaritan" statutes, 68 A.L.R.4th 294 (Originally published in 1989).

[141] Dahl v. Turner, 458 P.2d 816 (Ct. App. 1969).

[142] Construction and application of "good samaritan" statutes, 68 A.L.R.4th 294 (Originally published in 1989).

[143] Deal v. Kearney, 851 P.2d 1353 (Alaska 1993).

[144] Liability of Church or Religious Organization for Negligent Hiring, Retention, or Supervision of Priest, Minister, or Other Clergy Based on Sexual Misconduct, 101 A.L.R.5th 1 (Originally published in 2002).

[145] Liability of employer generally for negligence in hiring or keeping employee known, or who should have been known, to be incompetent, 6 Am. Jur. 2d, Assault and Battery § 134.

[146] Ira C. Lupu & Robert W. Tuttle, <u>Sexual Misconduct and Ecclesiastical Immunity</u>, 2004 BYU L. Rev. 1789, 1792 (stating "The legal fallout from the scandal of the Catholic Church may be even more widespread and enduring than the religious consequences. Priests have gone to prison for lengthy terms. Many courts have upheld tort claims against dioceses and their officers, and First Amendment defenses once thought likely to insulate defendants against such claims have been aggressively advanced and explicitly rejected..." continuing at 1797-98, "At the beginning of the twentieth century, a person sexually molested by someone acting on behalf of a religious organization would not have contemplated legal action against the religious organization and would not have been successful in such an action had she tried. By the beginning of the twenty-first century, however, a person who had suffered such an injury might well be a successful plaintiff in a suit against the wrongdoer, the ecclesiastical officials, and the religious entity in which the individual defendants served.").

[147] 27 Am. Jur. 2d, Employment Relationship § 473.

[148] <u>Negligent Hiring</u>, 27 Am. Jur. 2d, Employment Relationship § 392.

[149] Ponticas v. K.M.S. Investments, 331 N.W.2d 907 (Minn 1983); Read v. Scott Fetzer Co., 990 S.W.2d 732 (Tex 1998); Southeast Apartments Management, Inc. v. Jackman, 513 S.E.2d 395 (Va. 1999).

[150] <u>Principle Negligent Or Reckless</u>, Restatement (Second) of Agency § 213, Comment d (1958).

[151] Evan F. v. Hughson United Methodist Church, 8 Cal App 4th 828 (Cal. App. 3 Dist. 1992).

[152] Janssen v. American Hawaii Cruises, Inc., 731 P.2d 163 (Hawaii 1987) (risk of sexual assault was not foreseeable, based upon role employee was hired to fill); *Ponticas*, 331 N.W.2d 907 (because employee would hold a passkey to 198 apartments was reason to do more thorough investigation into his fitness); Di Cosala v. Kay, 450 A.2d 508, 518 (Ga. App. 1982) (stating "employer, knowing of its employee's unfitness, incompetence or dangerous attributes when it hired or retained its employee, should have reasonably foreseen the likelihood that the employee through his employment would come into contact with members of the public, such as the plaintiff, under circumstances that would create a risk of danger to such persons because of the employee's qualities."); Welsh Mfg., Div. of *Textron, Inc.* v. Pinkerton's, Inc, 474 A.2d 436, 440 (R.I. 1984) (stating "The greater the risk of harm, the higher the degree of care necessary to constitute ordinary care.").

[153] Negligent Hiring and Retention of An Employee, 29 Am. Jur. Trials 267 (May 2007) (stating "Although no individual case has stated exactly what connection is required between the employment relationship at issue and the plaintiff before a duty will be imposed on an employer, it has been suggested that there are three requirements concerning the plaintiff and the employment relationship which must be satisfied before the law will impose a duty upon the employer to use due care in hiring and retaining employees on its behalf. These requirements are that (1) the incompetent employee and plaintiff are in places where each have a right to be at the time that the plaintiff sustains injury; (2) the incompetent employee and the plaintiff came into contact as a direct result of the employment; and (3) the employer has received or would have received some benefit, either direct, indirect or potential, from the meeting of the employee and the plaintiff," quoting The Responsibility of Employers for the Actions of Their Employees: The Negligent Hiring Theory of Liability, 53 Chi-Kent LR 717 (1977)).

[154] Negligent Hiring and Retention of An Employee, 29 Am. Jurisdiction. Trials 267 § 6 Duty Owed Plaintiff by Employer (updated May 2007); Donald K. Armstrong, Negligent Hiring and Negligent Entrustment: The Case Against Exclusion, 52 Or. L. Rev. 296, 298 (1973).

[155] Similar to types of relationships described in Negligent Hiring and Retention of An Employee, 29 Am. Jur. Trials 267 (May 2007) (where the successful negligent hiring case examples include employees of a landlord committing a wrong against a tenant or other person legally upon the landlord's premises, an employee violates a customer or business invitee of the employer, or situations where the injured plaintiff is a fellow employee of the incompetent employee.)

[156] Liability of Church or Religious Organization for Negligent Hiring, Retention, or Supervision of Priest, Minister, or Other Clergy Based on Sexual Misconduct, 101 A.L.R.5th 1 (Originally published in 2002).

[157] Cause of Action for Injury or Death Resulting From Negligent Hiring, 25 Causes of Action 2d 99 (2006); see, e.g. C.C. v. Roadrunner Trucking, Inc., 823 F. Supp. 913 (D. Utah 1993); Detrick v. Midwest Pipe & Steel, Inc., 598 N.E.2d 1074 (Ind. Ct. App. 3d Dist. 1992); Narney v. Daniels, 115 N.M. 41, 846 P.2d 347 (Ct. App. 1992).

[158] Odenthal v. Minnesota Conference of Seventh-Day Adventists, 657 N.W.2d 569 (Minn. Ct. App. 2003).

[159] Joyner v. B & P Pest Control, Inc., 853 So. 2d 991 (Ala. Civ. App. 2002).

[160] Carney v. Roberts Inv. Co., Inc., 837 S.W.2d 206 (Tex. App. 1992), writ denied, (Nov. 11, 1992).

[161] Knicrumah v. Albany City School Dist., 241 F.Supp. 2d 199 (N.D. N.Y. 2003).

[162] Foster v. Loft, Inc., 526 N.E.2d 1309 (Mass. App. Ct. 1988).

[163] Smith v. Orkin Exterminating Co., Inc., 540 So. 2d 363 (La. Ct. App. 1st Cir. 1989).

[164] Cutter v. Town of Farmington, 498 A.2d 316 (N.H. 1985) (court declared breach of duty by the town when new police officers were not given training in use of handcuffs, and improperly applied them, causing permanent nerve damage to plaintiff.).

[165] Through the doctrine of *respondeat superior*, discussed in section 8.1.

[166] Fernquist v. San Francisco Presbytery, 313 P.2d 192 (Cal.App. 1957).

[167] *Id.* at 195.

[168] Negligent Hiring and Retention of An Employee, 29 Am. Jur. Trials 267 (May 2007) (stating "The tort of negligent hiring is distinct from tort liability predicated upon the doctrine of respondeat superior in that the two theories differ in focus; under the latter, an employer is vicariously liable for an employee's acts committed within the scope of employment, whereas the tort of negligent hiring is a doctrine of primary liability, and employer is principally liable for placing an unfit individual in an employment situation that involves an unreasonable risk of harm to others," in reference to *Interim Personnel of Central Virginia, Inc. v. Messer*, 559 S.E.2d 704 (Va. 2002)).

[169] Predator in the Primary: Applying the Tort of Negligent Hiring to Volunteers in Religious Organizations, 2006 BYU L. REV. 569.

[170] Morgan Fife, Predator in the Primary: Applying the Tort of Negligent Hiring to Volunteers in Religious Organizations, 2006 BYU L. REV. 569, 570; James S. Barber, Workplace Violence: An Overview of Evolving Employer Liability, 83 Ill. B.J. 462, 462-63 (1995).

[171] Jones v. Trane 591 NYS2d 927 (N.Y.Sup. 1992).

[172] *Id.* at 932-33.

[173] Gil B. Fried, Illegal Moves Off-the-Field University Liability for Illegal Acts of Student-Athletes, 7 Seton Hall J. Sport L. 69 (1997) (stating "Once convicted of a crime, especially sexual abuse or related crimes, the prospect of repeat offenses is substantial.").

[174] Enserch Corp. v. Parker, 794 S.W.2d 2, 6 (Tex. 1990); Redinger v. Living, Inc., 689 S.W.2d 415, 418 (Tex. 1985).

[175] Baptist Mem'l Hosp. Sys. v. Sampson, 969 S.W.2d 945, 948 (Tex. 1998).

[176] Marble Falls Hous. Auth. v. McKinley, 474 S.W.2d 292, 293 (Tex.Civ.App. 1971) (rehearing denied Dec. 1971).

[177] Restatement (Second) of Agency § 267 (1958); Baptist Mem'l Hosp. Sys. v. Sampson, 969 S.W.2d 945, 947 (Tex. 1998) (stating "Liability may be imposed in this manner under the doctrine of ostensible agency in circumstances when the principal's conduct should equitably prevent it from denying the existence of an agency.").

[178] Vincent R. Johnson, <u>Americans Abroad: International Educational Programs and Tort Liability</u>, 32 J.C. & U.L. 309 (2006).

[179] <u>Negligence As To Danger Inherent In The Work</u>, Restatement (Second) of Torts § 427 (1965) (current through April 2007) (stating "One who employs an independent contractor to do work involving a special danger to others which the employer knows or has reason to know to be inherent in or normal to the work, or which he contemplates or has reason to contemplate when making the contract, is subject to liability for physical harm caused to such others by the contractor's failure to take reasonable precautions against such danger."); Hatch v. V.P. Fair Found., Inc., 990 S.W.2d 126, 134 (Mo.Ct.App. 1999) (quoting 41 Am. Jur. 2d Independent Contractors § 41 (updated May 2007) (stating "The theory upon which this liability is based is that a person who engages a contractor to do work of an inherently dangerous character remains subject to an absolute, nondelegable duty to see that it is performed with that degree of care which is appropriate to the circumstances, or in other words, to see that all reasonable precautions shall be taken during its performance, to the end that third persons may be effectually protected against injury.").

[180] <u>Americans Abroad: International Educational Programs and Tort Liability</u>, 32 J.C. & U.L. 309, 335 (2006);

[181] Foster v. Roman Catholic Diocese of Vt., 70 A.2d 230 (Vt. 1950).

[182] *Id* at 235.

[183] *Id.*

[184] *Foster*, 70 A.2d at 234.

[185] *Id.*

[186] *Foster*, 70 A.2d 233.

[187] *Foster*, 70 A.2d at 235.

[188] Sullivan v. First Presbyterian Church, Waterloo, 152 N.W.2d 628 (Iowa 1967); *Fernquist*, 313 P.2d 192.

[189] *Sullivan*, 152 N.W.2d 628.

[190] *Fernquist*, 313 P.2d 192; Note that the "invitee" standard is most applicable to this discussion. If the entering party is a "licensee," meaning they are the one receiving the sole benefit from entering the property, the standard is different. To show the owner's liability there, "wanton and willful" misconduct must be present. Garnier v. St. Andrew Presbyterian Church, 446 S.W.2d 607 (Mo. 1969). Of course, if the injured individual were a trespasser, the standard of safety would be lower. The invitee standard is the highest.

[191] *Sullivan*, 152 N.W.2d 628.

[192] Garnier, 446 S.W.2d 607.

[193] *Fernquist*, 313 P.2d at 193.

[194] *Id.*

[195] *Fernquist*, 313 P.2d 192.

[196] Coates v. W.W. Babcock Company, 560 N.E. 2d 1099 (Ill.App. 1 Dist. 1990).

[197] *Id.*

[198] Haugen v. Central Lutheran Church, 361 P.2d 637 (Wash. 1961).

[199] Geiger v. Simpson Methodist-Episcopal Church of Minneapolis, 219 N.W. 463, 464-66 (Minn. 1928).

[200] *Id.*

[201] When Master Is Liable For Torts Of His Servants, Restatement (Second) of Agency § 219 (1958) (stating that masters are not liable for the tort of a servant if that servant was "acting outside of the scope of employment unless the master (a) intended the conduct or the consequences, or (b) the master was negligent or reckless...."); *Garnier*, 446 S.W.2d 607 (Rule that nongovernmental charitable institution is liable for its own negligence and for negligence of its agents and employees acting within scope of employment is applicable to churches).

[202] Liability of charitable organization under respondeat superior doctrine for tort of unpaid volunteer, 82 A.L.R.3d 1213 (Originally published in 1978); Person Serving Gratuitously, Restatement (Second) of Agency § 225 (1958) (stating "One who volunteers services without an agreement for or expectation of reward may be a servant of the one accepting such services.") (illustration given: "A, a social guest at P's house, not skilled in repairing, volunteers to assist P in the repair of P's house. During the execution of such repair, A negligently drops a board upon a person passing upon the street. A may be found to be a servant of P.").

[203] *Fernquist*, 313 P.2d at 196 (stating "These [volunteers] were acting as agents of the defendant even though their services were performed gratuitously and both their knowledge and negligence can be imputed to their principal.").

[204] Person Serving Gratuitously, Restatement (Second) of Agency § 225 (1958).

[205] Liability of charitable organization under respondeat superior doctrine for tort of unpaid volunteer, 82 A.L.R.3d 1213 (Originally published in 1978).

[206] *Id.*

[207] Timmons v. Assembly of God Church of Van Nuys, 40 Cal.App.3d 31, 34 (Cal.App.2.Dist. 1974).

[208] *Id.*

[209] Decedent-spouse as provider of household services, 1 Stein on Personal Injury Damages Treatise § 3:36 (3rd Edition); Terveer v. Baschnagel, 445 N.E.2d 264 (Ohio.App. 1982) (parents of 22-year-old dental hygienist were entitled to recover for loss of her services in helping with rental properties, cutting her brothers' hair, and cleaning her family's teeth); *Gilbert v. Root*, 294 N.W.2d 431 (S.D. 1980).

[210] Child's Wrongful Death; 1 Stein on Personal Injury Damages Treatise § 3:37 (3rd Edition); U.S. D'Ambra v. United States, 481 F.2d 14 (C.A.1 1973), cert. den., 414 U.S. 1075 (FTCA where state wrongful death act is inapplicable because partly punitive); Tucson v. Wondergem, 466 P.2d 383 (Ariz. 1970) (Widow, hospitalized from an emotional condition which required psychiatric treatment as result of death of husband who drowned when his automobile was washed into arroyo by flood, was entitled to recover for anguish, sorrow, mental suffering, pain and shock); Krouse v. Graham, 562 P.2d 1022 (Cal. 1977) (husband allowed to recover "reasonable compensation for loss of wife's love, companionship, comfort, affection, society, solace or moral support, any loss of enjoyment of sexual relations, or any loss of physical assistance in the operation or maintenance of the home," despite contention that such items were not "pecuniary.").

[211] Decedent-spouse as provider of household services, 1 Stein on Personal Injury Damages Treatise § 3:36 (3rd Edition); Wilson v. Lund, 491 P.2d 1287 (Wash. 1971) (In enacting 1967 amendment providing that damages may be recovered for loss of love and companionship of and for injury to or destruction of parent-child relationship, the legislature authorized recovery of damages for parental mental anguish in cases involving wrongful death of or injury to a child.).

[212] Sanchez v. Schindler, 651 S.W.2d 249 (Tex. 1983), *reh'g of cause overruled* June 15, 1983 (rejecting pecuniary loss rule in actions for death of minor child).

[213] Loss of companionship and the like—Loss of consortium, 22A Am. Jur. 2d Death § 223 (April 2007).

[214] Hitaffer v. Argonne Co., 183 F.2d 811 (D.C. Cir. 1950), *cert. denied*, 340 U.S. 852, partially overruled on other grounds by Smither & Co. v. Coles, 242 F.2d 220, 221 (D.C.Cir. 1957); Loss of companionship and the like—Loss of consortium, 22A Am. Jur. 2d Death § 223 (April 2007).

[215] Maureen Ann Delaney, What About the Children? Towards an Expansion of Loss of Consortium Recovery in the District of Columbia, 41 Am. U. L. Rev. 107 at 114 (Fall, 1991); Loss of companionship and the like—Loss of consortium, 22A Am. Jur. 2d Death § 223 (April 2007).

[216] States include Alaska, Massachusetts, Michigan, Texas, Vermont, Washington, West Virginia, and Wisconsin.

[217] Hibpshman v. Prudhoe Bay Supply, Inc., 734 P.2d 991, 997 (Alaska 1987) (allowing four minor children an independent cause of action for loss of parental consortium as result of on-the-job injuries suffered by their father); Ferriter v. Daniel O'Connell's Sons, Inc., 413 N.E.2d 690, 696 (Mass. 1980) (allowing children to recover for loss of consortium for father's negligent injury if child can demonstrate dependence on parent) superseded by statute on other grounds as stated in Lijoi v. Mass. Bay Transp. Auth., 548 N.E.2d 893 (Mass.App.Ct. 1990); Berger v. Weber, 303 N.W.2d 424, 427 (Mich. 1981) (allowing minor daughter to receive damages for loss of society, companionship, love, and affection when mother was permanently injured in automobile collision); Reagan v. Vaughn, 804 S.W.2d 463, 465-66 (Tex. 1990) (allowing minor child to recover against bar management for loss of parental consortium); Hay v. Medical Center Hosp., 496 A.2d 939, 946 (Vt. 1985) (allowing minor child to recover for loss of parental consortium when mother became permanently comatose); Ueland v. Reynolds Metals Co., 691 P.2d 190, 195 (Wash. 1984) (allowing two minor children to recover for loss of love, care, companionship, and guidance when father suffered permanent mental and physical disabilities); Belcher v. Goins, 400 S.E.2d 830, 841 (W. Va. 1990) (indicating that minor children or handicapped children of any age that are dependent on their natural or adoptive parents be allowed to succeed in an action for loss of parental consortium); Theama v. City of Kenosha, 344 N.W.2d 513, 522 (Wis. 1984) (allowing minor children to recover for loss of parental consortium where father suffered severe injuries to head and internal organs in a motorcycle accident).

[218] Ferriter v. Daniel O'Conner's Sons, Inc., 413 N.E.2d 690, 692 (Mass. 1980) (stating that "a minor child has a strong interest in his parent's society, an interest closely analogous to that of the wife...") (superseded by statute on other grounds

as stated in Lijoi v. Mass. Bay Transp. Auth., 548 N.E.2d 893 (Mass.App.Ct. 1990)).

[219] Ueland v. Reynolds Metals Co., 691 P.2d 190 (Wash. 1984).

[220] *Id.*

[221] Assumption of Risk, Elements, 65 C.J.S. Negligence § 369 (updated June 2007).

[222] *Id.*, stating "Elements of assumption of the risk that must be shown by the defendant include that the plaintiff had knowledge of the facts constituting a dangerous condition, the plaintiff knew the condition was dangerous, the plaintiff appreciated the nature and extent of the danger, and the plaintiff voluntarily exposes himself or herself to the danger."

[223] Timmons v. Assembly of God Church of Van Nuys, 40 Cal.App.3d 31 (Cal.App.2.Dist. 1974).

[224] Davenport v. Cotton Hope Plantation Horizontal Property Regime, 508 S.E.2d 565 (S.C. 1998); *Timmons*, 40 Cal.App.3d 31.

[225] Bennett v. Gitzen, 484 P.2d 811, 813 (Colo.App. 1971).

[226] *Bennett*, 484 P.2d at 813.

[227] Okianer Christian Dark, Tort Liability and the "Unquiet Mind": A Proposal to Incorporate Mental Disabilities Into the Standard of Care, 30 T. Marshall L. Rev. 169, 174 (stating "Courts have consistently recognized the inherent unfairness of asking children to act like adults when in fact they are not.").

[228] Jarrett v. Woodward Bros., Inc., 751 A.2d 972 (D.C. 2000).

[229] *Id.*

[230] *Id.*

[231] Note that there are more than two alternatives—some states have a hybrid form—but these are the main categories; Modern development of comparative negligence doctrine having applicability to negligence actions generally, 78 A.L.R.3d 339 (Originally published in 1977).

[232] Modern development of comparative negligence doctrine having applicability to negligence actions generally, 78 A.L.R.3d 339 (Originally published in 1977).

[233] Legal Effect of Plaintiff's Fault, 65 C.J.S. Negligence § 262 (June 2007); Litchford v. Hancock, 352 S.E.2d 335 (Va. 1987).

[234] Injured Person's Fault, 65 C.J.S. Negligence § 227 (updated June 2007).

[235] Rosendahl v. Lesourd Methodist Church, 412 P.2d 109 (Wash. 1966).

[236] Injured Person's Fault, 65 C.J.S. Negligence § 227 (updated June 2007).

[237] <u>Modern development of comparative negligence doctrine having applicability to negligence actions generally</u>, 78 A.L.R.3d 339 (Originally published in 1977).

[238] Aguallo v. City of Scottsbluff, 678 N.W.2d 82 (Neb. 2004).

[239] *Id.*

[240] L & K Holding Corp. v Tropical Aquarium, 192 A.D.2d 643 (N.Y.A.D. 1993); Davis ex rel. Davis v. Government Employees Ins. Co., 775 A.2d 871 (Pa. Super. Ct., 2001).

[241] Schutkowski v Carey, 725 P.2d 1057 (Wyo. 1986).

[242] Paralift, Inc. v Superior Court, 23 Cal App 4th 748 (Cal.App.4.Dist. 1983).

[243] <u>Avoiding the Effect of a Recreational Activity Liability Release</u>, 33 Am. Jur. Proof of Facts 3d 421 (January 2007).

[244] Even though releases resemble contracts, "lack of consideration" would not void the contract on a mission trip release, rather the mere privilege of participation would likely be considered sufficient; See for example, Grbac v Reading Fair Co. (W.D. Pa. 1981) 521 F.Supp 1351, *affd*, 688 F.2d 215 (auto-racing accident).

[245] *Grbac*, 521 F.Supp. 1351.

[246] <u>Voidableness of Release</u>, 8 Am Jur. Proof of Facts 2d 617 (July 2006).

[247] "Void" sometimes means that no return of consideration is required in avoiding the release; see Bonacci v. Massachusetts Bonding & Ins. Co., 137 P.2d 487 (Cal.App. 1 Dist. 1943), State ex rel. Order of United Commercial Travelers of America v. Shain, 98 S.W.2d 597 (Mo. 1936); Picklesimer v. Baltimore & O.R. Co., 84 N.E.2d 214 (Ohio 1949).

[248] <u>Factors Rendering a Release Voidable</u>, 8 Am Jur. Proof of Facts 2d 617 § 2 (July 2006).

[249] Franco v. Neglia, 776 N.Y.S.2d 690 (N.Y.Sup.App.Term 2004).

[250] <u>Voidableness of Release</u>, 8 Am Jur. Proof of Facts 2d 617 § 1 (July 2006).

[251] Hojnowski ex rel. Hojnowski v. Vans Skate Park, 868 A.2d 1087 (N.J.App. Div. 2005), *cert. granted*, 878 A.2d 853.

[252] Hawkins ex rel. Hawkins v. Peart, 37 P.3d 1062 (Utah 2001).

[253] Gillespie v Papale, 541 F.Supp 1042, 1046 (DC Mass 1982) (stating that "[I]n no event may a person be relieved of liability for willful and wanton negligence"); Falkner v Hinckley Parachute Center, Inc., 533 N.E.2d 941, 946 (2d Dist 1989); Simmons v American Motorcyclist Ass'n, 69 Ohio App 3d 844, 846 (Allen Co. 1990); Gross v Sweet, 400 N.E.2d 306, 308 (N.Y. 1979).

[254] "Voidable" sometimes means that a return of consideration is required in avoiding the release; see Bonacci v. Massachusetts Bonding & Ins. Co., 137 P.2d 487 (Cal.App. 1 Dist. 1943); Trokey v. U.S. Cartridge Co., App., 222 S.W.2d 496 (Mo.App. 1949); Frehe v. Schildwachter, 45 N.E.2d 427 (N.Y. 1942); Haller v. Borror Corp., 552 N.E.2d 207 (Ohio 1990), reh'g denied, 555 N.E.2d 322.

[255] Ryan v Industrial Comm'n, 623 P.2d 37 (Ariz. 1981) (aviation accident); Simkin v Heil Valley Ranch, Inc., 765 P.2d 582 (Colo.App. 1988), rev'd on other grounds, 784 P.2d 781 (Colo. 1989) (horseback riding accident); Zimmer v Mitchell & Ness, 385 A.2d 437 (Pa.Super. 1978), aff'd, 416 A2d 1010 (snow skiing accident).

[256] Prosser and Keeton on the Law of Torts § 49 (5th ed. 1984).

[257] La Frenz v Lake County Fair Board, 360 N.E.2d 605 (Ind.App. 1977) (auto-racing accident).

[258] Coughlin v T.M.H. Int'l Attractions, 895 F.Supp. 159 (W.D.Ky. 1995).

[259] Eelbode v. Chec Medical Centers, Inc., 984 P.2d 436 (Wash. Ct. App. Div. 2 1999).

[260] Young v Gadsden, 482 So 2d 1158 (Ala. 1985), (overruled in part on other grounds by Barnes v Birmingham Int'l Raceway, 551 So 2d 929 (Ala. 1989) (go cart racing accident)).

[261] McCorkle v Hall, 782 P.2d 574 (Wash.App. 1989), review denied, 790 P.2d 168 (health club accident).

[262] Hewitt v Miller, 521 P.2d 244 (Wash.App. 1974), review denied, 84 Wash.2d 1007 (scuba diving accident); Baker v Seattle, 484 P.2d 405 (Wash., 1971) (golf cart accident).

[263] Provence v Doolin 414 N.E.2d 786 (Ill.App. 1980) (auto-racing accident); Moore v Sitzmark Corp., 555 N.E.2d 1305 (Ind.App. 1990) (snow skiing accident).

[264] Atkins v. Swimwest Family Fitness Center, 691 N.W.2d 334 (Wis. 2005).

[265] Mettler ex rel. Burnett v. Nellis, 695 N.W.2d 861 (Wis.App. 2005).

[266] Vaughn v Didizian, 648 A2d 38 (Pa Super Ct. 1994); Hammer v Road America, Inc., 614 F Supp 467 (E.D.Wis. 1985), affd. without op., 793 F2d 1296; Haines v St. Charles Speedway, Inc., 689 F.Supp 964 (E.D.Mo. 1988) aff'd, 874 F.2d 572; Murphy v North Am. River Runners, 412 S.E.2d 504 (W.Va. 1991); In re Waikiki Hobron Associates, Bkrtcy.Hawaii, 51 B.R. 406; Carona v. Illinois Cent. Gulf R. Co., 561 N.E.2d 239 (Ill.App. 5 Dist. 1990) appeal denied 567 N.E.2d 329; Harris v. Lapeer Public School System, 318 N.W.2d 621 (Mich.App. 1982); Goncalvez for Goncalvez v. Patuto, 458 A.2d 146 (N.J.Super.A.D. 1983); Sparler

v. Fireman's Ins. Co. of Newark, New Jersey, 521 A.2d 433 (Pa.Super. 1987) *appeal denied*, 540 A.2d 535; Arnold v. Shawano County Agr. Soc., App., 317 N.W.2d 161 (Wis.App. 1982) *aff'd*, 330 N.W.2d 773.

[267] Neely v. Club Med Mgmt. Servs., Inc., 63 F.3d 166, 185 (3d Cir. 1995) (stating that "[P]arties may generally consent to application of American law to govern their relations, as evidenced by a choice of law clause."); National Ass'n of Sporting Goods Wholesalers, Inc. v. F.T.L. Marketing, 779 F.2d 1281, 1285 (C.A.7 (Ill.) 1985) (stating "[U]nless the court's subject-matter jurisdiction is affected, parties may generally stipulate to the substantive law to be applied.").

[268] Americans Abroad: International Educational Programs and Tort Liability, 32 J.C. & U.L. 309, 319 (2006); The Issue Involved, Restatement (Second) of Conflicts § 145 cmt. d (1971).

[269] Mary Ann Connell & Frederick G. Savage, Releases: Is There Still a Place for Their Use by Colleges and Universities?, 29 J.C. & U.L. 579, 617 (2003).

[270] White v Rhodes, 607 N.E.2d 75 (Ohio App. 2 Dist. 1992), *motion overruling* 598 N.E.2d 1171.

[271] Gillespie v Papale, 541 F Supp 1042 (D.C.Mass. 1982); Barker v Colorado Region - Sports Car Club, Inc, 532 P.2d 372 (Colo.App. 1974); Bowen v Kil-Kare, Inc., 585 N.E.2d 384 (Ohio 1992) *reh. denied*, 589 N.E.2d 46; Arnold v Shawano County Agricultural Soc., 317 N.W.2d 161 (Wis.App. 1982) *aff'g* 330 N.W.2d 773.

[272] Hardy v. St. Clair, 739 A.2d 368, 371 (Me.1999).

[273] White v Rhodes, 607 N.E.2d 75 (Ohio Ct. App 1992), *motion overruling* 598 N.E.2d 1171.

[274] *See, e.g.*, Brotherhood Mutual Insurance's policy entitled "Foreign Travel & Mission Trip Insurance" described at http://www.brotherhoodmutual.com/insPrograms/passportToMinistry/default.htm (last visited June 2007).

[275] Suzanne Craig Robertson, Dangerous Liaisons, 42-JAN Tenn. B.J. 16 (January, 2006).

[276] Proverbs 1; Psalms 1

[277] Matthew 25:14-28

[278] Matthew 10:16b

[279] Romans 3:23

[280] Revelations 7:9-10

CHAPTER 17

LESSONS FROM THE SAPLING: REVIEW OF QUANTITATIVE

RESEARCH ON SHORT-TERM MISSIONS

KURT ALAN VER BEEK

Introduction[1]

To what extent do short-term missions (STMs) bring about lasting positive change in participants? Conventional wisdom, repeated in Christian magazines and from many pulpits on Sunday mornings has it that an STM trip will create lasting change in the lives of both those who "receive" the trip and also in the short-term "missionaries." Eyes will be opened, hearts will be transformed, and lives will be changed forever. An estimated 1.5 million people a year (Priest 2006) are investing billions of dollars on STM trips, based on this perception. This truism is seldom questioned or challenged.

My recent study (Ver Beek, 2006—summarized below) of nearly 200 North Americans who came to Honduras after Hurricane Mitch to build houses found that these STMs trips had resulted in very little lasting positive change in either the lives of the North Americans or the Hondurans. As a result, I was curious if my study was an exception or if it was supported by other research. My review of STM research found another thirteen quantitative studies of STM which used some sort of independent measure to corroborate the changes in the participants' lives.

The review of these studies below demonstrates that eleven of these thirteen studies found little or no significant positive impact from the STM trip in the lives of participants. And despite the fact that the principal beneficiary of these trips is ostensibly to be the "recipients" of the STM, of the fourteen studies, only mine looked at the impact of the trip on the recipient churches and communities. Given the millions of short term missionaries, and the billions being spent, these results are disconcerting. However, a review of these studies demonstrates that while short-term missions, as currently practiced, may seldom result in lasting positive change—the experience *can* be structured to become a catalyst for such change. Research demonstrates that lasting positive change is possible, but it requires that participants are held accountable, and are encouraged to translate their good intentions into long-lasting actions.

My research on short-term missions with CIDO

My study (Ver Beek, 2006) sought to explore the long-term impact of STM on both the communities served as well as on the short-termers themselves: Do they pray more, study more, or give more? The results of the study took me and many others by surprise.

Background

In October 1998, Hurricane Mitch devastated Honduras, leaving more than 5,000 dead and 1.5 million homeless or displaced. Hurricane Mitch also created tremendous sympathy among North Americans. The Christian International Development Organization (CIDO)[2] raised over $2 million for reconstruction in Honduras, most of it used to build 1,082 new homes. CIDO channeled the majority of these funds through their partners in Honduras—Christian development organizations that normally receive CIDO funding for programs in areas such as health and agriculture. Most of the homes were built in regions where these organizations already worked and for people with whom they already had a relationship. Nearly all of the recipients were required to help build their own homes and pay back part or all of the home's cost. CIDO also had thirty-one STM teams (twenty-six from Canada and five from the United States) assist in building homes. Each team spent an average of $30,000 in airfare, lodging and local expenses. While in Honduras, each team built one house, which normally cost $2000 to build if STM was not involved. These work teams were coordinated by CIDO and CIDO partners in Honduras.

Impact of STMs on Hondurans

Nearly all STM research examines only the North American participants, despite the fact that local participants are the intended beneficiaries.[3] This study presented us with uniquely advantageous circumstances in that we were able to compare two groups of new homeowners: those whose homes had been built by STM groups and those whose homes had been built by Honduran Christian development. By comparing these two groups, we could isolate the effect that a STM group's presence (or absence) had on Honduran families and communities. To collect data on both groups, we sent out a Honduran social worker as well as a North American social worker fluent in Spanish to visit six regions in Honduras. They interviewed the fifteen CIDO partner employees (all Honduran) and seventy-eight beneficiaries, about half of whom lived in homes built by STM groups and half in homes built by local Christian organizations. These interviews were taped and then reviewed and summarized by both researchers.[4] We tried to determine how having the home built by an STM group rather than by local builders had impacted the beneficiaries' views of their homes, their relationships to their neighbors, and their faith. These interviews resulted in three principal conclusions:

1) *The North American work teams seemed to have no greater impact on the communities than the Honduran Christian organizations—either positive or negative.* When asked about sense of ownership of the new homes, spiritual life, loan repayment, motivation to participate in community projects, and other factors, neither beneficiaries nor development organizations could identify any noteworthy difference between families whose homes were built by STM groups and those whose homes were built otherwise. So while it seemed to make little difference who built the house, the houses built by locals only cost $2000, while the STM groups invested over $30,000 to build the same house.

2) *The work of Honduran agencies has substantial, lasting impact.* While the study did not find a significant difference in impact on the new homeowners based on who built their homes; the strategies used by the Honduran agencies for training, construction, loan repayment, and follow-up did have a lasting impact on the self-concept and motivation of Honduran individuals and on the unity of Honduran communities. The factors which appeared to have the most positive impact were (a) following through on a clearly defined strategy, (b) accompanying the construction process with a training program, and (c) managing funds and resources involved in construction and loan repayment transparently. Doing these three activities well, made families (a) more grateful for their homes, (b) feel more ownership of their homes, (c) more motivated to participate in other community projects, and (d) more likely to pay off their loans on time. So while the one week with the STM group did not result in lasting positive change, the continuing work of the local Christian NGO did make a significant lasting difference.

3) *Nearly all Hondurans surveyed gave reasons why it was good for STM groups to come to Honduras, but in the end they believed that*

rather than using up resources on plane tickets, food, and lodging, North Americans could better spend their money on building more homes. Hondurans made it clear they valued the relationships built and the changes brought about in the STM participants. Hondurans also hoped these participants would become more committed supporters. But in the end, when faced with the great need for housing around them and the shortage of construction work for their neighbors, they believed sending money to build more houses would be the greater good than spending so much on airfare, lodging and food.

Impact of STMs on North Americans

All 162 participants in the STM project in Honduras were sent a survey and 127 responded (a 78% response rate). They were asked to rate how they had changed their everyday actions such as the amount of time they spent in prayer, time spent volunteering, level of financial giving, and interest in poor countries as a result of their work in Honduras. On average, about 16% reported a significant positive impact and about 45% a slight positive impact, and the other 40% no change. These findings are very similar to most of the studies based on participants' self-perception. (See, for example, McDonough and Peterson 1999).

However, we also triangulated these results with the giving records of CIDO, the organization which had sponsored their trip. In the survey about 60% of the respondents (63 individuals) claimed that their level of donations to CIDO had increased significantly or somewhat. We then asked CIDO for the giving records for the year before the respondents went to Honduras and for two years after. According to CIDO giving records, 75% of them had not sent a single direct donation to CIDO after their trip, the total giving from the participants went up only 6%, from $31 to $33 per year among all participants, and from $169 to $179 per year among those who donated. Since it was possible that individuals were not sending direct donations to CIDO but were giving through their church's regular offerings for CIDO, we also looked at their churches' giving for the year before and two years after the Honduras trips. CIDO's records showed that the yearly giving average for the seventeen churches that sent groups to Honduras went up by about 1% ($20,427 to $20,635). Six of the seventeen churches increased giving after their trips, while eleven decreased giving. These results are certainly less than would have been predicted given the respondents' answers to the questionnaire and also were definitely smaller than CIDO would have hoped for, given the resources it invested in these trips.

It appears that the participant's perceived/reported changes in giving after their experience in Honduras, were much higher than their actual changes/actions.[5] Obviously this calls into question the respondent's other answers. If they perceived their change in giving as much more positive than it actually was, were their perceptions of their increases in volunteering, prayer and interest in Third World issues also exaggerated? And finally, if the respondents in *this* survey perceived their changes as more positive than they actually were, did this mean that many of the other studies of STM which reported very positive lasting change in participants were also exaggerated? I was curious. Were my findings just a fluke? I decided to look at other studies.

Review of Quantitative Studies of Short-term missions

Nearly all quantitative studies of STM have been done since 1990. We were able to find only forty-four quantitative studies, many of questionable quality. Of these studies, only thirteen applied at least one of the following basic research procedures for measuring change in a population: a pre and post-test of standardized questions, a post-test with a control group, or triangulation of the respondent's answers with secondary data sources. I will review here the results of these thirteen studies.[6]

No significant positive change in participants

Eleven of the thirteen studies which fit the criteria for this literature review found little or no change in short-term mission trip participants. I will begin by summarizing the results of the studies which found little or no significant change and which applied a pre-test/post-test format for standardized surveys.

Pre and Post-test without Control

Wilson (1999)

Wilson (1999) surveyed twenty-seven youth who went on a nine-day mission trip to Mexico before and after their trip and forty-five days later using the *Faith Maturity Scale*. Wilson found no significant changes in the scale as a whole. He did find significant changes in three out of the forty-one questions including self-perception of: time spent reading Bible, giving time and money to help others, concern about poverty in U.S. and in world. Wilson did not apply the survey to a control group.

Kirby (1995)

Kirby (1999) was the researcher and also the leader of two evangelism-oriented STMs in Romania[7] in May 1994. All participants—sixty-two Americans in the first group and forty-four in the second (there were also nationals participating, but they were not surveyed)—were given a pre-trip survey testing eight factors including: knowledge of, and attitude towards, missions, self-reported level of giving, and time spent in private prayer. The same questions were asked by mail or telephone three months after their return.[8]

Participants' self-reported change in all eight factors was very positive. For example nearly all participants stated that the amount of time they spent in prayer had increased after the trip. However, before and after their STM trip they were also asked to estimate rates for each of the eight factors. For example, before and after the trip they estimated how much time they actually spent in private prayer. So while their perception was that they had increased in all eight factors, the changes in their actions (also self-reported) was very minimal—two items increased, five stayed the same and one decreased. They reported an increase in private prayer and understanding of missionaries' problems. But their involvement in the promotion of missions, communal prayer, general knowledge of missions, sense of vocation as missionary and their financial giving stayed the same (although 36% perceived they were giving more, or significantly more[9]) and their overall attitude toward mission was more negative. The survey was not given to a control group and the use of phone interviews to increase response rate most likely increased the self-reported change (see footnote 5).

Pre and Post-test with Control

Beers (1999)

Beers (1999) studied 171 students from Taylor University—comparing seventy-two who participated in one-month school-sponsored "study abroad missions" (SAM) during their January term with ninety-nine who stayed on campus during the same time (a non-matched control group). Both groups were given the *Faith Maturity Scale*, and the *Growth in Mature Faith Index (GMFI)*. No significant differences emerged between pre-trip and post-trip scores on either faith scales or between the two groups, but there were significant changes in seven of fifty-five specific questions.[10] "The lack of a statistically significant increase in the SAM students' GMFI [Growth in Mature Faith Index] was surprising to the researcher" (122).[11]

Blezien (2004)

Blezien (2004) attempted to answer the question, "to what extent, if any, is the cross-cultural sensitivity of undergraduate college students influenced by participation in summer international short-term mission experiences?"

> The quantitative portion of the research involved pretests and posttests of 159 students from five different Christian colleges that are members of the Council for Christian Colleges and Universities. The instrument utilized in this portion of the study was the entire Quick Discrimination Index (QDI) (Ponterotto & Bukard, 1995; Utsey & Ponterotto, 1999) and a portion of the Crown-Mueller (1960) Social Desirability Scale. A non-matched control group of 151 students also completed the pretest and posttest (ii).

The pre-test was given approximately one month before their STM trip, and the post-test was applied approximately six weeks after their return. Blezein concluded that "no statistically significant difference was found between the pretest and posttest scores of the students who traveled overseas for summer short-term mission projects" (110). In fact, the Attitudes Toward Women's Equity scores of the QDI test actually decreased for the summer short-term mission participants.

Tuttle (1998)

Tuttle (1998) carried out a study of 131 students at four schools of the Coalition for Christian Colleges and Universities. The Belief and Commitment Scale (BCS) and the Faith Maturity Scale were administered to sixty-four test participants both one month before and several weeks after they went on short-term mission trips[12], and also to sixty-seven non-matched control participants. Twenty students who had been on at least one STM were also interviewed.

There was no significant change in either of the scales—either within the short-term mission group or between groups. "The change scores of only one BCS item out of thirty-five showed significant difference (236)." This item examined the extent to which respondents were moved by the beauty of creation.

Manitsas (2000)

Manitsas (2000) administered the *Spiritual Well-Being Scale* (Paloutzian, 1983; Paloutzian & Ellison, 1982), the *Tennessee Self-Concept Scale, Second Edition* (Fitts and Warren, 1996), and a Likert-Scale survey of his own design with questions about the STM experience to twenty-five members of a Baptist Church who went on a mission trip to Mexico. The test was administered three times (pre-trip, post-trip, six months after trip) to three groups: to seven who had previous experience in STM, seven who were going on a trip for the first time and eleven who served as a non-matched control.

Manitsas' found that,

> comparison between the STM groups and the control group did not show significant difference on Spiritual Well-Being or Self-Concept scales; in the Likert-Scale questions and anecdotal responses, however, STM participants reported feeling closer to God, being more committed to Christian service, and more likely to participate in another STM than they had been previously.

The author also notes that "except for being more likely to participate in a future short-term mission trip, these gains [feeling closer to God and being more committed to Christian service] were not sustained through a six month follow-up." (38)

Triangulated Studies

In addition to my study (Ver Beek, 2006) there were four other studies which compared STM participants' perceived changed with an external (triangulated) data source, all of which did not find significant lasting change in participants.

Purvis (1993)

Purvis (1993) surveyed seventy-nine short-term volunteers from the thirty-eight churches of the Caldwell/Lyon Baptist Association (sub-group of the Kentucky Baptist Convention) who had gone on short-term mission trips to Brazil and Kenya.[13] Sixty-eight participants responded to a post-trip survey and twenty-four were interviewed before, immediately following, and six months after returning from their trip. These volunteers reported that they had "experienced a positive impact in mission giving, mission knowledge, attitude towards career missionary service, and view of future short-term service" (i). In fact, a local pastor stated that "personal mission giving has virtually exploded" (36). In part due to the growth in this partnership, the Kentucky Baptist Convention hired a full-time staff person in 1985 to coordinate the trips, produce a monthly newsletter and recruit and supervise volunteers.

While volunteers reported a positive impact of the trip on various areas of the spiritual life, Purvis found no relationship between the number of trips and the reported positive changes—which appears to mean that participating in more STM trips would not result in greater amounts of giving, prayer, etc. Secondly, 76% of respondents claimed that their missions giving had either increased greatly or somewhat. He then triangulated these answers with thirteen years of mission's giving records from these thirty-eight churches and reported that their giving had increased by 66.8% from 1981 until 1992.[14] However, Purvis did not adjust for inflation. After adjusting for inflation, mission giving increased only 7% over eleven years, or 0.7% a year (see my calculations in Appendix 1). In addition, 89%

of the participants were given subsidies amounting to up to half the cost of their trip by the Kentucky Baptist Convention,[15] funds which came out of this same mission's fund—so the total amount given to long-term missionaries would necessarily have gone down over these years.

In summary, despite the fact that this STM effort enlisted a full-time staff person to promote the work, produced a monthly newsletter and represented a twelve-year partnership between the churches in Kentucky and the churches in Kenya and Brazil—my re-analysis of Purvis' data found that while 76% of the STM participants believed that the impact of the trip had significantly impacted their giving, this was not the case. In addition, increasing participation in STMs did not result in greater church growth in the U.S. And finally the funding received by overseas missionaries actually decreased during this period because mission fund income was used to cover airfare for short-term groups.[16]

Priest, Dischinger, Rasmussen, and Brown (2006)

Priest et al. (2006) present the results of three different surveys which examine the impact of STM on six different issues. One of the surveys found three significant positive changes in the 169 High School students who took a pre and post test surrounding a one-week trip to Tijuana. After their week in Mexico the students had a significant a) increase in interest in serving as a career missionary b) improvement in their perception of Mexicans and c) decrease in ethnocentrism. However, Priest et al. cite their own survey to question this decrease in ethnocentrism, and I would argue it calls into question the first two results as well.

> However, at the beginning of the trip, when we explored the relation of ethnocentrism to how many STM trips they had been on previously, STM participants did not score lower on

ethnocentrism. These latter results were similar
to our results with M. Div. seminary students
using a nine-item measure of ethnocentrism, with
ethnocentrism scores no lower for those with STM
experience abroad. One possible interpretation of
the above results is that STM trips tend to produce
temporary changes only. On the other hand,
there may be variability in outcomes due to other
factors (444).

The authors go on to argue that proper orientation and training
during the event may account for these changes where other STM
trips fail. I would argue however that all three of the changes are
most likely the result of a temporary bump resulting from the trip,
and that the survey needed to be reapplied a few weeks or months
after the trip to determine if any of those three changes would have
remained significant.

Priest et al. also present the results of two other surveys, one of
120 seminary students and the other of a mixed group of 565 Sunday-
school participants, college undergrads and seminary students. In
these studies Priest et al. were exploring whether or not there was
a correlation between the number of STM trips and changes in a)
increase in giving to missions b) levels of materialistic tendencies
and c) the number of interethnic relationships at home. Priest et
al. did not find, in either of the two studies, that people who had
participated in more STM trips gave more money to missions, were
less materialistic, or had more interethnic friendships.

Significant Positive change in participants

Two of the thirteen studies showed significant positive change in
the STM participants. Both of the studies applied pre and post-test
surveys.

Hopkins (2000)

Hopkins (2000) used Starrett's *Global Social Responsibility Inventory* to survey sixty-four George Fox University students who participated in one of five week-long service/mission trips in the Northwest United States [17] and a non-matched control group of thirty-six students in a general psychology class. Hopkins applied a pretest, posttest and a follow-up test four weeks later.

> [Even] when pretest social responsibility scores are controlled, the service ministry trip participants continue to differ from the members of the control group in social responsibility scores at the posttest.

Students who participated in the mission trips demonstrated a stronger sense of social responsibility than did a control group immediately after trip, and this effect persisted four weeks later. Contrary to Hopkin's hypothesis, increased opportunity to interact with marginal populations did not result in greater increases in social responsibility. [18]

Jones (1998)

Jones (1998) surveyed 852 U.S. middle and high school students who participated in week-long, summer STM projects in "high-need" communities in the United States. In the mornings the young people repaired homes and in the afternoons they helped with local inner-city ministries. Jones applied the *Faith Maturity Scale* and the *Multidimensional Self Concept Scale* on the first day and the last day of their week-long missions project and found that all groups had significant increases in both scales. Jones then analyzed the impact on the subgroups: junior and senior high, and males and females. Each of these groups also showed statistically significant increases in both scales. Jones did not apply the surveys to a control group and did not reapply either of the scales after a period of time to determine if the increases were lasting.

Analysis and Future Research

Why such difference between qualitative and quantitative results?

It is very curious that every qualitative study I have found concluded that there are significant positive changes in the participants in STM. Yet the quantitative studies reviewed above are heavily slanted toward no significant change. There are at least two possible explanations: 1) the participants may be significantly changed but the tests used may not be effective in measuring that change, or 2) the self-perception of the change was much greater than the actual changes in their lives. While more research is necessary to answer this question, claiming that these tests are failing to capture real change seems less likely given that the fourteen studies above use a wide variety of survey measures which have accurately detected change in many other settings. One further piece of convincing evidence is that while STM is often promoted as increasing interest in long-term missions, despite the skyrocketing number of STM participants in the last twenty years, the number of long-term missionaries has remained stagnant at about 40,000. As a result, I would argue that participants did have a very positive experience and intended that the experience would translate into action—but most often it did not. But when questioned, their positive view of the experience and their intention to make changes in their lives colored their answers. I would call for more studies which used verifiable secondary sources—giving or volunteering records, membership in voluntary groups, career choices, etc… as well as comparing the participants to a *well-matched* control group.

Why are results of even the quantitative studies reviewed still mixed?

It is also interesting that the findings in the studies above which fit my criteria were not unanimous. While the vast majority found very little or no significant change, two of the fourteen studies did find significant change. What can explain that?

I would like to take a closer look at the experiences surveyed in this research, and I would invite others to do likewise. The studies which found significant positive change should be replicated, to see if the findings are consistent. If they are, then the experiences themselves need to be examined more closely. There may well be something extraordinary in certain projects that do result in lasting positive change—certain program components, structures or leaders who enable others to overcome the human tendency to resist change and to not follow through on good intentions. These components may or may not be replicable, but examining what is working will likely help us learn how to design STMs experiences that bring about lasting positive change.

Why are there not more studies of the recipients of STM?

It is very distressing that only two of forty-four STM studies to date include data on those who receive STM trips. While this trend is beginning to change, we need more high quality research regarding the lasting impact of STM on the receiving communities.[19] One of the challenges in this research is to avoid the assumption that the communities have no options regarding how their needs can be met. For example, we should not be asking, would you rather a STM group came and built you a water system or would you rather keep drinking dirty water? But rather we need to consider together what would be the "best" way to build a new water system—the method which results in the most positive change for all involved—privileging marginal populations. Another challenge is how to carry out more systematic and "objective" research in communities unaccustomed to surveys or in places where literacy levels are low. I am confident that both of these obstacles will be overcome as researchers begin to pay more attention to the recipients of STM.

Hard to change people–the sapling

Before beginning my own study I believed that the North Americans who went on STM trips were somewhat fragile/vulnerable—that is to say, a one-week experience in Honduras, Kenya or Thailand could quite easily "shake-up their world" and result in lasting changes in areas such as social action, prayer or financial giving. This hypothesis is common among proponents of short-term missions.

I now question this belief. Rather than believing North Americans (or Hondurans, Kenyans or Thais) are so easily changed, I wonder if they do not more closely resemble young saplings, which can be bent and even held in one place for a week or more, but once let loose quite quickly go back to their original position. Those saplings need to be held in place for a much longer period of time for the change in growth to become permanent.

While my original assumptions seemed plausible, the new perspective seems much more logical. We all know that making changes in our lives is difficult, and that exciting experiences and good intentions often do not translate into lasting change. This perspective would have predicted that the majority of the North Americans who go to Honduras or Kenya or Thailand for a few weeks, upon returning to their jobs, families, mortgage payments, etc., would not follow through on their good intentions to significantly change their lives.

This new perspective contradicts the conventional wisdom and much of the non-quantitative research that has been done on short-term missions. However, both my own research and the majority of the studies reviewed above support this new perspective. It is very difficult to bring about lasting positive changes in our own, or our neighbors' lives.

What will bring lasting positive change?

So if short-term missions as they are currently being practiced are not resulting in lasting positive change in participants, what would? Many of our everyday experiences and lots of research, including my own, have shown that two *factors* are key in helping people bring about lasting positive change in their lives. I will call these two factors accountability and encouragement.

I believe all of us have had experiences which result in decisions to change our lifestyles, actions or attitudes. We step on the scale and then commit to exercise three times a week. Or we go on a retreat and decide to pray everyday or give sacrificially to a cause we care about—but as time goes by our resolve dissolves. But most of us have also set goals like these with the difference that friends, colleagues or family hold us accountable and encourage us—knocking on the door to take us jogging or meeting weekly to talk about our prayer lives or our giving practices—and as a result we are more successful in keeping those goals. Accountability and encouragement help us meet our goals.

The importance of accountability is very well documented by research. Over the last 35 years, Locke and Latham's (2002) goal-setting theory has been repeatedly[20] tested and time and again researchers have found that when individuals set goals and regularly get feedback (accountability) regarding their progress, they are much more likely to achieve those goals. Locke and Latham's theory provides several other interesting results to consider. Individuals are more motivated and will work harder to achieve their goals if: a) their goals are made public, b) if the goals are specific (not just do your best), c) if the goals are more demanding as long as it is within the individuals capability (most people have little motivation to achieve simple goals). In addition, it matters little if the individual sets their own goal or if the goal is set for them, as long as they accept and commit to the logic and importance of the goal. In summary, goal-setting theory would argue that short-term missions participants are much more likely to successfully experience lasting positive change in their lives if they set specific, public, demanding goals and then are regularly held accountable for their progress.

The importance of encouragement or social support is equally well documented in helping people accomplish what they would otherwise be unable of doing. Research has shown social support to result in increased test-scores in students (Lee and Smith 1999), improved college student's ability to adapt (Sandler and Barrera), reduced stress in cancer patients, and so on (Zea, Jarama and Bianchi, 1995). While social support networks do provide the challenges of accountability and public pressure to achieve outcomes described in goal-theory above, they also provide encouragement, understanding, friendship—in short positive social relationships—which provide the motivation to do things we would not do on our own.

My own research supports these points. While my own research did not find lasting positive change in North American participants, it did find lasting positive change in some Honduran communities. It was not the involvement of North American short-term groups that were the cause of these differences, but it was the long-term relationship with the Honduran Christian development organization. When the relationships between the community and the organization were healthy (with accountability of all parties to their mutual goals and encouragement and support in meeting those goals), the communities were motivated and paying their loans, but when there was a lack of clear goals, accountability and encouragement, the communities were complaining, not paying their loans and not working together.

Based on common life experiences as well as substantial amounts of research, I would argue that in seeking to make lasting change in the participants, the key ingredient is the creation of a structure which will provide accountability and encouragement to the participants before and especially after their experience.

How can STM contribute to lasting positive change in others and ourselves?

If it is true that lasting positive change will most likely happen within a long-term relationship of accountability and encouragement, then to contribute to real change in the churches, and communities they visit, STM groups need to do everything possible to ensure that they are partnering with organizations, missionaries, and churches that are involved in excellent, life-changing long-term work with those they serve. While the STM trip may be a catalyst or detractor from the intended changes—it is the long-term excellent relationships which will contribute most to creating lasting positive change.

Similarly, to create lasting positive change in their own lives, STM groups need a structure of accountability and encouragement in place in order to translate their good intentions into action. Such structures will likely include components such as written goals that they share with the group, accountability pairs, mentors, regular newsletters and meetings where they could do a mixture of things including: share progress on goals, make plans as a group for continuing support, or pray and worship together.

Conclusions

The research outlined above demonstrates that STM, as they are currently being practiced, create very little lasting positive change in the participants, whether North Americans, Hondurans, or Kenyans. While the STM trip is often a mountaintop experience for the participants, a few weeks or months later their good intentions to raise money for world missions, work for social justice, or deepen their faith have not been translated into actions. If we hope to see those good intentions translated into accomplishments something needs to change.

Our own experiences, and extensive research on goal-setting theory and social support networks provide us with strong evidence on how STM should be changed. Participants will be much more likely to change their lives in lasting ways if they set specific, demanding and public goals and then are regularly held accountable and encouraged to put them into practice. Creating a structure which holds *all* STM's participants accountable, and encourages them, will increase the likelihood that the STM trip will not be just a mountaintop experience but a catalyst which *will* result in dramatic increases in prayer, giving, and volunteering among North Americans, Hondurans and Kenyans.

Further research is required to confirm the very clear trend here which says that STM, as currently practiced, does not result in lasting change in the participants. Second, researchers and practitioners need to work together to demonstrate what goal-setting theory has proven in many other fields—that providing participants with accountability and encouragement will make it much more likely that participants will convert their goals and good intentions into lasting positive change. Finally, for this research to actually change practice, it will take practitioners and opinion shapers to recognize the problems with the current STM model and design and implement one which comes closer to meeting the expectations of opening eyes, transforming hearts and changing lives forever.

References Cited

Beers, Stephen Thomas. 1999. *Faith development of Christian college students engaged in a one-month study abroad mission trip.* Doctoral Diss., Ball State University.

Blezien, Paul. 2004. *The impact of summer international short-term missions experiences on the cross-cultural sensitivity of undergraduate college student participants.* Doctoral Diss., Azusa Pacific University.

Cecil, James W. 1981. *A critical analysis of the foreign mission board's procedures for the involvement of short term volunteers in personal presence overseas ministries.* Doctoral Diss., Southwestern Baptist Theological Seminary.

Hopkins, Sarah Mott. 2000. *Effects of Short-Term service Ministry Trips on the Development of Social Responsibility in College Students.* Doctoral Diss., George Fox University.

Jones, Karen. 1998. A study of the differences between the Faith Maturity Scale and the Multidimensional Self Concept Scale scores for youth participating in two denominational ministry projects. Doctoral Diss., Southwestern Baptist Theological Seminary.

Kirby, Scott Harrison. 1995. *Short-term volunteer foreign mission experiences: What difference do they make in the lives of the participants?* Doctoral Diss., Southeastern Baptist Theological Seminary.

Lee, Valerie E. and Julia B. Smith. 1999. Social support and achievement for young adolescents in Chicago. *American Educational Research Journal* 36: 907-945.

Locke, Edwin A. and Gary P. Latham. 2002. Building a practically useful theory of goal setting and task motivation: A 35-year odyssey. *American Psychologist* 57: 705-717.

Manitsas, David L. 2000. *Short term mission trips: A vehicle for developing personal and spiritual well-being.* Doctoral Diss., George Fox University.

McDonough, Daniel P., and Roger P. Peterson. 1999. *Can short-term mission really create long-term missionaries?* Minneapolis: STEM Ministries.

Priest, Robert, Terry Dischinger, Steve Rasmussen and C.M. Brown. 2006. Researching the short-term mission movement. *Missiology: An International Review* 34: 431-450.

Priest, Robert and Tito Paredes, Guest Editors. 2007. *Special Issue on Short-Term Missions in Latin America* of the *Journal of Latin*

American Theology: Christian Reflections from the Global South, Vol 2.

Purvis, Tommy G. 1993. *Partnership in cross-cultural mission: The impact of Kentucky Baptist short-term, volunteer missions.* Doctoral Diss., Asbury Theological Seminary.

Sandler, Irwin N. and Manuel Barrera. 1984. Toward a multimethod approach to assessing the effects of social support. *American Journal of Community Psychology* 12: 37-52.

Tuttle, Kathryn A. 1998. *The effects of short-term missions experience on college students' spiritual growth and maturity.* Doctoral Diss., Talbot School of Theology, Biola University.

Ver Beek, Kurt Alan. 2006. The impact of short-term missions: A case study of house construction in Honduras after Hurricane Mitch. *Missiology: An International Review* 34: 477-496.

Wilson, Dean Edward. 1999. *The influence of short-term mission experience on faith maturity.* Doctoral Diss., Asbury Theological Seminary.

Zea, Maria Cecilia, Lisbeth S. Jarama and Fernanda Trotta Bianchi. 1995. Social support and psychological competence: Explaining the adaptation to college of ethnically diverse students. *American Journal of Community Psychology* 23: 509-31.

Appendix 1

Reanalysis of Purvis (1993) data on reported giving vs. actual missions giving as a result of a STM experience.

Taken from Purvis, Tommy G. *Partnership in cross-cultural mission: The impact of Kentucky Baptist short-term, volunteer missions.* dissertation. Wilmore, Kentucky: Asbury Theological Seminary, 1993.

Appendix D, page 187

Per capita missions giving from Caldwell/Lyon Baptist Association

	average	inflation rate	average in 1980 dollars
1980	$ 29.13		$ 29.13
81	$ 32.93	-0.094	$ 29.83
82	$ 35.76	-0.146	$ 30.54
83	$ 40.49	-0.173	$ 33.49
84	$ 41.29	-0.207	$ 32.74
85	$ 42.54	-0.234	$ 32.59
86	$ 43.65	-0.248	$ 32.82
87	$ 46.29	-0.275	$ 33.56
88	$ 47.06	-0.303	$ 32.80
89	$ 48.50	-0.335	$ 32.25
90	$ 51.62	-0.37	$ 32.52
91	$ 53.52	-0.395	$ 32.38
1992	54.92	-0.413	$ 32.24

inflation rates calculated with:

http://www1.jsc.nasa.gov/bu2/inflateCPI.html

before adjusting	% change in 12 years	47%	
	% change per year	4%	
adjusted for inflation	% change in 12 years	9.6%	9.7%
	% change per year	0.8%	0.8%
before adjusting	since 1981 (11 yrs)	40%	
	change per year	4%	
adjusted for inflation	since 1981 (11 yrs)	7%	
	change per year	0.68%	

Endnotes

[1] I would like to thank Abram Huyser-Honig, Maree Ness, Grace Miguel and Jo Ann Van Engen for their assistance in this research. I would also like to thank Calvin College for generously granting me support for this project which I completed in part during a sabbatical year.

[2] The development agency that was the subject of this study prefers to remain anonymous. The Christian International Development Organization (CIDO) is a pseudonym.

[3] I have documented over 50 quantitative research papers on STMs. Of those only 4 surveyed the effect of the STM trip on the beneficiaries.

[4] We were hoping to get a mix of qualitative and quantitative data from the communities. We made several attempts to collect quantitative answers about topics such as: was the community more united, had it grown spiritually or which group of homeowners felt more ownership of their homes? The fact that the majority of the interviewees were illiterate or had very low levels of formal education, had little or no experience with surveys, as well as the difficulty of quantifying these topics with any audience, led us to abandon the quantitative questions in favor of a qualitative methodology. This resulted in a much more comfortable, conversational interview with the beneficiaries.

[5] Another study which reinforces the idea that observers often believe short-term mission will increase donations was carried out by Cecil (1981). Cecil found that the missionaries who hosted short-term missionaries had a much more optimistic perspective on the possibility of receiving increased donations from the participants after the trip than did the participants themselves. Sixty-eight percent of the missionaries thought the participants' donations would increase greatly and 30% thought they would increase somewhat, compared to just 17% of the participants who thought their donations would increase greatly and 55% who thought the increase would be moderate.

[6] I have not included four studies here which are often cited to support the claim that short-term missions result in significant increases in items such as prayer for, and giving to, missions. All four of these studies use the same survey form and very similar methodology. The best known of the four studies is McDonough and Peterson (1999). This study did not meet my criteria because it is only a post-experience survey and does not use a control group nor does it attempt to triangulate the responses to secondary data. The results are reported in a manner which may give the reader the impression that the authors used a

pre and post-test methodology; however, the participants were sent a survey after their short-term missions experience, in which in the left hand column they are asked to estimate the amount of time they spent in prayer or amount they gave to missions before their short-term missions trip (as much as 3 years earlier) and in the right hand column they are asked to estimate those same factors after their missions trip. Their results find that participants consistently increased one category in nearly every area. While these results may be accurate, I believe it may well be the result of the respondents attempting to be perceived and to perceive themselves in a good light. This is one of the principal reasons that I have only included in this literature review studies which used a standardized pre and post test or sought to triangulate respondents' answers with secondary data sources. For further critique of the methodology employed in this study, see Priest et al. 2006, 435-436.

[7] Kirby was both the leader and researcher (as with Peterson, see McDonough and Peterson 1999)—a combination which is full of conflict. Kirby led these 2 groups—each group was "doing missions" for 5 days and had no language training but worked through translators. Kirby (1995, 79) states "We recorded approximately 1600 decision for Christ during this project."

[8] None of the pretests were done by phone, but the author called people who had not responded by mail. This introduced potential error into the study since these 12 were non-respondents and their answers by phone to the researcher and the leader of the trip may have not reflected what they would have answered by mail. Cecil (1981) compared results from responses by mail and by phone to the same survey on STM and found the mean scores were 10-12% higher when the survey was done by phone.

[9] The participants were asked in the pre- and post-test their level of giving to missions—so while it was self-reported, these two figures were compared. They were also asked in the post-test to rate the impact of the trip on their giving and 36% claimed it had increased greatly or somewhat, but when their self-reported giving figures were compared, there was no significant difference (10 increased, 9 stayed the same and 10 decreased).

[10] The control group did have a significant positive change in one of the sub-scales; the short-term mission group did not. Of the seven questions which showed significant changes, four were questions in which the control group went down in score and all were related to stress levels and lack of time—congruent with a group of students taking classes on campus. The other three questions

included: acceptance of self, acceptance of other religions and God's role in the world/suffering.

[11] Beers has reviewed and agreed with this summary of his study (email communication, July 31, 2006).

[12] Eight of the sixty-four were involved in service tasks (such as construction or performance art) and the rest were involved in relational tasks (discipleship, teaching and evangelism).

[13] The relationship between Kentucky and Kenya churches lasted from 1982-1987. Kentucky churches sent 721 volunteers and saw 50,000 professions of faith, 600 churches started. From 1988-1992 the Kentucky churches formed a partnership with a region in Brazil. During this period the Kentucky churches sent over 677 volunteers to do evangelism, medical, music and construction work.

[14] My calculations in appendix 1 put the actual increase over these years at 40%.

[15] In 1983, "$450,000 was requested to cover the costs for which the individual volunteers could not be expected to pay. KBC directors of missions had their expenses subsidized up to half the cost, up to $1000. Pastors were assisted at $400 each (39).

[16] Purvis has reviewed this summary of his research and confirmed that he did not adjust for inflation.

[17] Four of the five groups were principally involved with serving inner-city populations (homeless, disadvantaged youth and battered women). The fifth group was focused on construction work and personal discipleship of the participants.

[18] There were two significant differences between the participants in the service experience and the control group—the service group had a higher history of previous community service (98% vs. 86% in control group) and were much older on the whole (14% freshmen vs. 81% freshmen in control group). In addition, doing a follow-up survey four weeks after the experience may not be long enough to determine the lasting impact on the participants.

[19] For example Trinity Evangelical Divinity School and the Facultad Evangelica Orlando Costas del CEMAA organized a conference on STMs with many Latin American STM researchers, with the papers subsequently published in English (Priest and Paredes 2007).

[20] With goal-setting theory, specific difficult goals have been shown to increase performance on well over 100 different tasks involving more than 40,000 participants in at least eight countries working in laboratory, simulation and field

settings. The dependent variables have included quantity, quality, time spent, costs, job behavior measures and more. The time spans have ranged from 1 minute to 25 years. The effects are applicable not only to the individual but to groups, organizational units and entire organizations. The effects have been found using experimental, quasi-experimental and correlational designs. Effects have been obtained whether the goals are assigned, self-set, or set participatively. In short, goal-setting theory is among the most valid and practical theories of employee motivation in organizational psychology. (Locke and Latham, 2002).

CHAPTER 18

RESEARCHING SHORT-TERM

MISSIONS AND PATERNALISM

KYEONG SOOK PARK

Introduction

The demographic center of global Christianity has shifted from the North and West to the South and East (Jenkins 2002a; 2002b). Asia, Africa, and Latin America have become the home of representative Christianity—that is, mainstream, norm-setting Christianity (Walls 2002, 68). Indeed, the Church worldwide is post-Western, polycentric and multicultural; and it is an extremely diverse collection of people from every country, ethnic group, and culture (Chandler 2000; Walls 2002). Furthermore, as Walls (p. 65) notes, the Christian faith will become more and more associated with, and more and more marked by, the thought and life of these continents. As a result, this new phase of Christianity has been raising new challenges especially when it comes to Christian mission. And these challenges concern traditional mission methods and practices, global missional theologies, missiological education and/or cross-cultural training, and paternalism.

Against this milieu of mosaic global Christianity, there have been new patterns of global connectedness affecting the global Church. STM provides one paradigm for such patterns, touching on many aspects of the challenges this post-Western, multiracial, and multicultural Christianity encounters. In view of the fact that STM participants and leaders often combine material resources (economic power) with naive optimism about the benefits of STM, some missiologists wonder whether STM represents a new form of colonialism or paternalism that benefits STM participants more than those they ostensibly serve.

The Purpose of This Paper

In the research I report on here, I chose to focus on the concept of paternalism and its relationship to STM experience and to formal education. The following were my core research questions.

Research Question 1: What is the effect of STM experience on paternalistic tendencies?

Since STM combines benevolent impulses with brief encounters in distant contexts where short-term missionaries necessarily lack contextual knowledge, one might hypothesize that the STM movement itself would foster paternalistic tendencies. When more money is spent on a young person's two-week trip than the total annual salary of host pastors, this again might easily signal an over-valuing of the brief and benevolent contribution of the short-term missionary, and a disrespect for the on-going and sustained contribution of local Christian leaders. Alternatively, it might be hypothesized that STM experience itself brings short-termers into relationship with indigenous Christians who clearly are exemplary, and thus that short-term mission experience would tend to lower paternalistic tendencies fostered by the STM rhetoric and funding patterns. Thus my first research question was: What is the effect of STM experience on paternalistic tendencies?

Research Question 2: What is the effect of STM experience on STM participants' subjective perception of the value of missiological and/or cross-cultural education?

Since STM experiences do not require professional missiological training or expertise, and indeed have been said to value the amateur, and since STM programs often involve brief package tours buffering participants from deep and sustained engagements with culture and cultural differences, one might hypothesize that STM experience contributes to a denigration of the importance of missiological education. Both Winter (1996, 5) and Hesselgrave (2005, 204) speak of short-term missions as a re-amateurization of missions, which emphasizes enthusiasm and experience at the expense of education. And certainly some short-term mission leaders have seemed to celebrate lack of education as a good thing (see Peterson, Aeschliman, and Sneed 2003, 15ff). Thus there are reasons to think that STM experience might actually make people less inclined to value intercultural and missiologically oriented education.

Alternatively, one might hypothesize that STM involves cross-cultural engagements which naturally lead the participant to realize how much they do not understand and to realize the value of further education related to cross-cultural ministry. Thus my second research question: What is the effect of STM experience on STM participants' subjective perception of the value of missiological and/or cross-cultural education?

Research Question 3: What is the effect of formal education, and missiological education, on paternalistic tendencies?

One possible effect of a Bible College/Bible Institute education is that one develops confidence in one's own education and credentials and understandings of the Christian faith in such a way as to treat other Christians with less respect. Alternatively, education may have a broadening effect, teaching people to respect Christian leaders of other societies. That is, one could justify alternative hypotheses as to the effects of Bible College/Bible Institute education on paternalistic tendencies. On the other hand, missiological education, specifically, ought to have a corrective impact on paternalistic tendencies. It was thus hypothesized that missiological/intercultural education would result in lower paternalism scores. I will examine how the subjects' majors, and the amount of education they receive, affect paternalism.

In addition to the above research questions, I will give a report on the findings related to the extent and nature of STM experiences among Christian college students in the U.S. Moreover, because of my professional background, I will incorporate into this paper some of the findings pertinent to the effect of STM experience coupled with missions education on paternalism. Before discussing the results in the order of (1) findings related to the extent of STM; (2) findings on the research questions; and (3) the effect of the synergy of short-term experience and missiological education, I will start with further discussion of my research methods.

Research Methods

Developing a Measure of Paternalism

At the core of my research lies the concept of paternalism. Paternalism is viewed as the dominance of the sending church and its representatives over the partnership churches who receive them. Paternalism involves an attitude, tendency, or disposition to relate to others in a fatherly manner, that is, to relate to adults of another culture as if they were children. Specifically, paternalism combines benevolence with an assumption of superior knowledge, experience, and skills (Van Rheenen 1996) giving one the right to make decisions and exercise authority on behalf of others, for their own good, without giving them full and equal respect and the right to determine their own agendas. The opposite of the paternalistic impulse is the desire to trust and respect others from another culture as adults, and is manifested in the willingness to serve under their leadership, respecting and accepting indigenous authority, decision-making, and responsibility.

There is a significant body of literature on paternalism in other settings (Cicirelli 1990, Jackman 1994, Stone 1977, Weiss 1985 Woodward 1998), and some of this literature includes quantitative measures of paternalism. However, quantitative measures of paternalism in medical contexts, for example, will not work to measure paternalism in mission settings. Thus I developed a series of seven situations and invited students to imagine themselves as a missionary in such situations. For example: *Indigenous Christians eagerly seek your advice on every ethical question they face, and believe you are a more trustworthy source of advice than their own indigenous pastors.* Students were then asked to indicate on a four point Likert Scale (rated from four to one) whether they "would eagerly accept this opportunity" or "would not accept this opportunity." An additional eleven items were listed, with level of agreement again intended as a means of measuring paternalistic tendencies. The survey respondent was asked to indicate whether they "strongly agreed," "agreed," "disagreed," or "strongly disagreed" (with Likert ratings from four to one) with statements such as: *When an indigenous church must decide between ministry projects, the missionary should have the final say in choosing one that he or she believes will help the church.* Missiologists were invited to give feedback on each question, indicating whether they felt it was a valid measure of paternalistic tendencies. The survey was also administered to several classes, and the results were examined statistically. Items which did not correlate highly with the other items were eliminated, as were items which missiologists rejected as invalid measures of paternalism. This resulted in a ten-item measure of paternalism, which received a high reliability score statistically (Cronbach's reliability alpha of .825) for the final scale (see Park 2007). The scores for each question were added together into a single measure of paternalism for each respondent. There was good variability in paternalism scores. Final paternalism scores ranged from a low of 10 to a high of 39, with a mean of 22.3.

Instrument

The survey questionnaire consisted of 44 items focusing on four major areas: (1) demographics; (2) the extent of STM experiences; (2) the nature of STM experiences; (3) college majors/emphases and the amount of education; and finally (4) the Paternalism Scale.

Subjects

The size of the sample population was 869 from four Christian Colleges: Moody Bible Institute (628 students—72.4%); Columbia International University (215 students—24.8%); Toccoa Falls Christian College (19 students—2.2%); and Nyack College (5 students—.6%). They represented all levels of undergraduate education, with 43.5% freshmen, 11.2 % sophomores, 18.4% juniors, and 26.9% seniors. While clearly freshmen were the largest group of students who filled out the survey, there were a sizable number of seniors represented in the data. Female respondents at 52% slightly outnumbered male at 48%. Only 7% of respondents were twenty-five years old or older.

Procedure

Faculty at Moody Bible Institute helped administer this survey to ten classes offered at different levels (from freshman to senior level), seven of which were required of all majors. Along with the survey and instructions, each student received a written explanation of the purpose of the research, and was assured of anonymity and confidentiality. While students were not required to fill them out, the vast majority did, and 630 were returned to me.

For the three other colleges, three names of missions professors and one theology professor were obtained and contacted to distribute the survey questionnaires in their respective classes. The questionnaires were mailed to three professors. Even though all four agreed to administer them in their classes, one did not respond, and, due to time constraints, was not followed up. This explains why the sample size from Nyack Christian College was particularly small. The courses at Columbia International University were also core required courses. Most of the respondents, then, were taking classes reflective of the general school population.

Findings: Descriptive Data

Number of STM Trips
Slightly over 25% of the respondents had never gone on STM trips outside of the United States; in other words 75% of these students had gone on at least one short-term service trip. This is seventy-five times the rate at which American undergraduate students travel outside the USA in the context of study-abroad programs (NAFSA 2003). Slightly less than 25% went on one short-term trip. Twenty percent had been on two trips, another 20% on three to four trips, 7% on five to six trips, and over 4% for seven or more trips, with a high a twenty trips taken by one student. Perhaps this last 4% exemplifies what some have called "short-term junkies" (McDonough 1996, 62).

Length of Most Recent Short-Term Trip
These mission trips are relatively brief. The following represents the amount of time students report having spent on their most recent STM trip.

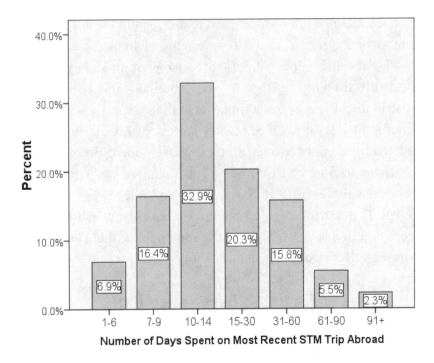

Figure 1: Amount of Time Spent on Most Recent Trip Abroad

Slightly over 23% of those who went on STM trips spent less than nine days on their latest short-term service trips; close to 33% spent between ten to fourteen days on their latest short-term service trips. In other words over 56% spent less than fourteen days; these blocks of time more or less fit within Spring break, Christmas holidays and so on. Like pilgrimages, these trips appear to be comparable to what Durkheim called "*rituals of intensification,*" or what Van Gennep termed "*rites of passage.*"

That is, STM can be regarded as a ritual of transformation similar to such practices as pilgrimage, camps and retreats, special revival services, or even as a rite of passage similar to other rites of passage associated with birth, marriage, death, and other transitions of life found in all religions of the world, including Christianity. Moreover, in the way that travel abroad now seems to be a part of the transition from youth to adulthood (Berger 2004, 37), STM phenomenon can also be explained as the sequential process of leaving the ordinary, that is, the sacralization that elevates the participant to the non-ordinary state ("away from home") where marvelous things happen (Graburn 1989, 26). This seems evident when participants in STM often describe their transformational experience as follows: "I was living it up, really living. I've never felt so alive." Such experiences are not only emotionally peak experiences, but they are intended as transformative rites. Young people are supposed to be changed in the process. Furthermore, unlike other forms of pilgrimage or rituals, these short-term trips explicitly intend to serve and help others in distant places. That is, they aim not only for self-transformation, but for change in the places to which they go (Priest et al. 2006, 434).

Total Amount of Time Spent on STM Trips

While individual trips are often brief, many students have been on multiple trips, so that the total time involved should also be noted. 41% of the students with STM experience spent a total of one month or less abroad; another 23% spent two months or less; and another 23% spent four months or less. Only 3.6% spent close to a year and 1.7% between one and three years.

These results, along with the amount of time spent on the most recent trip, may be a significant indicator of a paradigm shift in how today's Church in the U.S. perceives mission. This paradigm shift has made it essential for the advocates of STM not only to redefine but also to attempt to exegete biblical narratives in defense of what should constitute STM; Peterson et al. (2003) have attempted to do both in their latest book entitled *Maximum impact short-term mission: The God-commanded, repetitive deployment of swift, temporary, non-professional missionaries.*

Destinations of STM Trips

In terms of the destinations of short-term trips, the following lays out the continents and geographical locations to which the sample population made at least one short-term trip.

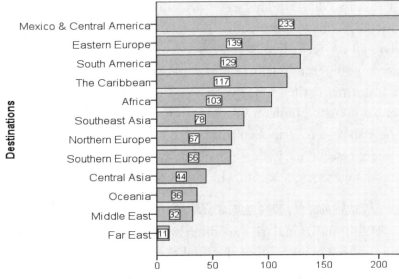

Figure 2: STM Trip Destinations

STM trips with destinations in the Americas are most frequent (566) for this sample population. Trips to Eastern, Northern, and Southern Europe add up to be 272. Next to the Far East, the Middle East turns out to have been least frequented by short-term service trips.

These results appear to be consistent with Tennent's (2004) observation that short-term mission trips often do not go to those places, nor work among peoples, that most need long-term workers. In this light, further studies will need to consider two things: (1) What is the relationship between the most popular destinations of short-term trips and their spiritual needs? (2) In what strategic and creative ways can STM be devised to be workable in least-reached areas, if possible at all?

Findings Related to the Research Questions

In the ensuing segment I will focus on a review of findings related to each research question.

Research Question 1: What is the effect of STM experience on paternalistic tendencies?

The independent variable, STM experience, can be measured either quantitatively (in terms of the sheer number of STM trips taken) or in more qualitative terms, such as by examining the nature of the experience itself. I do a little of each here.

First, what is the effect simply of taking trips? As indicated earlier, not only has 75% of my sample taken at least one STM trip, but many have taken multiple trips. Does participation in the STM movement tend to increase paternalistic tendencies, or to decrease them? To examine data bearing on this question, I examined the correlation between total number of STM trips taken and paternalistic tendencies. The correlation between the two was negative ($r = -.190^{**}$, $p \leq .01$; $n = 783$), indicating that STM involvement is associated with somewhat lower levels of paternalism. Correlation, of course does not prove causality. But it does seem unlikely that paternalism makes people uninterested in STM. That is, a stronger case can probably be made that STM experience is the independent variable affecting, and reducing, the level of paternalism. In either case, STM experience is not positively associated with paternalistic tendencies.

Since paternalism involves hierarchically organized relations, with the short-termer wishing to adopt the one-up position, I also wondered what would happen if the STM experience actively brought short-termers into respectful relationships with indigenous leaders. That is, might a certain kind of STM experience result in lower levels of paternalism? Alternatively, does limited exposure to the national Christian leaders and their ministry sites on STM trips result in higher levels of paternalism? To measure this I developed four questions about STM participant exposure to national Christian leaders and to their own ministry sites, measured in terms of a six-point Likert scale ranging from "Strongly Disagree" to "Strongly Agree." The results indicated that STM exposure to national Christian leaders and their ministries was in fact negatively correlated with paternalism ($r = -.091^*$, $p \leq .05$, n =577), although the relationship was weak.

This result seems to underline the importance of successful partnerships where partners from different cultures work together to achieve common goals based on mutual respect for each other. As far as implications for short-term service trips, these trips can be designed to reduce the danger of assuming that national Christians of other cultures are incompetent to carry out God-given ministry. In other words, if STM can be structured in a way that participants will be given more opportunities to understand the challenges, struggles, and triumphs indigenous leaders experience in their ministry, the results will be more beneficial to the global Christian Body of Christ. In turn, participants are likely to return home with a more realistic, rather than a staged picture of missions, thus becoming less paternalistic.

Research Question 2: What is the effect of STM experience on STM participants' subjective perception of the value of missiological and/or cross-cultural education?

One might naturally expect that cross-cultural experience would lead people to value the importance of studying and understanding cultural differences. But Livermore (2006, 68) notes that more than three-quarters of the short-term participants he surveyed commented on the similarities they had observed in the new culture with what they experienced at home or in another place. Accordingly, these participants did not sense a need to spend more time to try and understand cultural differences, even though they probably interpreted everything they saw through their own cultural framework without having time to learn to identify with another cultural framework due to the brevity of the trip.

What about multiple trips? Will they help participants see the cultural differences and interpret them accurately? According to Livermore, even multiple short trips to the same place do not necessarily correct inaccurate assumptions and interpretations about culture and people. Rather, "continued brief encounters in the same place can result in continued observation of the same similarities rather than exposing the vastly different cultural paradigms at work" (Livermore 2005, 70). These observations seem to suggest that at the heart of the problem lies the brevity of these trips. Regarding the brevity of these trips, over 56% of the sample population spent less than fourteen days on the most recent trips (Figure 1); and this will continue to be the trend as this block of time fits within Spring Break, Christmas holidays, and so on.

Thus, I raised the following question: "In what ways does the number of trips affect participants' attitude toward cross-cultural training and missiological education? Questions 23 and 24 were added together to form a measure for the dependent variable, "valuing of cross-cultural and missiological education." Question 23 stated: "Cross-cultural education/training is critical to cross-cultural ministry"; question 24 stated: "It is critical for someone who wants to be a missionary to get missions education." These questions ask for a level of agreement on a six-point Likert scale ranging from "Strongly Disagree" to "Strongly Agree."

Despite the fact that STM brings people into relationship with cultural and economic and social realities which cry out with the need for understanding, the amount of experience with STM (measured in terms of number of STM trips taken) had no relationship to whether respondents felt such knowledge was needed ($r = .032$, $p < .360$; $n=830$). That is, the number of trips has no effect on participants' attitude toward cross-cultural training and missiological education one way or the other.

Therefore, it can be argued that STM experience itself, *as currently practiced*, is not leading the participants to value cross-cultural training or missiological education. We might well ask, based on this finding, whether leaders of STM are themselves designing these experiences in ways which give the illusion of simple and impressive results, which buffer people from the reality of culture, which fail to help people grapple with the profound economic disparities they encounter, and so on. Should not a core test of whether an STM experience has authentically engaged be whether or not STM participants find themselves wishing that they better understood the social worlds that shape and constrain us?

Again, I examined the effects not only of the amount of STM experience, but the nature of the experience – measured in terms of STM exposure to national Christian leaders and their ministry sites. Again it was found that exposure to national Christian leaders and their ministry sites was positively associated with valuing of missiological and intercultural education ($r= .108^{**}, p < .01, n=627$). To interpret the result another way, it indicates that as short-term participants have more exposure to the national Christian leaders, they are more likely to value the importance of cross-cultural training and missiological education. This seems to be consistent with findings from research on study abroad. As Sells (1983) reports, well-designed study abroad programs turn students into active learners. These programs give students the hands-on introduction to global issues and reap better results if accompanied by a basic language requirement and interaction with the host family as an instrumental part of the cultural learning experience of the students. In terms of implications for STM, this result indicates that having participants interact with national Christian leaders can be a preliminary step in helping participants start understanding the importance of cultural learning in mission.

Research Question 3: What is the effect of formal education, and missiological education, on paternalistic tendencies?

Here I examined the effects of two independent variables (amount of education, and the subject focus of education) on paternalistic tendencies. So first I look at the effects of the amount of education on paternalistic tendencies.

Christian colleges, such as Moody Bible Institute and Columbia International University, have played a leading role in world missions in terms of motivating, preparing, and equipping their students. And a great number of their graduates have been serving around the globe as missionaries. Undoubtedly, these schools will continue to be a principal source of future U.S. missions personnel.

Since students at such U.S. Christian colleges are frequently told that they are the cream of the crop, that they will be future leaders in Christian ministry at home and abroad, and since such schools are sometimes stereotyped as training people in overly rigid models of the Christian faith, one might well expect students at these schools to become increasingly paternalistic towards those of other cultures as a result of their education.

In the following chart, then, we examine the changes in average paternalism scores of freshmen, sophomores, juniors, and seniors.

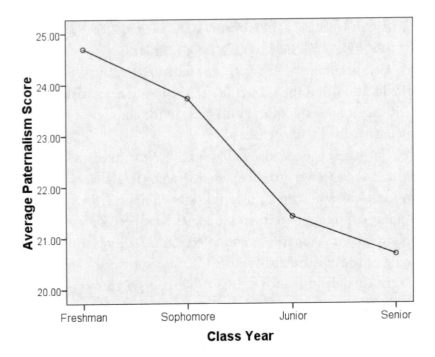

Figure 2: Amount of Education and Paternalism

There is a strong negative correlation between school year and paternalism ($r = -.368$**, $p \leq .01$), n =775), indicating that level of paternalistic tendency diminishes in proportion to the amount of education received at these institutions. Again when the 209 seniors are compared with the 342 freshmen in an Independent Samples T-test, there is a strong and statistically significant difference between these populations [$t(549) = 9.953$, $p \leq .001$]. Freshmen are significantly more paternalistic in their inclinations than seniors.

It would be interesting to see whether these patterns hold for other institutions of higher education (liberal arts colleges, seminaries). These are all schools with an unwavering commitment to world missions, dating back to the period of faith missions in the late 19th century. The overall educational curricula of these institutions may reflect what Elliston (1999) calls the integration of theological education and missiology, ranging from an institution-wide annual missions conference to an introductory missions course required of all majors.

As a second part of this research question, I examined the relationship of college majors, and especially of missions/ intercultural studies majors, on paternalistic tendencies. Here two tests were administered. First, mission majors were compared with non-mission majors on paternalism. With the lowest individual paternalism score a 10 and the highest a 39, the mean paternalism score for non-missions majors was 23.7 and the mean for missions majors was 20.8, indicating that missions majors are less paternalistic. The Independent Samples T-test indicated that this difference was statistically significant $[t\,(765) = 7.464, p \leq .001]$.

Second, the mean scores of each department are reported as follows (Table 2), including only majors for which there were at least thirty respondents, and listing them in order from highest paternalism scores to least.

Departments/Majors	Mean	N	Std. Deviation
Music	25.3	32	4.2
Pastoral Studies, Pre-seminary	24.2	59	5.5
Educational Ministry, Youth Min, Counseling	23.8	226	4.4
Communications	23.8	53	3.9
Bible, Theology	23.1	144	4.7
Missions & Inter-cultural Studies	20.8	212	4.8

Table 2: Paternalism Mean Scores of Each Department

The mean scores for the department of missions and world evangelism is at 20.8. It is the lowest among all departments, showing that students in that department are the least paternalistic. This is a statistically significant difference.[1]

These results corroborate the importance of formal missiological education and cross-cultural training in lowering paternalism. To put it succinctly, formal missiological education, in tandem with cross-cultural internship programs, and practical Christian ministry opportunities, has its merits, regardless of a certain degree of trepidation among some Christian leaders concerning the professionalization of the ministry (namely, the increase in education required for ministry).

Findings of the Effect of STM Combined with Missions Education

I did not originally intend to explore the combined effects of STM experience and missiological education on paternalism, but since each of them independently affected paternalism, it struck me that I should also examine the effects of both combined on paternalism.

To explore this, the sample population was recoded according to the combinations of both STM experience and missiological/intercultural education. In the following bar graph one can see the way in which STM experience and a missions/intercultural studies major combine to affect the paternalism score.

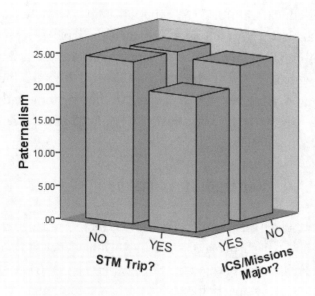

Figure 3: Paternalism of Those with STM Experience and/or ICS/Missions Majors

Those without either STM experience or ICS education score a 24.3 (n = 166). Those with only ICS education score 24.5 (n = 23), and those with only STM experience score 23.5 (n = 389). But those with both STM experience and whose major involves ICS/missions studies score 20.4 (n = 189).

It should be pointed out that the number of people with only an ICS/missions major was small (twenty-three) and was made up primarily of freshmen, who would not yet have taken many missions courses, and who tend to score higher simply by virtue of being freshmen. Little weight should thus be attached to this high score. Since almost no missions majors reach their senior year without taking a short-term missions trip (only two individuals in my sample), I simply do not have good data on people who have a missions education without STM experience.

The important point to observe in this chart is that neither missiological education, nor STM experience, by themselves, are strongly predictive of lowered rates of paternalism, but that when both are combined – then the rates of paternalism are significantly lower. Those with BOTH STM experience AND mission/intercultural studies are significantly less paternalistic than those without either [t(353) = 8.3, p ≤ .001] or than those with only STM experience [t(576) = 7.25, p ≤ .001].

Concluding Remarks

The research reported on here supports the idea that STM experience has a positive effect on participants, lowering their tendencies towards paternalism. Furthermore, when the STM experience is structured in a way which brings participants into first-hand contact with indigenous leaders, this is even more likely to lower participants' tendencies towards paternalism.

On the other hand, STM experience by itself did not have a positive effect on people's attitude toward the value of intercultural and missiological education. The way STM is currently being carried out does not appear to convince participants that cultural and social and missiological understandings are needed. I suggest both that further research is needed on this, but also that one test for the success of an STM experience is whether participants come away from their experience with a deep desire to understand the social and cultural worlds they have just experienced. By this test, STM as currently practiced appears to be failing.

But again, when the STM experience brought participants into first-hand contact with indigenous leaders and their ministries, STM participants were more inclined to value missiological and intercultural education. One element, then, in helping STM participants begin to recognize the importance of better understandings, is that they have an experience that brings them into close connection with indigenous leaders.

My research demonstrated that the education being provided in Bible Colleges is having a positive impact on students, with seniors significantly less likely to exemplify paternalistic tendencies than are freshman. But it also indicated that there is a significant difference between college majors in the extent to which this is true. Some majors appear to be taught in a way which is supportive of paternalistic tendencies. In the schools examined, those who studied missions or intercultural studies were significantly less paternalistic, on average than other majors.

Finally, my research demonstrated that education plus experience synergistically produces better outcomes than experience alone, or education alone. That is, an integrated program involving STM experience and intercultural education had significantly better results.

In short, to ensure the optimal outcomes of the STM movement, both practitioners and missiologists from the academy need to work together to ultimately serve the Global Church, knowing that the synergy of both STM experience and missiological education can be a powerful formula for, and solution to, the problem of paternalistic tendencies and problems associated with the re-amateurization of the Christian mission.

References Cited

Bernard, H. Russell. 2002. *Research methods in anthropology: Qualitative and quantitative approaches.* Walnut Creek, CA: Altamira Press.

Berger, Arthur Asa. 2004. *Deconstructing travel: Cultural perspectives on tourism.* Walnut Creek, CA: Altamira Press.

Chandler, Paul Gordon. 2000. *God's global mosaic: What we can learn from Christians around the world.* Downers Grove, IL: Intervarsity Press.

Cicirelli, Victor G. 1990. Relationship of personal-social variables to belief in paternalism in parent-caregiving situations. *Psychology and Aging* 5: 458-466.

Corwin, Gary. 2007.Missiology—good medicine and a fourth leg. *Evangelical Missions Quarterly* 42, no. 3: 282-283.

Elliston, Edgar J. 1999. Moving forward in missiological education. In *Teaching them obedience in all things: Equipping for the 21st century,* ed. Edgar J. Elliston, 240-278. Pasadena, CA: William Carey Library.

Graburn, Nelson H. H. 1989.Tourism: The sacred journey. In *Hosts and guests: The anthropology of tourism,* ed. Valene L. Smith, 21-36. Philadelphia, PA: University of Pennsylvania Press.

Graburn, Nelson H. H. 2004.Secular Ritual: A general theory of tourism. In *Tourists and tourism: A reader,* ed. Sharon Bohn Gmelch, 23-24. Long Grove, IL: Waveland Press.

Hesselgrave, David, J. 2005. *Paradigms in conflict: 10 key questions in Christian missions today.* Grand Rapids, MI: Kregel Academic & Professional.

Hiebert, Paul G. 1994. *Anthropological reflections on missiological issues.* Grand Rapids, MI: Baker Books.

Jackman, Mary R. 1994. *The velvet glove: Paternalism and conflict in gender, class, and race relations.* Berkeley, CA: University of California Press.

Jenkins, Philip. 2002a. The next Christendom. *Atlantic Monthly,* October 2002.

Jenkins, Philip. 2002b. *The next Christendom: the coming of global Christianity.* New York, NY: Oxford University Press.

Livermore, David A. 2005. *Serving with eyes wide open: Doing short-term missions with cultural intelligence.* Grand Rapids, MI: Baker Books.

McDonough, Daniel Patrick. 1996. The role of short-term missions in the Great Commission: a study of the effects of STEM ministries' short-term mission program on the participants. MA Thesis. Calvin Theological Seminary.

NAFSA. 2003. Securing America's future: Global education for a global age. Report of the Strategic Task Force on Education Abroad. NAFSA: Association of International Educators.

Park, Kyeong Sook. 2007. Researching the effect of short-term missions experience on paternalism among students from selected Christian colleges in the United States. PhD Diss., Trinity Evangelical Divinity School.

Peterson, Roger, Gordon Aeschliman, and R. Wayne Sneed. 2003. *Maximum impact short-term mission: The God-commanded, repetitive deployment of swift, temporary, non-professional missionaries.* Minneapolis, MI: STEMPress.

Priest, Robert J., Terry Dischinger, Steve Rasmussen, and C. M. Brown. 2006. Researching the short-term mission movement. *Missiology: An International Review* 34 (4): 431-450.

Sell, D. K. 1983. Research on attitude change in U.S. students who participate in foreign study experiences. Past findings and suggestions for future research. *International Journal of Intercultural Relations* 7:131-147.

Stone, Clarence N. 1977. Paternalism among social service employees. *Journal of Politics* 39: 794-807.

Tennent, Timothy C. 2004. Six dangerous questions about short-term missions. J. Christy Wilson Jr. Center for World Missions. Accessed 24 August 2004. Available from *www.gordonconwell. edu/ockenga/missionscenter/articles/resources-trips-dangerous*; Internet.

Van Rheenen, Gailyn. 1996. *Missions: Biblical foundations and contemporary strategies.* Grand Rapids, MI: Zondervan Publishing House.

Ver Beek, Kurt. 2005. "The impact of short-term missions: a case study on college students' spiritual growth and maturity." *Missiology: An International Review*. 34: 477-495.

Walls, Andrew F. 2002. *The cross-cultural process in Christian history*. Maryknoll, NY: Orbis Books.

Weiss, G. B. 1985. Ethics briefing: Paternalism modernized. *Journal of Medical Ethics* 11: 184-187.

Winter, Ralph D. 1996. The gravest danger: the re-amateurization of mission. *Missions Frontiers Bulletin* (March-April) 5.

Woodward, V. M. 1998. Caring, patient autonomy and the stigma of paternalism. *Journal of Advanced Nursing* 28: 1046-1052.

Endnotes

[1] The Independent Samples T-Tests, comparing the Missions department with other departments with $n \geq 50$, give scores of $t\,(545) = 4.426$, $p = .000$, $n = 212$ and $n = 144$ respectively (Bible/Theology), $t\,(269) = 4.277$, $p = .000$, $n = 212$ and $n = 59$ respectively (Pastoral Studies), $t\,(436) = 6.754$, $p = .000$, $n = 212$ and $n = 226$ respectively (Educational Ministries), and $t\,(263) = 4.683$, $p = .000$, $n = 212$ and $n = 53$ respectively (Communications).

CHAPTER 19

THE IMPACT OF URBAN
ON THE SOCIAL

SHORT-TERM PROJECTS CONNECTIONS OF EVANGELICAL COLLEGE STUDENTS

RICK RICHARDSON

Many evangelical college students are going on urban immersion experiences in order to serve the city, learn about justice and poverty, and grow in their connectedness to poor and ethnically diverse people. These trips cost less than international trips, present fewer language and culture barriers, and often are experienced as life changing events much like international trips. But little research has been done on these urban short-term immersion experiences. This article explores the impact on social capital for evangelical college students who participate and provides recommendations to project leaders for maximizing social capital gains.

Introduction

One of the key strategies for any religious leader or group of leaders who want to influence the future direction and shape of their religious movement is to shape the thinking, priorities, relationships, goals, and skills of the future leaders of that movement. In U.S. society and for Evangelicalism as a movement, that often means shaping the thinking, priorities, relationships, goals, and skills of contemporary Evangelical college students.

Toward that goal of leadership development, as well as toward the more general goal of spiritual formation and discipleship, campus ministries are taking large numbers of students on short-term mission projects, including short-term urban projects. As a result, urban immersion projects are a significant phenomenon. Researchers have found that at least 1.6 million people are going on short-term mission projects overseas each year, and some substantial percentage of this 1.6 million are serving in urban contexts.

What's more, many churches and parachurch groups and most Christian colleges are sending teams of young people to major U.S. cities for urban ministry and service projects each year. For instance, on the Association of Gospel Rescue Missions website alone, fifty-five organizations host opportunities for short-term domestic urban missions trips during Spring Breaks and summer vacations. Each of the fifty-five organizations helps anywhere from 100 to 500 people get connected to urban short-term service opportunities. In addition, all the major campus ministry organizations help students serve in the city. For instance, InterVarsity Christian Fellowship sent 2469 undergraduates on urban short-term projects in 2006, or 9% of the total number of students involved in InterVarsity nationally, and many of these students represent the most influential leaders in their IV groups. The other major campus ministries send a similar number of students. In addition, Christian colleges are also sending many evangelical students on urban ministry projects. For this article, we called twenty Christian colleges and discovered that they all send groups on urban service opportunities, anywhere from twenty-five to a couple hundred students each. What's more, many of these colleges are strongly encouraging their students to go on such trips with their churches. And many of these churches are also engaging with urban ministry contexts in substantial numbers, though often for shorter periods of time. For instance, Willow Creek Church estimates that they mobilize 10,000 people a year to volunteer locally for an afternoon, a day, or longer in ministries that serve under-resourced people. But with all of the activity and involvement, researchers have done very little solid research on the impact of these urban immersion projects on participants.

The research on international short-term projects has grown far more than the research on domestic urban short term. But domestic urban settings are geographically closer, cost less to get to, provide opportunities for ongoing involvement and investment, present fewer language and culture barriers, have the potential to accrue many of the same benefits to participants, and can more easily be turned into regular mutual relationships and partnerships. So urban immersion projects represent an important focus for short-term research because of their potential benefit to all involved, including senders, hosts, churches, and communities.

I researched the experience of a cohort of Northwestern InterVarsity students involved in urban immersion experiences over a several year period. One of my central research questions was the following:

> How do theologically informed short-term urban projects focused on service, justice and diversity influence the social capital of Evangelical college student participants?

Social capital refers to connections among individuals—social networks and the norms of reciprocity and trustworthiness that arise from them (Field 2003, 12). I explored the social connections that developed through the influence of these projects across racial, cultural, ethnic and class identities.

In these urban contexts, participants encounter relative poverty, racial diversity (African American or Latino), cultural difference, and justice and diversity oriented theology, possibly for the first time. In addition, hosts and recipients encounter people who have relative wealth, are often of European or Asian ethnicity and associated phenotype, and are proficient in the dominant middle class culture of the U.S. These encounters then are encounters with "perceived others." These encounters have great potential for creating important social capital, between people with different ethnic identities and people with different statuses and influence levels.

I chose to focus my research on urban projects led by InterVarsity Christian Fellowship staff in Chicago for students from Northwestern University. Sixty Northwestern students, about thirty each year, attended a one-week urban plunge experience during their Spring breaks over two successive years. The one-week plunge experiences took place in the predominantly Black Austin community.

One of my reasons for choosing this situated context was personal access. I have had a twenty year relationship with many of the key leaders, even helping to launch the Chicago Urban Project twenty years ago, and maintaining involvement with InterVarsity at Northwestern over the same period. But this access, though very important of course, is not the sole or even primary reason I chose this particular setting for research. A number of factors make this setting an especially helpful site for research:

1. InterVarsity has been at the vanguard among evangelical campus ministries in its theological engagement with issues of justice, poverty, diversity, racial reconciliation,

and wholistic ministry ever since its founding in the U.S. in 1939.

2. The Chicago Urban Project has a long history, having been launched in the late 1970s as the third InterVarsity urban project after the one in Los Angeles and the one in New York. Therefore, it is well established, and its values and theological perspectives are well articulated.

3. The Chicago Urban Project Director John Hochevar founded the urban project in 1983, and has been involved in many of the theological discussions and debates within InterVarsity about justice, diversity and the poor over the years. He is very intentional about influencing the theological understanding students have of the gospel, and how their understanding ought to influence their priorities and lifestyles.

4. Northwestern has had a three-year overarching strategy of intentional involvement in the Chicago Urban Project, including sending a total of sixty students on week-long Spring break plunges during March of 2005 and 2006 and sending nine students and three staff on the summer two-month-long internship program during the summer of 2005. The Northwestern strategy has included intentional plans for on campus follow up, thus providing support for ongoing change in participants' lives.

5. Northwestern has four different campus fellowships that have been involved in the urban project strategy, including a multi-ethnic (mostly Asian and White) campus fellowship, a fraternity/sorority (mostly white) campus fellowship, an Asian American (mostly Korean) campus fellowship, and an African American fellowship called the House. As a result of this diversity among the Northwestern students involved, I was able to gauge the impact of short-term urban experiences on a diversity of racial and ethnic evangelical college students.

Research Method and Plan

I tracked Northwestern University InterVarsity students who have been in a three-year process of engaging in short-term urban ministry. I did my research in three phases:

Phase I: March 2005

I attended the two-week Chicago Urban Spring Break Plunge during March of 2005, and engaged in participant observation and informal interviewing, both at the project site, and at some of the service sites. I also administered a questionnaire at the end of one of the weeks, and collected this data from 100 participants, forty of whom were Northwestern students.

Phase II: March 2006

I attended the Spring Break Urban Plunge Weekend in March of 2006, attending all the parts of the program I missed in the prior year, and having another opportunity to research the Northwestern InterVarsity commitment to urban project engagement. I also interviewed face to face two of the Northwestern Spring Break participants in April of 2006, after they had been back at school for a month.

Phase III: Fall 2006

As a final step in my research, I visited the Northwestern campus in early October for one more round of face-to-face interviews with students who had been on the Spring Break Plunge. Having been through the week-long plunge and seen how effective it is at getting the students to consider fundamental changes in their understanding of the gospel, their social change strategies and their identity and status-bridging relational patterns, I wanted to explore how much had carried over into their lives on an individual and a group level since the project. Some students had attended the Spring Break plunge in 2005, and some in 2006, so these interviews gave me a good idea of what changes persisted.

Relevant Social Capital Theory

Robert Putnam, the American political scientist, can plausibly claim much of the credit for popularizing the idea of social capital, rescuing it from the abstraction of social and economic theory (Field 2003, 4). In summary, Putnam has defined social capital as:

> features of social organization, such as trust, norms, and networks, that can improve the efficiency of society by facilitating coordinated actions (Field 2003, 4; Putnam 1993a, 169).

Putnam's central theme since the mid-1990s has been that, from the 1960s onwards, Americans have chosen to steadily withdraw from civic life. Critics have emphasized that Putnam looked at older forms of social connectedness (e.g. the Elks Club) and missed contemporary forms (see Field 2003, 111; Paxton 1999, 114-116; Stengel 1996, 35; Wellman 2001, 2032). In light of the under-researched area of social capital that is generated by religion, might these kinds of projects be one of the generators of new forms of connectedness?

What makes this idea of social capital distinctive as compared with the long tradition of reflecting on the value of community and associational life (e.g. De Tocqueville 1832 [1969])? What is unique is the combining of the social idea of association with the economic idea of capital. Social capital produces returns that in some way benefit its holders. In a weak sense, the claim is simply that social capital is a resource, which can be used by actors to help them achieve their goals. In a more ambitious sense of the term, social capital is to be taken, quite literally, as denoting an embodied productive investment in social relationships, leading to a measurable return which may then benefit those who made the investment (Schuller 2000).

Putnam, a leading researcher and advocate of the concept of social capital, has recognized that faith communities in which people worship together are arguably the single most important repository of social capital in America (Putnam 2000a, 66). Yet, despite this recognition, Putnam and others have treated religion primarily as one form, among many such forms, of association. Not enough attention, as yet, has been devoted to the unique role that religion may play in building social capital.

For instance, church-based social organizing in urban settings has proven more successful than other types of organizational efforts, due, in large part, to the demise of other forms of civic associations in urban areas (Smidt 2003). Religious institutions play a distinctive role within the inner-city contexts because those settings that previously generated trust and sustained broad social networks have deteriorated badly: unions, blue-collar workplaces, cultural associations, families and so forth" (Wood 1997, 601). In fact, within many inner-city neighborhoods, religious institutions are among the few institutions that still are trusted.

A growing number of scholars, joined by Putnam recently, have identified three primary forms of social capital (Putnam 2004, 142; Woolcock 2004, 186):

1. Bonding social capital, links among people who are like one another, crucial for "getting by."
2. Bridging social capital, links among people who are unlike one another, crucial for "getting ahead."
3. Linking social capital, vertical links to people in positions of authority, plays a special role in development and poverty alleviation. These are ties that span power differentials.

Wuthnow also makes the distinction between bridging and linking capital, but uses slightly different language. His language is especially helpful for my work given his concern for the American multi-ethnic and urbanized context. Wuthnow distinguishes between two types of bridging social capital: identity-bridging across racial, ethnic, cultural, religious, sexual and national differences and status-bridging across vertical arrangements of power, influence, wealth and prestige (Wuthnow 2002). I explored the influence of this urban project in producing both identity-bridging and status-linking capital.

Many scholars have also investigated the downside or dark side of social capital (see Portes 1998, 11; Portes and Landolt 1996). In essence, high levels of bonding capital can be associated with homogeneity and the dynamics of exclusion. Quibria (2003, 9-10) identifies four potentially destructive dimensions of networks, norms and reciprocities, especially focusing on urban and ethnic communities:

1. Social capital that opens up opportunities for the members of the network, which is often based on ethnicity, religion, language, and profession, can at the same time constitute an enormous barrier to entry for others outside the network.
2. While a close-knit group can be a source of economic dynamism for its membership, it can also dilute personal incentives to work hard, as in the case of a community that is substantially supported by welfare.
3. Group membership of the community can enforce strict conformity when it infringes on individual freedoms, and can thus create pressure for submission to mediocrity
4. Network and group coordination can often lead to the establishment of negative norms and values that are self reinforcing, such as teenage pregnancy and drug addiction.

These negative outcomes are most closely related to bonding capital in the absence of bridging and linking capital. So urban immersion experiences provide students and community people an opportunity for developing the kinds of social capital that can be an antidote for the dark side of bonding social capital. But I also want to stress that bridging and linking capital, without a strong foundation of adequate bonding capital are often not sustainable, as Weisinger and Salipente (Adler and Kwon 2002; Weisinger and Salipante 2005), point out.

Findings

So what is the impact of the Plunge experience on accruing social capital for these evangelical college students?

There are two primary components of the Plunge urban immersion experience that students cited as most central in producing increased levels of social connectedness: the team experience with others from their campus, and the service experience with people from the community. So first I explore outcomes from the team relationships, and then look at the service relationships, recognizing that this second dimension is in many ways the raison d'être for the whole urban immersion project.

The Plunge is structured such that students spend significant amounts of time with other students from their fellowship group. For a significant percentage of students (22%), the desire to go along with the crowd and to get to know other fellowship group members better was the primary reason they went. So their primary goal for going is developing bonding capital within their own fellowship group. Several aspects of the project facilitate well the development of intra-fellowship bonding capital.

Students from each group were housed together in rooms at an apartment building next to the Circle Urban Ministries main building. So for many of them, they slept in a room that held six to eight members from their fellowship group. They also tended to eat together, hang out on their free time together, and even often serve together. Students described the extended opportunities they had for interaction with others from their own fellowship group.

> The Plunge did have a strong social and
> communal element where we did share personally
> what we were going through and learning, but also
> we prayed for these things and personally shared
> a lot. We spent nights talking, especially the guys
> shared a lot because they roomed together.

The closeness that fellowship group members experienced still had purchase on relationships 9 months later.

> Those of us who went are definitely closer. We're
> all serving together, too. When God brings you
> through an experience that has so much impact
> on your life and the way you see certain things in
> the world, you're drawn naturally close together,
> you relate better, and you work better as a team.

This sense of team closeness and productivity, based on a shared experience and resulting shared values and perspectives, points to the strength and durability of the bonding capital produced through participation in the urban immersion experience.

This increase in bonding capital does help students fit in and get ahead since the students grew in perspectives and values that are prioritized by staff and by others who choose leaders. So many of the students who go on the Plunge are subsequently chosen for leadership roles in the fellowship group.

> It was a really good opportunity for members of
> my chapter, not just to get closer, but to prepare us
> for our vision for next year. Most of us that went
> are small group leaders this year. So this was a
> good experience for us to redirect how our chapter
> interacts with campus.

Do urban immersion experiences build more or less or similar amounts of bonding capital as international projects? I got some evidence from students who had been on both domestic urban and international short-term experiences that the international trip tends to build higher levels of bonding capital. The external dynamics pressing people together are stronger for short-term international projects, for which travel takes longer, people experience more uncertainty and less control over where they sleep and what and when they eat, orientation gatherings prior to the trip are more extensive because of the complex logistics, and language and culture barriers push people to spend more time with one another and less time with hosts and community people. Nevertheless, students built a significant level of bonding capital through the one-week urban experience.

The other primary component that influences the production of social capital the most on the urban Plunge is the service experience, and the interaction with diverse people from the community that happens on the service experience. This dimension has the potential to produce bridging and linking capital and not just bonding capital, and so goes to the heart of my research question on social capital. So I want to explore that experience in some detail, since the service component is also especially central in the justifying discourse for these projects.

In the week-long projects I studied, there were as many as ten different sites for service located in five different primarily Northside urban neighborhoods, including North Lawndale, East Garfield and West Garfield Parks, Cabrini Green and the Austin community.

Service activities included helping with kids' programs, painting walls, sorting clothes, teaching computers to adults, distributing leaflets on the street, and filing and other administrative work. The predominant service assignment was to work with kids in after-school programs or daycare situations (54% of the students), with most of the others working on facility improvements (40%). I visited a number of the service sites, and then spent intensive time at one of them, the Primo Center on the West side of Chicago. The site hosted nine college students, three from University of Wisconsin River Falls and six from Northwestern, during the 2005 Spring Break Plunge.

The students at Primo House and other sites where students worked with kids had three primary sets of interactions on the service experience. First, they interacted with the kids. Second, they interacted with the community people involved in the ministry. Third, they interacted with other InterVarsity students. In the case of students who worked on facilities, in contrast, they had two primary sets of interactions, with community leaders and with other InterVarsity students, but not with kids.

One result from the urban Plunge experience especially stood out. Students spoke of having stereotypes radically altered, and of interacting with people that inspired or humbled or taught them, whether they were talking about kids or adults. This impact on stereotypes through interaction with kids and adults from the community was the most significant and oft repeated consequence of the urban project in relation to social capital. Stereotypes were exposed and changed. Stereotypes influence trust, a foundational component of social capital (Leonard and Locke 1993; Stone 2001).

Trust can be defined as "the expectation that arises within a community of regular, honest, and cooperative behavior, based on commonly shared norms, on the part of other members of the community—these communities do not require extensive contractual and legal regulation of their relations because prior moral consensus gives members of the group a basis for mutual trust" (Baron, Field, and Schuller 2000, 16; Fukuyama 1995, 26). As negative stereotypes, which are in part a reflection of a lack of shared norms, are changed, trust increases. One of my goals in my qualitative study was to identify what kinds of quantitative research would be most helpful in subsequent research. I would suggest that one of the most fruitful ways to measure the impact of week-long urban immersion experiences would be to administer an instrument that tests for changes in trust. Clearly, the urban immersion students I researched could be expected to score fairly high on such a measure.

What's more, students expressed this change toward a range of community people, including the following:

- **Kids**
  The children: They are sooooo smart and beautiful and talented and unique.

- **The Homeless**
  I've changed how I view people on the street, more like they're people. Someone was talking about how they need to be touched, so shaking their hand is helping them get through their time. And I guess I have less fear going up to someone who is homeless and talking to them.

- **Drug Addicts**
  I worked at the shelter for receiving narcotics addicts. It stood out just how "normal" and "regular" these people at the shelter were. They were not crazy and intimidating as one would stereotypically cast a drug addict. In fact, I found that most of these people were broken and deprived people in need of healing.

- **Black Males**
  The supervisor at the church I was serving at really humbled me. He is an African-American male who is light-hearted, diligent, and multi-talented. I'm ashamed to admit, but if I saw him on the streets and didn't know who he was, I might actually have been afraid of him; he's very dark, tall, and muscular. But in reality, he's very gentle.

- **People in the Austin community more generally**
  I expected much more hostility and an unwillingness to interact, but I have been pleasantly surprised. The majority of people have been friendly and welcoming. This is just through normal interaction on the streets overall.

Scholars who measure trust empirically have identified three types of trust, particularized (toward particular people like neighbors), generalized (toward a whole group or population), and civic or institutional (toward the institutions of a community) (Stone 2001, 26). These students grew in both particularized trust toward the individuals associated with the hosting ministries, but they also grew in generalized trust, since stereotypes influence trust toward a population as a whole. They also decreased in levels of institutional trust, partly as a result of their orientation to the role of community institutions in creating and reinforcing systemic injustice.

I also need to mention that this positive interaction with people from the community was not universal. Especially several Asian Americans experienced being stereotyped and even experienced some hostility.

Last year I had four negative encounters with locals. I was called a M-F Chinese, skinny M-F, etc., etc. I wasn't surprised, but it makes you somewhat apprehensive and further realize the brokenness of this community. It reminds me that when I'm in a white church, I feel that these feelings are there too, but unmentioned. It reminded me of my minority status, and that God cares about issues of race, and that God calls the Asian-American church to root out racism in its congregations as well.

The first guys we met, we were talking with him and then a couple minutes into it he just yelled out to his friends, "Yo, Jackie Chan's cousins are here." It was like, I can't believe this, I mean I was actually kind of laughing, cause if I had been someplace like Northwestern, I would have been really offended, but I think we understood that we're going to this different context. So I don't think any of us were really like that offended. But that was actually really the only time that we were actually out in the community. I felt like the rest of the time I spent with kids tutoring them, or painting walls.

I would suggest that in the controlled environments within the host ministries, where students often encounter women and children and experience a hybrid subculture shaped largely by African American women and by a few white leaders, like the founder of the host ministry for the urban plunge, students had very good interactions and their stereotypes were changed. At the same time, students rarely experienced the urban Black predominantly male street culture (for more on Black predominantly male street culture, see Anderson 1992, 1999), and when they did, they were not nearly as likely to have a positive interaction. Those encounters tended to reinforce negative stereotypes and presumably decrease levels of trust. But these encounters were few and far between. And even when the students had negative experiences, they tended to put a positive spin on what they learned, as in the comments above.

In the service experience, students also interacted with one another across racial and cultural boundaries, and in some cases, this interaction influenced identity-bridging social capital.

> I helped paint/clean New Mount Pilgrim Church. I was most blessed through my interactions with Christians from other schools and fellowships. This may sound surprising, but I've never served with non-Asian Christians before. It was a new and truly touching experience. I learned a lot about faith and passion for God just by observing my non-Asian brothers and sisters in Christ.

Overall, changes in stereotypes especially hold true for the 54% of students who served kids, but still partially hold true for those who worked on facilities (40%), particularly if they still had meaningful contact with community people through their service. Meaningful contact can be defined as contact through which students were able to hear who the community people were, how they got involved in the ministry the students were serving, and some story of how God was at work in their lives to help them overcome the obstacles they faced. Generally, students who did not have any meaningful contact with community people through their service experience did not express this change in their stereotypes.

In contrast to the clear changes in stereotypes and trust, some changes I looked for did not materialize. Behavior and actions back at school did not change very much, which was an unexpected result, given how strong the claims for life change were on the part of the students (see also Ver Beek 2006, 490). Most students did not have any more friendships with people of different ethnicities than they had before the project (see also Priest et al. 2006, 444), although many expressed more appreciation for cultural and racial diversity and a higher level of commitment to being in multiethnic relationships.

> Interviewer: Do you have any on-going cross-cultural or cross-racial friendships?
>
> Student: Not a whole lot that I interact with on a consistent basis. Most of my friends are Asian. I think that's a tendency for a good amount of students here, to gravitate to the culture that they're used to.

What's more, few students had continued to be involved in their place of service, although students at the time of the Project expressed that they planned to volunteer after the project, and the sites for service are accessible by 'L' train:

> As a group we tried to do some things, like go back there and do tutoring, and two of the students did it, but it was an hour and a half 'L' ride, and I never did it…they did it for a couple months, and then they couldn't do it anymore.

Students were not giving any more money away after the project than they were before the project. Their lifestyle, for instance amount of money spent on fast food restaurants and clothes, had not changed appreciably. Most changes in behavior were still talked about in the future tense, when the students got a job or were making more money.

Since behavior didn't change, how could students still claim their lives had so radically changed through their involvement in an urban immersion experience? Apparently, students who claim changed lives are really talking about changed perceptions, attitudes and feelings, but not changed behavior.

One significant exception to this general lack of behavioral change was that a number of students had left their mono-ethnic church and joined a multiethnic church. This change was quite significant, and had led to students having stronger multi-ethnic friendships.

> I go to the Vineyard in Evanston. It's a pretty
> multicultural church. I like it a lot. I was going
> to the Well there, which is their Sunday night
> worship/prayer thing, and in the car there was
> myself (white), my friend Jen, who's also white,
> my friend Tiffany, who's African-American, my
> friend Deborah, who's Hispanic, and Helen, who's
> Korean. And I was like, "Oh, yeah! We did it!" And
> I really thought that was the coolest thing.

Students are demonstrating a similarly increased connectedness through their involvement with two other multi-ethnic urban churches, River City Church and especially New Community. Since 25% of the Plunge students change from a mono-ethnic church to a multi-ethnic church, this increase in identity-bridging capital is significant.

In addition, the InterVarsity staff have initiated a follow-up structure that has also had an impact in building persistent identity-bridging capital.

> IV's doing a new thing at Northwestern. We have
> leadership training all in the same room, with
> the leadership teams from the Asian American
> Fellowship, the Black Fellowship, the Multi-ethnic

Fellowship (mainly white and Asian), the Hispanic Bible study, and the Fraternity and Sorority Fellowship.

The staff people decided to hold the joint leadership training meetings. For an hour, one staff person trains student leaders using an InterVarsity leadership training curriculum, and the other staff person teaches regularly about the kingdom of God. Then the students meet within their leadership teams for the other hour. One Plunge alumna discussed the results.

> It's such a case study in ridiculousness. The first week we had it, the Greeks were shouting and off the wall and answering every question and raising our hands and all these quiet Asian kids were just sitting there thinking that, a) these Greek white folks are so rude they can't stand it, and b) they are so overwhelmed by how loud we Greeks are that there's no way they're ever going to say anything. So, we fraternity and sorority leaders had to have a little powwow after the fact and say, "Okay, we need to not talk so much because this is so counterproductive." It's mostly the people who went on CUP who recognize the cultural dynamics and say "shh" and don't talk as much, and the people who didn't go don't understand how white they're being.

Two other follow-up structures stand out: a follow-up large group meeting within each fellowship group and the fall retreat for the multi-ethnic fellowship held back at Circle Urban Ministries, the host site for the Plunge. The students use the InterVarsity large group gathering to share what happened and motivate other students to share their new values and to attend the Plunge.

> We had a CUP large group after we came back, and we invited Miss Frita. She led a kids' club in the Cabrini Green community, and that was one of our best large groups ever. It got a lot of upperclassmen thinking about it, and I know a lot of friends who are interested in CUP next year. There was definitely an impact.

In terms of social connectedness, the large group reconnects students with a community leader (Miss Frita) and with other past Plunge participants as they plan the group meeting and share their testimonies. Thus, follow-up structures in the fellowship group reinforced and intensified identity-bridging capital between racially different students. On the other hand, there are no established follow-up structures that foster ongoing linking capital, and there is little evidence that students maintain any ongoing relationships across power and status differentials.

In summary, students change in their stereotypes of racial and economic others, leading to higher levels of trust. They also gain in bonding capital within their fellowship across the board. Finally, they gain in identity-bridging capital where there are specific follow-up structures in the fellowship group or in a local church that foster ongoing identity-bridging relationships. On the other hand, in the absence of strong follow-up structures that support specific changes in social connectedness, post-Plunge participants tend to rejoin the self-segregated structures that are part of their university context. And apparently, they do not gain in active status-bridging capital under any circumstances, at least as the experience presently takes place.

My findings go to the heart of one of the debates in short-term missions on whether the quality of orientation can affect results. My data supports the conclusion that the orientation and project proper can influence people's attitudes and perspectives, including their stereotypes and trust levels, but follow-up structures are necessary for producing persistent and productive levels of identity and status-bridging relationships.

Implications

I want to end by drawing out some recommendations that emerge from my findings and that are especially relevant for people who are leading short-term urban immersion experiences. These recommendations are aimed at maximizing the development of social capital:

1. Intentionally foster bonding capital before, during and after the project by housing people together, placing them in small groups, giving them opportunity to share, play and pray together, and gathering them several times after the experience to establish an ongoing connection.

2. Make specific goals for also developing identity-bridging and status-bridging capital, and share those goals and their importance with participants during orientation and during the project.

3. In orientation, focus on influencing attitudes, perceptions and stereotypes. That's what orientations do best. Good orientations help frame the experiences people will have. If orientation teachers expose stereotypes and provide a framework for understanding cultural differences, participants will be much more likely to interpret their experiences with cultural and racial others in positive ways. Specifically:

    a. Give participants the opportunity to identify and express their stereotypes and attitudes.

    b. Discuss these stereotypes directly and honestly.

    c. Explore cultural differences and how behaviors by community people that seem "unnatural" are often very natural given the context and history of a community and often play an important positive function in the life of the community.

    d. Invite community people to speak during orientation or during the project, and to share their experiences of encountering stereotypes and cross cultural insensitivities and what impact those encounters had. Have community people tell their stories, even when the community people speak in a different language and need to be interpreted, as when whites visit Latino communities. Story telling is a very powerful and influential pedagogical strategy.

4. In service assignments, insure that participants have the opportunity to relate directly to community people and to hear their stories. These interactions happen naturally when participants work with kids, but when participants work on maintenance, construction or administration, the project director needs to be intentional about brokering such interactions.

5. In follow-up, focus on changed behavior and changed patterns of relating. If there are no follow-up structures, research suggests that there will be no behavioral changes. So specific goals need to be set and specific structures for fulfilling those goals need to be established. Since developing follow-up structures is difficult and takes time, resources and leadership, the goals for behavioral change should be manageable and specific, not general and overwhelming. It is better to make specific and institutionally supported

goals to increase giving a little, or to establish a few identity- and status-bridging relationships, for instance through one local partnering ministry or one ethnically or economically different neighborhood, than to have ambitious goals and no specific structures for fulfilling them.

References Cited

Adler, P.S. and S. Kwon. 2002. Social capital: Prospects for a new concept. *Academy of Management Review* 27: 17-40.

Anderson, Elijah. 1992. *Streetwise: Race, class, and change in an urban community.* Chicago: University of Chicago Press.

_____. 1999. *Code of the street: Decency, violence, and the moral life of the inner city.* New York: W.W Norton.

Baron, Stephen, John Field, and Tom Schuller. 2000. Social capital: A review and critique. In *Social capital: Critical perspectives,* ed. Stephen Baron, John Field and Tom Schuller, 1-38. New York: Oxford University Press.

De Tocqueville, A. 1832 [1969]. *Democracy in America.* New York: Harper.

Field, John. 2003. *Social capital.* New York: Routledge.

Fukuyama, Francis. 1995. *Trust: The social virtues and the creation of prosperity.* New York: Free Press.

Leonard, R. and D. C. Locke. 1993. Communication stereotypes: Is interracial communication possible? *Journal of Black Studies* 22: 332-343.

Paxton, P. 1999. Is social capital declining in the United States? A multiple indicator assessment. *American Journal of Sociology* 105: 88-127.

Portes, Alejandro. 1998. Social capital: Its origins and applications in modern sociology. *Annual Review of Sociology* 24: 1-24.

Portes, Alejandro and Patricia Landolt. 1996. The downside of social capital. *American Prospect* 26: 18-21.

Priest, Robert, Terry Dischinger, Steve Rasmussen, and C.M. Brown. 2006. Researching the short-term mission movement. *Missiology* 34: 431-450.

Putnam, Robert D. 1993. *Making democracy work: Civic traditions in modern Italy*. Princeton, N.J.: Princeton University press.

_____. 2004. Using social capital to help integrate planning theory, research, and practice: Preface. *Journal of the American Planning Association* 70, no. 2, Spring: 142-142.

Schuller, Tom. 2000. Human and social capital: The search for appropriate technomethodology. *Policy Studies Journal* 21: 25-35.

Smidt, Corwin E. 2003. Introduction. In *Religion as social capital: Producing the common good*, ed. Corwin E. Smidt:1-18. Waco, TX: Baylor University Press.

Stengel, Richard. 1996. Civic engagement in America isn't disappearing but reinventing itself. *Time* 148: 35ff.

Stone, Wendy. 2001. *Measuring social capital: Towards a theoretically informed measurement framework for researching social capital in family and community life*. Research paper number 24. Melbourne, Australia: Australian Institute of family studies.

Ver Beek, Kurt. 2006. The impact of short-term missions. *Missiology* 34: 477-495.

Weisinger, Judith and Paul Salipante. 2005. A grounded theory for building ethnically bridging social capital in voluntary organizations. *Nonprofit and the voluntary Sector Quarterly* 34: 29-55.

Wellman, B. 2001. Computer networks as social networks. *Science* 293: 2031-2034.

Wood, R.L. 1997. Social capital and political culture: God meets politics in the inner city. *American Behavioral Scientist* 40: 595-605.

Woolcock, Michael. 2004. Why and how planners should take social capital seriously. *Journal of the American Planning Association* 70: 183-9.

Wuthnow, Robert. 2002. Religious involvement and status-bridging social capital. *Journal for the Scientific Study of Religion* 41: 669-84.

CHAPTER 20

STUDENT SOJOURNERS AND UNDERSTANDING THE CULTURAL ADJUSTMENT

SPIRITUAL FORMATION: INTERSECTION OF CROSS- AND SPIRITUAL DISORIENTATION

MURRAY S. DECKER

It is a curious fact that the church has, by and large, continued to sing songs of orientation in a world increasingly experienced as disoriented. That may be laudatory. It could be that such relentlessness is an act of bold defiance in which these psalms of order and reliability are flung in the face of the disorder. In that way, they insist that nothing shall separate us from the love of God. Such a "mismatch" between our life experience of disorientation and our faith speech of orientation could be a great evangelical "nevertheless" (as in Hab. 3:18).

But at best, this is only partly true. It is my judgment that this action of the church is less an evangelical defiance guided by faith, and much more a frightened, numb denial and deception that does not want to acknowledge or experience the disorientation of life. At least it is clear that the church that goes on singing "happy songs" in the face of raw reality is doing something very different from what the Bible itself does.

Walter Brueggemann, *The Message of the Psalms of Faith*
(1984:51-2).

Introduction

Much has been written about the process of adjustment experienced by cross-cultural sojourners transitioning from one culture to another. The catchall term "culture shock" has been loosely given to the loss, disorientation and sensory overload experienced when a person loses many of their familiar cultural cues upon entering into a new and unfamiliar place. However, little has been written on the spiritual dynamics of sojourner adjustment, specifically, what is the impact of a cross-cultural immersion experience upon the soul?

The growth of the short-term mission phenomenon has made cross-cultural sojourners out of an increasingly broad cross-section of the North American church. Most evangelical churches readily embrace sending their parishioners on a short-term mission. Rare is the Christian college student that hasn't participated in a trip to Mexico. This paper is not another attempt to assess the legitimacy of this trend (I think it's fair to say that we've beaten that poor topic to death). Rather, given that STM's are here to stay, what are the emotional, spiritual and cultural issues that arise as short-term sojourners return to their country of origin and process the experience they just had abroad? How do the rigors of making a healthy adjustment to a foreign culture, and the equally difficult experience of readjusting to one's home culture upon return, interface with the operation of the Holy Spirit at work within the Christian's life?

This paper seeks to explore the intersection of these two internalized processes. Is there any correlation between the two, and if so, how can we more fully appreciate what God is doing in the midst of what is often a disorderly personal experience? More specifically, my concern is for student sojourners who experience significant disequilibration in the process of cultural transition, which in turn has a corollary impact upon their spiritual life. Naturally such an experience is more common for short-term mission stays of a few months or more, rather than for STM trips of a few days taken with large groups from home. So this paper will focus specifically on forms of STM which bring practitioners into more sustained engagement with another community and culture. It is my thesis that the messy emotions and overwhelming sense of disorientation common to such sojourner adjustment are also evidence that God is at work within the life of the student at a critical time in their emotional and spiritual development.

I work closely with undergraduate college students to assist them emotionally and spiritually as they transition to and from living in another culture. Most of these students are Intercultural Studies or Anthropology majors preparing for a career of cross-cultural service. Most feel a specific calling to serve cross-culturally and have already experienced significant exposure to people of other cultures as a result of short-term mission experiences, study-abroad opportunities, or various cultural emersion encounters. They usually range in age from eighteen to twenty-two, are both male and female, and come from a wide variety of cultural and socio-economic backgrounds. As these students complete their required summer internship or spend a semester abroad, many begin to experience a growing awareness of spiritual and emotional disorientation and frustration. They struggle to articulate exactly what they are experiencing, but commonly speak of feeling that God is distant, that their prayer life is cold, that God seems to have pulled away leaving them in a very dry place, and that the answers and spiritual formulas that always seemed to work for them (just pray more, recommit yourself to daily scripture reading) not only fail to work, but create anger, guilt, frustration, and resentment.

In the pages ahead I draw upon the similarities between spiritual disorientation and cultural readjustment. One does not necessarily cause the other, nor should we expect or predict that a cross-cultural sojourn will impact everyone similarly on a spiritual level. However, there appears to be more than just a coincidental correlation between the two. Similar things are taking place in both spheres, and thus, these two experiences frequently overlap and feed into one another. To split the two would be an artificial reduction; to force causality would appear overstated. This paper will stroll between these poles.

What is Sojourner Adjustment?

The first season living in a new culture is frequently an inordinately difficult personal experience. Adjustment to a new culture occurs over an extended period of time, from months to years, depending upon the degree of immersion in the culture, the degree you interact on a daily basis with the new culture, and the individual personality of the expatriate. Predictably, the first year is the most difficult, as the cumulative effects of culture stress overwhelm even the most adaptive sojourner. The recovery process follows the acquisition of language skills, building bridge relationships with host nationals or seasoned expatriates, a growing understanding of the host culture and growth of cultural competence. Stated more simply, once you can speak enough of the language to make your way through the market, once you've established a couple of good friendships to provide you with emotional support and the feedback of a cultural insider, and once you finally understand why everyone keeps laughing at you, things get much easier. The first year can be tremendously difficult but the vast majority of sojourners do recover to a higher sense of well-being and cultural competence.

Cora DuBois first coined the term "culture shock" in 1951. Christian anthropologist Kalvero Oberg used the term to describe the difficulties of American expatriates serving in Brazil in making a healthy adjustment to their host culture. Oberg called it "an occupational disease of people who have suddenly been transported abroad [which] is precipitated by the anxiety that results from losing all our familiar signs and symbols of social intercourse" (1960,

177). The term "culture shock" is something of a misnomer, as "shock" implies that it occurs suddenly—ZAP!—you've been culture shocked. Through the years, other terms such as homesickness, adjustment difficulties, or uprooting attempted to capture the same phenomenon: (Zwingmann and Gunn, 1983). The anxiety Oberg speaks of is a growing sense of being overwhelmed by all the new stimuli, cultural cues, and social adjustments. In varying degrees, all sojourners experience some of this anxiety. Many individuals experience something of an emotional shut-down, overwhelmed by the constant confusion and uncertainty of life in a new culture. Like drinking from a fire hose, the onslaught of the new and unfamiliar eventually overwhelms them.

Most sojourners are able to negotiate these anxieties and eventually return to a positive sense of well-being. However, upon return to their home culture, many experience reverse culture shock. Life back in their country of origin has changed, or perhaps more accurately, they have changed. The dissonance of that change causes a similar experience of anxiety as when they first arrived on foreign soil. Sojourners remark that they anticipated that life in the foreign culture would be hard, but didn't think their return to the United States would actually be more difficult. The longer an individual's sojourn abroad, the more emotionally difficult it is to transition back to the home culture.

The most commonly accepted model describing the sojourner adjustment process is the "U-Curve" model (figure 1). This model is descriptive, not necessarily predictive, yet is helpful to understand the common experience of many sojourners (Lysgaard, 1955; Oberg, 1960; Thomas & Harrell, 1994; Torbiorn, 1982). The model illustrates how a sojourner's initial sense of optimism and euphoria upon entry into the new culture dissipates over time as the discomfort and anxiety of life abroad begins to overwhelm them. But given time and the opportunity to develop adaptive strategies, their sense of well-being begins to "curve" back upward with growing feelings of ease and fit in the new culture. This U-Curve adaptive process is repeated when the sojourner returns to their culture of origin, creating a "W-Curve" of adaptation and re-adaptation (Gullahorn and Gullahorn, 1963). This second season of readjustment—the other half of the "W"—is often unexpected, as sojourners are not prepared for the disorientation they experience "back home."

U-Curve Model of Adjustment

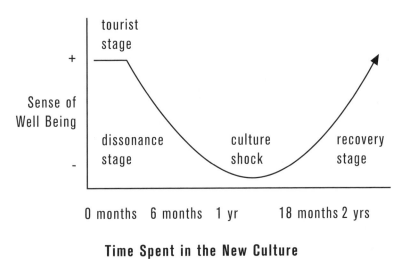

Figure 1: U-Curve Model of Adjustment

The first "honeymoon" stage of the sojourner's entry into the new culture is typified by elevated feelings of optimism and a positive sense of personal well-being. This initial stage of positive well-being might be called "the tourist stage" or "the honeymoon stage" because the differences and challenges of the new culture are seen as novel, entertaining, curious and exotic. Life in the new culture is fun, adventurous and even a bit romantic. This stage may last weeks or even months depending upon how soon the dissonance of the culture begins to wear-down the expatriate.

The next "dissonance stage" of the U-Curve model is typified by the sojourner's ongoing encounters with a confusing, unfamiliar and sometimes hostile culture. Tension, embarrassment, confusion, loneliness, and frustration emerge during this season of disequilebration (Mayers 1987, viii). The fatigue of daily life in an unfamiliar culture wears upon the sojourner. As weeks pass in the new country, the initial sense of optimism evaporates as the difficulties of daily life chip away at the sojourner. This second stage leads the sojourner to a greater and greater sense of personal loss. Loss of cultural familiarity, loss of control over the environment around them, loss of friendship and support from family and friends, loss of confidence, loss of comforts they had always taken for granted, and hundreds of other loses, great and small begin to pile up. They miss so many things they once found familiar—worship services that spoke to their soul, simple daily conversations where you walk away with a confidence that you understood what just took place, Christmas music and decorations, the Super Bowl, and the smell of Mom's kitchen on Thanksgiving. Healthy sojourner adjustment will require resolution of this bereavement; failure to negotiate their bereavement may break the sojourner's will to carry on.

The third stage of the U-Curve model is "culture shock." As mentioned above, culture shock isn't a sudden realization that something is wrong, but an overwhelming sense of fatigue. Culture shock is that season where the dissonance of change and bereavement washes over the sojourner. Culture shock is the bottom of the U-Curve, where the sojourner's sense of well being reaches its lowest ebb. It is stimulus and change overload as coping systems begin to shutdown.

During my own experience of culture shock as a teacher in Cameroon West Africa I remember the constant exhaustion and sense of doubt as to how I was coping. I would crash unto my bed, pull my Walkman over my ears and escape for a class period or two before I would walk back down to the classroom and somehow summon the strength for another class. Standing before sixty clever and bored teenagers, I maintained my composure and a bold front. Like sharks, I knew that if these kids sensed weakness—blood in the water—I would be torn apart. My inner world was insecure and confused, but I felt I could not expose this to my students or Cameroonian colleagues. Returning from class, I would once again collapse on my bed, grab the head-phones, hit the play button and return to a place familiar and safe.

In time I grew more confident in the culture and began to have successful experiences in the classroom, the church, the market and in the informal interactions of daily life. Close friendships developed. Putting away the Walkman, I invited national friends into my home more frequently and shared in their lives. They also invited me into their homes to eat and celebrate and share their lives. I cannot point to a day when those feelings of fatigue and dissonance began to subside but they eventually did. True to adjustment theory, my darkest days were from nine months to about a year in the new culture. The second year marked my recovery.

The final phase of the U-Curve model is the "recovery" stage. Recovery occurs with the growth of relationships, language skills, cultural knowledge, and cultural familiarity. The better you can function within the culture, the better you begin to feel about yourself. Recovery from culture shock can take a year or longer. Some never do recover but return home broken by the experience—perhaps we could call it the "Half U-Curve" model of maladjustment. Some sojourners never go through a deep trough of depression and culture shock but adjust quickly—the "Minor Pot-Hole in the Road" model of easy adjustment. Still others take years to fully recover from their bottomless experience of cultural bereavement—the "Deep Chasm of Despair and Loss" model of belated adjustment. I have known sojourners who still struggled with adjustment difficulties eight years after they first entered the culture but faithfully remained in the new culture. Most sojourners take far less time—two to three years—to recover to a functional state of interpersonal wellness.

Orientation, Disorientation, and Reorientation

Walter Brueggemann, in his books *The Psalms and the Life of Faith* and *The Message of the Psalms: A Theological Commentary* describes a "scheme" of three types of Psalm. Brueggemann speaks of the Psalms of orientation, Psalms of disorientation, and Psalms of reorientation.[1] This taxonomy of Psalms is also helpful to understand seasons or stations within the spiritual life. Brueggemann's classification of Psalms give reference to movements within the soul where the faith and identity of the individual shifts from orientation to disorientation, and then ultimately toward reorientation (Figure 2). As with the above-mentioned model of adjustment, this taxonomy or model is not necessarily predictive, but it is descriptive of a personal experience common to many.

ORIENTATION ➡	DISORIENTATION ➡	REORIENTATION
Ps. 30: 6-7a When I felt secure, I said, "I will never be shaken." O Lord, when you favored me you made my mountain stand firm;	Ps. 30:7b-10 ... but when you hid your face, I was dismayed. To you, O Lord I cried for mercy: "What gain is there in my destruction, in my going down to the pit? Will the dust praise you? Will it proclaim your faithfulness? Here, O Lord, and be merciful to me; O Lord, be my help.	Ps. 30:11-12 You turned my wailing into dancing; you removed my sackcloth and clothed me with joy, that my heart may sing to you and not be silent. O Lord my God, I will give thanks forever.
Examples: 1, 8, 33, 37, 100, 104, 112, 119, 128, 131, 133, 145	Examples: 13, 35, 50, 74, 79, 81, 86, 88, 109, 130, 137, 143	Examples: 23, 27, 30, 40, 47, 65, 66, 97, 98, 99, 114, 135, 138.
Songs of Creation, Songs of Torah, Wisdom Psalms, Songs of Retribution, Occasions of Well-Being	Songs of Personal Lament, Communal Laments, "A Second Opinion" on the Disorientation	Thanksgiving Songs, Thanksgiving Songs of Community, The Once and Future King, Hymns of Praise
Emotional posture: gratitude, praise, joy, delight, goodness, coherence, reliability of God.	Emotional posture: lament, deep loss, rage, resentment, suffering, self-pity, hatred, ragged disarray, abrasiveness.	Emotional posture: deliverance, transformation, surprise, joy breaking through despair, light dispelling the darkness.
Cultural Posture: Affirmation of the greater cultural and spiritual status quo. Going "from strength to strength," yet in denial that there is anything difficult in between.	Cultural Posture: "Profoundly subversive of the dominant culture which wants to deny and cover the darkness we are called to enter."	Cultural Posture: Darkness is strangely transformed, "not by the power of easy light, but by the power of relentless solidarity" with Christ who meets us in the despair and darkness.
Christ Jesus, "Who, being in very nature God..."	"... he emptied himself."	"Therefore God exalted him to the highest place. . ."

Figure 2: Spiritual Movement from Orientation to Disorientation to Reorientation

Brueggemann's (1984, 9-10) scheme of orientation— disorientation—new orientation is not intended to be a straitjacket in the interpretation of the Psalms, nor some master key in understanding psalmic spirituality, but a helpful paradigm that serves the heuristic function of classification in the mess of our spiritual story. These orientations become "voices of faith in the actual life of the believing community" (10). Brueggemann is cautious about any neat grid or prescribed set of passages that the spiritual life must take. In this same way, the correlation I attempt to make in this paper should never be seen as a prescriptive path that all cross-cultural sojourners walk upon re-entry. However, it is clear that there are seasons and movements in the life of faith where you are left with the clear impression that you have crossed over into a new spiritual place. The movement from orientation to disorientation is, well, disorienting. There is a sense that we have driven off the map; this is new emotional territory, uncharted spiritual waters. Everything we may have understood to "make it all better" no longer works. It is in this movement (wildly careening off the road into mystical badlands, our hands frantically clutching the wheel that no longer responds to our futile attempts to steer) where Brueggemann's scheme is most useful to returning sojourners.

Psalms of orientation affirm the goodness of God, prescribe a predictable formula that promises prosperity and health to the righteous, and clarify the correct relationship between God, our shepherd and Lord Almighty to his faithful sheep. Brueggemann states (1995, 10): "what mainly characterizes them is the absence of tension. The mind-set and worldview of those who enjoy a serene location of their lives are characterized by a sense of the orderliness, goodness, and reliability of life." They describe the goodness and continuity of life, a "voice of genuine gratitude and piety for such rich blessings" (11).

Psalm 128 would be an example of a Psalm of orientation:

> *Blessed are all who fear the Lord, who walk in his*
> *ways.*
> *You will eat the fruit of your labor; blessings and*
> *prosperity will be yours.*
> *Your wife will be like a fruitful vine within your*
> *house;*
> *your sons will be like olive shoots around your table.*
> *Thus is the man blessed who fears the Lord.*
> *May the Lord bless you from Zion all the days of*
> *your life;*
> *may you see the prosperity of Jerusalem,*
> *and may you live to see your children's children.*
> *Peace be upon Israel.*

The Psalms of orientation reaffirm a sense of a good world, a predictable Heavenly father who rewards the good and punishes the wicked, and an anticipation of ongoing continuity. Spiritual orientation is that place of feel-good faith, simple formulas, and easy answers. It is the bright day before the dark night.

The second phase in the scheme would be Psalms of disorientation. In this type of Psalm, there is a realization that the old order has collapsed, as the Psalmist laments the dislocation and distress of a new reality. Life is no longer orderly. God is no longer predictable ("Have you not rejected us, O God?" Ps. 60:10). God is not even discernable ("Will you hide yourself forever?" Ps.89:47). There are memories of better times ("These things I remember as I pour out my soul: how I used to go with the multitude, leading the procession to the house of God, with shouts of joy and thanksgiving among the festive throng." Ps. 42:4) but now the Psalmist protests that things are no longer good.

Psalm 77:1-9 would illustrate this kind of disorientation and lament.

I cried out to God for help; I cried out to God to hear me.
When I was in distress, I sought the Lord;
at night I stretched out untiring hands and my soul
refused to be comforted.
I remembered you, O God, and I groaned; I mused
and my spirit grew faint.
You kept my eyes from closing; I was too troubled to
speak.
I thought about former days, the years of long ago; I
remembered my songs in the night.
My heart mused and my spirit inquired: "Will the
Lord reject forever?
Will he never show his favor again? Has his
unfailing love vanished forever?
Has his promise failed for all time? Has God
forgotten to be merciful?
Has he in anger withheld his compassion?"

The Psalmist is not trying to protect God or burnish his reputation in this passage. His questions are immediate and pointed: God, where have you gone during this time of need? He references his former "songs in the night"—perhaps former Psalms of Orientation—but now those songs are found lacking. The six questions that form the heart of his discontent question the very character of God.

As with many of the Psalms, there is a "turn" that takes place in verses. 9b-10 when he states:

Then I thought, "To this I will appeal: the years of
the right hand of the Most High."

I will remember the deeds of the Lord; yes, I will
remember your miracles of long ago.
I will meditate on all your works and consider all
your mighty deeds.

Many of the Psalms of lament transition from disorientation to reorientation at some point within the text. This is common; there may actually be aspects of all three movements within the same passage (as shown in Figure 2 with Psalm 30).

Spiritual disorientation takes many forms, but is characterized by a sense of lostness and dryness. The songs that used to reassure now bring anger. The chapel services that used to encourage now illicit frustration. In disillusionment and rage the individual may rebel against the status quo, openly question and defy the conventions of the group and perhaps even openly live counter to the morality of the church. There is a reasoning that "since it seems that God has abandoned me, then I might as well abandon all this stuff I've been taught." Disorientation is a time of stripping away pretense and performance-based Christianity, leaving the individual to face their God and their questions without the distraction of having to keep up appearances. People moving through this stage are raw and confused and upsetting to the status quo (perhaps those who feel a need to protect their place of orientation).

The Psalms of reorientation or new orientation mark a movement toward a quieter and resolved place, and a surprise hope that emerges from the darkness. Brueggemann (1984, p. 20-21) describes these Psalms as:

> a new coherence made present to us just when we
> thought all was lost. This move entails a departure
> from the "pit" of chaos just when we had
> suspected we would never escape. It is a departure
> to us, to be credited only to the intervention

of God. This move of departure to new life
includes a rush of positive responses, including
delight, amazement, wonder, awe, gratitude, and
thanksgiving.

One such reference to "the pit" comes from Psalm 40; David was
a man familiar with hiding in pits:

> *I waited patiently for the Lord;*
> *he turned to me and heard my cry.*
> *He lifted me out of the slimy pit,*
> *out of the mud and mire;*
> *he set my feet on a rock and gave me a firm*
> *place to stand.*
> *He put a new song in my mouth,*
> *a hymn of praise to our God.*
> *Many will see and fear and put their*
> *trust in the Lord.*

To understand the context of many of David's Psalms, it is helpful
to see him as a man on the run for his life. The Psalms of lament are
"yells" from the back of a cave or the bottom of a pit, scratched-out
on the back of an envelope by a guy who isn't sure who he can trust
anymore. He questions what ever happened to him, the shepherd
boy with the magic touch—everything he had ever done had turned
out well—and now it seems as though God has abandoned him.
It appears that David loses confidence that God is still for him,
that God's hand is still upon him. The very foundation of his faith
was shaken; he is experiencing disorientation. After years on the
run, years of sleeping in caves and pits, surrounded by the other
misfits and malcontents of Israel (these losers later to be elevated to
"mighty men" status), it seems as though David is actually surprised
by this move from the pit to the solid rock. The hymn of praise is

a *new* song, not the old song of orientation nor the angry rant of disorientation. These songs sound differently on the other side of the wasteland. Perhaps they are softer or less arrogantly confident; perhaps the songs are more about God and less about us. David is clearly a different person when he took the throne than he was when he first fled from Saul. Something had been fundamentally reoriented in his life.

Reorientation may take the form of thanksgiving for the grace that carried the individual through the dark night. It may be a quieting of the soul after their season of discontent. There is an element of surrender or abandonment that precedes reorientation, giving up the spiritual prescriptions and cliché formulas and recognizing that God often works in sovereign mystery in our lives. Anger that used to be directed toward the church or God himself now begins to dissipate. Where these individuals may have left the organized church during their time of disorientation, they now find themselves drawn back, albeit, now they bring with them a voice for the hurting and desperate. They cannot be silent about the cruelty in the world. They find a bit more grace to listen to the pastor who used to anger them; they are more patient with fellow Christians whom they had dismissed during their dark night. They find comfort in the fellowship of the saints, and are willing to give testimony to the faithfulness of God, even as the Psalmist often ends many of his Psalms of lament with a reassurance that God *is* good and His faithfulness endures to all generations.

Describing three types of Psalm or these three movements in this sort of language has proven to be an insightful tool in the lives of cross-cultural sojourners. The heuristic function of these Psalms assists the sojourner in the process of self-discovery and self-awareness. For evangelicals who have never been given permission to count their lament as a form of praise, this taxonomy is liberating. "Do you mean to tell me that God is worshiped not only in Psalm 100, but also in Psalm 77?" Few people truly want to stay in the desert once they come to the honest realization that they actually are in that place of disorientation. But that simple acknowledgement can make such a difference to the person who thinks that there is something "wrong" with them.

Sojourner Readjustment and Spiritual Disorientation

The central premise of this paper is simply that the "symptoms" of sojourner adjustment and spiritual disorientation look very similar. In both, there is a sense of lost-ness; the familiar has slipped away and the landmarks are now unfamiliar. Lisa Espinelli Chinn works extensively with cross-cultural teams and individuals in the reentry process. Chinn (1998, 19) writes that many returning sojourners experience is characterized by

- anger, rejection and isolation
- negatively viewing their home culture
- pulling away from being in a stressful situation by being alone or with like-minded people (other former cross-cultural sojourners or mission participants)
- continuing to identify with the home culture but for the most part having negative attitudes and reactions to it
- expressing a strong judgmental posture toward the values and lifestyle of the home culture (church, family, friends, national and foreign policies)
- feeling a strong guilt or anger over their home culture's materialism and affluence

The sojourner understands that they are no longer in the "foreign" culture, yet they no longer feel at home in their home culture. The spiritually disoriented have also left home, so to speak, never to return as they once were.

In both reentry and disorientation, the individual begins to doubt if what you used to know was ever true to begin with. The sojourner begins to think: "I used to rest peacefully knowing that my way, and the way of my family and church was *the* way. There was a time when I felt a great deal of security having all the correct answers, and knowing my place within the greater circles of family, church, culture, and ultimately the spiritual world." That certitude has evaporated. Through cultural exposure, their core presuppositions are challenged. Values they once unquestioningly accepted are now weighed and found wanting. At a core level, even one's epistemology is challenged; how can I know what is true, when so much of what I used to think was correct and the answers I was taught are no longer adequate to explain the complexity of this world and the God who works within it?

In both sojourner disorientation and spiritual disorientation control is being stripped away. As one reads the Psalms of lament, there is an anger and frustration at God's silence in the face of injustice and personal persecution. The Psalmist is recognizing that he is out of control and cries out for help to a God who, at times, appears reluctant to offer assistance. Perhaps control is antithetical to the spiritual life. Surrender and abandonment should be the normative posture of the spiritual pilgrim, not tight-fisted control. "Against all of this the Psalms issue a mighty protest and invite us into a more honest facing of the darkness. The reason the darkness can be faced and lived in is that even in the darkness, there is One to address" (Brueggemann 1984, 12).

In the same way, control is antithetical to healthy cross-cultural adjustment. Sojourners who have a high tolerance for ambiguity have a much easier time learning to adapt and cope in their new cultural context. The movement from one culture to another might be described as moving from one canoe to another midstream . . . you have a foot in each canoe, but your weight isn't securely resting in either. It is a bit precarious. The adjustment process reduces the most competent and mature adult to the status of a child. Sojourners with a strong personal need to maintain their status and self-esteem based upon their ability to perform in the culture will have the greatest difficulty humbly learning the language and making the many necessary mistakes needed to become bi-cultural.

The recent rise in the popularity of apologetics and more confrontational approaches to evangelism (*contending* for the faith) within the evangelical church has also given rise to new concerns in the way we deal with spiritually disoriented Christians. Unfortunately, the students of such courses and programs are often equipped with a set of "truths" which they wield like sticks to whack the spiritually disoriented, attempting to somehow *prove* orientation to them. The failure of this approach is that as God is at work in the midst of the disorientation, the argumentative apologist usually fails to appreciate the nature of the problem. They frame the "problem" as, "You just need to get your beliefs straight," when in fact, it is an issue of the heart, not the head. As David was on the run from King Saul, his problem was not that he wasn't thinking straight. In fact, in the eternal scheme of things, it wasn't a concern at all; it was the hand of God at work within his soul to conform him to the image of Christ. You could make a stronger argument from the scriptures that the work of God in the desert (or dark night) is primarily a work of the heart. To swing the stick of apologetics and clobber a spiritually disoriented sojourner is usually spiritually counter-productive, and perhaps even abusive. To tell David "quit writing those depressing psalms of lament and just sing the old songs of orientation" completely misses what God was doing in the disorientation. The old saying is "truth without discernment is cruelty"; apologetics without grace is spiritually abusive.

Lament and Honesty

One contributing factor in the experience of culture-stress could be attributed to the individualism that so often characterizes our lives in North America. The rugged individualism and stoic independence that is expected of those "strong souls" willing to brave the trials of life abroad are actually enemies of the spiritual life. A thousand cultural voices call out to us daily to be strong, independent, self-reliant, master of our solo course and dependent upon no one. Vulnerability is considered weakness, and weakness is the enemy. But the spiritual life is not lived in rugged independence and self-contained isolation.

As a culture we celebrate the strong and write biographies lauding the feats of missionaries with the pluck, courage, and individual fortitude to trek out into the unknown by themselves. This kind of heroicism even trickles down to the level of short-term missions and student sojourners. Yet when you read these biographies, you are often left with the impression that these were not healthy individuals. The task of missionary service provides a great deal of spiritual and psychological cover for a person running away from the unrestfulness of their soul. If there is no place for weakness in our psychological and spiritual life, then we will go to great lengths to hide from it, cover it up, convince ourselves that we must be strong, and project to others that we've never been better. "But I'm doing the Lord's work" is the ultimate trump card of denial when the voice of the Spirit begins to reveal that our soul is ragged and dry. Vibrant and active service to the Lord should not be mutually exclusive from an honesty that takes a candid assessment of the condition of our soul. We may recognize that we need the nurture of others in our arid place, but pride or erroneous perceptions of self and Christian service keep us from moving with grace toward others in our weakness.

Two classic missionary biographies come to mind. First, Adoniram Judson is one of the most famous American missionaries of the 19th century. Judson is considered the father of the church in Myanmar (formerly Burma) for his forty years of service to the Burmese people. Biographers celebrate his individualism and fortitude, yet have a difficult time knowing how to write about some of the darker seasons in this man's emotional and spiritual life. In addition to the considerable loss that accompanies cross-cultural transition, Judson lost his wife of many years and three children to the rigors of tropical life, imprisonment and disease. Following the death of his dear wife Ann and his infant daughter Maria, he was so distraught that he walked back into the forest with a shovel and dug a grave for himself. His son later wrote:

> It is also true that during this period of his life Mr. Judson withdrew himself from general society. When not directly engaged in missionary work, he spent many of his waking hours alone in a bamboo hermitage, built in the jungle far from humankind among the haunts of tigers. Here in his endeavor to crucify his passionate love of life he had a grave dug, and "would sit by the verge of it and look into it, imagining how each feature and limb would appear, days, months, and years after he had lain there" (Judson 1883, 304-5).

To even the most casual observer this appears to be severe depression. As I read the story, I do not imagine him endeavoring to "crucify his passionate love of life," but rather grieving in extreme measure the loss that he had endured. For six months, Judson knelt beside the grave he had dug for himself and waited to drop into it. He wasn't crucifying his love of self; he was picturing what his decomposing flesh might look like in a couple of years. Yet we like our saints and heroes without blemish, and certainly without severe emotional disorientation. We dare not speak of the saints (or the prophets of the Old Testament) in such "negative" psychological language regardless of how depressed or neurotic they appear to the reader. We tolerate only the least amount of unflattering honesty about our heroes. Judson's actions are euphemismistically smoothed over by the sympathetic biographer. Another biographer wrote:

> "Little Maria, cared for by Mrs. Wade, was for six months the solace of her father's loneliness, and then this fragile flower faded, and after two years and three months of earthly life, the little one was laid by her mother under the hopia tree. So great was Dr. Judson's mastery over himself that he did not allow even his great sorrow to interfere with his missionary labors, though he could not help it's effect upon his own life. He continued his regular duties faithfully, holding worship, teaching, preaching and translating" (Johnston 1887, 42-43).

Were this story not so tragic, one could find this kind of euphemismistic "spin" laughable. "So great was his mastery over himself"? He was leaning over his own grave for a year, waiting for a divine nudge to end his misery! Can we not allow the poor man to be human? Sadly, this only serves to artificially raise the bar for all who follow. The hidden curriculum in this biographical classroom of the heroes is to keep up a brave front and hide our weakness behind a clever mask of spiritualized stoicism. Tragically, we teach all who follow to be distant from their own hearts, disconnected emotionally, and stoic in their sadness. Sadly, this becomes our model of the heroic missionary.

The missionary service of Australian Stan Dale is chronicled in the book "Lords of the Earth" (Richardson 1979). Raised in an emotionally distant family by a surly and abusive father, the scrawny and weak boy takes comfort and inspiration in Kipling's classic poem "If." Dale is a survivor who learns to be tougher than nails and, true to the advice of the poem, master of his own course. His relationships with wife and children, and every other missionary he worked with was characterized by unresolved conflict in which Dale could never back down and rarely asked for forgiveness. His self-reliant grit and determination, while seemingly laudable for the tenacity with which he sought to reach the lost tribes of Irian Jaya, was abrasive, reckless and anti-social. Time and again he picked petty fights and caused trouble until there was no one in the mission community who desired to work with him. Dale's life ended when he forced his way into a dangerous tribal situation and would not back down. In the end, Yali tribesmen filled his body with so many of their long arrows that he wouldn't even fall over. Mission history is filled with such men; hard, determined, aggressive, harsh, and uncaring for their wives and families (and while their biographies are not as plentiful, more than just a few unhealthy women as well). While they were Christians, one is left to question the health and condition of their souls, and grieve at the way they consistently moved against others.

The simple point of this history lesson is that we become like that we celebrate. If an unbalanced telling of these stories reinforces a relational posture that is at odds with spiritual growth, we will need to learn to be honest. Tell the stories again, but this time do not leave out the difficult parts. As we prepare sojourners for cross-cultural service, they need to hear and read the full story—your spiritual journey will most likely lead to a dry and difficult place even as so many before you have crawled through that same desert. The good news is that God's ways are higher than our ways, and His purposes are good. The spiritual desert which so frequently accompanies the cross-cultural sojourn is a good place to be. We must encourage outgoing and returning sojourners that as they find themselves in a spiritually dry place, they are in good company with countless saints before them. Our word of encouragement: "Remain in that place and let the full work of the Spirit be done in your soul."

Shelter and Rest for the Dry and Weary

The movement through disorientation and dark seasons of adjustment and readjustment should not be seen in terms of a person's solo struggle. The spiritual life is not lived in isolation. Even as the Trinity is characterized by loving relationship, so also we have been created in that relational image of God. For many of us, our first inclination during times of spiritual dryness is to pull away from others, away from relationships, and away from the support that should characterize the church. Pride, fear that others will not understand or support us, or self-pity may cause us to refuse the comfort and wisdom others might offer. Solitude during the dry season of disorientation is a healthy thing, but not if that solitude is driven by feelings of shame, fear, a need to maintain an unrealistic image of ourselves, or pride which dishonestly keeps us from facing the truth.

There certainly is a time for solitude and isolation. Christ pulled himself away from his friends to a lonely place to pray. Solitude that makes space to hear the voice of God and to quiet the many other competing voices is necessary (Nouwen, 1974). But we also read that Christ knew how to ask for and receive the support, prayer and comfort of his friends. Jesus didn't pull away from the nurture and support of others, neither did he attempt to maintain a stoic facade of relational indifference. He made himself vulnerable and accepted their concern.

One of the most significant difficulties of re-entry is when the sojourner finds that none of their friends or family understand what questions to ask of the returning sojourner, or frequently, simply do not care. Many returning sojourners are simply asked "So, how was it?"—and little more. The harsh realization that the majority of people will not take the time to listen to anything more than a two minute synopsis of your time abroad can be a devastating experience. The disequilebration of cultural re-entry, and the corresponding spiritual disorientation that frequently accompanies the experience are heightened when you realize that there is no one who honestly cares to listen. It can further bruise a soul that is already weary and hurting.

For this reason, the sojourner will often need to take a proactive hand in their own support system (Chinn 1998). This may actually include going so far as telling several friends, "This is what I will need of you when I return." Several wonderful resources have recently been written for the returning missionary which outline questions to ask the returnee and provide helps for easing their transition (see Lisa Espineli Chinn's *Re-Entry*, and Neal Pirolo's *The Re-entry Team*). These kinds of conversations and friendships are water to the weary soul. Returning missionaries need at least one person to meet them and say, "I've made a pot of coffee; now sit with me and begin to tell me everything. And tomorrow night we will do the same, and we will continue to do so until you have shared all you care to share."

In addition to questions about their time abroad, about ministry, and the culture this re-entry friend might ask of the returning sojourner questions such as:

- How is your soul? What is the condition of your inner world right now? What words would describe your spiritual state?
- Are you aware of what your soul desires right now? Rest? Comfort? Forgiveness? Hope? Assurance?
- While you were abroad, what sorts of things nurtured you spiritually? What sorts of things bruised you?

- Is there anyone you need to speak with and forgive? How has this impacted your spiritual condition?
- What have you been praying about? Do you hear anything from God in these things? Is the Lord silent, or does he feel distant?
- What new realizations have you grasped as a result of your sojourn (about God, about yourself, your family or parents, your past)?
- How do you think this experience has changed the way you view the spiritual life and the way God is at work within your life? Can you sense that He is doing something in your soul?
- When was the last time you had a solo day to spend in solitude? Do you need to schedule this? How might I support you in this?
- What disappointments did you face in your sojourn? Were you disappointed with God? Have you honestly expressed those feelings to God? If so, how did He respond?
- Do you have a community to return to who will love you and with whom you can be honest?

Finally, the returning sojourner must realistically expect that their identity will be permanently altered as a result of their time cross-culturally. Theorists have proposed that the sojourner experiences considerable changes that alter their "core sense of personal and cultural identity" (Adler, 1975, 1982; Bennett, 1993). Sojourners returning to America from abroad no longer "feel American," whatever that once meant to them. They may openly question the assumed values of the majority (i.e. materialism, inordinate busyness, political policy, etc.) or have difficulty knowing where they fit within the greater social game. They re-enter their home culture but stand on the periphery, viewing the world through new lenses acquired abroad.

In my work with student sojourners, I have come to several convictions. First, there is a great deal of hope in the midst of the disorientation they are experiencing—our work is to help them find this hope. Second, the dry and disagreeable place—the spiritual desert—is not a bad place. In fact, they are in a very good place, and a desert that God earnestly desires for them to enter. It is He who has put them there, and no amount of protest can remove them from a divinely ordained place of testing and trusting. Third, what they are experiencing is not unique to them; the spiritual stories of most Christians speak of these kinds of seasons, but this is often the first time they have personally gone through something so disorienting. Mentors can offer hope that "you are not alone in this," and even share how we ourselves have passed through similar experiences. Fourth, on another level, they *are* alone in this. They are the only one waking-up with this sense of disconnect and abandonment every morning, and in the mystery of the way the Lord works in the life of the believer, the journey is frequently lonely. Fifth, there is something about the transition from late-adolescence into early adulthood, including emancipation from parents that precipitates this kind of spiritual searching in Christian young people. This experience is so common to college sophomores and juniors that they refer to it as "junior meltdown." If re-entry from an STM is the agency by which they first experience such disorientation, then there is a critical role to be played by a mission mentor in nurturing the souls of these young adults.

It is important to note that this paper blurs the distinction between long-term and short-term sojourners, as individuals in both groups experience this kind of spiritual movement. The distinction I want to make is that young adults may be going through this kind of spiritual dryness for the first time in their spiritual journey. Coupled with the trauma of seeing real poverty, injustice, and death for the first time in their life, a nineteen year-old isn't going to have the emotional and spiritual resources to cope the way a long-term (thirty-year old) sojourner will. Further, a long-term missionary will often have a member-care safety net strung below them, whereas short-termers often return to little support. They may be especially vulnerable. Looking at this positively, this is a tremendous opportunity to nurture them spiritually to a deeper place of commitment and maturity.

I conclude this paper with the encouragement that patience with messy sojourners in their time of spiritual dryness is time well spent. Time and again we see in scripture that God's greatest work is often done in the most difficult seasons. I have seen this to be true in the lives of so many students. Many return years later to give testimony that the disorientation was, in fact, a gift from a gracious God intent on surprising them (and crushing them) with a new realization of His grace in their lives. Their time in the desert stripped many things away from them, including resistances they once held to deflect the grace and mercy of God away from themselves. Years later, they finally come to understand this, accept it, and find reorientation in that mercy and love.

Any responsible agency, school or church commissioning short-term missionaries for any significant length of time (five weeks or more) should expect their returning missionaries to experience spiritual and cultural disorientation. Not all returning sojourners will go through this, but expect it none-the-less. Expect denial—again, if most of our evangelical churches are not equipped to accept messy missionaries who openly doubt the goodness of God in the midst of their re-entry, these short-termers will deny (to themselves, others, and God) that they are, in fact, in disorientation. Mission pastors, mentors, professors, member care workers, and friends must gently move toward these people in their time of lament. Let them give testimony to what they are experiencing, even if it isn't resolved. Let scripture be our guide here: Psalm 88 is just as valid as Psalm 1. Let them sing the sad songs, and reassure them that these songs of lament are worship.

Where the church so often responds in "a frightened, numb denial and deception that does not want to acknowledge or experience the disorientation of life" (the Brueggemann quote at the beginning of this paper), we must model honesty. Our reminder to these broken sojourners and lost short-termers is: Christ has not left you in the desert—He moves toward you there. This world can be cruel, heartless and crushing to our souls, but rather than rescue us from the darkness, Christ meets us in the midst of it.

References Cited

Adler, Peter S. 1975. The transitional experience: An alternative view of culture shock. *Journal of Humanistic Psychology* 15:13-23.

Austin, Clyde. 1983. *Cross cultural reentry: An annotated bibliography.* Abiline, TX: Abilene Christian University Press.

Brueggemann, Walter. 1984. *The message of the Psalms: A theological commentary.* Minneapolis, MN: Augsburg Press.

Chinn, Lisa Espineli. 1998. *Reentry guide for short-term mission leaders.* Centreville, VA: VISSTA Publications.

Gullahorn, John T. & Gullahorn, Jeanne E. 1963. An extension of the U-curve Hypotheses. *Journal of Social Issues* 14:33-47.

Johnston, Julia H. 1887. *Adoniram Judson: Missionary to Burma, 1813 to 1850.* Chicago, IL: Fleming H. Revell Company.

Jordon, Peter. 1992. Re-Entry: Making the transition from missions to life at home. Seattle, WA: YWAM Publishing.

Judson, Edward. 1883. *The life of Adoniram Judson.* Philadelphia, PA: American Baptist Publication Society.

Loss, Myron. 1983. *Culture shock: Dealing with stress in cross-cultural living.* Winona Lake, IN: Light and Life Press.

Lysgaard, S. 1955. Adjustment in a foreign society: Norwegian Fulbright grantees visiting the United States. *International Social Sciences Bulletin* 7:45-51.

Mayers, Marvin K. 1987. *Christianity confronts culture: A strategy for cross-cultural evangelism.* Grand Rapids, MI: Zondervan.

Nouwen, Henri J. M. 1974. *Out of solitude.* Notre Dame, IN: Ave Maria Press.

Oberg, Kalvero. 1960. Culture shock: Adjustment to new cultural environments. *Practical Anthropology* 7: 177-82.

Pirolo, Neal. 2000. *The reentry team.* San Diego, CA: Emmaus Road International.

Richardson, Don. 1979. *Lords of the Earth.* Ventura, CA: Gospel Light Publications.

Smalley, W. A. 1963. Culture shock, language shock, and the shock of self-discovery. *Practical Anthropology* 10:49-56.

Thomas, Kay and Teresa Harrell. 1994. Counseling student sojourners: Revisiting the U-Curve of adjustment. In *Learning across cultures,* ed. Gary Althen. Washington D.C.: NAFSA; Association of International Educators.

Torbiorn, Ingemar. 1982 Living *abroad: Personal adjustment and personal policy in the overseas setting.* New York, NY: John Wiley.

Weaver, Gary R. 1993 Understanding and coping with cross-cultural adjustment stress. In *Education for the Intercultural Experience.* Yarmouth, ME: Intercultural Press.

Weissman, D. and A. Furnham. 1987. The expectations and experiences of a sojourning temporary resident abroad: A preliminary study. *Human Relations* 40(5): 313-326.

Zwingmann, Charles A. & Gunn, A. D. C. 1983. *Uprooting and health: Psycho-social problems of students from abroad.* Geneva, Switzerland: Geneva World Health Organization, Division of Mental Health (WHO/MNH/83.8).

Endnotes

[1] Brueggemann's analysis of the Psalms drew initial inspiration from the work of Paul Ricoeur. Ricoeur's fundamental categories of suspicion and retrieval, and displacement and recapture informed Brueggemann's descriptive model of movement from praise to lament to deliverance.

CHAPTER 21

FROM "WHATEVER" TO WHEREVER: IN YOUNG ADULTS THROUGH

ENHANCING FAITH FORMATION SHORT-TERM MISSIONS

FRAN BLOMBERG

The essential developmental tasks of young adults in 21st century North America may be described as establishing self-identity, finding "place" in community, finding purpose in vocation and forming integrity of faith in a coherent Christian worldview.

The role of the mentoring community in young adult faith development is vital for transformational growth. Such a mentoring community can occur within the context of STM service. STM trips, while maintaining the priority of serving the host community, can be structured in order to maximize the faith development of young adults participating. Team dynamics, spiritual formation and training, execution of a viable task, debrief and follow up should be considered from the perspective of nurturing the young adult's sense of belonging, integrity and contribution in a manner consistent with their developing Christian faith.

Young Adults

Defining a new generation

Young adults—ages eighteen to thirty-ish. They are often called Twentysomethings, and they are about 40 million strong in America today. They are remarkably diverse. The U.S. Department of Commerce states that between 1980 and 2000, the population of fifteen to nineteen-year old Caucasians dropped 19%, while that of African Americans dropped 6%. The Hispanic population of the same age group grew 42% and that of Asian-Americans grew by over 100% (Colatosi 1998, 9). Are these young adults simply the spoiled Peter Pans of the 21st century, raised on privilege and unwilling to grow up and take responsibility? Are they the inevitable product of dysfunctional, self-centered Boomer and Gen X parents? Are they really leaving the church in droves, without faith and incapable of commitment?

I begin in a deliberately pessimistic tone only to mimic the despair and anxiety I frequently find as I talk to my peers about Twentysomethings. I am incredibly privileged to work with young adults at both Denver Seminary and Scum of the Earth Church in Denver. I am thankful for the way their questions force me to a vigorous study of Scripture, their willingness to affirm my own sometimes rocky navigation of Christian life, and the boldness and vitality of their faith which gives me immense confidence for the future of the church.

This is a new and distinct generation. Our culture has created it. The number of broken and dysfunctional homes by most measures is increasing. In some homes children are being asked to assume the role of adult. In others they are restricted and protected by well-intentioned mothers and fathers who are determined not to repeat the mistakes of their own parents. None would deny the pervasive influence of media and industry in creating a distinctly youth-oriented consumer culture which is purposefully set apart from the "boring" adult world. Life spans are increasing, and typical adult milestones of marriage and parenthood are being delayed. Some put relationships on the shelf to pursue careers; others simply choose partners without commitment to marriage and ensure there are no children. Undergraduate education, once the privilege of a select few, is now accessible to most, but consequently has depreciated in value even while escalating in cost. This depreciation, along with other economic factors such as college debt, does not allow independence as readily, and many young adults are forced back home into poorly paying jobs with insufficient benefits (Blomberg et al 2005). In our globalized world, change is constant, choices are overwhelming, and stability and commitment can seem impossible.

This life stage genuinely exists and is significantly different from "when I was that age..!" Whether you are a Baby Boomer, born between 1946 and 1964, or a Gen Xer born between 1965 and 1980, you are not imaging it—Millennials, born after 1980 and coming into adulthood in the new millennium, ARE a genuinely different generation.

Developmental tasks of the young adult

Eric Erikson, in his seminal work *Childhood and Society* (1950) described the crisis and task of adolescence as that of *forming identity* in the midst of *role confusion*. The young adult will hopefully choose *intimacy* over *isolation*, and learn to make appropriate commitments in areas such as faith, marriage and career. The mature adult will then achieve fulfillment, or *generativity* rather than *stagnation*.

James W. Fowler (1981) postulated the faith development of the mid-twenties to mid-thirties as *individuative-reflective faith*. Here the young adult experiences the struggle to stand apart from previously accepted values and beliefs in order to reflect on and eventually "own" his or her own faith and take personal responsibility for beliefs, feelings and ethics. According to Fowler, *conjunctive faith* occurs in midlife when the mature adult comes to grip with the existence of unsolvable paradoxes in faith and life and encounters differing viewpoints with steadfast confidence in his or her own faith.

In 1986, Sharon Daloz Parks jumped off from Fowler's individuative-reflective stage and proposed a detailed theory of young adult faith development in her book *The Critical Years.* She expanded and updated her work in her excellent volume *Big Questions, Worthy Dreams,* published in 2000. She offers many paradoxical images of the developmental task of the young adult, including journey and home, pilgrimage and stability, shipwreck and reconstruction, dissolution and recomposition.

Parks contends that it is necessary for the young adult to intentionally challenge the integrity and viability of the faith which he or she has been given by parents and other authoritative adults (Parks 2000, 31). Some may question their derived faith with quiet reasoning, others with flamboyantly obvious rebellion; but without opportunity to deliberately assess the conventional faith of adolescence, a mature Christian worldview cannot develop. We may say a necessity of the young adult years is that of learning to evaluate the coherence of his or her Christian worldview, to reformulate understanding and expression of belief and ethics, and to continually recalibrate faith (Parks 1987, 95). Children can be taught stories and rules, teens can be taught principles, but young adults must be taught to learn, to question and to compose faith for themselves.

There are a number of steps in the journey to mature adult faith. From the idealistic, unqualified relativism of "whatever," "I can do anything," the young adult comes to the shocking conclusion that he or she has to make choices. You have to choose a major. You can't live in two cities at once. You can hold two or three jobs, but you will have to choose which bills your meager combined salaries will pay. And those are the relatively easy decisions; what about belief in

God, choice of a life mate, or whether or not your lifestyle promotes global justice?

It is terrifying to move from trusting external authorities to the necessity of trusting one's own judgments. The Christian rock/ Rap band DC Talk asks, "What if I stumble? What if I fall? What if I lose my step and I make fools of us all? Will the love continue if the walk becomes a crawl?"(DC Talk 2000). It can easily take a decade to move from the rebellious independence of adolescence through forming this fragile inner-dependence in young adulthood. Tentatively, with what Parks calls "probing commitment" (Parks 2000, 66), the young adult tackles the essential tasks of these years: establishing self-identity, finding "place" in community, finding purpose in vocation and forming integrity of faith in a coherent Christian worldview.

	Adolescent	> > >	Young Adult	> > >	Mature Adult
Forms of Knowing	Under authority	Anti-authority	Probing commitment	Testing commitment	Convicted commitment
Forms of Dependence	Dependent	Refusing dependence	Fragile inner-dependence	Confident inner-dependence	Inter-dependence
Forms of Community	Conventional	Diffuse; "whatever"	Supportive mentoring community	Opening to the other	Embracing the other

Figure 1. Adapted from Parks 2000, 91.

As the journey continues, maturing adults will develop, by the grace of God, a convicted commitment of faith/meaning, and a healthy inter-dependence in a broadened community (Parks 2000, 86).The maturing young adult has a stronger self-identity, and more readily considers others as contributors to, not determinants of, this personal identity. This strong self-identity learns to hold firmly to convictions and truth amidst the diversity, paradox and unanswerable questions in this fallen world—Fowler's conjunctive faith.

The developmental stage of young adulthood cannot be circumvented, but tragically, it is often denied or short-circuited. How can the church and Christian mentors facilitate Twentysomethings' necessary process of dissolution and discovery? How can STM trips contribute to the essential tasks of these years: establishing self-identity, finding "place" in community, finding purpose in vocation and forming integrity of faith in a coherent Christian worldview? It will first be necessary to examine the realities of young adults' involvement with the church.

Why Are the Pews Empty?

Again, it is not one's imagination—young adults are conspicuously absent from church. The Barna Group reported in September 2006 that 61% of those who had been churched as teens report themselves "spiritually disengaged (i.e., not actively attending church, reading the Bible, or praying)" at some point in or following college. "Twentysomethings were nearly 70% more likely than older adults to strongly assert that if they 'cannot find a local church that will help them become more like Christ, then they will find people and groups that will, and connect with them instead of a local church.'" Interestingly, a University of Texas study completed in June 2007 demonstrated that college-educated young adults were less likely to disaffiliate from church and organized religion than their peers who did not attend college (Uecker, Regnerus and Vaaler 2007).

In the past many churches accepted this disengagement as inevitable, expecting that most adults would return to the church as parents. Yet parenthood is being delayed by many, and no more than half of today's parents report taking their children to church. To take the confident position that "they'll be back" is to deny the reality that the church is failing in its crucial responsibility to nurture the emerging faith of young adults.

The focus of young adult ministry should not be programs to "get them back to church;" the focus must be people who will accompany the young adult on the necessary pilgrimage and exploration (Gribbon 1990, 13). Stephen Garber puts it this way: along with the need for a coherent and truth-filled worldview to sustain them in a pluralistic society, young adults need mentors who will incarnate the worldview, and a community that will practice and demonstrate the viability of the worldview (Garber 1996). The church's welcome to young adults cannot be without a willingness to be personally invested in their often messy, rollercoaster lives of discovery. The promise of mentoring is invaluable to a generation that has experienced fragmentation, broken homes, and fallen "role models." If the Christian lifestyle is truly viable, the young adult will expect to see it followed with integrity by those who presume to be their spiritual leaders.

Some might fear allowing young adults the freedom to construct their Christian worldview apart from direct imposition of tried and true orthodox beliefs and practices. However, "a transition from one faith stage to another does not necessarily mean a change in the *content* or the *direction* of one's faith. It does mean, however, changes in the way one holds, understands, and takes responsibility for living one's faith" (Fowler 1996, 68). We should fear the rejection of orthodox faith if it cannot be seen to hold integrity in the world in which these emerging leaders will themselves be called to live and minister.

> Values cannot be passed from one person to another. We can only aid the younger generation in understanding the process and acquiring the skills and tools that will make it possible for them to develop their own faith commitments. Seen in

> this light, true values and ethical behavior have
> much more to do with freedom and choice than
> they do with obedience and conformity (Dudley
> 1999, 11).

Where better than in a healthy, hospitable local church could the freedom of faith exploration and recalibration be found? Where better to receive nurture and support in establishing self-identity, finding "place" in community, finding purpose in vocation and forming integrity of faith in a coherent Christian worldview? STM trips, lasting from as little as one week up to two years, offered in the context of the local church, can be effective and intentional tools for the faith formation of young adults.

Designing Short-term Missions Trips to Enhance Faith Formation

Abrupt change or momentous events, are often encountered on STM trips. When sensitively handled and thoughtfully reflected upon, these can dramatically accelerate faith formation. "The educational significance of these experiences is vast. The challenges to their worldview, their heightened cultural sensitivity, and increased self-awareness brought about by these trips cannot easily be replicated by other experiences" (Johnstone 2006, 525).

The team leader as mentor: A key to faith formation

Given the need for Twentysomethings to lead and take responsibility for their own faith discovery, the role of the leader needs to be that of mentor. The mentor creates a place of safety, hospitality and inquiry where the participants can bring their tough questions, startling observations, frustrations and joys. Within this haven, the young adult can ask hard questions, face his or her own prejudices and shortcomings, recognize and appreciate gifts and strengths, and deliberate about the relative merits of the host culture's values and behaviors. The mentoring team leader can even introduce dissonance and conflict to the mind and experience of participants in order to provoke thought, although it is necessary to also provide a supportive environment for the discussion and resolution of those conflicts. Laurent Daloz offers a helpful grid for understanding the potential benefits and pitfalls that a challenge given with or without support can offer in an adult's growth process:

	Low support	High support
Low challenge	Stasis—no change provoked	Confirmation of belief without personal ownership—identity foreclosure
High Challenge	Retreat—culture shock!	Growth in faith, with appreciation of others

Figure 2. Adapted from Daloz 1999, 208.

It is as important to know when to interject one's leadership as it is to know when to be hands-off. In one secular travel journal's interesting study of over 1400 young adults in eleven countries, it was noted that this population not only likes to travel off the beaten track, but prefers adventures found through independent sources. Web research accompanied by personal online recommendations from former participants and the input of friends scored much higher as methods of choosing a particular trip than any form of publicity, brochure, or promotion. It could be that a leader's one-on-one recruitment, rather than impersonal advertising in traditional church communications would actually have greater appeal to those more prone toward risk-taking and open to genuine life transformation (Pizam 2004).

Team leaders who serve as mentors will be acquainted with the potential for faith development appropriate to the ages represented among the team. They will be ever on the alert to facilitate the young adult's learning in four key areas: that of forming self-identity, finding a place in community, finding purpose in meaningful work, and discovering a coherent worldview that appreciates but is not threatened by the input of others of differing worldviews.

Discovering self-identity in choosing what to value

The distilled life experience of a short-term trip is an excellent, concentrated opportunity for developing skills in assessing and choosing values, accepting responsibility for one's own growth, and learning to probe and question in constructive ways. It "allows one a standpoint from which conflicting expectations can be adjudicated and one's own inner authorization can be strengthened" (Fowler 1996, 63). In other words, the participant learns to both strengthen and recalibrate faith, a core, essential task of young adulthood.

Almost inevitably, the short-term trip will involve exposure to new people, places and circumstances. In these unprecedented situations, each significant observation and each decision the young adult makes can be formative in molding identity. When the participant decides it is not "stupid" for women in the host culture to wear a head covering, but can appreciate the value that drives the behavior, she has gained the ability to make more of her own decisions based not on the common dictates of her culture but on self-selected values. As the leader guides, reflects, corrects and affirms the *process* by which young adults make decisions and draw conclusions, he or she gives courage for more intensive scrutiny of personal choices, and broadens the young adults' ability to choose according to God-honoring criteria. A healthy identity is formed not when the person simply conforms to the leader's standards of behavior on the trip, but when he or she is nurtured in the process of choosing to humbly serve and honor the customs of the culture being visited. When "I had to" becomes "I chose to," character is strengthened.

Discovering a place in community in team dynamics

Unfortunately, often what passes for "community" today is simply dozens or even hundreds of individuals gathered together with common interests and little interaction. On an STM trip, the dynamics of teamwork can be paradigmatic of forming and sustaining genuine community. With the common focus of short-term service, the young adult has a group offering the security of like-mindedness and initial acceptance. This community then becomes a launching pad from which he or she can probingly commit to hearing, evaluating, accepting and incorporating the views of others. "The task of building community," says Johnstone (2006, 527), "is a solemn mandate."

It is not only Twentysomethings that long for genuine community, but this generation is intentionally structuring ministries to foster it. Study reveals the resurgence and growth of explicitly incarnational mission agencies such as Word Made Flesh, Servant Partners, as well as a "new monasticism" establishing intentional Christian communities in America's cities and slums (Bessenecker 2006; Moll 2005). This generation will not be content with forays from and nightly retreats to the mission compound or five-star hotel. They will want to live with and among the people, practicing incarnation and humbly recognizing that they too are being served by the ones they have come to serve.

Hawthorne's edited volume *Stepping Out* (1997) offers short but deeply insightful articles from several practitioners on such difficult topics as brokenness, surrender to God, giving up personal rights for others, and disappointment with God and others. These spiritual practices are often counter-intuitive to the emerging inner-dependence of the young adult, and are best formed in the concerned safety and support of a nurturing community. Again the team dynamics of a short-term trip can be invaluable to the concentrated formation of such difficult spiritual disciplines.

Yong adults will respect the need for holy living as a requirement for application and service—but the trip leaders better be prepared to be held accountable themselves by the community for their attitudes and actions! "Authenticity" is a new buzzword for the timeless maxim "practice what you preach," and it is truly necessary. "The team leader is naturally under constant observation. They are required by the nature of their position to live a life of transparency" (Johnstone 2006, 527). Be prepared for young adults to recommend new and surprising standards of holiness among the teams on which they serve. While the leaders may emphasize outward appearance and behavior, the young adult will be more concerned with integration of outward behavior and inner attitude. "No, I didn't finish my journal assignment, I went for a walk this morning and wound up helping a woman carry water back to her home." "The pastor told me I can't give my testimony unless I take out my nose ring. What's that got to do with my heart?"

Discovering purpose in meaningful task

Along with a thirst for authentic community comes the desire to see that community makes a genuine difference in the world. Traveling with a group in the formative stages of choosing careers and vocations is like turning children loose at the pick-and-mix candy counter—it is a phenomenal chance to experiment with gifts and skills, take calculated (and protected) risks and savor new flavors of success. But beware: "success" for this group is not simply completing a building project, or even adding a few good lines to a future résumé. Studies of Millennials show an increased interest in defining success as helping others and making a difference, and contributing toward collective well-being rather than simply individual advancement (Arnett 2004, 243). Task alone, without concurrent opportunity to build relationships among teammates and hosts, will likely prove unsatisfactory to a generation accustomed to group projects and incarnational ministry (Gascho 2005, 29).

On the other hand, this generation will demonstrate resourcefulness and adaptability toward the trip's inevitable delays, unexpected turn of events, and otherwise frustrating inability to complete the project. "Success" will come with friendships established with other team members and the host community. What team leader and host wouldn't appreciate the ability to "chill out" without the pressure to produce opportunities for ministry and events for an anxious, time-and-cost-conscious group of short-termers?!

Discovering worldview in the challenge to accept "other"

Most significant to the needs of young adults is the need to develop a coherent, sustainable Christian worldview that will carry them through the unpredictable challenges of a world that is changing with exponential rapidity. In the midst of exploding technologies, the world is shrinking to a global village and yet fragmenting into innumerable competing ideologies and ethnic rivalries. When in the throes of developing a stable self-understanding and determining the validity of Christian faith, how can we assist young adults to begin to embrace "the other," those outside their own tribe, those considered to be different and potentially suspect? Train them, nurture them and shake them up on an STM trip!

Pre-field training:

Training for task is an important component of preparation for effective service and ministry on the field. Perhaps more importantly, training for intentional learning and spiritual growth must be introduced to participants so that in the heat of the moment, they can draw from their cognitive backgrounds, and hopefully integrate prior learning with current experience. Young adults must learn *how* to learn for themselves. Peter himself offers a model of bringing principles learned to practical fruition at a later time: the same man who preached at Pentecost needed a succession of dreams and a personal encounter with a Gentile family to proclaim, "I now understand [that God does not show partiality]!" (Acts 10:34). When the light goes on long after the lesson was originally taught, may those who lead short-term trips replace the strong temptation to say "I told you so!" with "You're right! Great observation, good response!"

Without proper training in how to observe culture, read social cues, prioritize time for tasks and people, and discern structures of power and relationships, participants in an STM trip will more than likely try—inappropriately and even offensively—to squeeze new ideas and observations into their already existing cultural framework.

> Organizing for learning rather than for teaching means that we take a long view of short terms: We affirm that earnest and idealistic young people with limited life experience and intercultural ability can be developed into valuable resources in Christ's church if they refuse to settle for simply being "tourists for Jesus" or unaffected "soul savers." What's required, however, is a fundamental shift in missioner disposition. Rather than relating to the host culture either as a hot adventure land or as a cold, dark place destined for ultimate destruction, missioners would aim at identifying the good, the true, and beautiful within the local culture as a means of broadening their comprehension of the kingdom of God (Slimbach 2000, 439).

On the field reflection

David Livermore's *Serving with Eyes Wide Open* (2006) brings the principles of cultural intelligence (CQ), popular in business and organizational psychology, to the field of missiology. Assuming adequate time has been spent gaining knowledge about the host culture and its values, Interpretive CQ comes into play as "the ability to connect our knowledge with what we're observing in the real world" (Livermore 2006, 131). Perseverance CQ describes the "level of interest, drive, and motivation to adapt cross- culturally. It is a traveler's robustness, courage, heartiness, and capability to persevere through cultural differences" (Livermore 2006, 142). Behavioral CQ is the ability to act properly and to see how the same behaviors have different meanings in different places. CQ would be demonstrated by the short-termer who resists Starbucks for the sake of trying local drinks, or who balances his or her greater technological competence with the need to sensitively save face for the older national leader who is ineptly handling a recalcitrant sound system or computer.

There is the need for development of self-identity (Fowler's individuation) but it must not result in individualism without the longer-term challenge of reflection and interaction with otherness being met. Even as Twentysomethings break the bonds of hand-me-down faith with the cautious acquisition of their own adult faith, they simultaneously feel an inquisitiveness to hear the perspectives of others. "Faith," contends Parks (2000, 139), "develops at the boundary with otherness," and is nurtured by a supportive environment that will "invite genuine dialogue, strengthen critical thought, encourage connective-holistic awareness and develop the contemplative mind."

The young adults must be guided in discerning between cultural plurality, which expresses the diversity of God's creative ability; Christian plurality, which reflects our varying traditions and interpretations; and religious pluralism, which is idolatry. The well-prepared mentor/leader will engage the difficult questions such as "but they are such good people—how can I really believe they 'need Jesus'?" and "how should we respond to the injustices we see perpetrated by local authorities and even church leaders?" This engagement does not need to find definitive answers—most participants will see through such a ruse!—but needs to teach the young adult how to assess, react and pray in light of such profound discoveries.

Perhaps most important for the "rich young rulers" who often make up our young adult teams would be the area of learning to deal sensitively with issues of poverty and wealth (Willimon 2002, 47). Can the participants endure the calamity of first learning to live without their conveniences, and then recalibrate their understanding of what is *need* and what is *convenience*? Can they be taught to practice ministry without what Paulo Freire calls "malevolent generosity," and without what David Livermore calls "petting the poor?" (Livermore 2006, 168). What a watershed opportunity for the dissolution of a pervasive consumerist mindset and the reconstruction of a lifestyle based on simplicity, community and justice!

An ongoing process of debriefing

The lessons of an STM trip cannot be absorbed in the space of time the trip itself allows. Not until there has been time for reflection and evaluation after re-entry to the home culture can the participant fully grasp the significance of all that was discovered. Debriefing can begin with daily sessions during the trip, and extend to face-to-face or virtual meetings over the following months. Again the mentor/ leader's role is crucial. As situations are analyzed and difficulties and joys discussed, the astute leader will urge the participants not simply to formulate conclusions but will guide them into re-imaging their understanding of God, self, community and others. Images and metaphors are provocative learning tools that give shape to, without finalizing, the ongoing process of understanding. Images honor the process of learning and the pilgrimage of discovery as they give voice to tentative understanding and probing commitments of faith and lifestyle. An image I have found useful with short-term teams is that of "dumpster-diving for Jesus"—a vivid picture of willingness to enter squalor and stench in order to discover lost treasure. Encourage images in art, words and other media in order to coalesce the experience of the trip with the substance of faith.

The necessity for multiple venues for debrief over a period of time cannot be overstated. Randy Friesen's study (2005) of over 100 trip participants ages 18-30 offers sobering statistics on the decline of the perceived efficacy of personal prayer, Bible study, church attendance and personal purity. Similarly, an earlier study by Kathryn Tuttle (2000) discovered that debriefing was a key component in effecting lasting faith formation in college students who had participated in summer STM trips. Spiritual leaders cannot consider their responsibility finished while there are still significant questions and issues of faith on the table from participants. It is in the months that follow time on the field that the participants will be able to articulate areas of growth such as ability to trust God's sovereignty when circumstances were unpredictable, unsafe or undesirable. Similarly, reflection accompanied by continuing experience at home will increase confidence that one's ability to serve and make a difference wasn't just a fluke, but a gracious gift of God that should be heartily cultivated through ongoing ministry opportunities.

Conclusion: Integrating a Short-term Trip into a Faith that Fits with Life

In summary, I believe the church is the locus of Christian faith development that should most willingly offer permission and accompaniment on the journey to mature adult faith that we desire for Twentysomethings. I would urge that STM trips be viewed as faith-forming discipleship experiences that offer promise of restoring young adults to belief in and participation in the local church.

With intentional construction and the grace of the Holy Spirit, the compressed life experience of the STM trip can offer occasion for the young adult to establish self-identity, find "place" in community, find purpose in vocation and form integrity of faith in a coherent Christian worldview. An incisive team leader, resolute in allowing the participants to question, discover, reflect and challenge presuppositions and experiences, will be an invaluable servant to the community. Learning how to question, assess and recalibrate prior values and beliefs through enlarged lenses will aid the young adult in defining himself or herself—"this is what I stand for, this is who I am." The team as community will further support inquiry, listen to frustrations, rejoice with success and pray continually for spiritual growth and maturity. Success with community on the trip, albeit for a short time, will favorably dispose young adults to continue to seek intimate face-to-face community, even as they utilize every technology available to continue in virtual community with teammates.

Meaningful tasks accompanied by opportunities to build relationships with the host culture for mutual edification will contribute to the young adults' discovery of vocation and agency for change. On a short-term trip, participants encounter "otherness" in a way that secures conviction in his or her own self-identity while increasing appreciation for the contribution the other can make to a broadened understanding of faith. The Christian worldview is tested in the fire of competing worldviews and values, and with careful mentoring will prove worthy.

Maturity, Erikson's generativity, Fowler's conjunctive faith or Park's convicted commitment are various ways of expressing the outcome of these vulnerable and promising years of young adulthood. May we invoke the power of the Holy Spirit in praying that as God's people are equipped for works of service, "the body of Christ may be built up until we all reach unity in the faith and in the knowledge of the Son of God and become mature, attaining to the whole measure of the fullness of God" (Eph. 4:12-13).

References Cited

Arnett, Jeffrey Jensen. 2004. *Emerging adulthood: The winding road from the late teens through the twenties.* New York: Oxford University Press.

Bessenecker, Scott. 2006. *The new friars.* Downers Grove: IVP.

Blomberg, Fran, Geoff Hart, Tae Kyoon Kim, George G. Robinson IV. "Generational socio-cultural shifts in the post-modern age: From boomers to Gen X and beyond." Global Missiology. January 2006. Accessed February 20, 2007<*http://www.globalmissiology.com*> Path: GM archives.

Colatosi, Camille. 1998. Young adults today: Optimistic but fearful. *The Witness* 81:9 (Sept): 8-11.

DC Talk. 2000. "What If I Stumble?" *Intermission: The Greatest Hits.* Emi Cmg Distribution.

Daloz, Laurent. 1999. *Mentor: Guiding the journey of adult learners.* San Francisco: Jossey-Bass.

Dudley, Roger. 1999. Understanding the spiritual development and faith experience of college and university students on Christian campuses. *Journal of Research on Christian Education* 8: 5-28.

Friesen, Randy. 2005. The long-term impact of short-term missions. *Evangelical Missions Quarterly* 41: 448-454.

Fowler, James. 1996. *Faithful change: The personal and public challenges of postmodern life.* Nashville: Abingdon Press.

Fowler, James. 1981. *Stages of faith: The psychology of human development and the quest for meaning.* San Francisco: Harper and Row.

Garber, Steven. 1996. *The fabric of faithfulness: Weaving together belief and behaviorduring the university years.* Downers Grove: IVP.

Gribbon, Robert. 1990. *Developing faith in young adults: Effective ministry with 18-30year olds.* New York: The Alban Institute, Inc.

Hawthorne, Steve. 1997. *Stepping out.* Monrovia, CA: Short-term Missions Advocates.

Johnstone, David M. 2006. Closing the loop: Debriefing and the short-term college missions team. *Missiology* 34: 523-29.

Livermore, David A. 2006. *Serving with eyes wide open: Doing short-term missions with cultural intelligence.* Grand Rapids: Baker.

"Most Twentysomethings Put Christianity on the Shelf Following Spiritually Active Teen Years." *The Barna Update.* 16 September 2006. The Barna Group. Accessed 20 September 1007. <*http://www.barna. org/FlexPage.aspx?Page= BarnaUpdate&BarnaUpdateID=245*>

Moll, Rob. 2005. The new monasticism. *Christianity Today* 49.9 (September): 38-46.

Parks, Sharon. 1987. Global complexity and young adult formation: Implications for religious and professional education. *Religion and Intellectual Life* 4: 86-104.

Parks, Sharon Daloz. 2000. *Big questions, worthy dreams: Mentoring young adults in their search for meaning, purpose, and faith.* San Francisco: Jossey-Bass.

Parks, Sharon Daloz. 1986. *The critical years.* San Francisco: Harper and Row.

Pizam, Abraham, et al. 2004. The relationship between risk-taking, sensation-seeking, and the tourist behavior of young adults: A cross-cultural study. *Journal of TravelResearch* 42: 251-60.

"Populations Pyramids Summary for the United States." *U.S. Census Bureau.* 16 July 2007. Accessed 17 September 2007. < *http://www. census.gov/cgibin/ipc/idbpyry.pl?cty= US&maxp=14348291&maxa =85&ymax=250&yr=2000.submit=SubmitQuery*>

Slimbach, Richard. 2000. First, do no harm. *Evangelical Missions Quarterly* 36: 428-436, 439-441.

Tuttle, Kathryn. 2000. The effect of short-term missions experiences on college students' spiritual growth and maturity. *Christian Education Journal* 4: 123-140.

Uecker, Jeremy E., Mark D. Regnerus, and Margaret L. Vaaler. 2007. Losing My Religion: The Social Sources of Religious Decline in Young Adulthood. *Social Forces* 85:4.

Willimon, William. 2002. Preaching to affluent young adults, or, Lord, help me shove this camel. *Journal for Preachers* 26: 46-48.

CHAPTER 22

SUPERVISORS FOR SHORT-TERM MISSION

EXPERIENCES: THINKING ABOUT SELECTION

VICKI GASCHO

The supervisor of a short-term ministry may be the most essential component of a successful mission experience, for it is that person who walks with participants during a slice of their lives in which great personal growth can occur—or alternatively, where they experience a sense of failure, loss, and despair. It is the supervisor who plans, directs, and stands at the center of a ministry task, signaling its significance to God's overall plan in the universe. And it is the supervisor who may be best positioned in the participant's life to challenge and guide discussions about the future. . . "Does this ministry seem to fit my gifts, passions, and experiences?" "Can I picture myself working in this culture and with such a team?" "Do I sense God tugging at my heart and perhaps calling me to something further?"

Ministry supervisors are essential to the short-term process. Yet they create effective programs and lead energized, successful participants only to the extent that they themselves are well selected, intentionally trained, and their efforts carefully assessed. This paper addresses the first of those concerns—the *selection of short-term mission supervisors*. Regardless of whether supervisors lead two-week church-led teams or year-long experiences in conjunction with a mission agency, supervisors should be selected on the basis of carefully considered foundational strengths and on well-articulated personal commitments.

Jesus commanded all believers to grow in righteous and in their outward service for him. Yet the Scriptures also consistently demand a heightened expectation *for*, and a stringent selection, assistance, and monitoring *of* those who will lead others. That demand is nowhere more evident than in the choice of short-term mission supervisors. We dare not end our search for those leaders when we have culled out those who are growing obediently, working faithfully, or who seem to exhibit the capacity to learn and the willingness to take on new challenges. We must also assess exceptional foundational capacities, gifts, attitudes, and experiences. Then, on the heels of such assessment, we must target those who will voice the commitment to personal growth and incarnational living; to facilitate growth, challenge, and future hope in others; to lead in productive ministry; to becomes students of cultures and of the cultural adjustment process; and, finally, to see themselves, others, and ministry through the grid of missiological reflection.

Foundational Capacities

Jim Collins (2001) reminds us that "getting the right people on the bus" is essential for work teams in organizations, and certainly for the selection of its leaders. Like human gene inheritance, should a man or woman exhibit large numbers of deficits going into a supervisory role, probably no amount of human preparation and monitoring will turn them into leaders who reproduce themselves in healthy people and effective work. Obviously a good selection assessment is in order.

Rick Warren's simple *S.H.A.P.E.* acronym is widely used by individuals seeking to find their unique fit for ministry. However, such a tool could also serve as part of an assessment that evaluates short-term supervisor capacities in light of the task and in considering the people who will participate. In using the *S.H.A.P.E.* model as one part of the assessment process, the church or mission leadership would look carefully at recognized spiritual gifting of potential supervisors, their heart or passion for the task, and additionally their aptitude, personality, and their life experiences that increase their suitability for the assignment.

Participants in Willow Creek's 2006 Leadership summit remember Bill Hybels' discussion of a "constellation of leaders" in ministry. In selecting his own constellation of leaders, in which effectiveness becomes exponential, Hybels says he assumes a foundation of personal rich and growing spirituality and an obvious commitment to ministry. Beyond that, he looks for the following four characteristics in leaders who will rise to unusual effectiveness and influence: (1) all around intelligence; (2) energy enough to energize others; (3) relational IQ; and (4) a "win-or-die spirit."

In reviewing the above thoughts about supervisory leadership choices, some would say, "Those capacities are only about *character*." Exactly. And particularly so if we define *character* as something more complex than merely choosing to do the right thing ethically. For Henry Cloud, *character* goes far beyond ethics and morality, encompassing also the whole of the way we relate to ourselves, to other people, and to the work God has given us. Character, Cloud says, is *the ability to meet the demands of reality*. Character is thus bound to *integrity*, especially when we consider the classic definition of the word … *wholeness, unity,* or *having internal consistency*. Cloud insists that when a person of character or integrity is at work, the atmosphere is one of completeness, with a pervasive sense that things will be "working well, undivided, integrated, intact, and uncorrupted" (Cloud 2006, 24-33). Thus we must ask, "What are the *realities* of life and work for the supervisor?" and "Do our supervisors have the personal *internal consistency* to meet those demands?"

When we consider the necessary foundational capacities of supervisors for short-term mission experiences, we arrive at an astounding list of qualifications:

- A rich and growing spirituality
- A life and life-style that is increasingly integrated, demonstrating internal consistency
- A personal commitment, heart, and passion for the Lord's work and for leading others
- An compelling and contagious energy for the work
- Spiritual gifts corresponding to the needs of the role
- An all-around intelligence as well as an aptitude or talent for the particular assignment
- A personality or makeup that values people and that lends itself well to influencing them—the "relational IQ" element
- Past experiences that result in suitability for the work and for leading in the task
- A calling, vision, capacity, and passion to press forward regardless of what difficult circumstances may intrude—a "heart-of-a-missionary resiliency" and a "win-or-die" attitude

Goals for the Ministry and Corresponding Personal Commitments

Assessing the most necessary, basic capacities of short-term supervisors is critical, as we have seen in the foregoing discussion. Yet it is only the beginning of the selection process. The above capacities are the things that good potential supervisors lay on the table. Those capacities form the foundation on which the real work must now begin.

When we consider great short-term supervision, we must do so in the context of three large goals for any short-term program:

1. Assisting in the personal growth of the participants regardless of their future ministry decisions
2. Contributing positively to the tasks or ministries in progress
3. Providing an accurate, yet hope-filled "test-the-waters" atmosphere for possible future participation in the ministry

Our own organization has discovered the above goals to be absolutely fundamental to every short-term mission in which we have invested ourselves or invited others. Probably every sending agency or sending church would agree. Whenever one or more of the goals is neglected or diminished, the total experience becomes jeopardized. Unless the supervisor understands, and is equipped and committed to facilitating the accomplishment of each of the three goals, loss of personal hope, a sense of ineffective ministry, tenuous relationships, and possibly overall failure will occur.[1]

Thus, beyond the foundational capacities and character required of short-term supervisors, future leaders must also demonstrate a commitment to personal growth and incarnational living, to facilitating development, challenge, and future hope in others, to leading in productive ministry, and to understanding cultures and the cultural adjustment process. Finally, supervisors must commit to life-long missiological reflection—to seeing themselves, others, and ministry through that grid as a model to others and as a guide for continuing wise, godly judgment in their own roles.

Commitment to Personal Growth and Incarnational Living

Short-term supervisors who are themselves reaching toward maturity are in the best position to live for others rather than for themselves. Though they are not perfect, they probably are strong enough to set personal agendas and egos aside in order to unselfishly infuse life into situations and people. They are learning to demonstrate personal transparency and an inner security that allows them to respond without a self-protective or authoritarian posture.

Supervisors must learn to relate sensitively and comfortably to various generations of short term participants, as well as to the sub-cultures and personalities that those participants represent. They therefore resist making negative judgments about the worth of those who disagree or who may believe or behave differently than other team members. Such supervisors show acceptance of differing opinions and ideas, modeling openness to inquiry. They do not play favorites but rather are committed to fairness, justice, and impartiality. They are able to trust the motives of others.

Good supervisors discern and act on the needs of the participants, not solely on the demands of the task. In that way they demonstrate that people are valuable, not only for what they produce, but for their position as people created in God's image.

The best supervisors not only tell; they become students themselves as they learn to hear the thoughts and priorities of the people under their care. Participants bring with them various ways of working, playing, and worshipping, and wise supervisors pick up and adopt many of those positive patterns, incorporating them into the life of the group.

Commitment to Facilitate Growth, Challenge, and Future Hope

The best supervisors intentionally allow encounters, conversations, and experiences for their people that go beyond the members' present level of comfort and comprehension. Supervisors, however, must be intentionally present to support, encourage, and facilitate the growth that can occur through such experiences. Educators often speak about *teachable moments*--those serendipitous times that arrive without warning, providing opportunity for the Holy Spirit to move powerfully, or for people to come to new levels of profound insight, or for grand commitments to be made. Every supervisor can point to a few of those moments. Probably more often, however, growth, challenge, and future hope is instilled through a combination of many small events, compassionate action, good humor, and gentle, leading questions.

One might presume that short-termers, particularly young adults fresh out of college or seminary, would come to their assignment eagerly enthusiastic, earnestly seeking God, wanting to serve Him and others, and hoping to find a signal about their future. We have found, however, that participants often arrive exhausted and spiritually dry, regardless of the nurturing environment or the circumstances from which they come. Frequently they may act like immature children when their expectations are not fulfilled. They probably will need a solid peacemaker to assist them in learning to relate to their team members, veteran missionaries, or national believers. They may require large inoculations of nurture, grace, and understanding in the context of good conversation and plenty of face time. The supervisor may be the one person who is most able to bring refreshment, cool water, correction, challenge, and hope to those very thirsty people.

Conversations regarding future hope and challenge should allow for the possibility that God will act outside the boundaries of the supervisor's own thinking. Team members, nationals, or others on location may have great insights to share, and rich, helpful relationships may be developed apart from the supervisor. Wise supervisors need to develop the ego strength to encourage that very thing rather than seeking to be the master of every situation. Nor are great leaders so protective of their own workers that they prevent them from testing the waters of various other ministries, other teams, and other team leaders. Neal Pirolo relates that on his first youthful mission experience, his team leader encouraged the participants to visit other ministries, both going and returning. As a result, ten out of the twenty team members had returned to the field within a year to become involved in longer term commitments of one kind or another (Pirolo 2000, 103).

Commitment to the Task

Excellent supervisors seek to strike a balance between the informal, friendly atmosphere of the team and, at the same time, an orderly, coordinated, well developed plan of work. They anticipate and prepare for challenges and obstacles. They may need to make very difficult decisions, either regarding the task or the people on the team. And, as all short-term team supervisors have learned, they will need to be open and flexible enough to change and modify their best-laid plans to fit the realities of the host culture, and the intrusions of life itself. Wise leaders will draw people into the work, sharing both dreams and practical examples of how God will be honored and people blessed through their efforts.

Commitment to an Understanding of Cultures and the Cultural Adjustment Process

Supervisors of short-term teams may not know all the particulars of the host culture and sub-cultures in which they are leading people, but the more integrated they are to those realities, the more likely it is that the participants themselves will learn cultural and personal sensitivity. Brynjolfson and Lewis (2006, 13) recommend that mentors, trainers, and coaches be skilled in missionary experience, demonstrating effectiveness in cross-cultural ministry, having gained the respect of fellow missionaries and national leaders, having participated in and contributed to the growth of the national church, having learned to share the Gospel in the culture, and having become skilled in leading and training out of their own mission experience.

Regardless of the depth of experience supervisors have in the particular culture in which they are working, they must have a broader understanding of cultural adjustment dynamics, both for themselves and for the team members. Supervisors must consider the short-termer's level of cultural adjustment in gauging participant responses to leadership, to team members, and to the ministry. No matter how long or brief an STM experience is, time seems to crunch the steps of cultural adjustment (honeymoon, depths of discouragement, a gradual return to normalcy, and productivity) into each experience. "*That's* normal" and "*You're* normal" need to be conveyed frequently. And sometimes, "So *deal* with it!" Organizations may want to look at Myron Loss' classic, *Culture Shock* (1983) for amazing wisdom regarding essential supervisory qualities for mission assignments in general, and for leading during cultural stress in particular.

Commitment to Missiological Reflection

Perhaps the commitment that will stand short-term supervisors in the best stead of all is a firm dedication to place themselves, others, and the ministry through the grid of ongoing missiological reflection. *Missiology* may be best understood as a thoughtful, balanced consideration and integration of *anthropology, history,* and *theology.*

Anthropology

God has constructed his highest creation uniquely but, at the same time, in a pattern common to humanity. Not only are men and women formed after his image, but they are also created in a way that follows generally predictable patterns throughout life. For example, we all recognize that people in their twenties normally have huge, idealistic (and we might even say, unrealistic) dreams, and that their expectations of their leaders are gigantic. They need—and acutely express their need for—*intensive mentoring and coaching.* They yearn for *a supportive community or team.* They ask for *respect,* which is played out in such things as a voice in decisions that concern them, and in recognizing that they are valued for their thinking even when they have not yet jumped through all the experience hoops. And they expect *meaningful work* from the very beginning, not being satisfied to check off tasks completed and thereby "earn the right." They believe that they can both learn and serve simultaneously. Should time permit, we could speak similarly of the unique needs of each generation, listing factors that, if ignored, result in chaos, lassitude, and eventually despair. However, if those same factors are discussed, understood, and nourished by leaders, people may move toward maturity and effectiveness in great and wonderful ways.

It will be important for short-term supervisors to understand these concepts in order to remember that *this is God's normal plan of development!* When we observe people at any stage of life responding in ways that are typical of their normal maturity level, we should honor it. We do not try to force development faster than should be expected, nor is it useful to try. We can, however, foster a supportive environment that lends itself to discovery, growth, and maturity. A rich supervised atmosphere, coupled with the cross-cultural ministry experience itself, can and frequently does lead to a more rapid maturing process. Supervisors need to become experts in the life-cycle development of people.

We may ask about the place of *trends* in order to understand the people coming to us today. The research and articles—well constructed or otherwise—are rampant. Everyone seems to be an expert on generational trends. But the best of supervisors—when they become students of cultures—begin to understand that while *trends* may exacerbate the inclinations of any generation, they are at best surface-level pointers. The underlying needs of any generation are those things that are true in every era, and possibly across cultures.

History

When we consider of the grand historical factors of missiology, we are thinking about our own experiences, the history of our own church or organization, the histories of the novices with whom we are working, the background and experiences of the supervising leader, and the history of the culture into which we are inserting ourselves. Dynamics that normally go unobserved may become great obstacles, threats, or on the other hand, wonderful blessings and growth experiences as supervisors intentionally bring those experiences into play and appropriately work with them. An obvious example is communication methodology. Effective supervisors are not bound by their own preferred ways of training, interacting, and monitoring, but rather commit to adapt their methods to the needs, preferences, and experiences of the new missionary participants. When we think missiologically, it is never appropriate to neglect the precedent histories of a culture or the histories of the participants who are working in the ministry. Supervisors should model a very intentional, careful consideration of the various historical, cultural dynamics into which they and the participants are moving, taking those foundations seriously as they approach supervision.

Theology

Supervisory leadership is not for spiritual novices, for good supervisors must commit themselves to the huge task of putting their ideas, planning, convictions, and outworkings through the grid of their increasing understanding of God. The Scriptures both model and teach that leaders are to be "above reproach"—not perfect, but examples of constant and continuing growth into Christ-likeness. Thus we must ask those who aspire to supervisory influence about the experiences of God's work in their own lives. How do they articulate the importance of passing that learning on to others? Are they committed to servanthood? Do they know where to give grace and when to stand firm in belief and practice? How healthy do their closest relationships appear? What is their history of conflict and resolution? Who has trained them, and how? (Answers to those kinds of questions will go far in determining how they themselves will supervise others.) Further, what is their history of modeling godliness in the face of difficulty, challenge, and hardship? Are they able to sustain—to practice what they preach—over the long haul? Do they exhibit holistic health (physical, emotional, spiritual, and social)? Are they committed to developing others and confident of reproducing themselves in others? Thinking theologically encompasses not only our doctrinal systematics, but also "the bottom line of the bottom line"—how we live out what we know about God.

Supervision of short-term teams is not for the international novice, the lazy, the socially inept, or the spiritual adolescent. Enough of selecting leaders based on their willingness, current availability, their need for recognition or encouragement, or because they may have accomplished some past task satisfactorily! Short-term participants are increasingly discovering their entrée into missions via the short-term route, and in the process they are developing toward maturity, and affecting God's work significantly. Should that trend continue—and it undoubtedly will only increase—short-term supervision will become one of the most significant assignments in the entire mission world. Thus, church and mission leadership must take their responsibility extremely seriously. Supervisory selections must be made in intentional consideration of potential supervisors' solid foundational strengths. Beyond that, supervisors will need to commit whole-heartedly to ongoing personal growth and incarnational living, to facilitating development, challenge, and future hope in others, to leading in productive ministry, and to understanding cultures and the cultural adjustment process. Finally, they must commit to life-long missiological reflection—to seeing themselves, others, and ministry through that grid as a model to others and as a guide for continuing wise, godly judgment in their own roles.

References Cited

Brynjolfson, Robert and Jonathan Lewis, ed. 2006. *Integral ministry training: Design and evaluation.* Pasadena: William Carey.

Cloud, Henry. 2006. *Integrity: The courage to meet the demands of reality.* New York: Harper Collins.

Collins, Jim. 2001. *Good to great: Why some companies make the leap. . . and others don't.* New York: Harper Collins.

Dettoni, John M. 1995. On being a developmental teacher. In *Nurture that is Christian: Developmental perspectives on Christian education,* ed. James

C. Wilhoit and John M. Dettoni, 249-63. Grand Rapids: Baker.

Elmer, Duane. 2006. *Cross-cultural servanthood: Serving the world in Christlike humility.* Downer's Grove, IL: IVP.

Gorman, Julie. 1995. Developmentalism and groups. In *Nurture that is Christian: Developmental perspectives on Christian education,* ed. James C. Wilhoit and John M. Dettoni, 235-48. Grand Rapids: Baker.

Krallmann, Gunter. 2002. *Mentoring for mission: A handbook on leadership principles exemplified by Jesus Christ.* Waynesboro, GA: Gabriel.

Lingenfelter, Sherwood G., and Marvin K. Mayers. 1986. *Ministering cross-culturally: An incarnational model for personal relationships.* Grand Rapids: Baker.

Livermore, David A. 2006. *Serving with eyes wide open: Doing short-term missions with cultural intelligence.* Grand Rapids: Baker.

Loss, Myron. 1983. *Culture shock: Dealing with stress in cross-cultural living.* Winona Lake: Light and Life.

Pirolo, Neal. 2000. Short-term missions. In *The reentry team: Caring for your returning missionaries.* 102-20. San Diego: Emmaus Road.

Smithgall, Daryl. 2006. *Short-term missions leadership handbook: Preparation and field guide.* Palo Alto, CA: Footsteps Missions.

Tiplady, Richard. 2003. *World of difference: Global mission at the Pic 'N' Mix Counter.* Carlisle, Cumbria, UK; Paternoster.

Endnotes

[1] We have discovered that when problems arise during a short-term field ministry, frequently one of the goals has been misplaced, or the three have not been kept in good balance:

- When supervisors do not take seriously the responsibility to build into the personal lives of their workers, the participants may feel neglected or cheated, may voice disappointment about unfulfilled expectations, and may themselves have difficulty responding appropriately toward others. God may yet do great things in them and through them, but holes will remain in their personal lives that could have been filled by a leader who models an incarnational life and work. A supervisor's task is not only about himself/

herself, nor only about the "ministry;" it is also about God's command to support the growth of those to whom He has entrusted us.

- Some supervisors go to the other extreme: they neglect the assigned ministry task in order to spend most of their energy on individual team members. That kind of experience may appear great to the participants at first: they may develop deep relationships with one another, and they may write lengthy journal assignments about the *deeper life*. But in the end both they and their supporters will wonder, "And the purpose of the sojourn was . . . ?" Frequently people leave the ministry site disillusioned, thinking, "Missions may have its place, but not for me—I prefer to do something more useful and challenging with my life. I don't want to live forever in a Sunday school environment!"

- Participants may experience great personal support during their assignment, and they may also come to its completion with a sense that they accomplished some things for the Kingdom. However, some supervisors hesitate to point to the future, in which participants could be challenged to consider whether and how God may be directing them. Frequently leaders believe that they will place undue pressure on short-termers, particularly at a vulnerable, emotional time in their lives. Thus, many short-termers come and go without having heard the encouraging word, "You could do this if God asked you to!"